WILLIAM

Selected Poetry and Prose

LONGMAN ANNOTATED TEXTS

GENERAL EDITORS

Charlotte Brewer, Hertford College, Oxford

H. R. Woudhuysen, University College London

Daniel Karlin, University College London

PUBLISHED TITLES

Lyrical Ballads Michael Mason

Women's Writing in Middle English Alexandra Barratt

Thomas Hardy: Selected Poems Tim Armstrong

King Lear: A Parallel Text Edition René Weis

Women Writers in Renaissance England Randall Martin

Chaucer's Dream Poetry Helen Phillips and Nick Havely

Alexander Pope: The Dunciad in Four Books Valerie Rumbold

Victorian Women Poets Virginia Blain

WILLIAM BLAKE

Selected Poetry and Prose

Edited by

DAVID FULLER

PEARSON
Longman

Harlow, England • London • New York • Boston • San Francisco • Toronto
Sydney • Tokyo • Singapore • Hong Kong • Seoul • Taipei • New Delhi
Cape Town • Madrid • Mexico City • Amsterdam • Munich • Paris • Milan

Pearson Education Limited

Edinburgh Gate
Harlow
Essex CM20 2JE
United Kingdom

and Associated Companies throughout the world

Visit us on the World Wide Web at
www.pearsoned.co.uk

Published in the United States of America
By Pearson Education Inc., New York

First edition published 2000
This revised edition published 2008

© Pearson Education Limited 2000, 2008

ISBN 978-1-4082-0413-9

British Library Cataloguing in Publication Data
A CIP catalogue record for this book can be obtained from the British Library.

Library of Congress Cataloging-in-Publication Data
Blake, William, 1757–1827.
  [Selections. 2008]
  William Blake : selected poetry and prose / edited by David Fuller. — Rev. ed.
      p.   cm. — (Longman annotated texts)
  Includes bibliographical references (p.   ) and index.
  ISBN 978-1-4082-0413-9
  I. Fuller, David, 1947– II. Title.
  PR4142.F75 2008
  821'.7—dc22

                                                              2008029799

10 9 8 7 6 5 4 3 2 1
11 10 09 08

Typeset by 35 in 9/12 pt Stone Serif Roman
Produced by Pearson Education Asia Pte Ltd.
Printed in Malaysia (CTP-VVP)

To
Tom Craik

CONTENTS

LIST OF PLATES

ACKNOWLEDGEMENTS

I am indebted to the University of Durham for a Sir Derman Christopherson Foundation Fellowship which gave me a year's research leave during which much of the work for this edition was done; and to the Yale Center for British Art for a fellowship which allowed me to work on its wonderful Blake collection, its director, Patrick McCaughey, and the staff of its Library and Prints and Drawings department. I am also grateful to the various institutions which have allowed the reproduction of plates from works in their collections. Some passages in the introductions have been re-worked from my *Blake's Heroic Argument* (Croom Helm, 1988) and 'Blake' in Michael O'Neill (ed.), *Literature of the Romantic Period* (Oxford, 1998): I am grateful to the publishers for permission to use this material.

One of the pleasures of working on this edition has been the generous help of various friends and colleagues who have read sections of the text or given information and advice: G. E. Bentley Jr., Steve Clark, Pamela Clemit, Robin Dix, Cynthia Fuller, Ben Knights, Andrew Lincoln, Michael O'Neill, Corinne Saunders, and Michael Schepers. Among my readers a particular acknowledgement is due to Michael Ferber who read three sections with great care and generously provided information from his own annotations gathered over time. It is also a pleasure to thank my copy-editor, Sarah Bury, for her excellent punctilious work on the typescript.

Daniel Karlin has been a model general editor, reading with unfailing care and a sharp eye for detail. He has improved both introductions and annotations at many points.

The Blake Society (London) and the North American Society for the Study of Romanticism provided helpful occasions on which I was able to talk through some of the problems of the edition. It is also a pleasure to thank Stuart Campbell for the gift of a copy of the Sloss and Wallis edition of Blake's prophetic books; and to thank the Inter-library loan staff of Durham University Library, particularly Trixie Khoja and Judith Walton, who procured dozens of items for me with great efficiency and good humour.

My greatest debt, expressed by the dedication, is to T. W. Craik, for his learning, his critical sense, and his friendship. He has read these pages with a care typical of his generosity in quietly improving what I (and many others) have written over many years.

ABBREVIATIONS

Most abbreviations are obvious shortenings of titles listed in full in the bibliography. As a complete text for reference I have used the edition of G. E. Bentley Jr., *William Blake's Writings*, 2 vols., Clarendon Press, Oxford, 1978. The two volumes are paginated continuously. The edition of David Erdman (see bibliography) is usually taken as the standard reference text, partly because of its ready availability in paperback. It is now even more widely available in being on-line. Nevertheless, the Bentley edition is, in my view, preferable as the only complete text to contain most of the significant illustrations of the illuminated books. The Tate Gallery/Princeton University Press facsimiles referenced under the names of the editors of the separate volumes are listed in the bibliography under the name of the general editor of the series, David Bindman. The following abbreviations are used throughout:

Bentley, *Writings*: G. E. Bentley, Jr. (ed.), *William Blake's Writings*, 2 vols., Oxford 1978.

BIQ: Blake: An Illustrated Quarterly.

Butlin, *Paintings and Drawings*: Martin Butlin, *The Paintings and Drawings of William Blake*, 2 vols., New Haven, CT, 1981.

Erdman, *Complete Poetry and Prose*: David V. Erdman, *The Complete Poetry and Prose of William Blake*, with a Commentary by Harold Bloom, New York, 1965; rev. edn., 1988.

Erdman, *Prophet Against Empire*: David V. Erdman, *Blake: Prophet Against Empire: A Poet's Interpretation of the History of His Own Time*, Princeton, NJ, 1954; 3rd rev. edn., 1977.

References to Shakespeare are to *William Shakespeare. The Complete Works: Compact Edition*, ed. Stanley Wells and Gary Taylor, Clarendon Press, Oxford 1988.

INTRODUCTION

(1) VERSIONS OF BLAKE

Poetry fettered fetters the human race.
(*Jerusalem*, pl. 3)

William Blake is a philosophical poet-painter. His central concerns are spiritual, artistic, political and personal freedom, and for him freedom is indivisible. His work presented basic challenges to many widely accepted ideas of his time about religion, politics, sexual morality, the nature of consciousness and the nature and value of the arts. In some areas the challenges presented by Blake have been absorbed by liberal opinion. In a degree Blake himself has even been instrumental in such developments. In the late 1960s some of the more exuberant proverbs of Hell were spray-painted on walls alongside sentences from other heroes of an intellectual and practical revolution, and these played their part in changing how people thought and acted. But not all Blake's challenges can be so absorbed. On his own view of consciousness and society there is inevitably a struggle in each individual and in each age with gravitations towards the mundane. One of the aims of his art is to play a part in that struggle on the side of the angels – or as Blake preferred to put it (since such a position is inherently oppositional, and power naturally presents itself as morally admirable), on the side of the devils. Blake accordingly wrote and designed with an intense moral passion, and criticism must respond to that. Attention to Blake's themes need not degenerate into treating poetry as propaganda. On the contrary, for Blake poetry, as well as painting, 'exists and exults in immortal thoughts' (*A Descriptive Catalogue*, IV; Bentley, *Writings*, 847). His work is an intellectual and artistic struggle – in his most famous lyric a 'mental fight' – which aims to build the utopian community, the New Jerusalem, and to build it, not at the end of time in heaven, but as soon as possible on earth – even (he is quite specific) in England. Criticism that shies away from such often fiercely direct engagement with religious, political, epistemological and other issues risks degenerating into narrow aestheticism. But Blake also wrote and painted with an equal commitment to the forms and techniques of his art. He constantly experimented with both, and discussion of both, like engagement with ideas, occurs throughout his writings. Form and technique were as important to him as content because they were inseparable from content. As he puts it in his 'Public Address':

> I have heard many people say, 'Give me the ideas. It is no matter what words you put them into,' and others say, 'Give me the design, it is no matter for the execution.' These people know enough of artifice, but nothing of art. Ideas cannot be given but in their minutely appropriate words, nor can a design be made without its minutely appropriate execution.

> (Notebook, p. 62; Bentley, *Writings*, 1041–2)

1

To abstract Blake's ideas from their particular articulations and contexts is therefore to be false to him as an artist. Truth is always to be found in attention to the particular; the general, necessarily indistinct, is the agent of Error.

Blake's fiery commitments have naturally attracted critics who are in tune with his moral and aesthetic passions, but it is rare for a critic to be equally in tune with the full range of them. One problem of Blake criticism is that a modern reader, in some senses highly attuned to Blake's politics (for example), may be positively antagonistic to important aspects of his religion, and vice versa. Blake attracts enthusiasts, and it is right that he should do so. As he put it in contradicting the hated neo-classical principles of Sir Joshua Reynolds, 'enthusiastic admiration is the first principle of knowledge, and its last' (Bentley, *Writings*, 1470). Because the virtues of enthusiasm are peculiarly demanded by Blake, and the virtues of enthusiasm can be positively at odds with those of judiciousness and balance, it is difficult to see Blake steadily and to see him whole. And yet all the various strands of Blake's work are, for him, of a piece. 'Are not religion and politics the same thing?', Los asks in *Jerusalem* (57.10). They are. And it is significant that Los, the artist, asks the question. 'The Old and New Testaments are the great code of art'; 'Art is the Tree of Life' (*Laocoön*): art and religion too are entirely intertwined. Blake's readers must attempt to make his variousness cohere if they are to respond to Blake on his own terms. Nevertheless, many of Blake's most notable critics need to be understood in terms of some predominant and partial interest. The filtering that the commitments of partisan readers necessitate is the price to be paid for the provocative engagement of their criticism.

Several extended critical accounts of Blake, including some of the earliest, have presented him as primarily a mythographer,[1] even as discovering a grammar of symbolism underlying all imaginative writing.[2] Blake invented his own myth, perhaps (as is often said) because existing mythologies carried with them unwanted implied values, but also because Blake's insistence on the uniqueness of individual experience meant that he could not take over and reshape classical or Christian narratives which – whatever their openness to new meanings in new contexts – grew up in situations of relative cultural consensus. While the invention of a structure of myth implies a degree of self-consciousness quite different from that of the artist who can adopt what Ezra Pound called 'the tale of the tribe',[3] still myth is for Blake an attempt to embody the whole nature of a subject, including its appeal to unselfconscious supra-rational powers. As Blake recognized by making the myth-making 'poetic character' central to his first attacks on Enlightenment values, the tractates of 1788, it shows a drive towards knowledge and understanding which is by its nature a form of opposition to the claims of rationalism. Through myth art can become a form of magic – a structure of emotional power and subtlety engaging the imaginative, intellectual and passional life of the reader with a disciplined freedom. One

---

[1] As in the books of S. Foster Damon (1924 and 1965), Harold Bloom (1963), and Hazard Adams (1963): for details see the bibliography.

[2] As in Northrop Frye's *Fearful Symmetry* (1947).

[3] *Guide to Kulchur* (London, 1938), 194.

of its aims is to conjure up a buried life of which the mundane demands of everyday make us usually at best semi-conscious. Blake distinguished between vision and fable or allegory,[4] between truly imaginative work arising from and addressed to the deepest levels of being and adaptations suited to culturally or authorially endorsed schemes of values – as with Ovid's sophisticated but (on Blake's view) degenerately fanciful accounts of Greek myth in the *Metamorphoses*, or Bunyan's narrow labelling of his grand nightmare personifications in *Pilgrim's Progress*.[5] Concentration on myth is clearly a critical response to Blake's own creative priorities and his own ways of discussing the imaginative faculty. Its characteristic limitations are to impose an unduly stable order on the multifarious structures Blake elaborated, and to imply that Blake's whole *œuvre* consists of fragments of one great work each part of which can only be understood in the context of the rest. Blake is in fact willing to invent and discard mythic schemes and personifications with considerable prodigality, and constantly to experiment with and find new meanings in structures which might otherwise become, from his own point of view, too rigidly systematized. Many of Blake's shorter poems, moreover, have nothing to do with his structures of myth, and even those poems that clearly share some mythic elements can be made to seem more obscure than they are when read in the supposed light of patterns or signficances elaborated in other works.

Notably different from this stress on myth and archetype is a criticism which attempts to see Blake in relation to his own times, situating him in the artisan culture to which, uniquely among the major Romantic poets, he belonged, and stressing his political engagements.[6] This line of thought has taken new forms in recent criticism, directing attention not so much to social conditions and historical events as to discourses shared with non-canonical or popular culture and to the importance of the material conditions of Blake's work as an engraver and printer.[7] Blake's early work is politically engaged. Poetry makes things happen, if not by affecting events directly then in the long term by changing consciousness. The aspiration implied by the cancelled lines of *America* plate 4 (the bard, 'ashamed of his own song,' smashes his harp), or the late proof title-page of *Europe* (a youthful figure is drawn on the printed design tugging at the stalled serpent of revolution),[8] may even suggest some disappointment that his own poetry had not reached out into the world of engagement with ideas that affect action. In the 1790s Blake was working on the fringes of a group of active political radicals and intellectuals in the circle of the publisher Joseph Johnson. He may or may not have had direct contact with Tom Paine or Mary Wollstonecraft, but he lived and worked close to a circle of writers

---

[4] 'A Vision of the Last Judgement', Bentley, *Writings*, 1007–9.

[5] The examples are Blake's: see 'A Vision of the Last Judgement', Notebook, pp. 79 and 68 (Bentley, *Writings*, 1011 and 1008).

[6] As in the books of Jacob Bronowski (1944/1965), Mark Schorer (1946), David Erdman (1954/1977), and Michael Ferber (1985). E. P. Thompson's *The Making of the English Working Class* (London, 1963) is a classic study of the whole milieu in which Blake worked.

[7] As in the books of Jon Mee (1992) and Joseph Viscomi (1993).

[8] David V. Erdman (ed.), *The Illuminated Blake* (London, 1975), 397.

who designed to push the world in a certain direction,[9] the direction of the ideals of the French Revolution. But this is one of the ways in which Blake's poetry does change: the redirection in the later poetry from the myth of Orc (associated with energy and specifically with revolution and transforming material conditions) to the myth of Los (associated with the imagination and with transforming mental attitudes) does indicate some shift in Blake's political engagements. His later writings can at times suggest that this is a very considerable shift, as when he confides to his Notebook: 'Princes . . . Houses of Commons and Houses of Lords . . . they seem to me to be something else besides human life. I am really sorry to see my countrymen trouble themselves about politics. If men were wise the most arbitrary princes could not hurt them' ('A Public Address'; Bentley, *Writings*, 1048). Whether comments of this kind really mean – as Blake's more transcendentally oriented commentators wish to suppose – that he came to see politics as a materialist delusion, and mind, not matter, as the whole ground of being, is doubtful. Even in Blake's later work, where he concentrates more on the transforming powers of the imagination and less is expected from social change, he continues to be aware of what he early on called 'omissions of intellect springing from poverty' (Marginalia to Lavater; Bentley, *Writings*, 1387): material conditions do circumscribe spiritual possibilities. Los the poet is haunted by the cry of the poor (*Milton*, 44.34), or investigates the London slums with a view to finding out what is wrong and taking action (*Jerusalem*, 31[45]) – though the actions adumbrated may be remote from those a politician would conceive. Historical criticism errs systematically only when it searches for a specific contemporary referent for all Blake's details. Attempts to trace consistent historical allegory – to present Blake as writing covertly about personalities whom he does not name and events which he does not specify – invert the proper method of his poetry which is, as Blake puts it, to give 'the historical fact in its poetical vigour so as it always happens' (*A Descriptive Catalogue*, V; Bentley, *Writings*, 851). Accepting a line of thought which goes back at least to Aristotle (*Poetics*, 9), Blake here distinguishes the contingent fact to which the historian is tied from the typical and eternal form, stripped of contingency: this is what the poet can reveal.

Blake has been presented as an eccentric solitary, a resourceful Robinson Crusoe putting together a philosophy from odds and ends which happened to be available.[10] It has also, on the other hand, been seen as a key to Blake that he needs to be understood within one or more of various esoteric religious or intellectual traditions.[11] The first task of criticism, on this view, is to situate Blake in the appropriate intellectual framework. Traditions stemming from Plotinus and the Neoplatonists have been the most fully investigated, but the net can be cast very wide – to include, for example, the *Bhagavad Gita*, Zoroastrianism, the *Hermetica*, and the kabbala. The esoteric nature of some of the traditions invoked means that Blake is once again

---

[9] The phrase is George Orwell's: 'Why I Write', *Collected Essays, Journalism and Letters*, 4 vols., ed. Sonia Orwell and Ian Angus (London, 1968), 1.23–30 (26).

[10] The view of T. S. Eliot, 'William Blake' (1920), *Selected Essays* (3rd edn., London, 1951), 317–22.

[11] As in the books of Milton Percival (1938), G. M. Harper (1961), and Desirée Hirst (1964). Kathleen Raine (1968) presents a similar line of thought more polemically.

– albeit in a quite different way – seen as more obscure than he need be: the aim of this now deliberate obscurity is to put off readers who hope for unduly easy access to spiritual truths. Given that there are few meanings that ingenuity cannot make some show of justifying, and that views of this kind can be in principle opposed to usual criteria about evidence, the difficulty is to distinguish between obscured meanings discovered by informed contemplation (informed, that is, by knowledge of the necessary traditions) and meanings that an interpreter simply wishes to find. Blake's work, it is (for example) argued, in some ways resembles the kabbala: he must have had a friend who was a rabbi who discussed with him secret traditional Jewish lore. The intuitions about this of those who have appropriate predispositions are evidence: those who do not have appropriate predispositions are, of course, held to be incapable of recognizing qualified intuition. None of this is necessarily false. Clearly people do learn by word of mouth as well as by reading, and *credo ut intellegam* ('I believe in order that I may understand') is an arguable principle of understanding spiritual knowledge. But the intuitions to be trusted are not always in sympathy with the more political and sexually radical areas of Blake's thought, and can sometimes show themselves careless of evidence where this conflicts with the views they wish to suppose are Blake's. Moreover, dragging Blake towards Neoplatonic sources conflicts with his lifelong antagonism to mystery in spiritual knowledge, and suggests a dualistic view of the relations between body and soul and a negative attitude towards sexual desire. Blake's aim is quite opposite: it is to not divide soul and body, and to develop with a holistic intelligence an integrated physical, intellectual and emotional life.

There clearly are resemblances between Blake and various esoteric traditions of thought. These may provide a vocabulary, a symbolic structure, an ideological stance, from which Blake explores, or with which he quarrels creatively. But Blake's marginalia indicate that he was more likely to be influenced by opposition than by identification. It is always daunting, and it is usually false, to imply that unless you have read some supposed source you cannot understand a given work. Blake expected his readers to know the Bible and Milton – as anybody likely to read Blake in his own lifetime would. Beyond this he knew that scholarly learning – whether about sources in ancient thought or English Civil War sectaries, contemporary discourses of the sublime or the visual vocabulary of political caricature – can be imaginative ignorance. Widely read but self-educated, Blake often scorned the learned: 'Christ and his apostles were illiterate men; Caiaphas, Pilate and Herod were learned . . . The beauty of the Bible is that the most ignorant and simple minds understand it best' (marginalia to Thornton; Bentley, *Writings*, 1514). Insofar as they represent learning in its ideal form, the universities are among the giant Albion's spiritual friends: but the actual schools and universities of Blake's age are useless to Albion, vitiated as they are by acquiescence in the age's dominant intellectual fashions (*Jerusalem*, 15.14–16). Blake saw the learned as likely to have investments in the status quo, and he was accordingly mistrustful. He is indeed in his major work a difficult poet. He makes great demands on the reader, but what he requires is not preparatory esoteric knowledge but responsiveness in the act of reading.

These ways of making fundamental sense of Blake – as universal archetypalist; as political polemicist, the ally of Cold War or 'flower power' radicals; and as anti-materialist perennial philosopher – all contested, all in a degree at odds with one another, have all commanded wide assent. They have become in some sense classic versions of Blake. However, though Blake as mythographer is a somewhat *ur*-structuralist creation, only the political Blake has proved to any high degree amenable to subsequent developments in general critical theory and practice, and productive of a Blake who can be cast in an image that fits with recent ideological preoccupations, especially those of race and gender.

Blake has been the darling, in the traditional canon, of explicitly left-wing criticism. Criticism of his sexual politics has been interestingly more divided in its verdict. Feminist critics have had a good deal to say about Blake, often with a suspicion that he is only dividedly liberationist. Any historical criticism must accept that a writer be read first in terms of his or her own age. That Blake's present-day readers should conceive of political emancipation in terms somewhat different from his own is inevitable. It is parochial to measure the past by the present on the implicit assumption that our own ideological embeddedness is sufficiently apparent to us for us to be confident that the present represents unalloyed progress, in whatever area. One has to look first at a writer's tendency in his or her own historical context: specific meanings anachronistically transferred directly to a contemporary context may be entirely false to this. That said, while Blake was clearly concerned with issues of women's emancipation, and while positive values in his work are often conveyed by women and negative values by men, still in some of his metaphors and in certain characters of his myth Blake is held by some feminist critics either specifically to mistake the social (what might be transformed by the radical stances he proposes in other spheres) for the natural, or more generally to betray a misogynistic animus. There are traditional answers: that Blake's male and female personifications are not equivalent to actual men and women; that all are aspects of a total psyche which in its ideal form Blake conceives as androgynous. But these answers have often led to further criticism of how that ideal is conceived. The implications of Blake's work as a whole in terms of sexual politics is a very current debate.[12]

Most of the critics who invented the classic views of Blake were discovering in him something deeply congenial to their own views of the world – in politics or in intellectual or spiritual life. Even Northrop Frye, who saw himself as developing from his reading of Blake a descriptive 'science' of criticism (in *Anatomy of Criticism*, Princeton, NJ, 1957), might be seen in 'The Case Against Locke' and other parts of *Fearful Symmetry* (1947) as blending his own voice with Blake's more than he was perhaps aware. One common element to recent versions of Blake is a desire to establish, on the surface at least, a greater distance between author and critic, the kind of view of which Jerome McGann's *The Romantic Ideology* (Chicago, 1983) is catalyst and symptom, that Romanticism is not a permanent human attitude as (on this view) criticism had taken it to be, but an historic one which criticism of

---

[12] For further discussion of feminist criticism, see the headnote to *Visions of the Daughters of Albion*, and the essay by Brenda Webster in Miller, Bracher and Ault (1987), reprinted in Punter (1996).

Romantic period works should help us to transcend.[13] Underlying this so-called New Historicist programme is an attack on the whole idea of poetry derived from the Romantics and passed into twentieth-century criticism by Matthew Arnold: poetry can no longer be seen as the best that has been known and thought or a human power to transcend circumstance; beauty is no longer a fundamental category of the artistic. The rediscovery of Romantic Irony has been important in this development;[14] and while the common reader and enthusiast – to whose continued existence Blake Societies and reading groups attest – may feel that an eagerness to assert historical distance, and an apparent fear of being seduced into commitments which are not hedged around with irony, sits oddly with taking an interest in Blake at all, nevertheless probably no English writer of the Romantic period has been found more amenable to ironic readings than Blake.

Earlier criticism felt some confidence in an ability to place Blake's own voice in the dramatic mêlée of his creations, or at least to place the dramatic voices in relation to some discernible centre. Blake was the impassioned mental fighter of the famous *Milton* lyric; his archetypal poet, Los, uttered 'ambiguous words blasphemous' in his fallen state, but inspired he demanded 'explicit words'; his archetypal prophet, Isaiah, sneered that 'many are not capable of a firm persuasion of anything'.[15] More recent criticism, given to perceiving centres as themselves structurated, all positions as equally open to ideological suspicion, and language as inherently disintegrative in itself and problematic in its relation to the world, has often perceived Blake as a dizzyingly Derridean ironist whose works can be construed with apparently equal plausibility as containing meanings which are not just various but which are positively opposite to each other.[16] A critical practice of attempting to 'solve' difficulties in Blake's text (by giving them a specific historical referent, or by fitting them into some pattern in relation to which they can be seen as meaningful) has given way to practices which emphasize difficulties and attempt to make them fruitful of meaning. Inventive critics, moreover, have not been satisfied with the difficulties that might seem obvious: the powerful effect of deconstruction on the *zeitgeist* has appeared in Blake studies no less than elsewhere.[17]

All readers of Blake at times experience bafflement, and it is right to insist that how Blake's texts and designs work – which is often by puzzling the reader and resisting ordinary sense-making operations – is in part what they mean. Symbolic

---

[13] For an extended discussion of McGann's view of Romanticism, see my 'Keats and Anti-Romantic Ideology', *The Challenge of Keats*, ed. Allan Christensen, Lilla Crisafulli, Giuseppi Galigani and Anthony Johnson (Amsterdam, 2000).

[14] In David Simpson, *Irony and Authority in Romantic Poetry* (London, 1979), and Anne K. Mellor, *English Romantic Irony* (Cambridge, MA, 1980).

[15] *Four Zoas*, 53.26; *Jerusalem*, 17.60; *Marriage*, plate 12.

[16] The eclectic commentaries in Andrew Lincoln's edition of the *Songs* (1991) are symptomatic: see, for example, the opposite meanings postulated for 'To Tirzah' (p. 201); cf. David Simpson's 'Teaching Ideology in *Songs*' in Robert F. Gleckner and Mark L. Greenberg, *Approaches to Teaching Blake's 'Songs of Innocence and of Experience'* (New York, 1989).

[17] See the books of Nelson Hilton (1983) and Edward Larrissy (1985), and the collections of essays edited by Hilton and Vogler (1986) and Miller, Bracher and Ault (1987).

translation and ideological paraphrase are valid critical activities, but they render only certain aspects of significance. One of Blake's aims is to disturb our usual sense making faculties through an art in which the sources of meaning are various and are combined in unusual ways. The deconstructive postulate that has been most applied to Blake is specifically that (his) language is irreducibly polysemous, that (his) words fly free of their supposed semantic content and connect with other words that look or sound somewhat like them (veil / vale / vein / vile / live / evil), or have semantic associations with them (veil / tabernacle / chastity / nature).[18] Evidently semantic associations can be free-wheeling. Whether this particular road of excess leads to a palace of wisdom is for each reader to decide. Michel Bréal, the founder of semantics, would have rejected it: he understood associative processes with language as working quite differently, not on the sounds of words but on their referents. But deconstruction directs attention to words not as referring to things but as objects in themselves. Since the claims of deconstruction are concerned with problems of meaning which reveal themselves at the most minute levels of language, they can only be examined at that level. The Santa Cruz Blake Study Group explains: 'The interpreter must see language differently, must stop before the accepted or expected meaning of a word in order to perceive language in its material density.'[19] The reader willing to be persuaded may enquire what those obedient to this fiat will gain. The Study Group's best example is the word 'sinew' in *The Book of Ahania* (4.33), which, on the basis of an oddity in Blake's 'w', it construes as 'sinerv' (sinews are the nerves of sin). Blake, it should be remembered, was writing backwards on a copper plate (and not, here, in his usual method of relief etching but in intaglio). Test cases which have begun to pass into scholarship are 'worshipped' with a supposed play on 'warshipped' (*Jerusalem*, 21.44), and 'Enitharmon' with a supposed play on 'Enitharman' (*The Book of Urizen*, 19.46). Before these are accepted as puns it must be recognized that it is a feature of Blake's 'o' that he sometimes joins it to the following letter with a lower stroke.[20] If not all such criticism is wrong, it is all out of proportion. The slogan Blake gave his own personification of the poetic faculty is not 'Consider my words in their material density: they may mean what ingenuity can devise', but 'Mark well my words: they are of your eternal salvation' (*Milton*, 5.18). Probably the deconstructive agenda with Blake is potentially larger than in practice it has yet turned out to be. Given Blake's own against-the-grain readings (of the Bible and *Paradise Lost*), deconstruction's claims about what the marginalized can reveal about supposed centres and what aporia can reveal about supposed coherence, and its technique of concentrating on the revelatory potential of (to use Blake's term) 'minute particulars', Blake presents apparently responsive possibilities for some of deconstruction's most characteristic themes. But in practice more important kinds of significance are lost in a search for meanings which Blake's

---

[18] These examples are taken from Nelson Hilton, *Literal Imagination: Blake's Vision of Words* (Berkeley, CA, 1983), 2.

[19] Review of Erdman (ed.), *The Complete Poetry and Prose of William Blake*, BIQ, 18 (1984–85), 4–30; partially reprinted in Hilton, *Essential Articles for the Study of William Blake* (1986).

[20] See Morton Paley's discussion in his edition of *Jerusalem* (1991), 126; cf. the Essick/Viscomi edition of *Milton* (1993), 110.

attitude to ambiguity suggests he would have deplored. Where every word is given so many potentials no word has the precise significance which allows error to be snared and truth to be told so as to be irresistibly understood. Just as Blake loved the sharp bounding outline in visual art so he loved the clarity of a precise language. Indefinite possibilities of meaning, suggestion and association are not, for Blake, sources of a perception of the infinite.

One alternative to deconstruction's serious play has been to concentrate on stabilizing meaning (at least relatively) not by features of a text and its designs in themselves but by establishing ever more precise historical contexts which might be held to delimit the possibilities of meaning; for example, by examining the interpretative traditions through which Blake's understanding of the Bible was mediated, and the ways in which he borrowed or deviated from these traditions; or to place him more precisely in a specific context of politico-religious dissent.[21] Among the areas in which really significant new information precisely contextualizes Blake's work, discoveries about his working methods have been the most fruitful.[22] Reconstruction of Blake's material practices in creating the illuminated books – factual in relation to his basic methods, though also interpretative in relation to specific works – takes us into Blake's workshop, shows him composing, and, far from hiding the compositional processes so that the material product is the transparent vehicle of an ideal vision, making aspects of the production process meaningful parts of the final product. The kind of scholarship involved in such reconstruction is consistent with the stress New Historicist critics of the Romantic period place on bibliography, and through that the importance to interpretation of the precise social relationships of a work which bibliography can help us to construct. However, in relation to Blake this kind of scholarship has in a degree been found consistent with paradigms of Romanticism which polemics about the historicity of Romantic discourses were designed to displace. The centrality of the not purely time-bound creative imagination; the poet as prophet interpreting the political and spiritual worlds; the artist's struggle with ideas that can be embodied in language so as to influence action in the material world – none of this has been found inconsistent with new information about the poet-painter as skilled craftsman.[23]

---

[21] The first in Leslie Tannenbaum's *Biblical Tradition in Blake's Early Prophecies: The Great Code of Art* (Princeton, NJ, 1982), the second in E. P. Thompson's *Witness Against the Beast: William Blake and the Moral Law* (Cambridge, 1993).

[22] The peculiar nature of Blake's work as author, designer, engraver, printer, colourist and direct-supply publisher has long meant that bibliography plays an unusually prominent role in Blake scholarship. The foundational work of Geoffrey Keynes was enormously extended and refined by G. E. Bentley Jr. (particularly in *Blake Books* and its supplement). This has been developed into new areas by Robert Essick and Joseph Viscomi (see bibliography for details).

[23] The headnotes to each work return variously to the issues about critical practice and views of Blake raised here, and discuss their consequences in particular cases. For a detailed account of Blake criticism to 1984, see the essay by Mary Lynn Johnson in Frank Jordan (ed.), *The Engish Romantic Poets: A Review of Research and Criticism* (4th edn., New York, 1985), 113–253; for a shorter account which also deals with more recent work, see my essay in Michael O'Neill (ed.), *Literature of the Romantic Period: A Bibliographical Guide* (Oxford, 1998), 27–44.

Blake met with incomprehension from his contemporaries, though he energetically sought a public. Nevertheless, when those best qualified to judge read him – Wordsworth, Coleridge, Southey – they showed little understanding. The incomprehension of Blake's contemporaries is the first major fact of his later reputation: knowledge of his perseverance in the face of apparent failure implied for later generations a guarantee of authenticity. Blake's first sympathetic readers read him in the context of Carlyle and the Pre-Raphaelites. They discovered him through Alexander Gilchrist's *Life of William Blake, 'Pictor Ignotus'* (1863; 2nd edn., 1880). Gilchrist was a disciple of Carlyle, and the *Life* is Carlylean: the poet is a figure of heroic integrity. Gilchrist's widow, Anne, who completed the biography, was assisted by Dante Gabriel and William Michael Rossetti, and the *Life* is Pre-Raphaelite: the artist-poet for whom the sensuous and spiritual worlds are a continuum is an admirer of Gothic who trained by copying the medieval. The *Life* is also proto-Whitmanic (Anne Gilchrist wrote one of the earliest English essays on Whitman), but this ethos struggles with a more obviously 'Victorian' moralistic didacticism: on the advice of Samuel Palmer, Anne Gilchrist omitted from her selection of texts the 'Proverbs of Hell' (from *The Marriage of Heaven and Hell*), which Palmer warned would 'at once exclude the work from every drawing-room table in England'.[24] The Ellis-Yeats *Works of William Blake, Poetic, Symbolic, and Critical* (3 vols., 1893), which was the first attempt at a complete edition of Blake's writings, made available much more of Blake's work than can be found in the Gilchrist and Rossetti selections, and in so doing shifted attention to the prophetic books. Its extended introductions and commentary presented Blake in the image of Yeats: he was an occultist with a symbolic system.

T. S. Eliot's Blake essay of 1920 – the first essay on Blake which is still widely read – was a prelude to those other symbols of Blake's arrival in the canon: the first full scholarly critical treatment, S. Foster Damon's *William Blake: His Philosophy and Symbols* (1924); the first truly complete edition, Geoffrey Keynes's Nonesuch volumes (London, 1925); and the Sloss and Wallis Oxford edition of the prophetic writings (1926). Those who read Blake before this found him an outlaw who could be newly discovered in the spirit of various *avant-garde* movements. This is, of course, a spirit in which Blake can be – and has been – perpetually rediscovered. But after the 1920s Blake's position in English letters was entering the new phases charted here.

'The words of a dead man / Are modified in the guts of the living,' wrote W. H. Auden ('In Memory of W. B. Yeats'). Any writer of real scope presents to different historical perspectives, to different kinds of interest in literature, and even to individual readers a somewhat different face. Blake seems peculiarly open to various constructions. Nevertheless, many are in some sense versions of what Edwin Ellis, with more confidence than modern perspectives can muster, called in his 1907 biography 'the real Blake'. Though criticism must realize such constructions in intellectual terms, they are not in the first place intellectual: when Auden describes a writer's words as 'modified in the guts of the living' he means that legitimate new readings arise from new experience. Worthwhile reading negotiates between different

---

[24] *The Letters of Samuel Palmer*, ed. Raymond Lister, 2 vols. (Oxford, 1974), II, 662.

modes of construing and constructing works and writers: reading which identifies, and helps one further to develop and articulate, one's own experience, with perhaps little or no sense of the writer's historical distance; reading which selects and modifies, often unconsciously, in relation to experience – what Harold Bloom calls 'strong misreading'; and reading which attempts fully to acknowledge and engage with the otherness of a vision different from one's own. Most actual readings partake of all three modes. Recognizing the variousness with which Blake has been constructed should make each reader more aware of the truth and value of each such construction, and more able to make for him or herself a living modification which is also a real Blake.

(2) POETRY AND DESIGNS

If the spectator could enter into these images in his imagination, approaching them on the fiery chariot of his contemplative thought; if he . . . could make a friend and companion of one of these images of wonder, which always entreats him to leave mortal things, as he must know – then would he arise from his grave, then would he meet the Lord in the air, and then he would be happy.

This is Blake's prescription for the viewer of his paintings and designs. He was writing at a time when his work – totally ignored – must have seemed to him a failure, and perhaps there is a tone of desperation. 'Truth can never be told so as to be understood and not be believed': thus the confident devils of his youth (*Marriage*, plate 10). But now, 'as he must know': though people appear to resist it (Blake implies) at some deep level they must see that art is transcendental and quasi-religious. In the final sentence he is quoting Saint Paul describing the expected imminent apocalypse: 'Then we which are alive and remain shall be caught up together with them [the dead] in the clouds, to meet the Lord in the air' (1 Thessalonians, 4.17). The grave from which art can raise us is the spiritual death of ordinary existence untransfigured by imaginative experience. 'Poetry, painting and music' are 'the three powers in man of conversing with paradise which the Flood did not sweep away.' The proper experience of art is transformative. Also, Blake immediately goes on, 'it is in particulars that wisdom consists, and happiness too, both in art and in life.'[25] The wonder, love and (in its religious sense) enthusiasm Blake wishes to provoke depend on seeing intensely and making sense of detail.

The annotations of each design in this edition aim to start from this – seeing what is there: describing in a quite literal sense the main elements of each design. This is not always so simple as it might seem. Blake's principle, 'as a man is, so he sees', or 'every eye sees differently: as the eye, such the object',[26] is true not only interpretively but also literally. Does *America* plate 6 show a beached whale (David Erdman), or a tree-trunk? In plate 7 is the central figure decapitated (Erdman again), or just not very clearly foreshortened? Is the figure at the base of *Europe* plate 3

---

[25] 'A Vision of the Last Judgement', Notebook, pp. 82, 81; Bentley, *Writings*, 1018, 1017.
[26] To Dr Trusler, 23.8.1799; and marginalia to Reynolds, p. 34 (Bentley, *Writings*, 1527, 1466).

entwined with a serpent (John Beer) or a strip of cloth? At the most literal level what critics see can sometimes be related to a desired interpretation: the whale or serpent may be found because they are political symbols; decapitation because it connects the American Revolution with the French. Sometimes differences of vision seem more random. Does the man in copy G of *Europe* plate 17 have an enormously long penis (Bentley), or are his genitals decently covered with some drapery (Dörrbecker)?

When the reader/viewer has looked carefully and seen what is there to see, two related questions arise. How do you interpret what you see in visual terms? And what relation do you see between a design and its texts? Interpreting what one sees in visual terms requires primarily the attention to particulars and unhurried imaginative receptivity Blake describes in relation to his 'Last Judgement': making a friend and companion of the design, seeing it as a thing of wonder. Colour as well as form will play its part in expressivity, but Blake coloured different copies of the same illuminated book quite differently: there is no convention or code of symbolic colours, though to some extent Blake's later copies are different kinds of work from his earlier – the earlier coloured simply, with the focus on the verse, the later often coloured richly, with the focus drawn more to the design.[27] The meaning of an image may be complicated (mildly) by Blake's use of conventions of expressive gesture, derived from Michelangelo (a relatively naturalistic convention in which emotion is expressed by the torso), and from Poussin (a more obviously conventionalized expression of emotion through a gestural code).[28] Both of these readily become familiar to anybody who looks at Blake's designs with the imaginative thoughtfulness he urges, but as with colour there is no key: competent interpreters may disagree over a gesture's expressive value. Morton Paley re-applies a suggestive phrase from Coleridge, one thoroughly in keeping with Blake's advice that we 'make a friend or companion of . . . these images of wonder', when he calls Blake's designs 'not hieroglyphs but educts of the imagination'.[29]

Interpretation should not be relentless: aspects of Blake's designs are often pure decoration. But the relation of text and design can be problematic. Blake published none of his mature poetry in a purely verbal form, and it is now generally accepted that Blake's is a composite verbal-visual art. In the context of this acceptance one

---

[27] For differences in colouring between early and late copies compare, for example, the supplementary illustrations from *Innocence*, copy B (1789) with the main copy facsimiled (*Songs*, copy X, 1827) in Andrew Lincoln's Tate/Princeton facsimile of the *Songs* (see bibliography for details).

[28] These conventions are discussed by Christopher Heppner, *Reading Blake's Designs* (Cambridge, 1995), Part 1. Conventional gestures, with suggestions about their interpretation, are remarked in the annotation. Janet Warner (*Blake and the Language of Art*, Kingston, Ont., 1984) proposes an approach, based on Blake's repeated visual forms, which moves in interpretation from design to poetry.

[29] The scriptures are 'living educts of the Imagination' (*The Statesman's Manual*, ed. R. J. White, Princeton, NJ, 1972, 29). The whole context in which Coleridge uses the phrase, an attack on 'the hollowness of abstractions . . . mechanic philosophy . . . [and] an unenlivened generalizing understanding', is aptly Blakean. For Paley's use, see 'Types and Symbols, or How to Read Blake's Pictures', *The Continuing City: William Blake's 'Jerusalem'* (Oxford, 1983), 98.

may remember that Blake apparently invented many poems purely as verbal texts. As well as the early works set in letterpress (*Poetical Sketches* and *The French Revolution*) the Notebook versions of poems in *Songs of Experience* were not accompanied by designs. Similarly, the *Songs of Innocence* which first appeared in *An Island in the Moon* (and the variant of 'Laughing Song' written into *Poetical Sketches*) were not illustrated – and in these cases there was presumably a gap of several years between the composition of the poems and the designs which eventually accompanied them. There is also sometimes a positively unfruitful clash between a poem and its design: for example, when the rose in 'The Sick Rose' rose is white Blake was surely just not paying attention to the poem's implications of erotic flesh-colour ('has found out thy bed of crimson joy'); or, more obviously, it probably seems to most readers that no interesting relation can be experienced between the great verbal creation of 'The Tiger' and the poor beast that slinks below it. Only very rarely, on the other hand, did a primarily visual invention find its way into the illuminated books.[30] And though Blake did print designs from the illuminated books without their accompanying texts, he did so reluctantly, 'to the loss of some of the best things: for they when printed perfect accompany poetical personifications and acts, without which poems they never could have been executed'.[31] The verbal texts are therefore – on Blake's own account, and as the purely verbal drafts in the Notebook and elsewhere testify – the bases of the eventual 'composite art'. Interpretation will usually, therefore, move from text to design.

In some cases the relation of design to text is that of simple illustration. A design gives the text in pictorial form. Text and design are entirely at one: each reinforces the other, as in *America* plate 8 where the resurrection figure shown is entirely consistent with the text immediately below. The complication here is that illustrative designs are not necessarily immediately juxtaposed with the texts to which they refer – an effect which Northrop Frye refers to as 'syncopation'.[32] This is the case, for example, with several largely illustrative designs in *The Book of Urizen*, designs which Blake moved to different positions in different copies, so their relations to the texts they illustrate are not fixed.[33] Equally simply, a design may be a form of

---

[30] The frontispiece to *Europe*, often known as 'The Ancient of Days', is such a design. An early version first appeared in the Notebook (p. 96) with the motto 'Who shall bind the infinite?' (which also found its way in *Europe*: 5.13). It is notable that, exceptionally among the designs from the illuminated books, Blake did occasionally print, colour and sell this plate separately.

[31] Letter, 9.6.1818; Bentley, *Writings*, 1648. Blake refers here to the so-called *Small* and *Large Book of Designs* which he printed *c.* 1796: Butlin, *Paintings and Drawings*, 260–2. In these collections some plates were given titles not used when the designs were printed in their original contexts. Where these exist they are given in the annotation.

[32] 'Poetry and Design in William Blake', *The Journal of Aesthetics and Art Criticism*, 10 (1951), 35–42; reprinted in Frye (ed.), *Blake: A Collection of Critical Essays* (Englewood Cliffs, NJ, 1966), 119–26 (124).

[33] See, for example (using the numbering adopted in this edition), plate 22: this can be most obviously connected with the text at 10.25, though also with 13.26–7, and in the majority of copies it was placed next to plate 13. Cf. the annotation of the designs for *The Book of Urizen* plates 12, 14 and 27.

underlining, depicting something that is consistent with the text though not sim
ply illustration, as in *America* plates 10 and 12 (*Plate 6*), where the principal mythic
antagonists of the text, Urizen and Orc, are shown in characteristic (and opposite
attitudes; or as in *Europe*'s illustrations of the effects of war, 'Famine' and 'Plague
(plates 9 and 10), where Blake unusually juxtaposes his myth with specifically con-
temporary exemplifications of his theme. A design may also contrast with its text,
as in *America* plate 9 (*Plate 5*), where a reactionary indictment of Revolution is
juxtaposed with an idyllic dawn. Blake's designs do not, however, always have so
immediate a relation to the texts with which they combine. Some are more purely
graphic presentations. Such designs can only be interpreted in relation to their text
obliquely, as in *America* plate 14, a design which Blake elsewhere called 'Death's
Door',[34] which has no obvious direct relation with surrounding text. Here inter-
pretation becomes more problematic. If one has already seen the figures of plates 10
and 12 as a contrasting and complementary pair, one might more readily see this
old man entering a vault as in a relation of contrast to the resurrection figure emer-
ging from a grave in plate 8. The fact that the two images were brought together by
Blake fifteen years later in his designs for Robert Blair's poem *The Grave* indicates
that Blake himself thought of them then in a relation of contrast – though not
necessarily that he did so in 1793. In terms of a principle of interpretation one can
only say that the relationship of text and design is here more complex, and that
evidence about whatever meanings a design held for Blake can sometimes be sought
beyond the text itself. Some designs are more puzzling still: for the swan of *America*
plate 13 no critic has suggested a significance which seems more than plausible,
while for the king and queen of the fairies as the central image of *The Song of Los*
(plate 5) no interpretation has been offered which is at all convincing. Here, as
often with Blake's texts, there is some tension between different understandings of
art, the artist and the interpreter. Blake's account of 'what is not too explicit as the
fittest for instruction' because it rouses the faculties to act'[35] may in some degree
suggest that the writer/painter should be understood as creating provocations for
the reader's imaginative play, and that the reader/viewer is a constructor of mean-
ing. But so passionately moral an artist as Blake clearly also espoused a view of the
writer/painter as communicating a vision, drawing the reader outside his or her
own presuppositions to understand things which he or she has precisely not brought
to the act of interpretation. All we bring to reading is bound in some measure to
determine what we receive: when Blake has his Bard summon Milton from eternity
to correct the errors of his life's work with the repeated cry, 'Mark well my words:
they are of your eternal salvation',[36] he more than implies that what we bring should
not determine what we receive wholly.

Blake's relativistic principles of perception mean that some latitude of interpreta-
tion must be admitted. The significance of Blake's images changed even for Blake
himself as he reworked them at different periods of his life. This is most obviously

---

[34] *The Gates of Paradise*, plate 17 (like *America*, 1793).

[35] To Dr Trusler, 23.8.1799; Bentley, *Writings*, 1526.

[36] *Milton*, 2.25, 7.16, 7.48, 9.7, 11.31.

true in the case of images transposed from one context to another: the children and serpent design of *Thel* (plate 8) is used in *America* (plate 13) in a completely different context; the preludium to *America* design (plate 3) is used in *The Four Zoas* (page 62) with its characters more obviously indentified and in a new narrative setting. Similarly, a comparison of different copies of the same book shows designs changing their significance – change pointed perhaps by a different style of colouring, by the emphasizing or painting over of different details, by a new inscription, or by a different juxtaposition of plates. Whenever Blake produced a new copy of one of the illuminated books, he developed as a later self and saw in it new possibilities of emphasis – or perhaps, in cases of extensive reworking, a radically different significance. This does not mean the more meanings the better. A valuable ambiguity has some form of coherence: at some level alternative meanings – faultlines, fractures, aporia – must signify in relation to one another. Morton Paley describes valid alternative interpretations in terms of 'analogues':[37] one image may properly suggest several related figures of Blake's myth; its significance lies not in the particular identification but in the kinds of issues or characteristics it embodies. But mutually exclusive readings of a design cannot both be accepted: the same figure cannot be both Orc and his antagonist, Albion's Angel, unless there is a meaning in so bizarre an identity. Multiple meaning does not mean there are no wrong readings – though by what principles readings can be excluded is, of course, problematic. 'Pertinacious critics have been able to invert most of Blake's meanings', the great historian E. P. Thompson complained;[38] and reading designs is even more fertile ground for misinterpretation than reading texts. Images have meanings less fixed than words: misinterpretation is, therefore, both more possible and more difficult to refute. General principles are few: one should trust to visual values – if a design looks in an obvious sense beautiful it should not be given negative meanings; and one should not derive from isolated detail meanings that contradict the overall thrust of a design. Moreover, source studies, while they may tell one something about how Blake's visual imagination worked, are rarely a guide to meaning because Blake often fundamentally altered the significance of what he adapted.[39] In the illuminated books meaning emerges from the particular articulations of the design itself and its context – the surrounding poetry, and the design's place in a visual sequence. There are no easy criteria: as with all problems of interpretation there is finally, as T. S. Eliot discouragingly puts it, 'no method except to be very intelligent'.[40]

The problems and possibilities are best illustrated by some typical examples. The frontispiece to *America* (*Plate 4*) is a design which has been variously interpreted. One can consider first some general analogies. Blake usually uses a frontispiece to epitomize central issues of the work it introduces. The frontispiece of *Visions of the Daughters of Albion* (*Plate 3*), for example, shows the three protagonists in

[37] 'Jerusalem', Tate/Princeton, 1991, 131.

[38] '"London"', in Michael Phillips (ed.), *Interpreting Blake* (Cambridge, 1978), 5–31 (16).

[39] See the essays of Irene H. Chayes in *Colby Library Quarterly*, 20 (1984) and 26 (1990) (full details in the bibliography).

[40] 'The Perfect Critic', *Selected Prose of T. S. Eliot*, ed. Frank Kermode (London, 1975), 55.

characteristic postures and relationships. It illustrates a particular passage of the text (5.5–7): the viewer knows who the figures are and what they are doing. Similarly, the frontispiece to *Europe* (the so-called 'Ancient of Days') shows the main protagonist in a characteristic posture. No specific passage of the text is illustrated, but the character and his action – circumscribing the universe with his golden compasses – can be confidently identified, and the general import of the image in relation to *Europe* is not in doubt: this is the origin and presiding genius of Error. We may presume that Blake intended the frontispiece to *America* to be a similarly suggestive introduction to the work as a whole, but its precise articulations as an epitome have been much disputed. The first problem is the identity of the great winged figure.[41] He is Urizen (S. Foster Damon); he is Albion's Angel (Jean Hagstrum); he is England (John Beer). These readings seem to me wrong. The proposed mythic identities (Urizen/Albion's Angel) Blake does not depict in this way elsewhere, and England is too narrow an identification because it is not only English liberty that *America* shows as restrained. For other critics the same figure has a basically opposite meaning. He is Orc (David Erdman); he is despair under the Old Order (David Bindman); or he is the human condition with its manacles of mental cowardice (Janet Warner).[42] These readings are on the right lines because they evoke the central situation of liberty universally restrained with which the work begins and ends. But Bindman and Warner are unduly general (they pitch interpretation at a level which omits the design's cannon and sword hilt); and Erdman discredits his desire for a specific identity when he interprets the woman in the design as Oothoon: this is entirely misleading because the reader of *America* never hears of such a character.[43] What the viewer sees in any design is to be understood not in terms of solving a puzzle but in terms of registering a certain kind of experience of the work's subject – here, war: material destruction, a prisoner–warrior's exhaustion or despair, a mother's suffering, her children's need for comfort. Best of all readings seem to me Essick's – 'a representation of the consequences of war'; or Dörrbecker's – 'an emblem of bondage . . . the consequences of the American War for the British people', assuming that this means the British people of the war period – the British and the American colonists, everybody involved.

Similarly disputed, though for different reasons, is *America* plate 10. The identity of the figure in this design is not problematic. It is Urizen – in a characteristic setting of clouds (they obscure clear vision), and in a characteristic posture, pressing down

---

[41] The various interpretations that follow are gleaned from and fully referenced in the materials assembled by Detlef W. Dörrbecker, *William Blake: The Continental Prophecies*, Tate/Princeton, 1995, 42–73.

[42] Why just mental cowardice is not clear, since Blake is evidently concerned in the poem with literal manacles as well. Janet Warner is also astray in suggesting that the figure represents a form of the Covering Cherub: Blake uses a great deal of biblical imagery in *America*, but he does not use the symbol of the Cherub until ten or more years later, in *Milton*.

[43] Erdman's readings of Blake's designs in the illuminated books have been the most often consulted as a result of the wide availability of his *Illuminated Blake* (London, 1975). It is characteristic of his readings to insist on specific identifications for figures which may have a more typical value or generic suggestiveness.

from above (he represents social and intellectual tyranny). Blake did not think of his figure as Urizen when he invented him: the same figure appears in exactly this posture and setting in *All Religions Are One* (*c.* 1788; plate 4) about five years before Blake named Urizen (in *Visions*); but Urizen is named in *America* (10.3; 18.2–5), and this iconography of the old, bearded, saturnine figure soon becomes familiar, in *Europe* and in *The Book of Urizen*. However, the text of this plate is a speech from Orc. What, then, is the relation of text and design? Appeals to the text are problematic because they can be stood on their head: sometimes the designs illustrate the text, but sometimes they contain images which are in direct opposition to it. According to W. J. T. Mitchell, *America* plate 10 is 'an image not of the speaker but of the speaker's *vision*'.[44] This is oversophisticated: it suggests that the design offers a view of Urizen from a perspective which is placed by the work as a whole, whereas both text and design of this plate present visions of the protagonist which the work as a whole endorses. Orc (text) and Urizen (design) are here, more simply, counterpointed. The similar contrast between text and design in plate 9 (*Plate 5*) has presented still greater interpretative problems. Some critics, ignoring the visual values of this beautiful design, see it as negative. David Bindman compares it with the previous plate (the resurrection figure): 'the children are at the bottom of the page instead of the top, and their slumber contrasts with his awakening'. But is everything at the bottom of a plate to be seen as negative? What of the contrast of plate 10 (Urizen – negative – top) and plate 12 (Orc – positive – bottom)? And is rest not permitted in the paradise that Orc's revolution will bring about? This is not indolence: it is peace, and the dawning of a new age. The plate again counterpoints text and design: reaction's raving indictment of revolution (text) is contrasted with revolution's image of itself (design).[45] *America* as a whole gives perspectives on both.

Basic to these problems of interpretation is that we should ask what kind of interpreter Blake himself was. How did Blake read? What did he see as the perimeters of viable interpretation? What is meant, for example, by the remarks in *The Marriage of Heaven and Hell* that Milton 'was of the Devil's party without knowing it', or by the infernal reading of the Bible threatened in that work, or by the contrary reading referred to in *The Everlasting Gospel*: 'Both read the Bible day and night, / But thou read'st black where I read white'? In his designs for the Bible Blake has been well described as responding at times to latent or repressed meanings.[46] Blake's myth of Los and his Spectre shows that Blake thought of himself as, like other writers, just such a fractured combination as this account presupposes: an imagination which could appeal to the eternal, and an everyday self vitiated by the temporal; a creator of imaginative texts and designs, and an interpreter who might understand his own

---

[44] *Blake's Composite Art: A Study of the Illuminated Poetry* (Princeton, NJ, 1978), 9. Mitchell took his title ('composite art') from Jean H. Hagstrum, *William Blake: Poet and Painter. An Introduction to the Illuminated Verse* (Chicago, 1964).

[45] Cf. the completely contrasting visions of revolution from different perspectives (as Leviathan and a singing harper) described in *Marriage*, plates 18–19.

[46] Ronald Paulson, 'Blake's Bible', in chapter 4 of his *Books and Painting: Shakespeare, Milton, and the Bible: Literary Texts and the Emergence of English Painting* (Knoxville, TN, 1983), 115–24.

myths and metaphors less than fully; when most in his Spectre's power, a repressiv commentator. Los, the creative spirit in Blake's myth, both keeps the divine visio in time of trouble and becomes what he beholds in the fallen world.[47] One task c interpretation is to be in tune with the divine vision and where necessary to releas it from the less than fully imaginative – which was how Blake sometimes saw hi task as a critic-illustrator of the Bible and other poets. But sometimes releasing latent sense does not mean refuting all plain meanings. When Blake illustrated othe poets (as in the series of designs for Gray, Young, Blair, Milton and Dante), or whei he illustrated the Bible (as in the Job series and the many separate watercolours an temperas), he often did so with the most careful attention to detail and an almos pedantic literalism.[48] He did not constantly imply unexpected and idiosyncrati senses addressed to a coterie audience reading always against the grain. Like th Renaissance painters he admired – Raphael and Michelangelo – Blake assumed ar informed audience: at times his designs draw on a knowledge of iconographic con ventions, and they always require a careful and knowledgeable reading of their texts But the main thing Blake aimed to do as an illuminator of his own poetry was a bottom simple: to excite the viewer to read with the fullest possible imaginative engagement by presenting aspects of the poetry, or complements to it – sometimes obliquely – in visual terms. The viewer/reader needs to look intensely and think imaginatively, and dwell on what he or she sees: 'make a friend and companion of . . . these images of wonder'. Interpretation of Blake's designs – as of his poetry – must be in a degree individual and open-ended. But, despite its inevitable variousness, personal contemplation is a disciplined form of knowledge. It should not be indistinguishable from an interpreter's preferences or fancies. The solipsism which is condemned to read into paintings or poems its own preoccupations, not seeing art's otherness, is the antithesis of a recognition that art 'entreats [the spectator] to leave mortal things . . . arise from his grave . . . [and] meet the Lord in the air'.

(3) MODERNIZING BLAKE'S TEXT

Blake can be read in a variety of material forms. Though most people cannot get access to original copies of the illuminated books (some of which are extant in only one or two copies), thanks to some dedicated labours (particularly those of the Trianon Press), and to modern technology (especially the Tate Gallery/Princeton University Press facsimiles and the Blake Electronic Archive),[49] Blake can now be read in the combined verbal-visual form he intended. But he cannot be so read entirely. Misprinted text in any individual copy has to be recovered from copies with different inking or printing failures; as does unreadable text that has been masked by paint or subject to other accidents. Destroyed text, which cannot be shown up by photolithography, can only be recovered by editors who are able to

---

[47] *Jerusalem*, 30[44].15 and 95.20; *The Four Zoas*, 53.24 and 55.49.
[48] See my 'Blake and Dante', *Art History*, 11 (1988), 349–73.
[49] For details see the bibliography.

xamine its residual indentations in originals. And, as most facsimiles implicitly onfess by providing transcripts of their texts, the illuminated books can be difficult for readers familiar with the regularity of letterpress, especially when the ncised lines impressed by the etched copper plate in the original are flattened out n reproduction. Facsimiles are probably more often accompaniments to letterpress eading than read in themselves.

Facsimiles apart, Blake might be read in letterpress which reproduces the text exactly as he engraved and printed it. But again this proves in practice problematic. Most letterpress texts do not attempt to reproduce Blake's spacing, though some critics regard this as important some of the time; and letterpress has no equivalents of Blake's eccentric marks of punctuation. Apart from the unique eccentricities sometimes taken for punctuation which may be the result of careless etching or poor inking, these include Blake's colons which merge into his exclamation marks, his full stops which merge into his commas, his sometimes uncertain distinction between lower case and capital letters, and his irregular spacings for all punctuation marks. All these irregular forms may imply irregular meanings. Editors who are committed to transcribing what Blake printed (or perhaps – though this can be quite different – to recovering from a comparison of many copies what he engraved) in fact make choices about which standard letterpress punctuation mark most nearly represents the non-standard mark in the original, and they make those choices in relation to contemporary expectations about punctuation in the relevant context.[50] The result is that Blake's two best modern editors, when transcribing the same work from the same copy, several times represent its punctuation differently.[51]

The problems are yet more complicated because in some texts Blake uses adorned scripts in which the adornments – nothing like letterpress forms of punctuation – act, and surely were intended by Blake, partly as forms of punctuation. How adorned Blake's script can be the opening text plate of *America* demonstrates (plate 3). Here, in every line, a number of letters are exuberantly decorated – for example the *d* of 'abhorr'd' (line 11), which develops into a long vine; or the *b* of 'limbs' (line 16), which ascends as though recording the flight-path of a large insect. This is the usual form of Blake's script in *America*: other plates show even more fantastic adornments – for example, the beings, creatures and shapes that grow out of 'who commanded this? What God' (13.7), or the similar beings that grow out of 'earth' (17.5). Decorations of this kind are characteristic of Blake's script in many texts. In some places they punctuate quite as much as what we might usually recognize as

---

[50] Both David Erdman (*Complete Poetry and Prose*, 786–7) and G. E. Bentley Jr. (*Writings*, xliii–xliv) discuss the problems. Erdman admits that he is 'inclined . . . to read commas or periods according to the contextual expectations'.

[51] See the Bentley and Erdman editions of *The Book of Los*, which exists in only one copy. The two editions differ over punctuation in several places largely because Blake's marks cannot be directly transcribed into standard typography. Differences of interpretation or of representation between the two editions can be readily multiplied: see E. B. Murray's review of Bentley, *BIQ*, 14 (1980–81), 148–61. Murray concludes (p. 160), 'In the long run, the problems and the contradictory solutions available for them probably exceed even a theoretic comprehension, much more any set of workable editorial principles.'

punctuation;[52] and conversely irregular punctuation, as one aspect of the decorate
character of a script, plays its part in adornment: it is not primarily syntactic o
rhythmic-rhetorical; it is visual *jouissance*. In these cases, the forms in which punc
tuation occurs, and the ways in which it functions in the original, are entirely mis
represented when all the other adornments are stripped away and only what can b
recognized as related to conventional punctuation remains, regularized in form an
position into letterpress 'equivalents'. Blake's punctuation has to be understood ir
the context of his script as a whole in a way that conventional typography simply
cannot reproduce.

Moreover, despite Blake's own insistence on the expressive importance of detail
in his texts, he was often not careful about punctuation. Most obviously, when Blake
inked in text which had not printed properly he often did not ink in punctuation,
and when he did he sometimes inked in punctuation different from that which
other copies show to have been the punctuation of the copper plate. Then, passages
adapted from one work to another – for example, the three appearances of the lines
describing Los's fixing of Urizen's fallen form[53] – have numerous differences of punc-
tuation. Most repeated lines are not punctuated in the same way in their different
appearances. The three-times-repeated choric line of *America* plate 11 is punctuated
differently at each appearance. The five-times-repeated choric line of *Milton* is likewise
never given with the same punctuation.[54] The lines repeated from *The Marriage of
Heaven and Hell* in *Visions of the Daughters of Albion* and in *America*[55] are punctuated
differently in their different appearances. The two 'Nurse's Song's, in *Innocence* and
in *Experience*, have three common lines, but two of these are punctuated in the two
poems differently.[56] It might conceivably be argued that some of these differences
are related to context, but no dispassionate consideration could suppose that most
are. Moreover, there is much more variation in punctuation between different
copies of the same work than is generally recognized, not only because of misprinted

---

[52] For punctuation by decorated script, see, for example, 'Nurse's Song' (*Experience*), l. 6, 'arise',
where a long tail on the 'e' filling the rest of the line functions as a stop; or *America*, where
the exuberant tails on the 'y' of 'sky' (line 10) and the 'h' of 'youth' (line 22), both words
which occur at the ends of paragraphs but are followed by no conventional punctuation,
act in these contexts as marks indicating conclusion.

[53] *The Book of Urizen*, plates 10–13; *The Four Zoas*, pp. 54–5; *Milton*, plate b.

[54] 3.25; a.20; 5.18; 5.50; 7.7.

[55] *Marriage*, 'A Song of Liberty', Chorus; *Visions*, 11.10; *Marriage*, 9.19; *America*, 10.14.

[56] In *Experience*, lines 1 and 5 have Blake's common non-syntactic intrusive full stop:

When the voices of children. are heard on the green
Then come home my children. the sun is gone down

The corresponding lines in *Innocence*, verbally exactly the same, are punctuated differently:
the first has no punctuation, the second a mid-point comma. A similar apparent indifference
about punctuation is suggested by different punctuations for parallel clauses in adjacent
stanzas: for example, 'A Cradle Song', stanzas 3 and 4, 'Sweet smiles Mothers smiles / All the
livelong night beguiles. // . . . / . . . / Sweet moans, sweeter smiles, / All the dovelike moans
beguiles.' (Erdman's text: cf. note 65: the differences between the two stanzas are present
irrespective of how the punctuation of the original is rendered.)

punctuation but also because, in later copies especially, Blake would often cover punctuation when he coloured the plate. With one of the few texts for which a variorum of the punctuation has been attempted, *The Book of Thel*, of the work's one hundred and twenty-five lines (only two of which are unpunctuated) only thirty-nine are punctuated identically in the seventeen extant copies (Bogen, 1971, 10). Much of the evidence derived from Blake's practices therefore – corrected and un-corrected misprinting, repeated lines, variations between copies – suggests that he was relatively indifferent about punctuation. While some of his punctuation may have been carefully considered and expressive, much of it evidently was not.

Different problems about editing and punctuation are presented by the manu-script poems – those in Blake's Notebook, and *The Four Zoas*. The illuminated books were intended as public documents. The Notebook was not. The manuscript of *The Four Zoas* may have been intended as a public document during some of the work's composition (see the headnote, p. 238), though almost certainly not during its later stages of development. The poems in the Notebook engraved in *Songs of Experience* are much more lightly punctuated in their manuscript forms, and this is also true of the lines of *The Four Zoas* which were engraved in *Milton* and *Jerusalem*. With these works there is therefore an even slighter case for preserving punctuation which Blake's practice elsewhere indicates he would have revised had he prepared them for publication in his usual way.

With all these considerations in mind, while there is evidently a need for the kinds of collected edition produced by G. E. Bentley and David Erdman, and for the kind of facsimile edition of all the illuminated books overseen by David Bindman (in which the text and punctuation of the individual copies used is transcribed),[57] it should be clear that any notion of 'Blake's punctuation' is highly problematic and cannot be treated as a shibboleth. There is not only one useful way of editing. Choices depend on an edition's purpose and audience.[58]

While modernizing involves some losses it also offers some important gains. Prin-cipally, it can clarify problems of Blake's syntax, problems to which a transcribing editor need not attend, but for which a reader must find solutions. A reader con-fronting the considerable difficulties of Blake's text for the first time is not helped by the presence of punctuation in the middle of syntactic units, the absence of punctuation at the ends of syntactic units, and other elements of syntactic struc-ture which are not marked by any form of punctuation, as well as a host of other idiosyncratic usages which cannot be explained in any systematic way,[59] all of which

---

[57] For details see the bibliography.

[58] Peter Middleton presents an argument for the importance of what he takes to be Blake's punctuation, but on the assumption that the forms and significances of the punctuation in the originals are those of letterpress. In the five-line passage mainly discussed, he contrives to misquote the punctuation, the lineation, the paragraphing and the words (*Oxford Literary Review*, 6 (1983), 35–51).

[59] For example, Blake's use and non-use of the question mark: contrast its complete absence from the questions of 'The Lamb' with its copious presence in the questions of the companion poem 'The Tiger'; or in 'Earth's Answer' contrast its absence where questions are asked in stanza 3 with its presence in the middle of questions as well as at their end in stanza 4.

can make the primary sense difficult to recognize. Modernizing means that the editor is doing some of the ideal reader's work – clarifying, for example, the syntactic possibilities which are always present as a base from which interpretation may knowingly deviate. Many readers are not ideal readers; many readers do benefit from having that work done for them. I had thought of myself as a careful reader of Blake. Certainly I have read him carefully enough to have filled the margins and destroyed the bindings of more than one collected edition. But in editing him I have noticed problems of syntax which I did not notice as a non-editing reader, and I suspect this is not unusual. Modernizing certainly runs the risk of producing meanings not intended by Blake, but then so can retaining Blake's punctuation;[60] and the occasional misreadings of modernizing editors – unless one considers such editors peculiarly obtuse – are themselves demonstrations of how often the reader unaided by editorial clarifications may misunderstand.[61] Sometimes where a choice of senses is available that choice has to be made not in terms of immediate sense and syntax but in terms of context.[62] Sometimes it has to be made in terms of what seems a preferable shape for the rhetoric – whether, for example, it seems characteristic in a given case for syntax and lineation to coincide or to be expressively at odds.

Syntactic ambiguity can, of course, produce a valuable interaction of different possible meanings. But it can also produce a mental haze antithetical to Blake's demand for the sharply precise. The editor as ideal reader is often called on to make choices. The common absence of punctuation at line endings, for example, often means that lines can be connected either backwards or forwards – as in the following.

> Albions Guardian writhed in torment on the eastern sky
> Pale quivring toward the brain his glimmering eyes, teeth chattering
> Howling & shuddering his legs quivering; convuls'd each muscle & sinew
> Sick'ning lay Londons Guardian, and the ancient miter'd York
> Their heads on snowy hills, their ensigns sick'ning in the sky
> (*America* 17.6–10)

Here Blake's punctuation (the semicolon in the middle of line 8) might suggest distributing the parallel phrases between the two candidates (Albion/London) – a choice no modernizing editor makes: the shape of the rhetoric (parallel phrases modify the same noun) and the form (line-ending is a type of punctuation) is allowed to

---

[60] See, for example, 'A Song of Liberty', Chorus: 'Let the Priests of the Raven of Dawn, no longer in deadly black, with hoarse note curse the sons of joy.' Blake's meaning is evidently '. . . no longer, in deadly black . . .': priests, indicatively black-gowned, should no longer curse (not, as the punctuation on a modern interpretation implies, priests, wearing something other than their usual colour, should continue to curse).

[61] A simple but representative case of misunderstanding shown up by modernization comes in *The Four Zoas*, 49.4, 'So Saying in a Wave he rap'd bright Enitharmon'. W. H. Stevenson at first modernized '. . . he raped bright Enitharmon' (*The Complete Poems*, London, 1971), correcting (properly) to 'rapt' (meaning 'carried off') in his revised edition (1989).

[62] See, for example, *Visions of the Daughters of Albion*, 7.2 and note; *The Four Zoas*, 34.94–5 and note.

predominate. Stevenson adds a full stop at the end of line 6 so as to apply lines 7–8 to London; Sloss and Wallis, Keynes, Bentley and Mason add a full stop at the end of line 8, and so apply lines 7–8 to Albion. Stevenson's choice seems to me definitely wrong, mainly because it involves an awkward shift from singular to plural within the same syntactic unit ('his . . . their'), partly because the lack of punctuation at the most probable point (line 8) has a possible material cause (the word 'sinew' only just fitted on to the etched plate). A similar problem occurs in *America* at 16.9–10. Here an intervening illustration can be taken as punctuation. Mason does so understand it; Sloss and Wallis, Keynes, Bentley and Stevenson agree in regarding the syntax as continuous across the illustration. Similarly in *America* Blake has no punctuation at the end of plate 17. Mason connects the last line of plate 17 and the first line of plate 18; most editors add a full stop, accepting that the plate-ending acts as a form of punctuation and that 18.1 begins a new syntactic unit.[63] In cases of serious doubt the annotation gives the original punctuation and the range of alternative possibilities.

Blake's punctuation is, however, often not syntactic. Where it has a discernible specific purpose it may also be intended to point the rhythm (for example, by marking a caesura); or it may be intended to point the rhetoric where the shapes do not coincide with the lineation.[64] Or non-syntactic punctuation was perhaps sometimes intended to signify what a twentieth-century poet might render by lay-out – a reading which considers each phrase or clause as a separate unit:

> Sweet moans,
>   dovelike sighs,
> Chase not slumber from thy eyes.
> Sweet moans,
>   sweeter smiles,
> All the dovelike moans beguiles.[65]

But these can be no more than hypotheses. Distinctive idiosyncratic feature of the text that it is, much of Blake's punctuation is not specifically explicable. And it can be actively misleading about syntax.

---

[63] Cf. *America*, 3.4–10, which Sloss and Wallis, Keynes, Stevenson and Mason all punctuate with striking differences.

[64] See, for example, *Visions of the Daughters of Albion*, 8.10–11: 'Does he who contemns poverty, and he who turns in abhorrence / From usury: feel the same passion', where the non-syntactic colon may be intended to point the parallelism of the antithetical phrases which is obscured by the lineation:

> Does he who contemns poverty
>   and he who turns in abhorrence from usury
> Feel the same passion . . .

[65] 'A Cradle Song'. This hypothetical lay-out is based on Bentley's reading of the original punctuation: 'Sweet moans. dovelike sighs. / Chase not slumber from thy eyes. / Sweet moans. sweeter smiles. / All the dovelike moans beguiles.' The stanza exemplifies the difficulties of rendering the punctuation of the original in letterpress. Erdman (*Complete Poetry and Prose*, 12) and Lincoln (Tate/Princeton facsimile, 1991) both represent the punctuation of this stanza differently from Bentley and from each other. Cf. note 67.

Blake's most notable and potentially misleading idiosyncrasy is his use of the full stop. A full stop can occur in the middle of a word (*America*, 6.11: 'atmo./-sphere'), and full stops commonly occur in the middle of grammatical units. This may sometimes be intended to mark an internal rhyme ('The Little Boy Found': 'Who in sorrow pale. thro' the lonely dale'),[66] though Blake often has internal rhyme unmarked by punctuation (as, for example, in 'The Little Vagabond'). But it apparently most often signifies the kind of minor syntactic disjunction which would now be rendered by a comma: 'And because I am happy. & dance & sing' ('The Chimney Sweeper', *Songs of Experience*); 'And Father. how can I love you' ('A Little Boy Lost'). Or a full stop can be (as it was commonly in the seventeenth century) an extra way of marking the end of a line, as in 'Night', which has full stops at the end of each of the last four lines though the syntax is continuous.[67] Or it can be an extra way of marking the end of a stanza, as in 'Laughing Song', which has full stops at the end of the first and second stanzas, though the grammar is continuous into stanza three.

There are, moreover, many examples of punctuation which actively misleads the reader about the syntax.

> On his head a crown
> On his shoulders down,
> Flow'd his golden hair.
> ('The Little Girl Found')

Here the presence of the syntactically redundant comma implies (absurdly) that 'down' is a noun parallel to 'crown' rather than as an adverb modifying 'Flow'd'. In 'The Little Black Boy' on the other hand, the absence of a comma where it is syntactically expected between two parallel phrases – 'Comfort in morning joy in the noon day' – momentarily confuses about the function of 'morning', which can be mistaken for an adjective modifying 'joy'. These examples the competent reader readily sees how to negotiate. But the long poems, often much more syntactically complex than the lyrics, provide many examples of syntactic problems which are much less straightforward. Bentley addresses the difficulty by frequently modernizing, with an elaborate apparatus to indicate where he does so. And even the relatively purist Erdman alters the most syntactically misleading punctuation, recording such changes in his textual notes.

There may be all sorts of meanings in Blake's punctuation. And in some of it there may be no meaning. Its meaning is often not syntactic, and it often misleads

---

[66] Cf. 'The Garden of Love': 'And Priests in black gowns, were walking their rounds, / And binding with briars, my joys & desires.' (On the 'gowns' / 'rounds' rhyme see the annotation.)

[67] Cf. 'Holy Thursday', *Songs of Experience*, stanza 1, in which each line ends with a syntactically redundant full stop. Also *Songs of Experience*, 'Introduction', 'That might controll. / The starry pole', and 'Earth's Answer', 'Break this heavy chain. / That does freeze my bones around' – though both of these are also examples of the ambiguous forms of Blake's punctuation. In the first case Bentley gives no punctuation (perhaps in error, but perhaps correctly interpreting the mark undoubtedly present in some copies as a spatter); Erdman gives a comma. In the second case Bentley gives a full stop, Erdman a comma: the mark is an indeterminate hybrid.

bout the syntax. Readers coming to Blake for the first time may have many needs. Guidance with his syntax is fundamental to other kinds of sense-making.

*   *   *

Modernization also helps with pointing Blake's rhythms by retaining his indica-tions of syllabic value: for example, 'ev'n', 'giv'n', 'black'ning', 'sick'ning', 'rav'nous', 'wintry' (not 'wintery'), and so on. While these forms can be obscured by modern-zation,[68] modernization which retains them, by the new context of more familiar forms, draws attention to them. This is particularly important from the point of view of Blake's rhythms with his distinction between final non-syllabic d or $'d$ and syllabic ed. It is not possible, of course, in the relatively free metres of the long-line poems to be conclusively sure simply from any given case that Blake's practice was entirely consistent. However, his practice in the metrically regular poems suggests that inconsistencies are at most very few.[69] The two forms are used throughout his work, and the only alternative to supposing the *intention* of a consistent distinction is to suppose that the distinction is meaningless – a supposition which its use in the metrically regular verse, where Blake's intention can be judged against recognized patterns of syllabic organization, entirely contradicts. The convention of pronounced final 'ed' in formal written usage was still very much alive in the late eighteenth century. It was still observed in the printed texts of the younger generation of Blake's contemporaries. It is observed consistently, for example, in Keats's 1820 volume. Rhymes on ed or d, in the few places where Blake uses them, indicate that the con-vention is being observed: 'bed' rhymes with 'ecchoed', 'mild' with ' beguil'd'. A more interesting and important test is provided by the poems and passages copied from one source to another – the two manuscripts of 'I askèd a thief to steal me a peach';[70] the poems in *Songs of Innocence* first included in *An Island in the Moon*,[71]

---

[68] Contracted forms are not retained by Stevenson, who regularly ignores all such indications of syllabic value. They are retained by Mason, as also in the more partial and conservative modernization of Keynes. (For details of these editions see the bibliography.)

[69] One exception to Blake's ed indicating $èd$ in his metrically regular verse comes in the 'Introduction' to *Songs of Innocence*: 'So I piped with merry chear, / . . . / So I piped, he wept to hear'. Here Blake perhaps thought of the 'e' as necessary to modify the 'i' and to dis-tinguish 'pipe' from 'pip': cf. *Songs of Experience*, 'The Little Vagabond', line 3, 'use'd' (Notebook, p. 105, 'usd'), and *Milton*, 11.47, 'tone'd' (where the 'e' is retained to modify the 'o'), both cases of other verbs which can function as nouns where the 'e' is necessary to distinguishing them from another common word. In these cases an apostrophe is used to indicate that the 'e' should not be pronounced. See also 'Ah, sunflower', *Songs of Experience*, line 5 note.

[70] Bentley, *Writings*, 996, 1071. In the fair copy Blake actually marks with an accent the 'e' of 'askèd' in line 1 (to distinguish it from monosyllabic 'asked' in line 3), and he maintains the distinction from the Notebook version between ed (line 2) and $'d$ (lines 7, 8, 12). 'Turned' (line 2) must be disyllabic: line 2 is not otherwise the trimeter required by the ballad metre stanza structure to match line 4.

[71] For example, 'Nurses Song', line 17, 'The little ones leaped and shouted and laugh'd', where the same ed / $'d$ distinction is made in the version in *An Island in the Moon*.

and the poems in *Songs of Experience* drafted in the Notebook;[72] the passages from the early prophetic books transposed into *The Four Zoas*,[73] and the passages from *The Four Zoas* transposed into *Milton* and *Jerusalem*. With reworkings to or from *The Four Zoas* one must allow for the fact that re-use is almost never simply transcription. Blake usually reworked material to suit the new context, or, one may deduce simply with an aim of aesthetic improvement. Nevertheless, practically without exception, when reworking material from one poem to another, and often in the context of making numerous other changes, Blake retains distinctions between *d* or *'d* and *ed*.[74] Those who have written on Blake's metrics have understood the distinction as meaningful.[75] Unnecessarily, modernizing editors have not, and have usually suppressed it, modernizing all forms without differentiation to *ed*.[76]

Contemporary readers are not accustomed to observing Blake's distinction between pronounced and unpronounced 'ed'. Without a modern way of rendering it, therefore, the rhythms Blake intended, for which he had this still widely recognized convention of notation, are probably often not observed. In some cases, I suspect, observing them may have results which are surprising even to Blake's most competent readers.

---

[72] Here the distinction is reproduced with almost complete consistency. The single exception is 'The Angel' where in the Notebook line 6 has 'wiped' (which, since it is metrically possible, may indicate only that in engraving the poem Blake changed his mind). In the draft of 'My Pretty Rose Tree', 'But my rose was turned from me' was altered to 'But my rose turnd away with Jealousy'; in the draft of 'London', 'The german forged links I hear' was altered to 'The mind forgd manacles I hear' – both changes which clearly indicate Blake observing the *'d* / *ed* distinction.

[73] See, for example, *The Book of Urizen*, plates 10–13; *The Four Zoas*, pp. 54–5; *Milton*, plate b: despite the changes of form between *The Book of Urizen* and *The Four Zoas* (short to long lines), and the overall abbreviation of the passage in *Milton*, there is only one single change of a verb form.

[74] See, for example, *The Four Zoas* 39.17–20, 40.1–20, 41.1–18, 42.1–19, which became *Jerusalem*, 29[43].33–82: in a context of several minor changes the *d* (or *'d*) and *ed* distinction is reproduced with complete consistency. Exceptions can be found: *America* 8.6–12 is repeated verbatim in *The Four Zoas* 134.18–24, except that one *ed* becomes *d*. Whether this indicates Blake's occasional inconsistency or a change of mind about the rhythm is, of course, impossible to tell.

[75] In one of the best discussions of Blake's metrics in his long-line verse (*The Continuing City*, pp. 42–57) Morton Paley is explicit: see p. 54, n. 1.

[76] The distinction is ignored by both Stevenson and Mason. The only edition actively to bring it out is that of Sloss and Wallis which retains the non-syllabic forms and renders the syllabic form *èd*.

CHRONOLOGY

1752

15 Oct.: marriage of James Blake (a hosier) and Catherine Harmitage. The couple were dissenters, in what sect is not known.

1753

July: birth of James Blake (died ?February/March 1827) (see 1809).

1755

12 May: birth of John Blake (presumed died in infancy since the Blakes' fourth child was also named John).

1757

28 Nov.: William Blake born at 28, Broad Street, Golden Square, Westminster.

1760

20 Mar.: birth of John Blake, referred to by Blake in 1802 as 'my brother John, the evil one' and as already dead; lived at 29, Broad Street from 1784 to 1793, apparently working as a baker, latterly in poor circumstances.

Ossian (James MacPherson), *Fragments of Ancient Poetry* (see *Visions of the Daughters of Albion* headnote).

Accession of George III.

Josiah Wedgwood founds pottery at Etruria, Staffordshire (see 1815).

1762

25 Apr.: birth of Catherine Sophia Boucher, later Mrs Blake, daughter of a market gardener in Battersea, the last of thirteen children (four of whom died in infancy). Such evidence as there is about the family suggests it was poor. Catherine probably could not read or write when she and William married.

19 June: birth of Richard Blake (died in infancy).

1764

7 Jan.: birth of Catherine Elizabeth Blake (died after 1833).

1765

Bishop Thomas Percy, *Reliques of Ancient English Poetry* (a collection of ballads, songs, and metrical romances, mostly written from the fifteenth to the seventeenth century; Blake's copy is still extant).

1767

4 Aug.: birth of Robert Blake, Blake's favourite brother. In this or the following year Blake begins to attend the drawing school of Henry Pars in the Strand, his only formal schooling (until 1772).

1768

Thomas Gray, *Poems* (see 1797).

1768–69

Begins to compose poems that later appeared in *Poetical Sketches* (1783), described in the advertisement to the publication as written between Blake's twelfth and twentieth years (1768–77).

1770

Birth of Wordsworth.

Death by suicide of the poet Thomas Chatterton at the age of eighteen. Blake professed himself an admirer of his pseudo-medieval poems 'equally with any poet whatever'.

1771

Arkwright's first spinning mill.

1772

4 Aug.: apprenticed to the engraver James Basire (until 1779), for whom he sketches from the tombs in Westminster Abbey. During his apprenticeship Blake probably lived in Basire's house, 31, Great Queen Street, Lincoln's Inn Fields (near his home, between Holborn and the Strand).

Birth of Coleridge.

1775

James Watt perfects his invention of the steam engine.

1776

Beginnings of the American War of Independence: Declaration of Independence signed (4 July) by eleven British colonies.

Edward Gibbon, *Decline and Fall of the Roman Empire* (–1788).

1779

8 Oct.: admitted to the Royal Academy of Arts as a student under the painter and Academy Keeper G. M. Moser.

Watercolours on English historical subjects, including 'The Penance of Jane Shore'.

David Hume, *Dialogues of Natural Religion* (published posthumously).

1780

Conception of the engraving known as 'Glad Day' ('Albion Rose'). Exhibits for the first time at the Royal Academy – watercolour: 'The Death of Earl Goodwin'. At about this time begins important friendships with the sculptor John Flaxman (1756–1826), the painter Thomas Stothard (1755–1834) and the painter, etcher and *amateur* of the fine arts George Cumberland (1754–1840s?). First engraving commissions from the publisher Joseph Johnson (later the publisher of Tom Paine, William Godwin, Mary Wollstonecraft, and other radical writers). Arrested on suspicion of spying for the French while on a drawing expedition on the Thames with Stothard and another friend; released within hours. June: Gordon Riots – civil disorder in London in response to proposed easing of anti-Catholic legislation during which Newgate prison was broken open and burned.

1781
Effective end of the American War of Independence with the British surrender at Yorktown. (Treaty of Versailles signed in 1783.)

Anna Laetitia Barbauld, *Hymns in Prose for Children*.

1782
18 Aug.: marriage to Catherine Boucher. The couple live first at 23, Green Street, Leicester Fields (later Leicester Square), and then at 27, Broad Street (next to Blake's parents). Begins to move in the literary and artistic circle of Mrs Harriet Mathew (a milieu satirized in *An Island in the Moon*).

William Cowper, *Poems* (see 1800).

1783
Poetical Sketches, printed at the expense of Flaxman and the Reverend A. S. Mathew and distributed privately.

1784
An Island in the Moon (containing early versions of three *Songs of Innocence*) probably dates from this time.

Exhibits at the Royal Academy: 'War Unchained by an Angel, Fire, Pestilence and Famine Following', and 'A Breach in a City, the Morning after a Battle'.

4 July: death of Blake's father. Blake begins to run a print-selling shop in partnership with James Parker (a fellow apprentice from Basire's) at 27, Broad Street; this fails in the following year.

1785
Blake and Catherine move to Poland Street, Soho. Exhibits at the Royal Academy: three biblical drawings (on the story of Joseph), and 'The Bard' (after Thomas Gray's poem).

James Watt and Matthew Boulton install the first industrial steam engine in a cotton-spinning factory in Nottinghamshire.

1787
Feb.: death of Robert Blake from consumption. Blake nurses his brother in his last illness. At about this time begins friendship with the Swiss-born painter Henry Fuseli (1741–1825).

Society for the Abolition of the Slave Trade formed (begins soliciting subscriptions in Nov. 1788).

1788

The probable year of Blake's first experiments with illuminated printing, the tractates *All Religions Are One* and *There is No Natural Religion*.

Annotations of Lavater's *Aphorisms on Man* (translated by Fuseli, published by Johnson, with a frontispiece portrait engraved by Blake after a design by Fuseli); also annotates (sympathetically) Swedenborg's *Wisdom of Angels Concerning Divine Love and Divine Wisdom*.

George Washington elected first President of the United States of America (inaugurated Jan. 1789). George III's first attack of mental illness (recovers 1789).

Act of Parliament attempts to ameliorate the conditions of child chimney sweeps, but proves difficult to enforce.

1789

Tiriel (?); *The Book of Thel*; *Songs of Innocence*.

13 Apr.: Blake and Catherine attend the first session of the general conference of the Swedenborgian New Church, and sign its manifesto.

Beginning of the French Revolution. Fall of the Bastille (14 July).

1790

The Marriage of Heaven and Hell (?).

Annotates (critically) Swedenborg's *The Wisdom of Angels Concerning the Divine Providence*. Blake and Catherine move to 13, Hercules Buildings, Lambeth (south of the River Thames).

Edmund Burke, *Reflections on the Revolution in France*.

1791

The French Revolution (set up in type by Johnson but not published).

Illustrates Mary Wollstonecraft's *Original Stories from Real Life*. Engraves plates for Erasmus Darwin's *The Botanic Garden*, and Christian Gotthilf Salzmann's *Elements of Morality* (translated by Mary Wollstonecraft). Begins work on engravings for John Gabriel Stedman's *Surinam* (see 1796).

Tom Paine, *The Rights of Man*, Part 1, published by Johnson.

1792

Engraves four plates for vol. 3 of Stuart and Revett's *Antiquities of Athens* (one of the most important works of eighteenth-century classical scholarship; vol. 1, published 1762, was a major source for neo-classicism).

7 Sept.: death of Blake's mother.

Paine, *The Rights of Man*, Part 2. Wollstonecraft, *A Vindication of the Rights of Woman*, published by Johnson.

)eath of the painter and first President of the Royal Academy, Sir Joshua Reynolds.
'rance proclaimed a Republic.

1793

Visions of the Daughters of Albion; *America*; the emblem book, *For Children: the Gates of Paradise*.

10 Oct.: prospectus advertising *Songs of Innocence*, *Thel*, *Visions*, *America*, and *Songs of Experience*. Probable first meetings with Thomas Butts, a civil servant who became one of Blake's most important patrons.

William Godwin, *An Enquiry Concerning Political Justice*.

21 Jan.: execution of Louis XVI.

Feb.: war declared between Britain and France. The period of the French Revolution 'Terror' (group trials without defence lawyers or witnesses; mass executions), culminating in the Great Terror of June/July 1794 during which 1,376 people were guillotined in Paris alone.

Eli Whitney invents the cotton gin.

1794

Songs of Innocence and of Experience, *Europe*, *The [First] Book of Urizen*.

Paine, *The Age of Reason*, Part 1.

28 July: execution of Robespierre brings the Terror to an end.

Nov.: trials, and popular acquittals, of the notable English radicals Thomas Hardy, Thomas Holcroft, John Thelwall and John Horne Tooke.

Habeas Corpus Act suspended (–1804) means the possibility of detention without trial.

1795

The Song of Los; *The Book of Los*; *The Book of Ahania*.

Blake prints in a uniform style sets of large-paper copies of his entire *œuvre* in relief etching. After this, apart from the two sets of *Songs* (and possibly *America* copy M), no copies of the illuminated books written up to this time are printed until 1818.

Commissioned to illustrate an edition of Edward Young's *Night Thoughts*; produces 537 watercolours from which only 43 plates are engraved (published 1797).

Twelve Colour Prints, including some of Blake's best-known images: 'Newton', 'God Judging Adam', 'Nebuchadnezzar'.

Speenhamland Act for poor relief (wages supplemented by dole).

1796

A Small Book of Designs and *A Large Book of Designs* (designs from the illuminated books printed without their accompanying texts).

John Gabriel Stedman's *Narrative of a Five Years Expedition against the Revolted Negroes of Surinam* published, with engravings by Blake (Blake's plates dated 1792–94).

Engraves plates for George Cumberland's *Thoughts on Outline.*

Paine, *The Age of Reason,* Part 2.

1797

Begins *Vala* (which later becomes *The Four Zoas*).

Illustrates the poems of Thomas Gray (116 watercolours, commissioned by Flaxman for his wife Ann).

1798

Annotations of Bishop Richard Watson's *Apology for the Bible* (a reply to Paine's *Age of Reason*). Probably also annotates Bacon's *Essays* at about this time.

Wordsworth and Coleridge, *Lyrical Ballads.*

Thomas Malthus, *Essay on the Principles of Population* (enlarged edns., 1803 and 1805).

1799

Exhibits at the Royal Academy (for the first time since 1785), the tempera 'The Last Supper'.

Flaxman introduces Blake to the art connoisseur and popular poet William Hayley (1745–1820): Blake is engaged to engrave designs for Hayley's *Essay on Sculpture* (1800).

Napoleon seizes power in France (*coup d'état* of 18th Brumaire).

1799–1800

Combination Laws, against trade union organization (repealed 1824).

1800

Exhibits at the Royal Academy, the tempera 'The Miracle of the Loaves and Fishes'.

16 Sept.: Blake and Catherine move to a cottage in Felpham, Sussex, owned by William Hayley. Blake works on engravings and miniature portrait painting under Hayley's patronage, and begins a series of portrait heads of the poets to decorate Hayley's library. During this period Blake continues work on *Vala* (*The Four Zoas*) until *c.* 1807, and begins *Milton* (see 1810). He also continues to work on commissions from Butts, and over the following five years paints about one hundred watercolours for him on biblical subjects.

5 Oct.: 'Little Tom the Sailor', a broadsheet ballad by Hayley with illustrations drawn and engraved by Blake.

Death of the poet William Cowper, of whom Hayley wrote a biography with designs drawn and engraved by Blake (published 1803).

Wordsworth and Coleridge: second edition of *Lyrical Ballads* with a new preface by Wordsworth.

London at this date a city of *c.* 864,000 inhabitants (Britain *c.* 10.4 million).

1801

Watercolour illustrations to Milton's *Comus* (a second set painted *c.* 1815)

Probably annotates Reynolds' *Discourses* for the first time at about this period (and see 1808).

1802

Designs for a series of *Ballads Founded on Anecdotes Relating to Animals* by Hayley drawn and engraved by Blake.

Mar.: Peace of Amiens: temporary cessation of war with France.

1803

Engravings for a new edition of Hayley's poem *The Triumphs of Temper*, after designs by Maria Flaxman (half-sister of the sculptor).

30 Jan.: letter to James Blake stating his decision to leave Felpham; also mentions that he is learning Latin, Greek and Hebrew.

25 Apr.: letter to Butts mentioning a poem of 'an immense number of verses on one grand theme' (perhaps *The Four Zoas*, perhaps *Milton*).

10 May: war renewed against France.

12 Aug.: Blake evicts a dragoon, Private John Scolfield, from his garden.

15 Aug.: Scolfield deposes that Blake assaulted him and made seditious remarks. Blake denies the charges and is bailed by Hayley and a local printer, Joseph Seagrave.

Sept.: the Blakes return to London, to new lodgings at 17, South Molton Street (off Oxford Street).

1804

Jan.: trial for sedition at Chichester Quarter Sessions which ends in Blake's acquittal.

Oct.: visits the Truchsession Gallery of Pictures, and describes himself as a result as 'again enlightened with the light I enjoyed in my youth'.

Title pages of *Milton* and *Jerusalem* dated 1804, though the first copies of *Milton* were not printed until *c.* 1810, and the first copies of *Jerusalem* not until *c.* 1820.

Napoleon becomes Emperor.

1805

Blake commissioned by the speculative publisher Robert Cromek to illustrate Robert Blair's poem, *The Grave*; the lucrative aspect of the project, the engraving of the designs, is later given to Louis Schiavonetti in what Blake regards as a swindle. Over the following five years Blake did little engraving work and was almost entirely dependent on the patronage of Thomas Butts.

Probable date of the watercolour illustrations to The Book of Job painted for Butts (though these may be later, *c.* 1810; a second set for John Linnell painted *c.* 1821).

Oct.: Battle of Trafalgar (Britain v. France and Spain) and death of Nelson.

1806

Benjamin Heath Malkin, *A Father's Memoir of his Child*, published, containing a biographical and critical essay on Blake with examples of his poetry from *Poetical Sketches* and *Songs*.

Blake writes to *The Monthly Magazine* defending Fuseli (and through Fuseli his own artistic principles) after an attack in *Bell's Weekly Messenger*.

Death of the painter James Barry whose work Blake admired.

The British cotton industry at this date employs *c*. 90,000 factory workers and 184,000 handloom weavers.

1807

Watercolour illustrations of Milton's *Paradise Lost* (a second set painted for Butts in 1808).

Entry in Blake's Notebook: 'Tuesday Jan. 20, 1807, between two and seven in the evening – despair.'

May: Thomas Phillips' portrait of Blake exhibited at the Royal Academy.

Petworth House version of *The Last Judgement* commissioned.

Wordsworth, *Poems in Two Volumes*.

Abolition of the British slave trade. First introduction of street lighting by gas in London.

1808

Publication of Cromek's edition of Blair's *The Grave*, with an engraved frontispiece of Phillips' portrait and a dedicatory poem by Blake addressed to Queen Charlotte (wife of George III). The designs are attacked by Robert Hunt in *The Examiner*. Second, more personal and hostile annotations of Reynolds's *Discourses* were probably made at about this time.

1809

Watercolour illustrations for Milton's 'On the Morning of Christ's Nativity' (a second set painted *c*. 1815).

May/Sept.: Blake's exhibition at 28, Broad Street (the family home and now the house of his brother James), with its *Descriptive Catalogue* describing the principles of Blake's art. The exhibition, which included Blake's watercolour of 'Chaucer's Canterbury Pilgrims', is visited by the journalist and diarist Henry Crabb Robinson and the poet (and associate of Wordsworth and Coleridge) Robert Southey. It is attacked in *The Examiner*, where Blake is described as an 'unfortunate lunatic'.

1810

Probable date of the first printings of *Milton*.

8 Oct.: engraving of 'Chaucer's Canterbury Pilgrims' published.

Drafts in the Notebook of a 'Public Address' and a description of Blake's largest picture (now lost), one of several versions of 'A Vision of the Last Judgement'.

1811

Tempera, *An Allegory of the Spiritual Condition of Man.*

Crabb Robinson records a visit to Blake with Southey during which they are shown parts of *Jerusalem*: he reports that Southey 'admired both [Blake's] designs and his poetic talents', but thought *Jerusalem* 'a perfectly mad poem'. Crabb Robinson's essay on Blake, 'Künstler, Dichter, und Religiöser Schwärmer' ('Artist, Poet and Religious Mystic'), published (anonymously) in the *Vaterländisches Museum*.

George III declared incompetent; his son becomes Prince Regent (George IV from 1820).

'Luddites' destroy industrial machines in the north of England.

1812

Blake exhibits at the Water Colour Society, including plates of *Jerusalem*.

May: Crabb Robinson reads some of Blake's poems to Wordsworth who admires them 'a thousand times more than either Byron or Scott'.

Shelley begins significant publishing at about this time, and Keats from 1816, but there is no evidence that Blake attended to the work of either poet.

1814

Begins work on engravings, to Flaxman's designs, for Longman's edition of *Hesiod* (published 1817).

Fall of Paris: Napoleon exiled to the island of Elba. George Stevenson constructs the first practical steam locomotive. St Margaret's, Westminster, the first London district to be illuminated by gas.

1815

Begins drawing and engraving for Josiah Wedgwood's Catalogue of Earthenware and Porcelain. Also for Abraham Rees, *The Cyclopaedia, or Universal Dictionary of Arts, Sciences and Literature* (published 1819/1820).

Wordsworth, *Poems* (includes *Lyrical Ballads*, a new preface and the 'essay supplementary' to the preface) (see 1826).

Napoleon escapes from Elba: his 'Hundred Days', final defeat at Waterloo, and exile to St Helena.

1816

Watercolour illustrations of Milton's *L'Allegro* and *Il Penseroso*.

1818

For the Sexes: The Gates of Paradise (revised version of the emblem book of 1793). Probable date of *The Everlasting Gospel*.

For the first time since 1795 prints a small number of copies of the early illuminated books including *Thel*, *Marriage*, *Visions* and *Urizen*.

6 and 12 Feb.: letters of Coleridge (the second with detailed opinions on many individual poems) mention admiringly Blake's *Songs* ('He is a man of genius').

June: Blake's first meeting with the painter John Linnell (1792–1882), the most important patron of his final years.

1819

Draws a series of 'visionary heads' for the painter John Varley (1778–1842).

1820

Probable date of the first printings of *Jerusalem*.

1821

Woodcut illustrations for Robert Thornton's *The Pastorals of Virgil*.

The Blakes move to 3, Fountain Court, on the River Thames side of the Strand. Blake sells his print collection to the dealers, Colnaghi.

Byron, *Cain: a Mystery*.

1822

The Ghost of Abel . . . To Lord Byron in the Wilderness (two sheets in illuminated printing, written in response to Byron's *Cain*).

Probable date of *On Homer's Poetry* [and] *On Virgil*.

Blake, described as 'labouring under great distress,' is made a grant of £25 by the Royal Academy.

1823

Financial agreement between Blake and Linnell in relation to Blake's Job engravings gives Blake a small secure income.

1824

Begins work on a series of watercolour illustrations for Dante's *Divina Commedia*.

At about this time Blake meets the young painters Edward Calvert (1799–1883), Samuel Palmer (1805–81) and George Richmond (1809–96), the core of a group which called itself 'The Ancients' and looked to Blake as a mentor. Frederick Tatham (1805–78) also becomes acquainted with Blake at about this time, probably through Linnell.

'The Chimney Sweeper' (*Innocence*) printed in James Montgomery, *The Chimney Sweeper's Friend and Climbing Boy's Album*.

1825

Engravings for The Book of Job completed (though not printed and published until the following year).

Apr.: death of Fuseli.

Dec.: Crabb Robinson begins making detailed notes of meetings and conversations with Blake.

1826

Laocoön, Blake's last work in illuminated printing.

Annotations of Wordsworth (*The Excursion* and *Poems*, 1815).

Dec.: death of Flaxman.

1827

Begins engraving Dante designs (only seven completed).

Annotations of Robert Thornton's *New Translation of the Lord's Prayer*.

12 Aug.: death of Blake, at the age of sixty-nine.

17 Aug.: as his parents had been, buried in the Dissenters' burial ground, Bunhill Fields.

1828

John Thomas Smith's account of Blake and his works printed in *Nollekens and his Times*.

1830

Allan Cunningham, Life of Blake, in his *Lives of the Most Eminent British Painters, Sculptors, and Architects*.

1831

17 Oct.: death of Catherine Blake.

1832

Tatham's manuscript 'Life of Blake'. Tatham inherited from Catherine Blake all Blake's effects – manuscripts, drawings, proofs of engravings, illuminated books and copper plates. Though the evidence is not perfectly clear it seems almost certain that he destroyed most of these on the grounds of his religious views.

THE WORKS

FROM
POETICAL SKETCHES

Poetical Sketches was published in 1783. About fifty copies were privately printed at the expense of Blake's friends, the Reverend A. S. Mathew, his wife Harriet, and the sculptor John Flaxman. According to a prefatory 'advertisement', the poems were composed when Blake was between the ages of twelve and twenty, that is between 1769 and 1777. (Blake's friend Benjamin Heath Malkin, who presumably had his information from Blake himself, records specifically that 'How sweet I roamed' was written before Blake was fourteen [*A Father's Memoirs of his Child*, 1806]). Though only the lyrics are represented here, the collection as a whole is notable for its variety: Blake experimented with the ballad form, Elizabethan dramatic verse, Ossianic prose poems, and with unusual metres and unrhymed verse. (On Ossian, see *Visions*, Introduction.) There are foreshadowings of his later manner in the metrical experiments, in the visionary quality in the poems addressed to the seasons – their perception of natural phenomena in terms of human forms, which goes beyond conventional personification – and in the thoroughgoing symbolic method, suggestive but inexplicit, of some of the lyrics. The poems show a variety of influences: there are echoes of Shakespeare (especially in the dramatic fragments, but also in the songs), Milton, and Bishop Percy's *Reliques of Ancient English Poetry* (1765),[1] as well as of some of Blake's elder contemporaries. The poems have often been passed over by critics interested in Blake's more characteristic qualities, but they have shown themselves correspondingly responsive to critics with a taste for poetry as distinct from a taste for Blake.[2] In 1924 S. Forster Damon was able to describe 'To the Evening Star' as one of the best loved poems in the English language.[3] The standard modern studies are those of Margaret Ruth Lowery, *Windows of the Morning* (New Haven, CT, 1940), and Robert Gleckner, *Blake's Prelude* (Baltimore, MD, 1982).

The last poem in this group, 'Song by an Old Shepherd', is one of three shepherds' songs (not in Blake's handwriting) found on the flyleaf of a single copy of *Poetical Sketches* inscribed, 'from Mrs Flaxman, May 15 1784'.

---

[1] See *Visions*, Introduction, note 10.

[2] See the brief studies by George Saintsbury (*A History of English Prosody* (1906–10), 3 vols., (2nd edn., London, 1923, 3.10–14); and Edith Sitwell (*The Pleasures of Poetry*, Second Series, London, 1931, 18–26).

[3] *William Blake: His Philosophy and Symbols* (London, 1924), 254.

To Spring

O thou with dewy locks, who lookest down
Through the clear windows of the morning, turn
Thine angel eyes upon our western isle,
Which in full choir hails thy approach, O Spring!

5   The hills tell each other, and the list'ning
Valleys hear; all our longing eyes are turnèd
Up to thy bright pavilions: issue forth,
And let thy holy feet visit our clime.

Come o'er the eastern hills, and let our winds
10   Kiss thy perfumèd garments; let us taste
Thy morn and evening breath; scatter thy pearls
Upon our love-sick land that mourns for thee.

O deck her forth with thy fair fingers; pour
Thy soft kisses on her bosom, and put
15   Thy golden crown upon her languished head,
Whose modest tresses were bound up for thee.

To Summer

O thou, who passest through our valleys in
Thy strength, curb thy fierce steeds, allay the heat
That flames from their large nostrils! Thou, O Summer,
Oft pitchèd'st here thy golden tent, and oft
5   Beneath our oaks hast slept, while we beheld
With joy thy ruddy limbs and flourishing hair.

---

1 *dewy locks*] Cf. *Paradise Lost*, 5.56–7: 'his dewy locks distilled / Ambrosia' (the angel in Eve's dream).

7 *pavilions*] A large stately tent, here used for the clouds; cf. Psalm 18, v. 11: 'His pavilion round about him were . . . thick clouds of the skies'.

15 *languished head*] Cf. *Comus*, line 744: Beauty 'withers on the stalk with languished head'. (Also in *Samson Agonistes* [line 119] Samson lies 'with languished head unpropped'). Cf. 'Song', line 2.

2 *steeds*] In classical myth the sun is associated with Apollo and his horse-drawn chariot ('car', line 9).

6 *ruddy . . . hair*] Cf. the Notebook fragment, 'Abstinence', line 2.

Beneath our thickest shades we oft have heard
Thy voice, when noon upon his fervid car
Rode o'er the deep of heaven; beside our springs
10   Sit down, and in our mossy valleys; on
Some bank beside a river clear, throw thy
Silk draperies off, and rush into the stream:
Our valleys love the Summer in his pride.

Our bards are famed, who strike the silver wire;
15   Our youth are bolder than the southern swains;
Our maidens fairer in the sprightly dance.
We lack not songs, nor instruments of joy,
Nor echoes sweet, nor waters clear as heaven,
Nor laurel wreaths against the sultry heat.'

To Autumn

O Autumn, laden with fruit and stainèd
With the blood of the grape, pass not, but sit
Beneath my shady roof. There thou may'st rest,
And tune thy jolly voice to my fresh pipe,
5   And all the daughters of the year shall dance.
Sing now the lusty song of fruits and flowers.

'The narrow bud opens her beauties to
The sun, and love runs in her thrilling veins;
Blossoms hang round the brows of morning, and
10   Flourish down the bright cheek of modest eve,
Till clust'ring Summer breaks forth into singing,
And feathered clouds strew flowers round her head.

The spirits of the air live on the smells
Of fruit; and joy, with pinions light, roves round
15   The gardens, or sits singing in the trees.'
Thus sang the jolly Autumn as he sat;
Then rose, girded himself, and o'er the bleak
Hills fled from our sight; but left his golden load.

---

8 *fervid*] Burning hot, glowing (often applied in verse, as here, to the sun).
14 *wire*] Strings (of harp or lyre).

To Winter

'O Winter, bar thine adamantine doors.
The north is thine; there hast thou built thy dark
Deep-founded habitation. Shake not thy roofs,
Nor bend thy pillars with thine iron car.'

5   He hears me not, but o'er the yawning deep
Rides heavy; his storms are unchained, sheathèd
In ribbèd steel. I dare not lift mine eyes,
For he hath reared his sceptre o'er the world.

Lo, now the direful monster, whose skin clings
10   To his strong bones, strides o'er the groaning rocks;
He withers all in silence, and his hand
Unclothes the earth and freezes up frail life.

He takes his seat upon the cliffs; the mariner
Cries in vain – poor little wretch, that deal'st
15   With storms – till heaven smiles, and the monster
Is driv'n yelling to his caves beneath Mount Hecla.

To the Evening Star

Thou fair-haired angel of the evening,
Now, while the sun rests on the mountains, light
Thy bright torch of love; thy radiant crown
Put on, and smile upon our evening bed.
5   Smile on our loves; and, while thou drawest the
Blue curtains of the sky, scatter thy silver dew
On every flower that shuts its sweet eyes
In timely sleep. Let thy west wind sleep on
The lake; speak silence with thy glimmering eyes,
10   And wash the dusk with silver. Soon, full soon,

---

11 *his hand*] Printed as 'in his hand' in the original, but corrected by Blake in several copies.

16 *Mount Hecla*] A volcano in Iceland; it appears in James Thomson's *Winter* ('Hecla flaming through a waste of snow'), part of his famous early eighteenth-century series on the seasons.

2 *while*] Printed as 'whilst' in the original, but corrected by Blake in one copy.

3 *love*] The evening star is Venus, planet of the goddess of love. It appears in the west briefly at sunset (lines 2 and 10–11).

Dost thou withdraw; then the wolf rages wide,
And the lion glares through the dun forest:
The fleeces of our flocks are covered with
Thy sacred dew: protect them with thine influence.

To Morning

O holy Virgin, clad in purest white,
Unlock heav'n's golden gates, and issue forth;
Awake the dawn that sleeps in heaven; let light
Rise from the chambers of the east, and bring
5   The honied dew that cometh on waking day.
O radiant morning, salute the sun,
Roused like a huntsman to the chase; and, with
Thy buskined feet, appear upon our hills.

Song

How sweet I roamed from field to field,
   And tasted all the summer's pride,
Till I the Prince of Love beheld,
   Who in the sunny beams did glide.

5 He showed me lilies for my hair,
   And blushing roses for my brow;
He led me through his garden fair,
   Where all his golden pleasures grow.

With sweet May dews my wings were wet,
10   And Phoebus fired my vocal rage.
He caught me in his silken net,
   And shut me in his golden cage.

---

1 *Virgin*] The morning star is usually also Venus, but Blake seems to be thinking of the star as her antithesis, the virgin huntress, Diana (for whom a salute from the huntsman-sun and 'buskined feet' are also appropriate).

4 *chambers . . . east*] Cf. 'To the Muses', line 3 note.

8 *buskined*] wearing half-boots.

3 *Prince of Love*] Cupid.

10 *Phoebus*] The sun; Apollo, god of poetry.   *rage*] Poetic inspiration (*OED*, *sb* 8).

12 *golden cage*] Cf. the song in *An Island in the Moon*, 'Hail matrimony made of love', line 27, sung by Quid the Cynic (usually identified with Blake himself).

He loves to sit and hear me sing,
　　Then, laughing, sports and plays with me,
15　　Then stretches out my golden wing,
　　And mocks my loss of liberty.

Song

My silks and fine array,
　　My smiles and languished air,
By love are driven away,
　　And mournful lean Despair
5　Brings me yew to deck my grave:
Such end true lovers have.

His face is fair as heaven
　　When springing buds unfold;
O why to him was't given,
10　　Whose heart is wintry cold?
His breast is love's all-worshipped tomb,
Where all love's pilgrims come.

Bring me an axe and spade,
　　Bring me a winding sheet;
15　When I my grave have made,
　　Let winds and tempests beat:
Then down I'll lie as cold as clay.
True love doth pass away.

Song

Love and harmony combine,
And around our souls entwine,
While thy branches mix with mine,
And our roots together join.

13–14] Cf. Vaux, 'I loath that I did love' (from Tottel's *Miscellany* [1557], printed in Percy's *Reliques*): 'A pickaxe and a spade, / And eke a shrouding sheet'; cf. *Hamlet*, 5.1.91–2.

4 *join*] Probably a true rhyme at this period with lines 1–3: both before and after Blake (in Pope and Byron, for example) it is used to rhyme with words ending in 'ine'.

5   Joys upon our branches sit,
Chirping loud and singing sweet;
Like gentle streams beneath our feet,
Innocence and Virtue meet.

Thou the golden fruit dost bear,
10   I am clad in flowers fair;
Thy sweet boughs perfume the air,
And the turtle buildeth there.

There she sits and feeds her young;
Sweet I hear her mournful song;
15   And thy lovely leaves among
There is Love: I hear his tongue.

There his charming nest doth lay;
There he sleeps the night away;
There he sports along the day,
20   And doth among our branches play.

Song

Memory, hither come,
    And tune your merry notes;
And while upon the wind
    Your music floats,
5   I'll pore upon the stream
Where sighing lovers dream,
And fish for fancies as they pass
Within the watry glass.

---

11 *perfume*] Accented on the second syllable.

12 *turtle*] The turtle-dove, conventional symbol of faithful love.

16 *his*] This is altered in three copies from the original 'her'; Blake seems to have had in mind two symbols of love, a female turtle-dove and Cupid.

17 *lay*] lie.

2] Perhaps echoing *As You Like It*, 2.5.1–3: 'Under the greenwood tree / Who loves to lie with me / And turn his merry note'. Eighteenth-century texts (following Rowe's edition of 1709) sometimes emended 'turn' here to 'tune'.

8 *the watry glass*] The idea of water as a mirror is conventional, but Blake may have recalled *A Midsummer Night's Dream*, 1.1.209–10: 'when Phoebe doth behold / Her silver image in the watry glass'. (The original spells 'watery', but 'watry' is Blake's invariable spelling in engraved and manuscript work.)

I'll drink of the clear stream,
10   And hear the linnet's song;
And there I'll lie and dream
    The day along;
And when night comes I'll go
To places fit for woe,
15   Walking along the darkened valley
With silent Melancholy.

Mad Song

The wild winds weep,
    And the night is a-cold;
Come hither, Sleep,
    And my griefs enfold.
5   But lo, the morning peeps
    Over the eastern steeps,
And the rustling birds of dawn
The earth do scorn.

Lo, to the vault
10   Of pavèd heaven
With sorrow fraught
    My notes are driven;
They strike the ear of night,
    Make weep the eyes of day;
15   They make mad the roaring winds,
    And with tempests play.

Like a fiend in a cloud
    With howling woe,
After night I do crowd,
20   And with night will go;

Title] There are several mad songs in Percy's *Reliques of Ancient English Poetry*.

4 *enfold*] Printed as 'unfold' in the original, but corrected by Blake in several copies (with the spelling 'infold').

7 *birds*] Printed as 'beds' in the original, but corrected by Blake in several copies.

9 *vault*] *OED* records several archaic spellings without *l* (vawte, vaught, vawght), which perhaps suggests that Blake pronounced this as a full rhyme with 'fraught'.

I turn my back to the east,
From whence comforts have increased,
For light doth seize my brain
With frantic pain.

To the Muses

Whether on Ida's shady brow,
 Or in the chambers of the east,
The chambers of the sun, that now
 From ancient melody have ceased;

5 Whether in heaven ye wander fair,
 Or the green corners of the earth,
Or the blue regions of the air,
 Where the melodious winds have birth;

Whether on crystal rocks ye rove,
10 Beneath the bosom of the sea
Wandering in many a coral grove,
 Fair Nine, forsaking poetry;

How have you left the ancient love
 That bards of old enjoyed in you!
15 The languid strings do scarcely move,
 The sounds are forced, the notes are few.

Title *Muses*] The nine classical goddesses of the liberal arts (only some of whom were specifically associated with poetry).

1 *Ida*] The mountain in Crete from which Saturn ruled the world during the Golden Age; or the mountain in Phrygia where the Judgement of Paris (which gave rise to the Trojan War) took place. Either could be associated with the Muses (through pastoral poetry about the Golden Age, or epic, which originates in poems concerned with the Trojan War).

3 *sun*] The abode of Apollo, god of poetry. Also the source of the element of fire; the three other conventional elements follow (earth, air, water). Blake might also have recalled Psalm 19, vv. 4–5: 'the sun, which is as a bridegroom coming out of his chamber' – though from this 'the chamber[s] in the east' had become conventional.

15–16] Cf. Blake's early narrative, *Tiriel*, in which the old and senile Har, who represents, among other things, the debilitated condition of poetry, goes into a cage to sing.

Song [3ᵈ] by an Old Shepherd

When silver snow decks Sylvio's clothes,
And jewel hangs at shepherd's nose,
We can abide life's pelting storm,
That makes our limbs quake, if our hearts be warm.

5   Whilst Virtue is our walking-staff,
And Truth a lantern to our path,
We can abide life's pelting storm,
That makes our limbs quake, if our hearts be warm.

Blow boisterous wind, stern winter frown;
10   Innocence is a winter's gown;
So clad we'll abide life's pelting storm,
That makes our limbs quake, if our hearts be warm.

1–2 *When . . . nose*] Adapted from lines 1–2 of 'Blind-Man's Buff' (a seventy-line narrative poem in *Poetical Sketches*). Blake perhaps recalled the opening of Winter's song at the close of *Love's Labour's Lost*: 'When icicles hang by the wall, / And Dick the shepherd blows his nail'.

3, 7] Cf. *King Lear*, 3.4.28–29: 'Poor naked wretches . . . / That bide the pelting of this pitiless storm'.

SONGS OF INNOCENCE AND
OF EXPERIENCE

Songs of Innocence was completed and the first copies made up in 1789, probably only a year after Blake's first experiments with his characteristic method, illuminated printing. Songs of Experience was offered for sale separately in Blake's prospectus of 10 October 1793. The two collections appeared with a common title page in 1794. But Songs of Experience was issued separately at least four times between 1795 and 1818, and probably no copy of the combined Songs was produced between 1796 and 1818. During this period Blake apparently thought that either collection could stand without the commentary of the other. However, after 1818 Blake did consistently print the two sets together. Because of the many paired poems and the common title page this is how they are best considered.

Both Innocence and Experience highlight by contrast each other's limitations. Songs of Innocence articulates primitive hopes and fears about the world which are exhibited with fewest qualifications in the uninhibited condition of childhood but which are also present in more partial or concealed forms in adults – living forces, fundamental roots of being which, however qualified by commonsensical knowledge of the world, continue to shape later life. Innocence reproaches us, as Blake puts it, with the errors of acquired folly (marginalia to Lavater, c. 1788). Its songs aim to re-awaken positive aspects of life lost amid the stultifying constrictions of experience. And in this world of earthly and heavenly guardians Innocence itself is a form of protection. As Blake put it, in a poem written into his Poetical Sketches (see above, p. 50), 'Innocence is a winter's gown; / So clad we'll abide life's pelting storm, / That makes our limbs quake, if our hearts be warm'. But Innocence also has its limitations. These are indicated by the opening of a lyric Blake at some stage contemplated as a motto for the two collections: 'The good are attracted by men's perceptions / And think not for themselves' (see Lyrics from the Notebook, p. 159). There are many things Innocence cannot take account of which the speakers of Songs of Experience see more clearly.

In both collections the speaker is usually not Blake though Blake's view is often implied, either by the counterpointing of a parallel lyric in the contrary collection, or by the contexts established by the two sets of poems as a whole. But Blake was an enthusiast of the firm persuasion, a critic of the doubter who is never capable of answering. He is not a writer to leave central values entirely to implication. Though some modern critics see him as a continuous ironist, some of the Songs can be taken straightforwardly, giving clear points of reference. In 'The Divine Image' and 'The Voice of the Ancient Bard' in Songs of Innocence, and 'London', 'The Garden of Love' and other poems of Songs of Experience Blake can be understood as speaking without implied qualification.

The order in which the poems are printed here is that of six of the seven copies produced between 1818 and Blake's death. However, this does not accord with Blake's one extant ordered listing of the poems (Bentley, *Writings*, 1319–20 [the order of only one extant copy, copy V, *c.* 1818]): it may represent simply the convenient duplication of an order originally no more authoritative than any other.

1. Title Page, plate 2 from 'Songs of Innocence: Innocence', 1789 (relief etching with w/c); Yale Center for British Art, Paul Mellon Collection, USA/The Bridgeman Art Library.
Original size: 7 × 11.1 cms

Songs of Innocence and of Experience

[Title-page]

Songs of Innocence and of Experience
Showing the Two Contrary States of the Human Soul

Design. Beneath the subtitle Adam and Eve are depicted surrounded by flames and with fig leaves round their loins – details which show that they are newly expelled from Eden (Genesis, 3.7 and 24), and so have just lost innocence and are confronting the world of experience with all its difficulties fresh to their view. Eve prostrate, looks out towards the reader; Adam just above her, supported on his right leg, holds his head in his hands in a posture expressing suffering or despair.

Songs of Innocence

[Frontispiece]

Design. This shows (as in the 'Introduction') the Piper looking upwards at a naked, wingless child, backed by a cloud, with arms and legs spread in a posture indicating exuberant flight. The Piper is surrounded by a flock of grazing sheep, and the scene is framed by trunks of trees to left and right.

[Title-page]

Songs of Innocence

1789

The Author and Printer W. Blake

Design (*Plate 1*). This shows, on the left, a young woman seated, with a boy and a girl standing at her knee and reading a book in her lap. To the right a fruit-bearing tree (round the trunk of which curls a vine) extends its branches above the children and between the words of the title. The piper of the frontispiece and the 'Introduction' (now wearing a broad-brimmed hat), pipe in mouth, leans with his back against the 'I' of 'Innocence'. Tiny figures disport themselves in the large capitals of 'SONGS', which issue in swirls of flame (above) and vegetation (below). The highly decorated script is typical of Blake's visual exuberance in the *Songs* and elsewhere: see Introduction (3), pp. 19–20.

Introduction

This account of the transition from spontaneous lyrical and poetic effusion to written poem stresses the joy of poet and child-auditor in both forms of composition. The same pastoral image of piper and flying (naked) child is depicted as frontispiece to the volume. Some critics see a hint of corruption in the poem's 'stained'

water, but a more neutral meaning ('impart colour to', *OED v.* 3) is implied both
by the pastoral and celebratory context and Blake's readiness to refer quite literally
to his own processes of composition (cf. 'The Little Girl Lost', 'Grave the sentence
deep'). Nicholas Williams offers a discussion which builds on the dark implica-
tions which have been found in 'stained' and elsewhere: *Ideology and Utopia* (1998),
54–8.

Design. Both left and right margins contain four oval vignettes formed by the
looped crossings of stem-like growths. These can be seen as referring to the figuration
used in medieval manuscripts and in stained glass known as the Tree of Jesse (a
genealogy showing the lineage of Christ from Jesse, father of King David [Matthew,
1.6–16]), and so as reinforcing the Christian frame of reference suggested by the
'song about a Lamb'. The detail of the vignettes varies from copy to copy. Those
that can be clearly and consistently identified include (right margin, reading from
the top) (1) a seated adult and standing child (as in the title-page); (2) a naked leap-
ing figure resembling that of Blake's engraving of 1780, 'Albion Rose' ['Glad Day'];
(left margin, reading from the top) (1) a bird flying upwards; (3) a figure reaching
towards (as if to feed?) two birds flying past. A river flows across the plate under-
neath both text and marginal designs.

> Piping down the valleys wild,
> Piping songs of pleasant glee,
> On a cloud I saw a child,
> And he laughing said to me,
>
> 5   'Pipe a song about a Lamb.'
> So I piped with merry cheer.
> 'Piper, pipe that song again.'
> So I piped; he wept to hear.
>
> 'Drop thy pipe, thy happy pipe;
> 10   Sing thy songs of happy cheer.'
> So I sung the same again,
> While he wept with joy to hear.

---

5 *Lamb*] Blake's capitalization may be no more than conventional eighteenth-century ortho-
graphy, but it may also indicate the Christian context in which *Songs of Innocence* is to be read
(cf. 'Shepherd' in the following poem). In 'The Lamb' (see below) the Christian meaning of
the symbol is explicit.

6, 8 *piped*] See Introduction (3), note 69.

8] Cf. line 12, and the Proverb of Hell, 'Excess of sorrow laughs, excess of joy weeps'.

10 *Sing*] The association of the *Songs* with music is not purely a convention of the lyric mode:
according to Blake's younger contemporary J. T. Smith, Blake sang his lyrics to melodies of his
own composition in the Mathews' circle (*c.* 1784) and somewhat later (see Bentley, *Blake Records*
(1969), 26 and 457).

'Piper, sit thee down and write
In a book that all may read.'
5   So he vanished from my sight.
And I plucked a hollow reed,

And I made a rural pen,
And I stained the water clear,
And I wrote my happy songs
:0   Every child may joy to hear.

The Shepherd

As with 'Lamb' in the 'Introduction', the capitalization of 'Shepherd' in this poem may be no more than conventional, or it may suggest the biblical tradition of imaging God as the Shepherd of Israel, most famously in Psalm 23 ('The Lord is my Shepherd; I shall not want'), and in Isaiah, 40.11 ('He shall feed his flock like a shepherd'); cf. Psalm 80.1, and Ezekiel, 34.11–15. This becomes the Good Shepherd of Christian symbolism, Christ as ideal guardian, as in John, 10.11 (Jesus speaks): 'I am the good shepherd: the good shepherd giveth his life for the sheep'; cf. 1 Peter, 2.25, 5.4, and the design on plate 2 of 'The Little Black Boy'.

Design. Under the poem a shepherd holding a crook and standing beneath a tree (which extends up the whole right-hand side of the plate) watches a flock of sheep, one of which looks up and bleats towards him. Left of the tree a large bird flies upwards.

How sweet is the Shepherd's sweet lot!
From the morn to the evening he strays;
He shall follow his sheep all the day,
And his tongue shall be fillèd with praise.

5   For he hears the lamb's innocent call,
And he hears the ewe's tender reply;
He is watchful, while they are at peace,
For they know that their Shepherd is nigh.

The Echoing Green

The echoes of this green are both literal and metaphorical: the games of the young echo those of the old, whose memories are as much enjoyed as the children's present activities. Nature is wholly in tune with this wholly harmonious community. The

---

2 *strays*] Roams, wanders free from control (*OED*, v^2 2a).

4] Cf. Psalm 71.8: 'Let my mouth be filled with thy praise' (and psalm 35.28: 'my tongue shall speak . . . of thy praise all the day long').

poem is printed on two plates. On the first, above the text, two men in hats an
two mothers with children at their knees or on their laps sit under a spreading oa
surrounded by five older boys playing and watching games. To the left of the tex
stands a boy with a bat; to the right a boy rolls a hoop with a stick. To the righ
of the text (and reaching up both sides) grows a vine. On the second plate, belov
the text (framed by a more substantial vine which grows from the bottom right c
the plate), 'Old John' directs homeward a party consisting of a mother (with bab
in arms) and six children. To the left of the text a boy standing on the vine reache
upwards for a bunch of grapes; to the right a boy reclining on the vine reache
down to give a bunch of grapes to the girl at the back of the group below – ar
action which may suggest that the green's darkening is, like its echoes, metaphoric

       The sun does arise,
       And make happy the skies;
       The merry bells ring,
       To welcome the spring;
5   The skylark and thrush,
       The birds of the bush,
       Sing louder around,
       To the bells' cheerful sound,
       While our sports shall be seen
10   On the echoing green.

       Old John with white hair
       Does laugh away care,
       Sitting under the oak,
       Among the old folk.
15   They laugh at our play,
       And soon they all say,
       'Such, such were the joys
       When we all, girls and boys,
       In our youth time were seen
20   On the echoing green.'

       Till the little ones, weary,
       No more can be merry;
       The sun does descend,
       And our sports have an end.
25   Round the laps of their mothers
       Many sisters and brothers,
       Like birds in their nest,
       Are ready for rest;
       And sport no more seen
30   On the darkening green.

The Lamb

This poem uses a traditional presentation of the Christ child (meek and mild), and a traditional symbol of Christ as surrogate sacrificial victim (the Lamb); but the child-speaker's delight in a non-symbolic lamb and vivid identification with the incarnate child obviate the sentimental and pious ethos (passivity and obedience; a gloomy consciousness of sin and guilt) with which these versions of Christ can be associated.

Design. Below the text a naked child addresses a lamb, which stands beside a river and in front of a flock of sheep. Behind the flock is, to the left, an oak, and to the right a thatched cottage. On either side a thin tree trunk, circled by a vine, rises to surround the text, above which the trees' upper branches mingle to form a covering arch. Contrary in *Experience*, 'The Tiger'.

> Little lamb, who made thee?
> Dost thou know who made thee?
> Gave thee life and bid thee feed
> By the stream and o'er the mead;
> 5   Gave thee clothing of delight,
> Softest clothing, woolly, bright;
> Gave thee such a tender voice,
> Making all the vales rejoice?
> Little lamb, who made thee?
> 10   Dost thou know who made thee?
>
> Little lamb, I'll tell thee,
> Little lamb, I'll tell thee:
> He is callèd by thy name,
> For he calls himself a Lamb;
> 15   He is meek and he is mild,
> He became a little child;
> I a child and thou a lamb,
> We are callèd by his name.
> Little lamb, God bless thee,
> 20   Little lamb, God bless thee.

1–3] On a Christian view, like all creation the lamb is made by Christ as the executive power of God (John, 1.3; Colossians, 1.16).

14] Jesus never actually refers to himself in these terms, but is so called, at his baptism, by John the Baptist (John, 1.29): 'Behold the Lamb of God, which taketh away the sin of the world'. The exalted Christ is imaged as a sacrificed lamb at various points in Revelation (5.6–13, 12.11, and 22.1).

The Little Black Boy

Even more than with the Songs of child sweeps, Blake is here writing in relation to a prominent contemporary social issue. The Society for Effecting the Abolition of the Slave Trade was formed in 1787, and began seeking subscriptions in November 1788. Shortly after *Songs of Innocence* Blake began engraving the illustrations of John Gabriel Stedman's account of the treatment of slaves in Surinam, which influenced his most extended presentation of the issue in *Visions of the Daughters of Albion* (1793). Looking back, Wordsworth described England in the year of that work as 'a whole Nation crying with one voice / Against the Traffickers in Negro blood' (*The Prelude*, 1805, X. 205–6). A number of other poets wrote on the issue at the time, most notably Cowper, in 'The Morning Dream' and other poems. But, as with the sweep of *Innocence*, Blake's approach is oblique. The black boy has been taught by his mother that God is infinitely generous and loving. Though she teaches a pagan religion derived from observation of natural facts, it seems from the design (plate 2) that the boy, inducted into the idea of a benign presiding power, learns Christianity. For Blake, as his early tractate has it, 'all religions are one'. We may even find in the mother's teaching on the purpose of earthly life – 'That we may learn to bear the beams of love' – the implication that 'the sun-burnt face' has learned the lesson of God's nature better than the 'little English boy'. Such an implication could be traced to Blake's interest in Swedenborg, who taught 'that the inhabitants of Africa had preserved a direct intuition of God' (Morton Paley, ' "A New Heaven is Begun": Blake and Swedenborgianism', *Blake: An Illustrated Quarterly*, 13 (1979–80), 64–90). But religion has also taught the black boy that white is the colour of angels, and therefore that black implies being bereft of spiritual light. He partly envisages heaven as freedom from differences of colour; but the white boy (with silver hair) seems still in his imagination to be white, and the black boy hopes to be like him. The pathos lies in what is said only indirectly – 'he will then love me': the white boy, whom the black boy admires and wishes to help and protect, rejects him now.

The poem is printed on two plates. The design of the first (above the text) illustrates stanza 2. That of the second (below the text) illustrates the last six lines: Jesus, haloed and with a crook, is presented as the Good Shepherd (cf. 'The Shepherd'), seated under an overarching willow, beside a river, with his flock in the background; the black boy (still black in most copies) presents to him the white, perhaps stroking his silver hair.

My mother bore me in the southern wild,
And I am black, but oh! my soul is white.
White as an angel is the English child,
But I am black, as if bereaved of light.

5   My mother taught me underneath a tree,
And sitting down before the heat of day,
She took me on her lap and kissèd me,
And pointing to the east began to say:

'Look on the rising sun: there God does live,
10   And gives his light and gives his heat away;
And flowers and trees and beasts and men receive
Comfort in morning, joy in the noon day.

'And we are put on earth a little space
That we may learn to bear the beams of love;
15   And these black bodies and this sunburnt face
Is but a cloud, and like a shady grove.

'For when our souls have learned the heat to bear
The cloud will vanish; we shall hear his voice,
Saying, "Come out from the grove my love and care,
20   And round my golden tent like lambs rejoice."'

Thus did my mother say, and kissèd me,
And thus I say to little English boy:
When I from black and he from white cloud free,
And round the tent of God like lambs we joy,

25   I'll save him from the heat till he can bear
To lean in joy upon our Father's knee;
And then I'll stand and stroke his silver hair,
And be like him, and he will then love me.

The Blossom

This simple poem uses the nursery rhyme convention that sparrows are cheerful and robins tragic (as in 'Who killed Cock Robin?' and 'A little cock sparrow sat on a green tree', *The Oxford Book of Nursery Rhymes*, ed. Iona and Peter Opie (1952), 130–3). The poem indicates the unity, in *Innocence*, of vegetable (blossom), animal (bird) and human (speaker).

The design is celebratory, and suggests an angelic protectiveness parallel to that of the poem's human. It shows a plant-like flame which rises up the right margin and curls above the text, issuing in cherubic figures, three leaping, one reading, and two exchanging a kiss. In the centre an angel sits sheltering a child on its breast. (Those for whom criticism means finding inexplicit depths follow Joseph Wicksteed in seeing the birds of the poem and the flame of the design as phallic symbols [*Blake's Innocence and Experience* (1928), 125–6].) 'The Sick Rose' can be seen as a contrary in *Experience*.

Merry, merry sparrow,
Under leaves so green,
A happy blossom
Sees you swift as arrow
5   Seek your cradle narrow
Near my bosom.

Pretty, pretty robin,
Under leaves so green,
A happy blossom
10   Hears you sobbing, sobbing,
Pretty, pretty robin,
Near my bosom.

The Chimney Sweeper

Chimney sweeping was among the worst forms of child labour. Porter's Act of 1788
set a minimum age of eight, limited the hours of work, stipulated that boys be pro-
perly washed once a week, and that they should not climb chimneys in which there
was a fire. But it was not enforced, and attempts to impose legislative controls con-
tinued throughout Blake's lifetime (and beyond). On the conditions in which sweeps
worked, and how closely Blake's poem reflects the plain facts, see Martin Nurmi in
Northrop Frye (ed.), *Blake: A Collection of Critical Essays* (1966). In the name Tom
Dacre, Blake possibly had in mind the Lady Anne Dacre alms-houses which stood
in James Street, Westminster (founded 1594, closed 1892): if so, it is ironic that the
boy is named after a local benefactress. Kathleen Raine notes a passage of Swedenborg
which may have suggested lines 13–14: spirits called sweepers of chimneys become
angels when, on the direction of an angel, they cast off their 'vile raiment' (*Blake and
Tradition*, 2 vols., 1968, I. 25–6). Tom Dacre is offered the pietistic view that divine
love is a reward for obedience; and, in his innocence, the speaker accepts a yet more
pious moral which the circumstances revealed by the poem contradict. The boys
are actually made happy by being able to imagine a life antithetical to the one they
lead. But the sweepers' faith, though from Blake's viewpoint false in its claims both
about divinity and the material world, provides for the suffering boys real comfort.

The design (below the text) may simply illustrate lines 13–16, though Erdman (*The
Illuminated Blake* (1975), 12), on the grounds that the figure has no wings, takes it
as Jesus, and so the design as 'a realization of the Angel's promise of "God for his
father"'. The poem was chosen by Charles Lamb for inclusion in James Montgomery's
The Chimney-Sweeper's Friend, and Climbing-Boy's Album (1824). Contrary in *Experi-
ence*, 'The Chimney Sweeper'.

When my mother died I was very young,
And my father sold me while yet my tongue
Could scarcely cry ''weep! 'weep! 'weep! 'weep!'
So your chimneys I sweep and in soot I sleep.

1–2 *very young . . . sold*] Boys were usually 'apprenticed' at ages between six and seven (though
sometimes as young as four), and were literally 'sold': a fee of between one and five pounds
was paid by the master sweep to the parent. (See Nurmi, above.)

3 *'weep!*] Punning on 'sweep!', the boy's street-cry when touting for work.

5   There's little Tom Dacre, who cried when his head
That curled like a lamb's back, was shaved, so I said,
'Hush Tom, never mind it, for when your head's bare
You know that the soot cannot spoil your white hair'.

And so he was quiet, and that very night,
10   As Tom was a-sleeping he had such a sight –
That thousands of sweepers, Dick, Joe, Ned and Jack,
Were all of them locked up in coffins of black,

And by came an angel who had a bright key,
And he opened the coffins and set them all free.
15   Then down a green plain leaping, laughing they run,
And wash in a river and shine in the sun.

Then naked and white, all their bags left behind,
They rise upon clouds and sport in the wind.
And the angel told Tom, if he'd be a good boy,
20   He'd have God for his father and never want joy.

And so Tom awoke and we rose in the dark,
And got with our bags and our brushes to work.
Though the morning was cold, Tom was happy and warm;
So if all do their duty they need not fear harm.

The Little Boy Lost / The Little Boy Found

The contrary to these two poems taken together is 'A Little Boy Lost' in *Experience*. There is an early version of the first poem only in *An Island in the Moon*, where it is sung by Quid the Cynic (a version of Blake himself). Taken alone (as in *An Island*) the first poem implies a desolate view quite unlike that of other *Songs of Innocence*. Taken together, however, the two poems imply both that faith will find the protective beneficence it conceives to resolve fears generated by the natural world, and also something about how we perceive that protective presence – in terms of the already known (God as father). The poems' patterns of caesura and internal rhyme give both an emphatic, ballad-like simplicity.

Design. Above the text of the first poem a boy in a hat and white gown underneath a bare tree chases a flaming will-o'-the-wisp; six protective angels surround the text. Above the text of the second poem the boy is led through a dark wood by a figure who is gowned, haloed and Christ-like (though perhaps also androgynous). A floating figure to the right of the text, wingless but nonetheless angelic (perhaps the boy's mother), gestures with outstretched arms and looks towards the illustration above.

The Little Boy Lost

'Father! father! where are you going?
O do not walk so fast!
Speak, father, speak to your little boy,
Or else I shall be lost.'

5   The night was dark, no father was there,
The child was wet with dew.
The mire was deep, and the child did weep,
And away the vapour flew.

The Little Boy Found

The little boy lost in the lonely fen,
Led by the wandering light,
Began to cry, but God ever nigh
Appeared like his father in white.

5   He kissed the child, and by the hand led,
And to his mother brought,
Who in sorrow pale, through the lonely dale
Her little boy weeping sought.

Laughing Song

An earlier version of this song was written in a copy of *Poetical Sketches* inscribed as a gift – 'from Mrs Flaxman May 15 1784'. In this version the present lines 1–2 and 5–6 are transposed, there is no stanza break after line 4, and the singers of line 7 have the more stylized pastoral names of 'Edessa, and Lyca and Emilie'. 'I hate scarce smiles; I love laughing' Blake wrote in his copy of Caspar Lavater's *Aphorisms on Man* (c. 1788): it is a pleasure in which here, as in 'The Blossom', the natural and human worlds participate jointly.

The design shows a pastoral group of young adults, with no nuts and cherries but drinking wine, seated at a table backed by a clump of trees. One stands with his back to the viewer, with raised glass and gesturing with his hat as though to conduct the others in song. (In one copy of the combined *Songs* this poem appears in both *Innocence* and *Experience*, perhaps accidentally: it shares none of the characteristics which led a small number of poems occasionally to be transferred to the later collection.)

When the green woods laugh with the voice of joy,
And the dimpling stream runs laughing by,
When the air does laugh with our merry wit,
And the green hill laughs with the noise of it;

5   When the meadows laugh with lively green,
        And the grasshopper laughs in the merry scene,
        When Mary and Susan and Emily
        With their sweet round mouths laugh 'ha ha he';

        When the painted birds laugh in the shade
10   Where our table with cherries and nuts is spread,
        Come live and be merry, and join with me
        To sing the sweet chorus of 'ha ha he'.

A Cradle Song

Blake's *Songs* are often contrasted with somewhat comparable but more conventionally moralistic poems in Isaac Watts's *Divine and Moral Songs* (1715), as, for example, by Nicholas Shrimpton, 'William Blake: Hell's Hymnbook' (in *Literature of the Romantic Period 1750–1850*, ed. R. T. Davies and B. G. Beatty (Liverpool, 1976)). Vivian de Sola Pinto argues, however, that this poem is closely paralleled by Watts's 'A Cradle Hymn'. This does indeed begin from the same point as Blake (the child in its cradle/Jesus in the manger), but it soon develops a moralistic tone and ends – unlike Blake – by contrasting the human and the divine ('William Blake, Isaac Watts, and Mrs Barbauld', in Pinto (ed.), *The Divine Vision* (1957)). As (pre-eminently) in 'The Divine Image', Blake stresses the unity of human and divine: not only is the child like the infant Jesus, but the mother too, in her guardianship, is like the Creator caring for his creation.

The poem is on two plates. The first shows swirls of stems and leaves which contain tiny forms, some sleeping, some perhaps angelic guardians of sleep. The second (contrastingly realistic) shows, below the text, a mother, seated, watching over a baby sleeping in its cradle. Contrary in *Experience*, 'Infant Sorrow'. A more direct contrary in Blake's Notebook (also called 'A Cradle Song') was not engraved for *Experience* (see below, p. 151).

        Sweet dreams form a shade
        O'er my lovely infant's head;
        Sweet dreams of pleasant streams,
        By happy, silent, moony beams.

5   Sweet sleep with soft down
        Weave thy brows an infant crown.
        Sweet sleep, angel mild,
        Hover o'er my happy child.

---

4 *By*] 'together with', or perhaps (elliptically) 'lit by'.

Sweet smiles in the night,
10   Hover over my delight.
Sweet smiles, mother's smiles,
All the livelong night beguiles.

Sweet moans, dovelike sighs,
Chase not slumber from thine eyes.
15   Sweet moans, sweeter smiles
All the dovelike moans beguiles.

Sleep, sleep, happy child;
All creation slept and smiled.
Sleep, sleep, happy sleep,
20   While o'er thee thy mother weep.

Sweet babe, in thy face
Holy image I can trace.
Sweet babe, once like thee
Thy maker lay and wept for me;

25   Wept for me, for thee, for all,
When he was an infant small.
Thou his image ever see,
Heavenly face that smiles on thee.

Smiles on thee, on me, on all,
30   Who became an infant small.
Infant smiles are his own smiles,
Heaven and earth to peace beguiles.

The Divine Image

In this central poem of *Songs of Innocence* Blake speaks in his own voice. The human and divine are identified, and (as Blake's early tractate has it) all religions are one: God can indwell Muslim, Jew and even non-believer as well as the Christian. Human and divine are identified throughout Blake's work, from his annotations of Lavater (*c*. 1788: 'Human nature is the image of God') to those of Berkeley (*c*. 1820: 'God is Man and exists in us and we in him') (Bentley, *Writings*, 1378, 1505). The

---

12, 16, 32 *beguiles*] charms away (*OED v* 5); in *Experience* the word usually carries the more sinister sense, 'deceives, cheats' (*OED v* 1). The singular form, not acceptable by eighteenth-century standards of correct grammar, is made necessary by the rhyme. Similarly with 'weep' (plural for singular), line 20.

27 *see*] Subjunctive: 'may you ever see . . .'

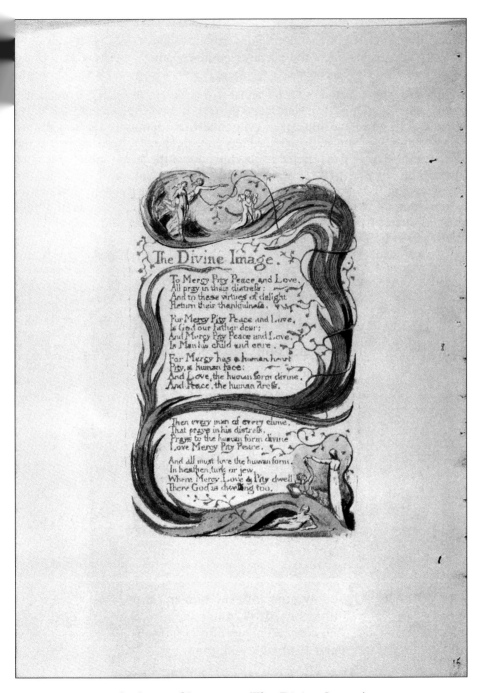

2. *Songs of Innocence*, 'The Divine Image'

idea can be linked to Blake's early interest in Swedenborg (cf. 'The Little Black Boy'), though it might as readily relate to more orthodox sources (see lines 19–20 note). E. P. Thompson interprets the poem as positively anti-Swedenborgian (*Witness Against the Beast* (1993), chapter 9).

Design (*Plate 2*). A flame-like form (similar to that in 'The Blossom'), round which a vine twines, curls up, around and above the text, and between the third and fourth stanzas. On it, above the title, two praying children are approached by two gowned female figures. Below right an aureoled figure (Jesus as divine-human) reaches out to touch the finger-tip of a naked figure rising out of the flame; another figure reclines or rises below. The postures suggest a scene of creation (the figures representing Adam and Eve, the human-divine, being brought into being), or possibly of resurrection. Contrary in *Experience*, 'The Human Abstract'. (A simpler and more direct contrary, 'A Divine Image', though not included in *Experience*, was also illustrated and etched: see pp. 108–9.)

> To Mercy, Pity, Peace and Love,
> All pray in their distress,
> And to those virtues of delight
> Return their thankfulness.
>
> 5 For Mercy, Pity, Peace and Love
> Is God, our Father dear;
> And Mercy, Pity, Peace and Love
> Is Man, his child and care.
>
> For Mercy has a human heart,
> 10 Pity a human face,
> And Love the human form divine,
> And Peace the human dress.
>
> Then every man of every clime
> That prays in his distress
> 15 Prays to the human form divine,
> Love, Mercy, Pity, Peace.
>
> And all must love the human form
> In heathen, Turk or Jew.
> Where Mercy, Love and Pity dwell
> 20 There God is dwelling too.

---

18 *Turk*] Muslim.

19–20] 1 John, 4.16: 'God is love; and he that dwelleth in love dwelleth in God, and God in him' – a verse of which Blake quotes the second part in his marginalia to Lavater (*c.* 1788), in an annotation beginning 'It is the God in *all* that is our companion and friend' and concluding 'every thing on earth is the word of God, and in its essence is God' (Bentley, *Writings*, 1384–5).

Holy Thursday

Contrary, 'Holy Thursday' in *Experience* (though the opening of 'The Human Abstract' is also relevant: 'Pity would be no more / If we did not make somebody poor'). The Charity Schools' service of thanksgiving, begun in 1704, was almost always held on a Thursday, though not on either of the important Thursdays of the church calendar (Maundy Thursday, Ascension Day). It is Blake (whether or not ironically) who associates the service with these festivals. The service, first held in Saint Paul's cathedral in 1782, was, with its associated procession, a notable public event attended by several thousand children. The poem was written for Blake's largely prose satire, *An Island in the Moon* (*c.* 1784), in which it is sung by Obtuse Angle (whose name may suggest limited vision). After its performance the riotous company 'all sat silent for a quarter of an hour' – a response indicating perhaps that they are both chastened and (like later critics) puzzled: does the poem simply enjoin charitable giving, or does it suggest that the children deserve better than their situation allows, even when alleviated by such charity? Charity Schools are seen by both Victorian and modern commentators as a socially conservative form of philanthropy, inculcating the quiescent virtues of diligence and humility. While they saved the children of the very poor from utter degradation, they did so commonly in brutal conditions, such as, in 1788, caused a riot leading to the arrest of the matron of the Greycoat Hospital in Blake's Westminster. Stanley Gardner, however, presents a quite different view of the Charity Schools, and so of this poem, arguing that it is entirely unironic and shows a hopeful Blake, temporarily persuaded by philanthropic activity in his own neighbourhood that social evil might be overcome in an evolutionary way (*Blake's 'Innocence' and 'Experience' Retraced*, 1986).

The design shows lines of paired children, boys above the text led by two beadles, girls below led by a matron (or perhaps a minister).

'Twas on a Holy Thursday, their innocent faces clean,
The children walking two and two, in red and blue and green,
Grey-headed beadles walked before with wands as white as snow,
Till into the high dome of Paul's they like Thames' waters flow.

5 Oh, what a multitude they seemed, these flowers of London town!
Seated in companies they sit with radiance all their own.
The hum of multitudes was there, but multitudes of lambs,
Thousands of little boys and girls raising their innocent hands.

Title] This designation was used of various Thursdays in the church calendar – Thursday in Rogation Week, Ascension Day, Maundy Thursday (*OED*, Thursday, 3).

2 *red*] 'grey' (*An Island in the Moon*).

6 *Seated in companies*] As at the feeding of the five thousand (Mark, 6.39).

Now like a mighty wind they raise to heaven the voice of song,
10 Or like harmonious thunderings the seats of heaven among.
Beneath them sit the agèd men, wise guardians of the poor.
Then cherish pity, lest you drive an angel from your door.

Night

'Night' is the Song of Innocence which most acknowledges the fact of suffering and death, though this is subsumed in the poem's references to Old and New Testament visions of restored paradise in which the cruelty and sorrow inherent in the natural world are overcome. The poem has been compared with various eighteenth-century evening hymns, in which nocturnal angelic protection is a common topic. It is most elaborately read by David Wagenknecht, as a key not only to the *Songs* but to a central aspect of Blake's work, in terms of pastoral tradition and its reconciliation of this-worldliness and otherworldliness (*Blake's Night*, Cambridge, MA, 1973).

The poem is etched on two plates. The design of the first shows angelic guards floating around the text, two in a tree which fills the right margin and surrounds the title, and below which a lion rests in a cave. On the second plate a tree in the left margin contains angelic figures, while below the text two groups of aureoled women stand beside a river.

The sun descending in the west,
The evening star does shine;
The birds are silent in their nest,
And I must seek for mine.
5 The moon, like a flower
In heaven's high bower,
With silent delight
Sits and smiles on the night.

9] Reversing the 'mighty wind' of Pentecost (Acts, 2.2) which brought the Holy Spirit from heaven to earth.

11 *Beneath them*] Special stands were erected for the children.   *the aged men, wise guardians*] 'the reverend men, the guardians' (*An Island in the Moon*).

12] Hebrews, 13.2: 'Be not forgetful to entertain strangers: for thereby some have entertained angels unawares' (referring, as the Authorized Version marginal reference points out, to Genesis 18 and 19, where Abraham's three angelic guests are often understood as the triune God – Father, Son, Holy Spirit).

Farewell, green fields and happy groves
10 Where flocks have took delight.
Where lambs have nibbled, silent moves
The feet of angels bright.
Unseen they pour blessing,
And joy without ceasing,
15 On each bud and blossom,
And each sleeping bosom.

They look in every thoughtless nest
Where birds are covered warm;
They visit caves of every beast,
20 To keep them all from harm.
If they see any weeping
That should have been sleeping,
They pour sleep on their head,
And sit down by their bed.

25 When wolves and tigers howl for prey
They pitying stand and weep,
Seeking to drive their thirst away
And keep them from the sheep.
But if they rush dreadful,
30 The angels, most heedful,
Receive each mild spirit
New worlds to inherit.

And there the lion's ruddy eyes
Shall flow with tears of gold,
35 And pitying the tender cries,
And walking round the fold,
Saying, 'Wrath, by his meekness,
And, by his health, sickness
Is driven away
40 From our immortal day.

---

11 *moves*] The form should properly be plural: cf. 'A Cradle Song', lines 12, 16, 32 note.

17 *thoughtless*] free from care or anxiety (*OED* 1c, citing this example).

27 *thirst*] for blood.

37 *his*] Christ's.

'And now beside thee, bleating lamb,
I can lie down and sleep;
Or think on him who bore thy name,
Graze after thee and weep;
45   For washed in life's river
My bright mane for ever
Shall shine like the gold
As I guard o'er the fold.'

Spring

The celebratory tone of this paean on corresponding births in the human and natural worlds is created by Blake's handling of form – the short rhythmically emphatic lines and quick chime of full rhymes, which may be intended to suggest a child-like speaker.

The poem is etched on two plates. On the first, above the text, a mother holds a naked baby which reaches enthusiastically towards a lamb surrounded by grazing sheep. On the second, below the text, a baby sitting between two sheep (and in some copies beside a river) pulls the wool of a lamb, which is perhaps offering to lick the baby's neck.

Sound the flute!
Now it's mute.
Birds delight
Day and night:
5   Nightingale
In the dale,
Lark in sky,
Merrily,
Merrily, merrily, to welcome in the year.

10   Little boy
Full of joy,
Little girl
Sweet and small,

41] Isaiah, 11.6: 'The wolf also shall dwell with the lamb, and the leopard shall lie down with the kid; and the calf and the young lion and the fatling together; and a little child shall lead them.' And cf. Isaiah, 65.25.

43] Cf. 'The Lamb', line 14 note.

45] The holy river seen by Ezekiel (47.1–12), by means of which 'every thing . . . shall live', and (typologically related) the 'river of water of life' of Revelation (22.1–2).

Cock does crow,
15   So do you:
Merry voice,
Infant noise,
Merrily, merrily, to welcome in the year.

Little lamb,
20   Here I am;
Come and lick
My white neck;
Let me pull
Your soft wool;
25   Let me kiss
Your soft face;
Merrily, merrily, we welcome in the year.

Nurse's Song

Perhaps even more evidently than in 'Laughing Song' and 'The Blossom' (and especially when contrasted with the 'Nurse's Song' in *Experience*) this poem implies that a healthy ethic allows human beings to participate with spontaneous joy in patterns of behaviour which parallel those of the natural world. The final echo is both literal and symbolic. As usual Blake does not indicate speakers by punctuation. Most editors assume that the nurse does not speak the first stanza; many critics assume that she does. (Some also assume that she speaks the last two lines of the poem.) The stanza begins in parallel with the first stanza of the contrary 'Nurse's Song' in *Experience*, which is clearly spoken by the nurse herself. The main design, underneath the text, shows the nurse sitting reading while seven dancing children play in a ring in front of her. (An earlier version of the poem occurs in *An Island in the Moon*.)

'When the voices of children are heard on the green,
And laughing is heard on the hill,
My heart is at rest within my breast,
And everything else is still.

5   'Then come home my children, the sun is gone down,
And the dews of night arise;
Come, come, leave off play, and let us away,
Till the morning appears in the skies.'

---

1 *voices*] 'tongues' (*An Island in the Moon*).

'No, no, let us play, for it is yet day,
10   And we cannot go to sleep;
Besides in the sky the little birds fly,
And the hills are all covered with sheep.'

'Well, well, go and play till the light fades away,
And then go home to bed.'
15   The little ones leapèd and shouted and laughed,
And all the hills echoèd.

Infant Joy

The design shows, above the text, a luxuriant open blossom in which a mother sits with a baby in her lap. A child-like, winged angelic figure stands in front of the mother with outstretched hands. A contrasting closed blossom hangs down to the right of the text. It is in keeping with the spirit of the collection as a whole (cf. 'The Shepherd', 'The Lamb') that the three figures be seen as analogous to the traditional Adoration scene: Madonna, Christ-child and worshipping angel. Either the mother or the angel may be thought of as speaking those parts of the poem not spoken by the baby. Contrary in *Experience*, 'Infant Sorrow'.

'I have no name,
I am but two days old.'
What shall I call thee?
'I happy am,
5   Joy is my name.'
Sweet joy befall thee.

Pretty Joy!
Sweet Joy, but two days old,
Sweet Joy I call thee;
10   Thou dost smile,
I sing the while.
Sweet joy befall thee.

---

15 *leapèd*] Possibly a monosyllable: the third line of each previous stanza is marked by rhyme, and this internal echo is more nearly retained if the word is treated as monosyllabic. However, it was spelt by Blake with a final 'ed' (in contrast to 'laugh'd'), and a disyllable better fits the predominantly anapaestic rhythm of the line. (On Blake's distinction between syllabic 'ed' and non-syllabic ''d' see Introduction (3), pp. 25–6.)

A Dream

As in the pair of poems on the little boy lost and found, the sequence here is of loss and distress in a threatening landscape followed by comfort. The speaker's belief in angelic guardians is confirmed by the dream – though some critics read the dream as revealing the fears which generate the speaker's need to believe in guardian angels. The main figure in the design is a small human watchman, with staff and lantern, lower right. Just above him is a flying beetle. 'The Angel' can be seen as a contrary in *Experience*. (In three copies Blake transferred the poem to *Experience*.)

> Once a dream did weave a shade
> O'er my angel-guarded bed,
> That an emmet lost its way
> Where on grass methought I lay.

5
> Troubled, wildered and forlorn,
> Dark, benighted, travel-worn,
> Over many a tangled spray,
> All heart-broke I heard her say:

> 'O my children! do they cry?
10
> Do they hear their father sigh?
> Now they look abroad to see,
> Now return and weep for me.'

> Pitying I dropped a tear;
> But I saw a glow-worm near,
15
> Who replied, 'What wailing wight
> Calls the watchman of the night?

> I am set to light the ground,
> While the beetle goes his round.
> Follow now the beetle's hum:
20
> Little wanderer, hie thee home.'

---

8 *heart-broke*] A standard archaic variant of 'heart-broken' (*OED* gives examples from the mid-seventeenth to the mid-nineteenth century).

15 *wight*] being (*arch.*).

16 *watchman*] The word was applied to angels (*OED* 3b; *OED*'s earliest entry for the sometimes supposed significance 'dor beetle' is 1864).

On Another's Sorrow

As in 'The Divine Image' divine and human are identified, here specifically through the figure of Jesus. As Jesus identifies with all living things in their sorrows (both historically, in his Incarnation, and also in the present: 'he becomes . . .'), so we too can sympathize with one another. However, though the poem acknowledges the reality of suffering, in not recognizing the possibility of indifference, or even the active cruelty shown elsewhere in the joint collection, it may be seen as exemplifying the limitations as well as the strengths of innocence.

The design shows, to the right, a leafy tree with a vine coiling up it, and a bird of paradise taking wing by stanzas six and seven; to the left, stems in which human forms clamber upwards, below them the piper of the frontispiece and 'Introduction'.

> Can I see another's woe,
> And not be in sorrow too?
> Can I see another's grief,
> And not seek for kind relief?

5
> Can I see a falling tear,
> And not feel my sorrow's share?
> Can a father see his child
> Weep, nor be with sorrow filled?

> Can a mother sit and hear
10
> An infant groan, an infant fear?
> No, no, never can it be;
> Never, never can it be.

> And can he who smiles on all
> Hear the wren with sorrows small,
15
> Hear the small bird's grief and care,
> Hear the woes that infants bear,

> And not sit beside the nest
> Pouring pity in their breast;
> And not sit the cradle near
20
> Weeping tear on infant's tear;

---

14 *Hear the wren*] Cf. Matthew, 10.29, 'Are not two sparrows sold for a farthing? and one of them shall not fall on the ground without your Father.'

And not sit both night and day
Wiping all our tears away?
O no, never can it be;
Never, never can it be.

25 He doth give his joy to all.
He becomes an infant small.
He becomes a man of woe.
He doth feel the sorrow too.

Think not thou canst sigh a sigh
30 And thy maker be not by.
Think not thou canst weep a tear
And thy maker is not near.

O, he gives to us his joy,
That our grief he may destroy.
35 Till our grief is fled and gone
He doth sit by us and moan.

---

22 *Wiping all our tears away*] Cf. Revelation, 7.17, 'God shall wipe away all tears from their eyes' (repeated at 21.4).

27 *man of woe*] Cf. Isaiah, 53.3, 'He is despised and rejected of men; a man of sorrows, and acquainted with grief' (part of Isaiah's account of the suffering servant, understood in Christian tradition as a prophecy of the sufferings of Christ).

Songs of Experience

One central critical problem with *Songs of Experience* is whether they are designed to characterize their speakers, trapped within Experience's embittering limitations, or whether they are to be understood as valid comments by the speaker on his or her world. Are they concerned with psychological or social landscapes? Evidently there need be no single answer to this question, and the two concerns are not mutually exclusive: human beings can be both oppressed by corrupt social structures and victims of their own interior failures. And either corruption or failure may generate or reinforce each other. The critical issue with each particular poem is one of primary focus. Decisions about focus can produce quite different, even contradictory meanings. Clearly some poems are primarily about their speaker: 'Nurse's Song', for example, has features of what would later be called a dramatic monologue. If poems such as 'Holy Thursday' or 'London' are understood in the same terms – as by many critics they currently are – social criticism becomes at most a secondary focus. Blake's other writings of the period 1790–94 suggest it should not be.

All but three of the poems written for *Songs of Experience* – 'Introduction', 'Ah, Sunflower' and 'A Little Girl Lost' – were drafted in Blake's Notebook. These drafts, often with layers of correction and development, are in many cases revealing about what Blake may have intended in the poems. Some material from these drafts is incorporated into the notes.

[Frontispiece]

Design. A contrary to that of *Innocence* – and so a visual parallel to the contrary poems of the two collections – this shows the piper, winged child and sheep of *Innocence*, but now in new postures: the piper has no pipe, the child sits on top of his head; both face outwards, confronting the reader. The symmetry of framing trees in the earlier design is replaced by asymmetry: a full tree in the background, left, is balanced by a bare trunk which cuts into the design diagonally in the foreground, right.

[Title-page]

Songs of Experience

1794

The Author and Printer W. Blake

Design. The design is constructed in contrasting sections: lightness, movement and happiness; heaviness, stasis and sorrow. The upper portion contains the title, the letters of which are extended into flowing tendrils and leaves; in the centre a male and a female figure dance in reciprocal postures of joy. The lower shows a woman and an aged bearded man lying on a bed, apparently dead, against the background of a rigidly symmetrical stone wall. On either side of the bed a boy and a girl bend in parallel postures of mourning.

78

Introduction

This poem and 'Earth's Answer' should be read together: both are written in the same unusual form (stanzas with five lines of 3 4 2 2 and 4 feet, rhyming abaab), and in the various orderings of the collection Blake always treated them as a pair – though his Notebook, which contains 'Earth's Answer' but not the 'Introduction', suggests that 'Earth's Answer' was composed as the response from a female perspective to a plea from a male perspective for ideally free sexual relationships ('Thou hast a lap full of seed'). 'Introduction' initiates a new tone and frame of reference: the authoritative bard and the Creator-Judge who expelled Adam and Eve from Eden replace the carefree piper and the Saviour-Comforter of *Innocence*. The poem has been variously interpreted, partly depending on how much, and which parts, of some usual Blakean associations are brought to bear, and how the problems of the poem's ambiguous syntax are resolved. Some critics see the Holy Word as a hypocritical tyrant – the Urizen of the prophetic books: he has the power to restore the fallen but instead weeps crocodile tears, offers a material world which is not all he implies and some unspecified better future (perhaps an after-life) which is a delusion; Earth rightly sees through his offers. Other critics see the bard as inspired witness to a God of compassion who offers a potentially redemptive creation as prelude to an apocalyptic consummation; Earth, trapped by the embittering trials of Experience, is unable to respond adequately. The text is inscribed on clouds in a night sky filled with stars. A female figure – Earth (though taken by some critics to be the bard) – in several copies aureoled by a sun-like halo, reclines on a pallet bed, with her back to the reader.

> Hear the voice of the bard,
> Who present, past and future sees,
> Whose ears have heard
> The Holy Word,
5   That walked among the ancient trees,
>
> Calling the lapsèd soul
> And weeping in the evening dew,

---

4 *Holy*] Blake often associates 'Holy' with hypocrisy (see, for example, 'A Little Girl Lost', lines 27–9), though it would be highly unusual for him to present the Son in such terms. *Word*] Usually used of the Logos, the Son, as in John 1.1, though Earth addresses her answer to the Father.

4–7] Cf. Genesis, 3.8: the newly fallen Adam and Eve 'heard the voice of the Lord God walking in the garden in the cool of the day'. In *Paradise Lost* the fallen pair are judged (as may be implied by 'Word' here) by the Son.

6 *Calling*] The allusion to Genesis (see previous note) suggests that this refers (as is grammatically simpler) to 'the Holy Word'; some critics take it as referring to the bard. The ambiguous syntax may suggest that ultimately the two possible grammatical subjects are one: the bard who sees past, present and future is a vehicle of divine knowledge.

That might control
The starry pole,
10   And fallen, fallen light renew.

'O Earth, O Earth, return!
Arise from out the dewy grass.
Night is worn,
And the morn
15   Rises from the slumberous mass.

Turn away no more.
Why wilt thou turn away?
The starry floor,
The watry shore,
20   Is giv'n thee till the break of day.'

Earth's Answer

A serpent underneath the poem associates the fallen earth with Eve. The design is otherwise a counterpoint to the bitter text: flowing tendrils of vine surround and mingle with each stanza, issuing in a bunch of grapes to the right of stanza two.

Earth raised up her head
From the darkness dread and drear,
Her light fled,
(Stony dread!),
5   And her locks covered with grey despair.

---

8 *That*] Probably parallel to 'That' in line 5, and so referring to the 'Holy Word'; some critics take it as referring to the 'lapsèd soul' (lines 8–10 are merely orthodox if applied to God or Christ, more startlingly Blakean – and relevant to the world of Experience – if applied to the fallen soul).

9 *pole*] The sky, heavens (*OED sb*² 4) – a Greek and Latin usage which Blake probably derived from Milton (*Paradise Lost*, IV, 724, 'starry pole'); Blake's is *OED*'s latest recorded use.

11] Earth is similarly addressed in Old Testament prophecy – Deuteronomy, 32.1 ('hear, O earth, the words of my mouth'), and Jeremiah, 22.29 ('O earth, earth, earth, hear the word of the Lord').

18 *floor*] That is, the floor of heaven, the sky.

4 *Stony*] 'petrifying', stupifying (*OED a* 5c).

'Prisoned on watry shore,
Starry Jealousy does keep my den.
Cold and hoar,
Weeping o'er,
10   I hear the Father of the ancient men.

Selfish father of men,
Cruel, jealous, selfish fear!
Can delight,
Chained in night,
15   The virgins of youth and morning bear?

Does spring hide its joy
When buds and blossoms grow?
Does the sower
Sow by night,
20   Or the ploughman in darkness plough?

Break this heavy chain
That does freeze my bones around.
Selfish, vain,
Eternal bane,
25   That free love with bondage bound.'

The Clod and the Pebble

If this poem is read as a contest of views then Blake clearly condemns the pebble:
the alliterating jingle of 'warbled out these metres meet' – and of course what the

---

7 *Starry*] Cf. 'Introduction', line 18 and design. Blake associated his archetypal oppressor, Urizen (see *Visions* 8.3 note), with the stars: see, for example, the starry sky of the contemporary emblem 'Air' (*The Gates of Pardise*, plate 6), associated with the anxious tyrant (Notebook, p. 94). But it would be difficult to grasp so esoteric an association in this context: Blake may mean 'Argus-eyed'.   *Jealousy*] The God of the Pentateuch is often described as a 'jealous God', as at Exodus, 34.14: 'the Lord, whose name is Jealous, is a jealous God' (cf. Exodus, 20.5; Deuteronomy, 4.24).

11 *men*] The rhyme scheme (abaab) breaks down at this point and yet further in the following stanza. In his Notebook draft Blake initially maintained a more complete (though different) rhyme pattern in stanza 4 ('Does the sower sow / His seed by night').

13–20] Cf. the Notebook lyric, 'Are not the joys of morning sweeter'.

15] 'virgins' is the grammatical subject ('Can the virgins . . . bear').

25 *free love*] *OED*'s first use of 'free love' in the sense 'the right of free choice in sexual relations without the restraint of marriage or other legal obligation' is 1814 (*OED* D 2), but it would be consistent with other works of this period (for example, *Visions of the Daughters of Albion*) that Blake should intend this sense here.

wretched thing actually says – cannot but mean that 'meet' is ironic. Some critic suppose that he also condemns the clod of clay, not because the poem says so but because it is supposed that Blake cannot mean something that might savour of self suppression. They forget the great proverb of Hell: 'The most sublime act is to se another before you'. What the clod of clay proposes is not self-suppression but the imaginative act of so entering into another consciousness that its fulfilment become one's own greatest desire – though not, of course, one's only desire, hence the poten tial for pain. It is 'trodden with the cattle's feet' because unselfish love will suffer it can still sing. Grant and Johnson well comment: 'The Clod's view recalls St. Paul'. praise of charity in 1 Corinthians 13' (*Blake's Poetry and Designs*, 1979). Andrew Lincoln puts the contrary view (*William Blake: 'Songs of Innocence and of Experience'* 1991). But the poem should perhaps not be read as a contest of doctrines but as an acknowledgement of love's disturbingly twofold character.

Design. Above the text four sheep (one a ram) and, to their right, two horned cattle drink from a stream with a leafless tree above them. Below the text a duck swims by two frogs frolicking on a bank on either side of a worm. From the bank a vine reaches up the right-hand margin to the title.

> 'Love seeketh not itself to please,
> Nor for itself hath any care,
> But for another gives its ease,
> And builds a Heaven in Hell's despair.'

> 5 So sung a little clod of clay,
> Trodden with the cattle's feet;
> But a pebble of the brook
> Warbled out these metres meet:

> 'Love seeketh only self to please,
> 10 To bind another to its delight,
> Joys in another's loss of ease,
> And builds a Hell in Heaven's despite.'

Holy Thursday

On the charity children's service of thanksgiving, see the introduction to the contrary poem in *Innocence*. A contemporary account from *The Times* (6 June 1788) indicates how the event was seen from a viewpoint antithetical to the poem's: the reporter praises 'the glorious sight of 6000 children, reared up under the humane direction of the worthy Patrons, and supported by the public contributions of well disposed persons . . . aiding to the nurture of a future generation to fight his

---

1–4] Cf. the speech of the clod of clay in *The Book of Thel*, 6.10–7.6, beginning 'we live not for ourselves', and 5.26–7: 'Every thing that lives, / Lives not alone, nor for itself'.

SONGS OF INNOCENCE AND OF EXPERIENCE

majesty's] battles – carry forward the commerce and manufactories of Great Britain' Erdman, *Prophet Against Empire*, 122). The speaker of the poem in *Experience* actually hears something different from the speaker in *Innocence* – 'a trembling cry' where the other hears a song 'like a mighty wind': each listens with a different ideological predisposition; their mental landscapes dominate their sensory experience. As Blake later put it (marginalia to Reynolds), 'as the eye, such the object' – and as the ear. Some critics suppose that the speaker of this poem, like others in *Experience*, can be placed: his 'partisanship falsifies by exaggeration' (E. D. Hirsch, *Innocence and Experience: An Introduction to Blake* [1964], (2nd edn., Chicago, 1975, 220)). This is wise only if we are sure Blake mistrusted outrage as a response to injustice. For his Isaiah, 'the voice of honest indignation is the voice of God' (*Marriage*, plate 12).

Design. Above the text, in a landscape dominated by a leafless tree, a woman stands looking down, with a stylized expression of horror (hands raised at the wrists), on a baby stretched out dead. The right-hand margin shows further victims of poverty: a woman sits with a weeping child standing next to her and a naked child hanging about her neck; below the text another child is stretched out dead.

> Is this a holy thing to see
> In a rich and fruitful land:
> Babes reduced to misery
> Fed with cold and usurous hand?
>
> 5   Is that trembling cry a song?
> Can it be a song of joy?
> And so many children poor?
> It is a land of poverty!
>
> And their sun does never shine,
> 10   And their fields are bleak and bare,
> And their ways are filled with thorns:
> It is eternal winter there.
>
> For where'er the sun does shine,
> And where'er the rain does fall,
> 15   Babe can never hunger there,
> Nor poverty the mind appal.

---

4 *usurous*] miserly, ungenerous; though perhaps also implying that the wealth with which the charity schools are endowed is generated by illicit financial dealings.

15–16] That is, true kindness (unlike charities which palliate, and so shore up, exploitative structures) will ensure that hunger and poverty are not causes of affliction – perhaps by ensuring they do not exist; perhaps by ensuring that such sufferings as exist are purely inevitable, not caused by social injustice, and so not spiritually embittering.

16 *appal*] Both 'shock' (the observer of poverty), and (taking line 16 as more fully parallel to line 15) 'make pale' (that is 'weaken', the mind of the person who experiences poverty); cf. 'London', line 10 note.

The Little Girl Lost

This and the following poem form a pair and are engraved as such continuously on three plates. Both were originally included in *Innocence* but were transferred to *Experience* in almost all copies after *c.* 1795. The voice of the bard with which the poem opens, with its echo of the visionary idealism of Isaiah, indicates that Lyca's story illustrates a general truth about how the world of experience might be transformed. Not everything that appears to the knowledge of experience as threatening turns out to be so: innocence reproves the errors of its supposed wisdom. The first plate's design suggests that Blake may have had specifically in mind parental fears about a child's entry into sexual experience, but in the poem the child is released from the constraints of civilization only by having her dress taken off: one does not wear clothes in Eden. Various allegorical readings of the poem have been suggested. Reading in a considerable amount by supposed implication and allusion, Kathleen Raine connects the poem with the Mysteries of Eleusis, and specifically a Neoplatonic interpretation of the myth of Persephone and Demeter as an allegory of the soul's descent into mortal life (*Blake and Tradition*, 2 vols. (1968)). Irene Chayes invokes the same myth in less esoteric terms, noticing differences as well as similarities (Northrop Frye (ed.), *Blake: A Collection of Critical Essays* (1966)). The child cared for by animals, and the animal endowed with characteristics of human personality, are traditional figures in folklore.

The design of the first plate shows, to the right, a youthful boy and girl embracing beneath a tree with two gracefully drooping branches; the girl turns slightly away and points upwards to a flying bird of paradise beneath the title. A vine grows up the left-hand margin and into the space between stanzas 2 and 3, where it supports a serpent, open-mouthed with forked tongue protruding. The second plate, in the middle, below the end of the first poem, shows Lyca, as a young woman rather than a girl, sitting in a forest: she is framed by trees and has a clump of three entwined trees behind her. In the right margin of the opening of the second poem stands a composite lioness-leopard-tiger under the overarching trunk of a bare tree. The design of the third plate shows, beneath the entwined trunks of two massive trees, the full-grown Lyca of plate 2 lying asleep, now naked, and three naked children playing with a lion and lioness, perhaps echoing the bard's opening stanzas in recalling the visionary idealism of Isaiah (11.6): 'The wolf also shall dwell with the lamb, and the leopard shall lie down with the kid; and the calf and the young lion and the fatling together; and a little child shall lead them'. The desert has become a 'garden mild'.

> In futurity
> I prophetic see
> That the earth from sleep
> (Grave the sentence deep)

---

4 *Grave*] Engrave. (Some critics suppose a pun on 'grave' as an adjective, 'serious'.)

5   Shall arise and seek
For her Maker meek,
And the desert wild
Become a garden mild.

———

In the southern clime,
10   Where the summer's prime
Never fades away,
Lovely Lyca lay.

Seven summers old
Lovely Lyca told;
15   She had wandered long,
Hearing wild birds' song.

'Sweet sleep, come to me
Underneath this tree;
Do father, mother weep
20   "Where can Lyca sleep"?

Lost in desert wild
Is your little child.
How can Lyca sleep
If her mother weep?

25   If her heart does ache
Then let Lyca wake;
If my mother sleep
Lyca shall not weep.

Frowning, frowning night,
30   O'er this desert bright
Let thy moon arise
While I close my eyes.'

7–8 *desert . . . garden*] Cf. Isaiah 35.1, 'The wilderness and the solitary place shall be glad . . . and the desert shall rejoice, and blossom as the rose'. Cf. *Marriage*, Argument, lines 6–8.

12 *Lyca*] An invented name, classical in type; Blake also used it in the draft of 'Laughing Song' found in one copy of *Poetical Sketches*.

14 *told*] counted.

20] Blake very rarely uses speech marks, but the indications here are from the engraved plate.

21 *desert*] uninhabited, uncultivated wilderness (*OED sb*² 1b). (In line 7 the word has its usual modern sense.)

30 *bright*] Refers to the moon.

Sleeping Lyca lay,
While the beasts of prey
35   Come from caverns deep,
Viewed the maid asleep.

The kingly lion stood,
And the virgin viewed,
Then he gambolled round
40   O'er the hallowed ground.

Leopards, tigers play
Round her as she lay,
While the lion old
Bowed his mane of gold,

45   And her bosom lick,
And upon her neck
From his eyes of flame
Ruby tears there came,

While the lioness
50   Loosed her slender dress,
And naked they conveyed
To caves the sleeping maid.

The Little Girl Found

All the night in woe
Lyca's parents go
Over valleys deep
While the deserts weep.

5   Tired and woe-begone,
Hoarse with making moan,
Arm in arm seven days
They traced the desert ways.

---

35 *Come*] having come.
45 *lick*] Substituted for 'licked' for the sake of the rhyme (cf. *Innocence*, 'A Cradle Song', lines 12, 16, 32).

Seven nights they sleep
10   Among shadows deep,
And dream they see their child
Starved in desert wild.

Pale, through pathless ways,
The fancied image strays,
15   Famished, weeping, weak,
With hollow piteous shriek.

Rising from unrest
The trembling woman pressed,
With feet of weary woe;
20   She could no further go.

In his arms he bore
Her, armed with sorrow sore,
Till before their way
A couching lion lay.

25   Turning back was vain;
Soon his heavy mane
Bore them to the ground;
Then he stalked around

Smelling to his prey;
30   But their fears allay
When he licks their hands,
And silent by them stands.

They look upon his eyes
Filled with deep surprise,
35   And wondering behold
A spirit armed in gold.

---

18 *pressed*] hastened onwards (*OED v*[1] 15a).

22 *armed with*] strengthened by (referring to 'he').

24 *couching*] couchant, lying ready to spring (*OED v* 16b).

29 *Smelling to*] Now archaic, but see *OED*, smell, *v* 6a.

30 *allay*] abate (*OED v*[1] 10; last recorded use 1723).

On his head a crown;
On his shoulders down
Flowed his golden hair.
40   Gone was all their care.

'Follow me,' he said;
'Weep not for the maid;
In my palace deep
Lyca lies asleep.'

45   Then they followèd
Where the vision led,
And saw their sleeping child
Among tigers wild.

To this day they dwell
50   In a lonely dell,
Nor fear the wolfish howl,
Nor the lions' growl.

The Chimney Sweeper

On the relevant social context see the introduction to the contrary poem in *Innocence*. Unlike the charity school children (who do not speak for themselves) the sweep is allowed to acknowledge that his miserable state does not preclude the possibility of happiness – though he also sees adults as provoked to cause his suffering by envy of his happiness ('Because I was happy . . .'). This chimney sweep's cry does not appal the Church as the speaker of 'London' thinks it should. As in many *Songs of Experience*, an underlying vision of the poem is of a conspiracy of Church and State (with which here the boy's parents have colluded) to oppress the poor. Seeing the Church as an instrument of his oppression the boy understands its promise of 'Heaven' – what Blake elsewhere calls 'an allegorical abode where existence hath never come' (*Europe*, 8.7) – as a postulate designed to make the injustice and misery of this life seem acceptable. Or 'Heaven' may be the life in this world of those godlike mortals who exploit labour such as that of sweeps.

The design, below the text, is realistic: a young sweep, with a soot-filled sack on his back, walks through a snow-driven townscape.

A little black thing among the snow
Crying ''weep, 'weep' in notes of woe!
'Where are thy father and mother, say?'
'They are both gone up to the church to pray.

---

2 *'weep*] Cf. 'The Chimney Sweeper', *Innocence*, line 3 note.

5   Because I was happy upon the heath,
And smiled among the winter's snow,
They clothèd me in the clothes of death,
And taught me to sing the notes of woe.

And because I am happy, and dance and sing,
10   They think they have done me no injury,
And are gone to praise God, and his priest and king,
Who make up a Heaven of our misery.'

Nurse's Song

This is a particularly close contrary to the 'Nurse's Song' of *Innocence* with which it shares three lines. More clearly than with many other *Songs of Experience* the subject here is not what the speaker sees but how she sees it (see headnote, p. 78). Her view of children (that their secrets must be about sex), her view of the social world (childhood play is a waste of time, adult life is a matter of assuming disguises), and – in contrast to the nurse of *Innocence*, who lets play continue – the kind of discipline she enforces, are based, the poem implies, on her own childhood repressions.

Design. A nurse combs the hair of a smartly dressed boy, presumably as the epitome of a more general training in social formalities. Behind them a girl sits reading. The tableau is framed on either side by luxuriant vines on which hang bunches of grapes suggesting the pleasures the combed approach to life is designed to suppress.

When the voices of children are heard on the green,
And whisperings are in the dale,
The days of my youth rise fresh in my mind,
My face turns green and pale.

5   Then come home, my children, the sun is gone down,
And the dews of night arise.
Your spring and your day are wasted in play,
And your winter and night in disguise.

The Sick Rose

The rose is, in poetry, a traditional symbol of love, though one need hardly interpret: the poem does not only mean that the figure Blake called Father of Jealousy, and Old Nobodaddy, author of conventional religion, destroys sexual love by puritanical

---

4 *green and pale*] A set phrase (*OED* A. 3a, citing this example); green is conventionally associated with envy.

regulation. Night, storm, invisibility, vermicularity characterize the destroyer, dark-ness and secrecy his methods. The rose is all the beauty such forces prey on.

The design surrounds the poem with an unusually thorny rose. Below the text a worm enters a luxuriant blossom from which a woman with arms outstretched extrudes her upper body. In branches above the text two female forms are slumped in postures expressing suffering and a caterpillar munches a leaf.

> O rose thou art sick.
> The invisible worm
> That flies in the night,
> In the howling storm,
>
> 5   Has found out thy bed
> Of crimson joy,
> And his dark secret love
> Does thy life destroy.

The Fly

It is clear from the drafts in Blake's Notebook that 'The Fly' gave him trouble. The elaborate and contrasting expositions of critics suggest that the poem gives readers trouble too. The problem is that the first three stanzas equate humans and flies as creatures able to enjoy life, drawing the moral that one should therefore be as care-ful of such rudimentary life as that of a fly as one would wish suprahuman forces to be of oneself. The concluding stanzas say, with an appearance of logical connec-tion, the opposite: since thought is immortal physical death is of no importance. Those who are confident that Blake wrested a coherent meaning from the struggles recorded in his Notebook include John Grant, for whom the speaker's confusions show him trapped in experience (Northrop Frye (ed.), *Blake: A Collection of Critical Essays* (1966)), and Jean Hagstrum, who attempts to save the speaker from confusion (Alvin Rosenfeld, *William Blake: Essays for S. Foster Damon* (1969)). Uniquely the stanzas are engraved, not continuously, but in two groups – stanzas 1 to 3 to the left, and stanzas 4 and 5 to the right of the plate.

The design, below the text, shows a woman who teaches a boy to walk, holding his hands to steady him. Behind them an older girl plays with a battledore and shuttle-cock. Two leafless trees frame both the illustration and the text. The design enforces the idea that, whatever the poem's coherence, its subject is not flies but the con-sciousness of human vitality to which proper attention to the fly might give rise. In writing this poem Blake may have had in mind Gray's ode 'On the Spring' (which he later illustrated), in which the poet-moralist sees 'the busy and the gay' as like flies who 'But flutter through life's little day, / In fortune's varying colours dressed; / Brushed by the hand of rough Mischance', and is in turn rebuked by them as merely 'a solitary fly'. Blake returned in *Milton* to the poetry of flies, as teachers and in a spirit of 'every thing that lives is holy' (*A Song of Liberty*; *Visions*, 11.10; *America*, 10.13) (see p. 297).

(see p. 297)

Little fly,
Thy summer's play
My thoughtless hand
Has brushed away.

5   Am not I
A fly like thee?
Or art not thou
A man like me?

For I dance
10   And drink and sing,
Till some blind hand
Shall brush my wing.

If thought is life
And strength and breath,
15   And the want
Of thought is death,

Then am I
A happy fly,
If I live
20   Or if I die.

The Angel

'What can it mean?': the speaker invites the reader to interpret, to understand that she was not beguiled but beguiled herself. She adopts a queenly posture of dominance and control, weeps at the pains of suppressed emotion (or perhaps with unconscious hypocrisy, to stimulate the pity she can deal with as a substitute for the love she cannot), but protects herself against the feelings that could cure her by hardening suppression into an inviolable habit.

Title *Fly*] Until the late eighteenth century 'fly' could signify any winged insect, as the bee, gnat, moth or butterfly (*OED sb*[1] 1a). The Notebook draft, with its reference to 'gilded painted pride', suggests that Blake began the poem thinking of a butterfly.

13–16] The Notebook draft shows that this stanza was a later insertion.

Design. A woman wearing a crown lies at full length under a leafless tree. Leaning in dejection on one hand, she turns away from and holds at arm's length a Cupid who nevertheless caresses the extended arm.

> I dreamt a dream! What can it mean?
> And that I was a maiden queen,
> Guarded by an angel mild.
> Witless woe was ne'er beguiled.

5
> And I wept both night and day,
> And he wiped my tears away.
> And I wept both day and night,
> And hid from him my heart's delight.

> So he took his wings and fled.
10
> Then the morn blushed rosy red.
> I dried my tears, and armed my fears
> With ten thousand shields and spears.

> Soon my angel came again.
> I was armed: he came in vain;
15
> For the time of youth was fled,
> And grey hairs were on my head.

The Tiger

Blake's tiger is what the eighteenth century called sublime: it combines beauty and terror; it astonishes. The poem's questions (so puzzled that their syntax collapses), its insistent, hypnotic rhythms, the imagery of the forge with its associations of physical energy and violent wrenching into form of the intractable, and the mysterious fifth stanza especially – all these suggest a cosmic fascinated wonder and horror at, and pity for the victims of, the creature whose creation may have satisfied its inscrutable and perhaps dark creator. 'What kind of a universe is it in which the creator of the tiger is also the God responsible for the Incarnation with all that signifies about mercy, pity, peace and love?' the poem asks. The question implies an affirmation: any adequate sense of the divine must take account of the extremes of creation and not shelter in the pieties of *Innocence*. The speaker of 'The Tiger' really knows more than the speaker of 'The Lamb', but part of his knowledge is his awareness of its limits in the face of the incomprehensible.

The design below the text shows a tiger which in some copies is a tame and smiling contrast with the beast of the poem.

5–6 *I wept . . . away*] Cf. 'On Another's Sorrow', line 22 and note.

Tiger, tiger, burning bright
In the forests of the night,
What immortal hand or eye
Could frame thy fearful symmetry?

5   In what distant deeps or skies
Burnt the fire of thine eyes?
On what wings dare he aspire?
What the hand dare seize the fire?

And what shoulder, and what art,
10   Could twist the sinews of thy heart?
And when thy heart began to beat,
What dread hand, and what dread feet?

What the hammer? What the chain?
In what furnace was thy brain?
15   What the anvil? What dread grasp
Dare its deadly terrors clasp?

When the stars threw down their spears,
And watered heaven with their tears,
Did he smile his work to see?
20   Did he who made the Lamb make thee?

---

5 *deeps*] abyss of space (*OED sb* 3c, citing this example – a usage Blake would know from Milton); perhaps also 'depths of the earth' (conceived as full of molten lava), cf. *OED sb* 4a.

8 *seize the fire*] In Greek mythology Prometheus seized fire from heaven. Blake also associated Orc, his spirit of desire and rebellion, with Prometheus (as in plate 3 of *America* where, like Prometheus, he is chained to a rock).

12] The line was altered in one copy to 'What dread hand formed thy dread feet?'. In the letterpress text issued by Blake's friend Benjamin Heath Malkin the line reads, '. . . forged thy . . .' (*A Father's Memoirs of his Child*, 1806). In the Notebook draft it was completed syntactically by the opening line of the following stanza: 'Could fetch it from the furnace deep'.

17–19] Cf. *The Four Zoas*, Night 5, line 224: 'The stars threw down their spears and fled naked away'. In *The Four Zoas* the stars are the Satanic Urizen's rebel angels. Blake would know of the association of stars and angels in a famous passage of Job (38.7) which he later illustrated: 'When the morning stars sang together, and all the sons of God shouted for joy'. In 'The Tiger' he perhaps had in mind the creation of the world as following (as in *Paradise Lost*) from the rebellion of Satan and his angels. The Notebook draft shows that this whole stanza was added later.

19 *Did he smile*] Perhaps with reference to Genesis 1 where, after each day's work, 'God saw that it was good'.

20 *the Lamb*] Blake's capitalization is erratic, but it seems very likely that he means here to recall not only the contrary *Song of Innocence* but also that poem's invocation of Jesus as the Lamb of God ('The Lamb', line 14).

Tiger, tiger, burning bright
In the forests of the night,
What immortal hand or eye
Dare frame thy fearful symmetry?

My Pretty Rose Tree / Ah, Sunflower / The Lily

These three poems are engraved on a single plate and evidently belong together in theme and mode: all are symbolic flower poems about love and sexual behaviour. Jealousy is bound up with the oppressive possessiveness which prefers to preen itself as fidelity; acquiescing in the codes of sexual restraint usual in Blake's society is spiritual suicide; true purity in love does not repel the beloved. The poems carry implications of this kind, but, because the reader is engaged to extrapolate from symbolic objects and all the implications of their treatment, the effect is radically different from that of ideological statement. Beneath 'My Pretty Rose Tree' a woman (the reverse image of the 'maiden queen' of 'The Angel') turns away from a man slumped in a posture of despair.

My Pretty Rose Tree

A flower was offered to me,
Such a flower as May never bore.
But I said, 'I've a pretty rose tree,'
And I passèd the sweet flower o'er.

5   Then I went to my pretty rose tree,
To tend her by day and by night,
But my rose turned away with jealousy,
And her thorns were my only delight.

Ah, Sunflower

Ah, sunflower, weary of time,
Who countest the steps of the sun,
Seeking after that sweet golden clime
Where the traveller's journey is done,

1, 8 *sunflower*] Pronounced as trisyllabic to match the anapaestic rhythms elsewhere in the poem. Similarly 'traveller' in line 4.

2 *countest . . . sun*] The sunflower is heliotropic.

5   Where the youth pined away with desire,
And the pale virgin shrouded in snow,
Arise from their graves, and aspire
Where my sunflower wishes to go.

The Lily

The modest rose puts forth a thorn,
The humble sheep a threat'ning horn,
While the lily white shall in love delight,
Nor a thorn, nor a threat, stain her beauty bright.

The Garden of Love

Surely a poem in Blake's own voice, though some critics find ways of condemning the speaker (Andrew Lincoln, for example, implies that he is almost in the state he protests about when he starts looking for love in a garden instead of in the open fields: *Songs of Innocence and of Experience*, Tate Gallery/Princeton, p. 191). The poem's central idea is entirely consistent with that of many other Blake poems of this period: the supposed Religion of Love destroys love by prohibiting its usual (sexual) form.

Design. Above the text a boy and girl kneel in an attitude of prayer beside a totally bald monk who reads from a book and gestures towards an open grave in front of them. Behind the monk is a gravestone and (above it) a church window. Below the text are criss-crossing briars.

I went to the Garden of Love,
And saw what I never had seen:
A chapel was built in the midst,
Where I usèd to play on the green;

---

5 *pined away with desire*] Blake may have had in mind the myth of Clytie, who, when deserted by Apollo (God of the Sun), was changed to a sunflower (Ovid, *Metamorphoses*, IV). Michael Mason notes that in Lemprière's *Classical Dictionary* (a standard reference work of the period) Clytie is described as having 'pined away' (*William Blake*. The Oxford Authors, 1988).

5 *pined*] Spelt 'pined' on the engraved plate, and so an exception to Blake's usual spelling of non-syllabic 'ed' (clearly required here by the metre).

1 *modest*] On modesty cf. *Visions*, 9.4–20.

2 *humble*] The original reading of the Notebook draft was 'coward'; on 'humble' cf. 'The Human Abstract', line 11.

1–2] A chapel was built 'on the green' in South Lambeth (where Blake lived while writing *Songs of Experience*) during 1793. Seating was exclusive – for shareholders who financed the building, and for others approved by the shareholders who paid rent for their pews (Stanley Gardner, *Blake's 'Innocence' and 'Experience' Retraced* (1986)).

4 *usèd*] This disyllabic pronunciation (retained from the same spelling in the Notebook draft) maintains the anapaestic movement of the second foot of each line.

5   And the gates of this chapel were shut,
       And 'Thou shalt not' writ over the door,
       So I turned to the Garden of Love,
       That so many sweet flowers bore;

       And I saw it was fillèd with graves,
10   And tombstones where flowers should be,
       And priests in black gowns were walking their rounds,
       And binding with briars my joys and desires.

The Little Vagabond

The poem is unusual in that the vagabond's is a voice from innocence – fresh and clear-sighted, not embittered – in the world of experience. The poem rightly belongs in *Experience*, however, because the boy proposes improvements of religion as it might be in this world.

Design. Above the text a kneeling haloed bearded figure – God as ideally benevolent Father – protectively embraces a naked boy who crouches before him, face to the ground, hands raised, perhaps in an attitude of prayer. Massive tree trunks to left and right, and a canopy of leaves overhead, set the scene in a dark wood. Below the text a father and mother, sitting in postures expressing dejection, and three children, at least one of them naked, warm themselves beside a blazing fire. (The first typographical edition of the *Songs*, ed. J. J. Garth Wilkinson (1839) omitted this poem from its second issue – if intentionally, presumably on the grounds that it is so subversive of early Victorian religious respectability).

       Dear mother, dear mother, the church is cold,
       But the ale-house is healthy, and pleasant, and warm;
       Besides I can tell where I am used well:
       Such usage in heaven will never do well.

---

6 *'Thou shalt not'*] The opening formulation of several commandments in the Mosaic Decalogue (Deuteronomy, 5.6–21).   *writ over the door*] Of the commandments in Deuteronomy 6 the Israelites are told 'thou shalt write them upon the posts of thy house, and on thy gates' (v. 9).

11 *priests . . . rounds*] That is, they are patrolling like watchmen or soldiers, in relation to whom 'to walk the rounds' is a set phrase (*OED*, round, sb^1 14a).

11–12] Both lines rhyme internally: *OED* records (as reflecting a colloquial pronunciation) the eighteenth-century spelling 'gownds'.

12 *binding with briars*] Binding newly filled graves with briars was actually practised into the nineteenth century: see Blake's illustrations of Gray ('Elegy in a Country Churchyard', plates 2 and 9) and Young (*Night Thoughts*, Night 3, p. 21); 'briars' also had a well-established figurative sense of 'troubles, difficulties' (*OED*, brier, sb^1 4, citing this example).

5   But if at the church they would give us some ale,
And a pleasant fire our souls to regale,
We'd sing and we'd pray all the livelong day,
Nor ever once wish from the church to stray.

Then the parson might preach, and drink, and sing,
10   And we'd be as happy as birds in the spring;
And modest Dame Lurch, who is always at church,
Would not have bandy children, nor fasting, nor birch.

And God like a Father rejoicing to see
His children as pleasant and happy as he,
15   Would have no more quarrel with the Devil or the barrel,
But kiss him, and give him both drink and apparel.

London

This poem is an impassioned indictment of the city, and as such can be placed in a tradition of urban satire and denunciation, one recent example of which was Samuel Johnson's poem of the same title, itself an 'imitation' (free translation) of Juvenal. That London is enslaved to commerce is everywhere manifest: in the church's tacit endorsement of exploited child labour, in state-sanctioned violence, and most of all in the corruption of sexual relations epitomized by the 'marriage hearse', the inevitable underside of marriage as here constituted – prostitution and its attendant evils. As Blake has it in *Jerusalem*: 'What is a wife and what is a harlot? ... / ... Are they two and not one? Can they exist separate?' They cannot: pre-marital virginity and exclusive sexual possession are, from Blake's point of view, mistaken ideals which necessarily give rise to prostitution. The poem presents a nightmarish vision with a prophet's preternatural consciousness of suffering, but that consciousness need not be seen, as some recent criticism has argued, as a corrupt one. The claim that 'in *every* face', 'in *every* cry' shows the speaker's error – that his sense of mental disorders as ubiquitous cannot but be a projection of his own paranoia – invokes a sense of life as less vitiated by the evils of Experience than the *Songs* show it to be. 'Many are not capable of a firm persuasion of anything' (*Marriage*, plate 12): it is difficult to conclude from the prophetic jibe of Isaiah that Blake is the dizzying ironist of some modern accounts. (Edward Larrisy espouses the opposite view – that

---

11 *Dame*] Title prefixed to the surname of a schoolmistress (*OED n* 6c).   *Lurch*] Clearly Blake wanted an internal rhyme to match those of lines 3, 7 and 15. However, *OED* records two senses of 'lurch' which involve pilfering food which rightly belongs to others (*v*¹ 2 and 3 [3 would be archaic, but the last recorded use of 2 is 1810]): Blake may mean to imply that this religious schoolmistress has rickety pupils because she eats their rations.

12] Bow-legs are a characteristic feature of rickets, a disease plausibly connected by Blake's contemporaries with poor diet and a lack of open-air exercise (as in William Buchan, *Domestic Medicine* [1770], 9th edn., 1786).

the speaker's perspective is severely limited: *William Blake* (1985), 42–55.) Parts of the poem are closely comparable to the Notebook fragment, 'An Ancient Proverb': 'Remove away that blackening church, / Remove away that marriage hearse, / Remove away that man of blood, / You'll quite remove the ancient curse.'

Design. Above the text a boy leads an old man who walks on crutches (an image Blake used again in *Jerusalem*, plate 84, where the old man is identified as 'London, blind and age-bent, begging through the streets / Of Babylon, led by a child'). To the right of the text a boy warms his hands at a blazing fire.

I wander through each chartered street,
Near where the chartered Thames does flow,
And mark in every face I meet
Marks of weakness, marks of woe.

5 In every cry of every man,
In every infant's cry of fear,
In every voice, in every ban,
The mind-forged manacles I hear.

How the chimney-sweeper's cry
10 Every black'ning church appals,
And the hapless soldier's sigh
Runs in blood down palace walls.

1, 2 *chartered*] Charters originally guaranteed freedoms, as in Blake's early *Edward III* (*Poetical Sketches*), which speaks of 'Liberty, the chartered right of Englishmen'. Blake's usage here points the irony: the commercial freedoms charters protected for a mercantile minority are exclusive of, and oppressive to, the majority. Erdman cites Paine in *The Rights of Man* (Part 1, 1791): 'Every chartered town is an aristocratical monopoly' (*Prophet Against Empire*). Cf. Blake's use of the word in the lyric beginning 'Why should I care for the men of Thames, / Or the cheating waves of chartered streams' (Notebook, p. 113). The whole poem is relevant (see p. 157). E. P. Thompson investigates this word, with further examples from Paine, as 'at the centre of Whig ideology'. He also discusses 'mark' (see following note), with further examples from the Bible, arguing against 'ambiguities . . . [which] are not fruitful multipliers of meaning' (Michael Phillips (ed.), *Interpreting Blake* (1978)). The Notebook draft originally read (in both lines 1 and 2) 'dirty'.

3 *mark*] notice, observe (*OED v* III). This is also sometimes understood as meaning 'put a mark upon' (*OED v* I), as by Harold Bloom, who sees a reference to Ezekiel 9.4–7: 'And the Lord said unto him, Go through the midst of the city, through the midst of Jerusalem, and set a mark upon the foreheads of the men that sigh and that cry for all the abominations that be done in the midst thereof . . . Slay utterly old and young . . . but come not near any man upon whom is the mark' (*Poetry and Repression*, New Haven, CT, 1976). This view is ably criticized by Michael Ferber (*ELH*, 48 (1981), 310–38).

7 *ban*] an imprecation expressing anger (*OED sb* 6, citing this example).

8 *mind-forged manacles*] The Notebook draft originally read 'German-forgèd links', referring to the Hanoverian king, George III, and the German mercenaries the British government employed during the 1790s. The change shifts the oppression from without to within.

10 *blackening*] The literal discoloration through soot is a symbolic index of the Church's moral culpability.   *appals*] Punning on the archaic sense, makes pale (*OED v* 5, last recorded use 1583).

But most through midnight streets I hear
How the youthful harlot's curse
15   Blasts the new-born infant's tear,
And blights with plagues the marriage hearse.

The Human Abstract

This poem revisits from a sceptical perspective the virtues of 'The Divine Image': mercy, pity, peace, and love can all can be seen as having corrupt forms, underlying which is a corrupt religion – encouraging quiescence, manipulating people by the fear of death: a religion of hypocrisy and placemen which opposes criticism with mystification.

Design. Beneath the text a bearded old man who resembles the Urizen of the prophetic books struggles with a net of thick ropes over his head (cf. *The Book of Urizen*'s 'Net of Religion', 'So twisted the cords, and so knotted / The meshes: twisted like to the human brain' [25.20–21], and plate 28 design).

    Pity would be no more
    If we did not make somebody poor;
    And Mercy no more could be
    If all were as happy as we.

5   And mutual fear brings peace,
    Till the selfish loves increase;
    Then Cruelty knits a snare,
    And spreads his baits with care.

    He sits down with holy fears,
10   And waters the ground with tears;
    Then Humility takes its root
    Underneath his foot.

13–16] It is clear from the disposition of the stanzas in the Notebook draft that this final stanza was not part of the poem as first conceived. Cf. the Notebook stanza left over from 'The Human Abstract': 'There souls of men are bought and sold, / And milk-fed infancy for gold, / And youth to slaughterhouses led, / And beauty for a bit of bread.'

13 *hear*] Literally and metaphorically: the speaker both hears the prostitute curse the child she did not want, and (with the same eerily nightmarish vision that a sigh heard became blood seen) perceives the effects of the prostitute's curse – venereal disease – on children and marriages.

15 *Blasts*] strikes with a curse; but the sense 'strikes the eyes with dimness' is also relevant (*OED v* 10a, 8d).   *tear*] Gonorrhoea in a mother can cause blindness in a baby.

Title *Abstract*] Contrary to the imaginative and particular nature of the image – the generalized product of the purely rational faculty, and therefore in Blake's terms less than fully human. In Blake's Notebook the poem was titled 'The Human Image', making it more clearly a contrary to 'The Divine Image' in *Innocence*.

> Soon spreads the dismal shade
> Of Mystery over his head;
> And the caterpillar and fly
> Feed on the Mystery.

15

> And it bears the fruit of Deceit,
> Ruddy and sweet to eat;
> And the raven his nest has made
> In its thickest shade.

20

> The gods of the earth and sea
> Sought through Nature to find this tree,
> But their search was all in vain:
> There grows one in the human brain.

Infant Sorrow

This poem comes from a much longer draft of nine stanzas in Blake's Notebook (p. 113), which focuses on the child's development under an oppressive religious tutelage. Parts of this draft were used in other songs. As it stands the poem is an exemplum: the new-born infant takes its first step in the characteristic processes of repression.

Below the text the design – which recalls that of 'A Cradle Song' in *Innocence* – shows a naked (entirely unswaddled) baby in a cradle waving its arms, about to be picked up by its mother.

> My mother groaned, my father wept,
> Into the dangerous world I leapt,
> Helpless, naked, piping loud,
> Like a fiend hid in a cloud.

---

14 *Mystery*] Cf. Revelation 17.5, the account of the Great Whore, the antagonist of the Lamb, who has written on her forehead 'Mystery, Babylon the Great, the mother of harlots and abominations of the earth'.

15 *caterpillar*] Cf. the proverb of Hell which connects the caterpillar with the clergy: 'As the caterpillar chooses the fairest leaves to lay her eggs on, so the priest lays his curse on the fairest joys.'

19 *raven*] Traditionally a bird of ill-omen associated with death.

22 *this tree*] Based on the poisonous upas tree of Java (which Blake mentions in the contemporary Notebook lyric, 'Let the brothels of Paris be opened') and the banyan tree, which grows by putting down branches which then re-enroot (of which Blake knew from *Paradise Lost*, IX, 1101–10). The seductive fruit also suggests the Tree of the Knowledge of Good and Evil (Genesis, 2.16–17, 3.1–7). The Tree of Mystery reappears further developed in the prophetic books: *Ahania*, chapter III, *The Four Zoas*, Night VII (lines 31ff.), and *Jerusalem*, plate 28.

4] The line is varied from 'Mad Song' of Blake's early *Poetical Sketches*.

5   Struggling in my father's hands,
       Striving against my swaddling bands,
       Bound and weary, I thought best
       To sulk upon my mother's breast.

A Poison Tree

This is a poem on the psychology of repression consistent with *The Marriage of Heaven and Hell*'s proverb that 'He who desires but acts not breeds pestilence'. Blake's Notebook title, 'Christian Forbearance', points to a quasi-Lawrentian satire of 'turn the other cheek' ethics, which Blake may have decided was simplistic: there could, on Blake's view, be versions of this ethic both corrupt (as here, suppressing anger) and heroic (like Jesus, transcending it). Blake may also have intended the Notebook title to imply a critique of the traditional Christian view of Wrath as one of the Seven Deadly Sins. But he would regard as simplistic any attempt to inflate such a critique into a generalization about Christian thinking on anger: his own account of what he later called a 'science of wrath' (*Milton*, 7.46) – a proper understanding of anger pure of egotism as psychologically cleansing – was perfectly consistent with the action of Jesus in cleansing the temple (as in Matthew, 21.12–13). Nevertheless, despite the change of title, a poem about a tree with an apple which tempts and slays the person who picks it almost inevitably suggests some reference to the Judeo-Christian myth of the origin of sin (Genesis, chapters 2 and 3). The relation can be variously interpreted (see Philip J. Gallagher, 'The Word Made Flesh: Blake's "A Poison Tree" and the Book of Genesis,' *Studies in Romanticism*, 16 (1977)). The poem's repeated structures magnificently express both the speaker's obsession and his fixated sense of movement towards an inevitable doom.

Design. Below the text, beneath an overarching, leafless tree, lies a naked body, arms outstretched, head to the reader.

       I was angry with my friend:
       I told my wrath, my wrath did end.
       I was angry with my foe:
       I told it not, my wrath did grow.

5   And I watered it in fears,
       Night and morning with my tears;
       And I sunnèd it with smiles,
       And with soft, deceitful wiles.

---

6 *swaddling bands*] Stanley Gardner gives quotations from William Buchan's *Domestic Medicine* (1770, 9th edn., 1786) recommending against swaddling (*Blake's 'Innocence' and 'Experience' Retraced*, London, 1986): the traditional practice had become controversial by the time of the poem.

10

And it grew both day and night,
Till it bore an apple bright;
And my foe beheld it shine,
And he knew that it was mine,

15

And into my garden stole
When the night had veiled the pole.
In the morning glad I see
My foe outstretched beneath the tree.

A Little Boy Lost

The central issue of this poem is religious hypocrisy. The boy is a voice from Innocence who speaks honestly about his experience. He denies that one can love one's neighbour as oneself as Jesus commanded, and rejects the conventional Christian idea of a transcendent God. Blake endorsed only the second of these ideas – though the first, to love one's neighbour as oneself, he would recognize as a counsel of perfection to which most people can only aspire. Although the boy is not wholly right, however, he is honest. He says what he thinks, not what he is supposed to think, while his accuser is a hypocrite whose actions show that he cannot truly understand what the boy denies, either about love or about God.

Design. Below the text a group of people – weeping parents and obedient worshippers – huddle, cowed before a fire. To the right one turns away with a gesture expressing horror. Spiky bird-like leaves ascend the right margin.

'Nought loves another as itself,
Nor venerates another so,
Nor is it possible to Thought
A greater than itself to know.

5

And Father, how can I love you,
Or any of my brothers more?
I love you like the little bird
That picks up crumbs around the door.'

---

14 *pole*] See note to 'Introduction', line 9.

1] See the commandment of Jesus to 'Love . . . thy neighbour as thyself' (Luke, 10.27, based on Leviticus, 19.18).

3–4] Cf. Blake's marginalia to Swedenborg's *Divine Love and Wisdom* (*c.* 1789): 'Man can have no idea of anything greater than Man as a cup cannot contain more than its capaciousness'.

The priest sat by and heard the child,
In trembling zeal he seized his hair;
He led him by his little coat,
And all admired the priestly care.

0

And standing on the altar high,
'Lo, what a fiend is here!', said he,
'One who sets reason up for judge
Of our most holy Mystery.'

15

The weeping child could not be heard,
The weeping parents wept in vain;
They stripped him to his little shirt,
And bound him in an iron chain,

20

And burned him in a holy place,
Where many had been burned before.
The weeping parents wept in vain.
Are such things done on Albion's shore?

A Little Girl Lost

There can be no doubt about this poem's point of view: it begins with the voice of the bard announcing a polemic for free love. Ambiguity arises from the poem's treatment of the Golden Age: is it not a myth but a present reality, always available to whoever is able to enter it? Ona and her lover seem to start there, but they know already that parents need to be afar and that the dark is thought proper for love. Ona is vulnerable because horrified holiness has begun to take hold before she encounters its full force in the person of her father.

The design presents contrasts: a barren tree grows up the right margin, but it supports a vine which shoots looping tendrils into the text, and there are numerous birds – mostly small, though three larger ones (two birds of paradise) fly around the opening stanza.

---

15 *reason*] common sense. (The word does not imply that the boy is a Urizenic rationalist of a kind to which Blake objected.)

24] The last burning for heresy in England was in 1612, but children were still threatened with being burned eternally as punishment for sin. Andrew Lincoln compares Watts's 'The Danger of Delay': 'Tis dangerous to provoke a God! / His power and vengeance who can tell!/ One stroke of his almighty rod / Shall send young sinners quick to hell' (*Songs of Innocence and of Experience*, 1991).

Children of the future age
Reading this indignant page,
Know that in a former time
Love, sweet Love, was thought a crime.

———

5   In the Age of Gold,
Free from winter's cold,
Youth and maiden bright
To the holy light,
Naked in the sunny beams delight.

10   Once a youthful pair,
Filled with softest care,
Met in garden bright
Where the holy light
Had just removed the curtains of the night.

15   There, in rising day,
On the grass they play;
Parents were afar,
Strangers came not near,
And the maiden soon forgot her fear.

20   Tired with kisses sweet,
They agree to meet
When the silent sleep
Waves o'er heaven's deep,
And the weary tirèd wanderers weep.

25   To her father white
Came the maiden bright,
But his loving look,
Like the holy book,
All her tender limbs with terror shook.

---

5 *Age of Gold*] An imaginary past time of innocence and happiness – though the following present tense ('delight') may imply that it could be a permanent condition. Blake described his own work as 'an endeavour to restore what the Ancients called the Golden Age' ('A Vision of the Last Judgement,' Bentley, *Writings*, 1009).

22–4] Contrast the Notebook lyric, 'Are not the joys of morning sweeter': 'Let age and sickness silent rob / The vineyards in the night, / But those who burn with vig'rous youth / Pluck fruits before the light'.

30   'Ona, pale and weak,
To thy father speak.
O, the trembling fear!
O, the dismal care
That shakes the blossoms of my hoary hair!'

To Tirzah

This poem does not appear in the earliest copies of *Songs*. How late it is has been disputed. Partly because its symbolism can be connected with the epics (see note on the title and line 3) Erdman and others place it possibly after 1805, but Bentley conjectures 1797, and an even earlier date, 1795, is suggested by Joseph Viscomi's researches about Blake's printing techniques (*Blake and the Idea of the Book* (1993), 238–9). In the manner of *The Book of Urizen*, the poem presents the world of the fallen senses as a snare, though the material world is also the necessary ground of spiritual recovery. The repetition of the speaker's question may suggest, however, that the problem of our relation to the sensuous world is not so easily disposed of as the doctrines invoked might seem to imply.

Design. To the left two women wearing long gowns raise and support a naked man slumped on the ground beneath them; to the right, an old man, bearded and gowned, reaches towards the man a pitcher. On the old man's gown is written 'It is raised a spiritual body' – from Saint Paul, 1 Corinthians, 15.44: 'It is sown a natural body; it is raised a spiritual body. There is a natural body, and there is a spiritual body.' Branches of a fruit-bearing tree, the trunk of which is to the right of the old man, stretch across the scene.

Whate'er is born of mortal birth
Must be consumèd with the earth
To rise from generation free:
Then what have I to do with thee?

Title *Tirzah*] Capital of the northern kingdom of Israel, the kingdom of the apostate Jeroboam (1 Kings 14); an antithesis therefore to Jerusalem, capital of the southern kingdom, home of true spiritual perception and spiritual liberty. In *The Four Zoas*, *Milton* and *Jerusalem* Blake associates Tirzah with the heathen tribes of Amalek, Canaan and Moab and their cruelties. Tirzah is also one of the daughters of Zelophehad, who had no sons, and so whose daughters were allowed to inherit from him (Numbers, 27.1–11). Cities are by convention female, and the primary sense here is that of the antithesis to Jerusalem; but the Numbers narrative of what could be seen as female usurpation may also be relevant.

3 *generation*] Like Tirzah, this term suggests the world of Blake's epics, where it is the usual term for the second level of his fourfold spiritual geography – Ulro, Generation, Beulah, Eden.

4, 16 *what . . . thee*] 'Woman, what have I to do with thee?' Christ's words to his mother during the wedding at Cana (John, 2.4). Here the speaker addresses Tirzah. Out of context the words can be taken as affirming that a person's 'mortal part' (what Christ derived from Mary) is not ultimately real. (The phrase also occurs in 1 Kings 17.18, but the context there is not consistent with its use here.) The line also appears in 'William Bond' (line 28), and in fragmentd (Bentley's lettering) of *The Everlasting Gospel* (line 32).

5   The sexes sprung from shame and pride,
                 Blowed in the morn, in evening died.
                 But mercy changed death into sleep:
                 The sexes rose to work and weep.

                 Thou mother of my mortal part
10   With cruelty didst mould my heart,
                 And with false self-deceiving tears
                 Didst bind my nostrils, eyes and ears;

                 Didst close my tongue in senseless clay,
                 And me to mortal life betray.
15   The death of Jesus set me free.
                 Then what have I to do with thee?

The School Boy

This poem was originally included in *Songs of Innocence*, and is somewhat poised between the two collections. It was transferred to *Experience* only in late copies. The speaker is not finally protected from the conditions of experience, as the speakers in *Innocence* usually are; but, though this is a song of protest – against the usual eighteenth-century view that compulsion in education is both necessary and beneficial – it has none of the bitterness of, for example, the song of the *Experience* chimney sweeper. It is perhaps closest in spirit to 'The Little Vagabond'. Among various doggerel verses of *c.* 1807–9, Blake gave thanks for his own lack of formal schooling: 'Thank God I was never sent to school / To be flogged into following the style of a fool' (though the reference seems to be primarily to graphic art, the one area in which Blake did have a formal training, at Henry Pars's drawing school from the age of ten). In 1825 Blake told the diarist Henry Crabb Robinson that he 'would allow of no other education than what lies in the cultivation of the fine arts and the imagination', and, more unequivocally, 'There is no use in education. I hold it wrong. It is the great Sin' (Bentley, *Blake Records* (1969), 543, 540). In the poem Blake presents the main content of formal education not as what but as how one learns: compulsion and fear eradicate spontaneity and joy. The music of the poem's stanza pattern, with its unexpected rhyme added to extend and clinch the quatrain, can be equally expressive of joy or melancholy. The diction is more smoothly eighteenth century than is usual in the *Songs*: this schoolboy gives an impression of having mastered polite accomplishments.

---

5 *sexes . . . pride*] As in *The Book of Urizen* (chapter V) the Fall and the separation into two sexes of the eternal androgynous being are treated as a single event.

12–13 *bind . . . clay*] Cf. the binding of Urizen: *The Book of Urizen*, chapter IV[b], vv. 8–11.

The design illustrates proper childhood joys. Below the text three boys sit playing
marbles or jacks. Vines grow up both the right- and left-hand margins. The two on
the right are looped: three boys clamber up the loops; a fourth sits at the top read-
ing, taking delight in learning's unofficial bower.

> I love to rise in a summer morn
> When the birds sing on every tree;
> The distant huntsman winds his horn,
> And the skylark sings with me.
> 5   O, what sweet company!
>
> But to go to school in a summer morn,
> O, it drives all joy away!
> Under a cruel eye outworn
> The little ones spend the day
> 10   In sighing and dismay.
>
> Ah, then at times I drooping sit
> And spend many an anxious hour,
> Nor in my book can I take delight,
> Nor sit in learning's bower,
> 15   Worn through with the dreary shower.
>
> How can the bird that is born for joy
> Sit in a cage and sing?
> How can a child, when fears annoy,
> But droop his tender wing,
> 20   And forget his youthful spring?
>
> O father and mother, if buds are nipped,
> And blossoms blown away,
> And if the tender plants are stripped
> Of their joy in the springing day
> 25   By sorrow and care's dismay,
>
> How shall the summer arise in joy,
> Or the summer fruits appear?
> Or how shall we gather what griefs destroy,
> Or bless the mellowing year
> 30   When the blasts of winter appear?

---

8 *outworn*] worn out (referring to 'the little ones').

18 *annoy*] hurt, harm (*OED v* 4b, citing this example).

The Voice of the Ancient Bard

Like 'The School Boy', this poem was originally included in *Songs of Innocence*. In the present arrangement *Experience* begins and ends with a bardic voice. The poem is unusual among the *Songs* in not being in stanzas but in lines of varied length (the first unrhymed). The bard announces the apocalypse as already begun, but nevertheless seems still taken up with denouncing error.

Design. A bardic figure plays a harp; in front of him a boy and girl and four young women listen; behind him a youthful boy and girl embrace.

> Youth of delight, come hither
> And see the opening morn,
> Image of truth new-born.
> Doubt is fled, and clouds of reason,
> 5   Dark disputes and artful teasing.
> Folly is an endless maze;
> Tangled roots perplex her ways.
> How many have fallen there!
> They stumble all night over bones of the dead,
> 10   And feel they know not what but care,
> And wish to lead others when they should be led.

Three early copies of the joint *Songs* end with a tailpiece, a small full-plate design which shows a male figure (Jesus?), his hands in an attitude of prayer, being borne upwards by six winged cherubs.

A Divine Image

In this arrangement of the combined *Songs* 'The Voice of the Ancient Bard' is the last poem of *Songs of Experience*. 'A Divine Image', conceived as a contrary to 'The Divine Image' of *Innocence* but superseded by 'The Human Abstract', was engraved

---

4 *Doubt*] Cf. 'Auguries of Innocence', 'He who shall teach the child to doubt / The rotting grave shall ne'er get out': scepticism as a settled attitude recognizes no limits, and as such is fundamentally at odds with imagination.

9] Cf. John 11.9–10 (Jesus speaks): 'If any man walk in the day, he stumbleth not, because he seeth the light of this world. But if a man walk in the night, he stumbleth, because there is no light in him.' Cf. *Marriage*, plate 7: 'Drive your cart and your plough over the bones of the dead.'

10] That is, though they can recognize in themselves sorrow or anxiety, they cannot (beyond this elementary recognition) understand their own feeings.

11] Probably a largely anapaestic line with (like the preceding lines) four feet, the third stress falling on 'they' to mark the antithesis others/they. (It can also be read as a largely iambic five-foot line, with the fourth stress falling on 'should', to mark the antithesis lead/led.)

presumably *c.* 1791–92) but was included in only one copy of the collection made up by Blake (copy BB, *c.* 1795). (It was also included in five posthumous copies.)

The design shows the character who became Los, a blacksmith and in Blake's later myth the spirit of poetry, kneeling naked, with a huge hammer thrown back behind his head ready to strike a wall which obstructs the sun. This design was re-worked in *Jerusalem* (plate 73).

> Cruelty has a human heart,
> And Jealousy a human face,
> Terror the human form divine,
> And Secrecy the human dress.
>
> The human dress is forgèd iron,
> The human form a fiery forge,
> The human face a furnace sealed,
> The human heart its hungry gorge.

5

THE BOOK OF THEL

The Book of Thel begins from Thel's fear of death, but it is mostly concerned, given the fact of death, with questions about the value of life. Meditations on death, and what one might learn from it about life, were a common subject in eighteenth-century poetry. Blake later illustrated Gray's 'Elegy in a Country Churchyard', Young's *Night Thoughts*, Blair's *The Grave*, and Hervey's *Meditations among the Tombs*, all on this subject, and all widely known when Blake was a young man. For most of *The Book of Thel* answers are offered to Thel's problem about transience and value in terms of an ethic propounded with little variation by a humanized lily, cloud, and clod of clay – an ethic of selfless giving as part of a natural cycle of death and rebirth, a doctrine to which Blake's biblical allusions give Christian resonances of faith in a controlling beneficence. At the end of the work these comforting answers are challenged by a sudden acknowledgement of the sufferings of ordinary experience, a voice from Thel's 'grave' which has nothing to say about literal death but much about being painfully alive to the stimuli of the senses. Blake's symbolism, as often, is open: the reader need not decide between possible meanings of Blake's metaphors, or even between literal and metaphoric senses. Thel confronts a transition between radically different states of being which presents itself as terrifying.

Interpretation of this potential transition from innocence to experience has been various. On one view Thel is an unborn soul who hears about the sufferings of the material world and flees from them in terror: Blake (it is argued) was influenced by the eighteenth-century Neoplatonist Thomas Taylor, and specifically his interpretation of the myth of Persephone's descent to the Underworld as representing the birth of a pre-existent soul into the material world. The final plate is a key: Thel's real fear is not of death but of birth.[1] The problems with this reading are that there is no sign of Thel's being unborn before the final plate, and that the final plate is more obviously about fear of sexual experience than fear of birth. Alternatively, Thel is human and afraid quite literally of death, but nevertheless recoils from the creative albeit painful experiences which might address this fear by giving life greater value. Different reactions typically attend these different views: sympathy (Thel's fears are valid), or condemnation (the consequence of not confronting pain is emotional and imaginative stultification). On this latter view Oothoon in *Visions of the Daughters of Albion* is Thel's instructive antitype: she seeks experience with openness, undergoes what is painfully forced upon her, and uses it creatively to deepen participation in what she discovers is valuable. Lyca and Ona in the *Songs* offer similar

---

[1] See George Mills Harper, *The Neoplatonism of William Blake* (1961), 246–56; and Kathleen Raine, *Blake and Tradition* (1968), chapter 4. Assuming that the final plate of *Thel* was not engraved until 1791, Harper supposes a specific source for it in Taylor's *Dissertation on the Eleusinian and Bacchic Mysteries*, 1790 (but see 8.1 note). On the probable date of plate 8, see the final paragraph of this introduction.

models of Blakean spiritual adventurers. For Thel the way down would be the way up: in her end is a beginning that she does not take.

Whether Thel's return to the valley from which she begins her quest is judged by implication a failure, or even whether any judgement is implied, has also divided interpreters.[2] As often, Blake allows a somewhat free interaction of points of view at odds with one another. How far such competing voices can be placed in a hierarchy not of the interpreter's imposition is, of course, disputed. One possible interpretative gloss is suggested by Blake's maginalium to Swedenborg: 'understanding or thought is not natural to man: it is acquired by means of suffering and distress, i.e. experience' (Bentley, *Writings*, 1388). As in *The Marriage of Heaven and Hell*, where improvement of sensual enjoyment will bring about the apocalypse, the sense-experience that terrifies Thel would be a source of legitimate pleasure and increased understanding.

The date of *Thel* is controversial, and the controversies have some bearing on interpretation. The title-page gives 1789, but because there is a change in lettering style in plates 1 and 8, and because those plates are not present in an early set of proofs (copy a), it has been argued that they were etched later than plates 2 to 7, probably in 1791. Clearly Thel's motto (plate 1) is in a different mode from the rest of the work – a poetic quatrain, and unillustrated; and equally clearly there is an abrupt shift of mode and tone at the beginning of plate 8 – from pastoral to grave-yard, and from pathos to sublime. But such changes can be understood as parts of single and coherent aesthetic intention, and on the basis of Joseph Viscomi's work on Blake's printing methods, the argument for later composition of plates 1 and 8 has been convincingly challenged: it now seems probable that *Thel* as it exists in all copies apart from proof copy a, as a work in eight plates, was completed in 1789 or early 1790, and is therefore contemporary with *Songs of Innocence*.[3]

---

[2] For Robert Gleckner, Thel fails to learn the wisdom offered by the lily, the cloud and the clay (*The Piper and the Bard: A Study of William Blake* (1959), 161–74); for Mary Lynn Johnson she retreats to make good use of it (*JEGP*, 69 (1970)). For Donald R. Pearce, on the other hand, Thel is the victim of false religious instruction (*Blake Studies*, 8 (1978), 23–35). W. J. T. Mitchell argues that the work makes all such judgements impossible (*Blake's Composite Art* (1978), chapter 3).

[3] Joseph Viscomi, *Blake and the Idea of the Book* (1993), chapter 23; Morris Eaves, Robert N. Essick and Joseph Viscomi, *William Blake: The Early Illuminated Books* (1993), 71–4.

The Book of Thel

[Plate 1]

Thel's Motto

Does the eagle know what is in the pit?
Or wilt thou go ask the mole?
Can wisdom be put in a silver rod?
Or love in a golden bowl?

Plate 1. Thel's motto. This plate is placed last in copies N and O, the only extant copies printed after 1795, c. 1818. Its text might be interpreted in terms of traditional wisdom as opposing the eagle's sharp sight to the mole's blindness, a reading supported by the symbolism of *The Marriage of Heaven and Hell* in which the eagle is 'a portion of genius'. But the idea that knowledge is derived from experience favours the mole's knowledge of the pit: relevant experience may be more important than innate gifts. *Visions of the Daughters of Albion* endorses this answer: 'Does not the eagle scorn the earth and despise the treasures beneath? / But the mole knoweth what is there' (8.39–40). The questions in lines 3 and 4 apparently mean 'can wisdom and love be adequately symbolized?', merely to ask which might seem to carry the implication that they cannot; but see Blake's concluding annotation to Lavater's *Aphorisms*: '. . . it is impossible to think without images of somewhat on earth' (Bentley, *Writings*, 1386). The phraseology of lines 3 and 4 is biblical, but none of the suggested sources indicates a conclusive answer to the question (see, for example, Ecclesiastes, 12.6–7: 'Or ever the silver cord be loosed, or the golden bowl be broken [. . . then shall the dust return to the earth as it was']; or Job, 28.12, 15: 'Where shall wisdom be found? . . . It cannot be gotten for gold, neither shall silver be weighed for the price thereof'). The silver rod may symbolize secular power (the sceptre) and the golden bowl religious wisdom (the chalice), but other possibilities have been suggested (the phallus, the womb, the skull), and to interpret the symbols may not be necessary to considering whether love and wisdom can be symbolized. The lines appear (as a single line) in a cancelled passage of *Tiriel* (also written c. 1789), where the immediately following question – 'Is the son of a king warmed without wool?' – clearly implies the answer 'no'. It is finally open to question whether Thel acts on her motto or whether its application to her own case is ironic. The lines are evidently riddling: interpretation both depends upon, and will in turn influence, the reader's understanding of the work as a whole. The riddles are teased out by A. G. den Otter, *Studies in Romanticism*, 30 (1991). The motto can be interpreted to mean that neither innate gifts nor eloquent symbols are any substitute for experience, its application to the poem then being that Thel's return to the vales of Har is a failure to live out this recognition.

[Plate 2]

The Book of Thel

The author and printer William Blake, 1789.

Plate 2. Title-page. The name Thel has been variously understood: as an anagram of Lethe (the Underworld river of forgetfulness); as derived from the Greek *thelos*, 'will' or 'wish'; or from the Greek *thelus*, 'female' (also 'fresh' and 'gentle'); from the Hebrew *thal*, 'dew'; or from the name of the Muse most associated with pastoral, Thalia. Given its radical proposals on subjects of interest to him – prostitution and polygamy – Blake may have come across the Greek *thelus* through Martin Madan's *Thelyphthora: or, a Treatise of Female Ruin* (1780), and the reply of William Cowper (Madan's cousin – who therefore published his response anonymously), *Anti-Thelyphthora: a Tale in Verse* (1781). One problem with such derivations is their very multifariousness: so many different possibilities can scarcely all be intended; and if all are equally probable all are equally improbable. Blake would know from the marginal glosses of the Authorized Version that biblical personal and place names often involve some etymological play, but he did not actually learn either Hebrew or Greek until after 1800. Michael Ferber objects to the whole idea of 'meaningful' names, arguing that strangeness and lack of existing associations are often the point of Blake's onomastic invention, and that the analogues suggested by scholars – if Blake knew them – have the opposite aim: Blake invents linguistic forms which suggest the world of an *Ur*-language lying behind Hebrew, Greek and Latin (*The Poetry of William Blake* (1991), 54–5). Vincent De Luca argues for a different but also non-etymological view of Blake's names, the importance of recognizing their 'phonetic and orthographic remoteness from the norms of expected naming in spoken or literary usage' and 'independence from . . . discursive significance' (*Blake Studies*, 8 (1978), 5–22 [6]).

Design. To the left, below the title, stands a young woman (Thel), gowned and holding a shepherd's crook in her left hand (cf. 3.1–2). She watches the human forms of two flowers: a naked male leaps from his flower to seize a gowned female, who leaps from her flower with arms raised, perhaps in alarm though possibly to express joy (in which case the design might be seen as illustrating the courtship of the cloud and the dew, 5.12–15). Above and around the title arches a thin tree round the whole length of which loops a vine.

[Plate 3]

Thel

I

The daughters of Mne Seraphim led round their sunny flocks,
All but the youngest. She in paleness sought the secret air,
To fade away like morning beauty from her mortal day.
Down by the river of Adona her soft voice is heard,
5   And thus her gentle lamentation falls like morning dew.

'O life of this our spring, why fades the lotus of the water?
Why fade these children of the spring, born but to smile and fall?
Ah, Thel is like a watry bow, and like a parting cloud,
Like a reflection in a glass, like shadows in the water,
10   Like dreams of infants, like a smile upon an infant's face,
Like the dove's voice, like transient day, like music in the air;
Ah, gentle may I lay me down, and gentle rest my head,
And gentle sleep the sleep of death, and gentle hear the voice
Of him that walketh in the garden in the evening time.'

15   The lily of the valley breathing in the humble grass
Answered the lovely maid and said, 'I am a watry weed,
And I am very small, and love to dwell in lowly vales;
So weak, the gilded butterfly scarce perches on my head.

3.1 *Mne Seraphim*] Bne Seraphim (the sons of the Seraphim, guiding intelligences of the planet Venus, angels of love) are among the spirits listed in *The Three Books of Occult Philosophy* of Cornelius Agrippa (1486–1535; English trans. 1651, II.22). Blake took from this the names Tiriel and Zazel which he used in the poem *Tiriel* (see Thel's motto, note). The change Bne to Mne is sometimes understood to hint at 'Mnemosyne', Memory, mother of the (to Blake false) classical Muses (or, less plausibly, Mnetha, a nurse-guardian in *Tiriel*).

3.4 *Adona*] Probably derived from Adonis, in classical myth the mortal youth loved by Venus. It may be relevant that in Spenser's *Faerie Queene* (III.6) the Garden of Adonis is a paradise from which spirits are born into the material world, and that it also provides the basis for a lament about transience. The river of Adonis is mentioned in *Paradise Lost* (I.450).

3.12–13 *gentle may . . . death*] Possibly a reminiscence of James Hervey's *Mediations and Contemplations* (1748, I.83): 'I would lay me gently down, and sleep sweetly in the blessed Jesus.'

3.13 *gentle hear*] A proof copy shows that Blake originally etched 'gentley' with the *e* under the *y*. He first corrected this to *y* only, and finally to *e* only.

3.14 *him . . . time*] Recalling Genesis, 3.8: 'they heard the voice of the Lord God walking in the garden in the cool of the day.'

3.15 *lily of the valley*] Blake apparently has in mind the flower usually known by this name, with racemes of white, bell-shaped, fragrant flowers (*Convallaria majalis*). Some commentators suppose a more exotic plant, by allusion to The Song of Solomon, 2.1; but Blake's lily can be eaten by sheep (4.5–6).

Yet I am visited from heaven, and he that smiles on all
Walks in the valley, and each morn over me spreads his hand,
Saying, "Rejoice thou humble grass, thou new-born lily flower,
Thou gentle maid of silent valleys and of modest brooks,
For thou shalt be clothèd in light, and fed with morning manna,
Till summer's heat melts thee beside the fountains and the springs
5   To flourish in eternal vales." Then why should Thel complain,

[Plate 4]

Why should the mistress of the vales of Har utter a sigh?'
She ceased, and smiled in tears, then sat down in her silver shrine.

Thel answered, 'O thou little virgin of the peaceful valley,
Giving to those that cannot crave, the voiceless, the o'ertirèd,
Thy breath doth nourish the innocent lamb: he smells thy milky
5   garments,
He crops thy flowers, while thou sittest smiling in his face,
Wiping his mild and meekin mouth from all contagious taints.
Thy wine doth purify the golden honey; thy perfume,
Which thou dost scatter on every little blade of grass that springs,
10   Revives the milkèd cow, and tames the fire-breathing steed.
But Thel is like a faint cloud kindled at the rising sun:

3.21–3 *Rejoice . . . clothèd in light*] Perhaps recalling Christ's use of the lily, 'clothed' by God (Matthew, 6.28–31), to epitomize a proper trust in God's providential care.

3.23 *morning manna*] The food provided for the Israelites in the wilderness (Exodus, 16.14–35).

Plate 3 design. The title word, 'Thel', is framed by figures: to the upper left a naked man reaches towards a flying eagle; to the lower left another naked man, looking upwards, lies on a leaf or ear of corn (suggesting that the figures are very small); above him, and to his right, a woman in a billowing gown swings a naked child upwards in her raised arms; to the right (below the title *l*) a naked man, seen from behind, carries a shield and brandishes a sword.

4.1 *vales of Har*] In *Tiriel* a place of innocence and simplicity (though there degenerated into a refuge for evasion and senility). In *Thel* the place apparently retains its idyllic quality.

4.2 *shrine*] that in which something dwells (not necessarily with primarily religious connotations) (*OED sb* 4). Blake uses the word similarly in *Visions* (4.10).

4.4 *crave*] ask, beg (for this intransitive use cf. *Poetical Sketches*, 'King Edward the Third', 6.45–6).

4.4 *o'ertirèd*] Apparently etched 'o'erfired', but the word is difficult to explain convincingly: it has no usual application outside of ceramics.

4.7 *meekin*] Not recorded by *OED*; apparently a nonce-formation from 'meek'.

4.11–12 *cloud . . . place*] Cf. Job, 7.9: 'As the cloud is consumed and vanisheth away: so he that goeth down to the grave shall come up no more.' Thel's next interlocutor here, and at 5.23, is suggested by the terms of her lament.

I vanish from my pearly throne, and who shall find my place?'
'Queen of the vales,' the lily answered, 'ask the tender cloud,
And it shall tell thee why it glitters in the morning sky,
15   And why it scatters its bright beauty through the humid air.
Descend, O little cloud, and hover before the eyes of Thel.'

The cloud descended, and the lily bowed her modest head,
And went to mind her numerous charge among the verdant grass.

[Plate 5]

II

'O little cloud', the virgin said, 'I charge thee tell to me
Why thou complainest not, when in one hour thou fade away:
Then we shall seek thee but not find. Ah, Thel is like to thee:
I pass away, yet I complain, and no one hears my voice.'

The cloud then showed his golden head, and his bright form
5   emerged,
Hovering and glittering on the air before the face of Thel.

'O virgin, know'st thou not our steeds drink of the golden springs
Where Luvah doth renew his horses. Look'st thou on my youth,
And fearest thou because I vanish and am seen no more
10   Nothing remains? O maid, I tell thee, when I pass away,
It is to tenfold life, to love, to peace, and raptures holy:
Unseen descending weigh my light wings upon balmy flowers,
And court the fair-eyèd dew to take me to her shining tent;
The weeping virgin trembling kneels before the risen sun,
15   Till we arise linked in a golden band, and never part,
But walk united, bearing food to all our tender flowers.'

Plate 4 design. Below the text Thel stands to the right in front of the trunk of a tree, the delicate branches of which arch over the whole scene. She looks down at the human form of the lily of the valley who 'bow[s] her modest head'.

5.7 *golden*] That is, suffused with sunlight.

5.8 *Luvah*] An important figure in Blake's later myth, but here little more than a name: his horses which drink from golden springs may suggest the horses of the chariot of Apollo as god of the Sun.

5.15 *golden band*] Cf. 7.2, 'nuptial bands' and the loves of the plants as depicted on the title-page: selfless giving begins to be imaged in erotic terms.

'Dost thou O little cloud? I fear that I am not like thee;
For I walk through the vales of Har, and smell the sweetest flowers,
But I feed not the little flowers; I hear the warbling birds,
20   But I feed not the warbling birds: they fly and seek their food;
But Thel delights in these no more because I fade away,
And all shall say, "Without a use this shining woman lived,
Or did she only live to be at death the food of worms?"'

The cloud reclined upon his airy throne and answered thus:

25   'Then if thou art the food of worms, O virgin of the skies,
How great thy use, how great thy blessing. Every thing that lives
Lives not alone, nor for itself: fear not and I will call
The weak worm from its lowly bed, and thou shalt hear its voice.
Come forth, worm of the silent valley, to thy pensive queen.'

30   The helpless worm arose and sat upon the lily's leaf,
And the bright cloud sailed on to find his partner in the vale.

[Plate 6]

III

Then Thel astonished viewed the worm upon its dewy bed.

'Art thou a worm? Image of weakness, art thou but a worm?
I see thee like an infant wrappèd in the lily's leaf.
Ah, weep not little voice: thou canst not speak, but thou
    canst weep.
5   Is this a worm? I see thee lay helpless and naked: weeping,
And none to answer, none to cherish thee with mother's smiles.'

5.23 *at death . . . worms*] A commonplace in relation to human mortality, but Blake may have
expected the reader to recall a repeated thought in Job (19.26, 21.26, 24.20).

5.26–7 *Every . . . itself*] The idea is reiterated by the clod of clay (6.10) and by the clod of 'The
Clod and the Pebble' in *Songs of Experience* that 'seeketh not itself to please, / Nor for itself
hath any care.'

6.3–4 *infant . . . canst not speak*] Blake may have known the derivation from L. *infans*, unable
to speak.

6.5 *lay*] lie.

6.6 *cherish*] take affectionate care of (*OED* 5); and, at 7.10, 'tend, cultivate' (*OED* 2b); but in
both cases with something also of the sense 'give comfort to' (*OED* 6).

The clod of clay heard the worm's voice, and raised her
  pitying head;
She bowed over the weeping infant, and her life exhaled
In milky fondness; then on Thel she fixed her humble eyes.

10   'O beauty of the vales of Har, we live not for ourselves.
    Thou seest me the meanest thing, and so I am indeed;
    My bosom of itself is cold, and of itself is dark,

[Plate 7]

But he that loves the lowly pours his oil upon my head,
And kisses me, and binds his nuptial bands around my breast,
And says, "Thou mother of my children, I have lovèd thee,
And I have given thee a crown that none can take away."
5   But how this is, sweet maid, I know not, and I cannot know;
    I ponder, and I cannot ponder; yet I live and love.'

The daughter of beauty wiped her pitying tears with her white veil,
And said, 'Alas! I knew not this, and therefore did I weep:
That God would love a worm I knew, and punish the evil foot
10   That wilful bruised its helpless form: but that he cherished it
    With milk and oil I never knew, and therefore did I weep;
    And I complained in the mild air, because I fade away,
    And lay me down in thy cold bed, and leave my shining lot.'

'Queen of the vales,' the matron clay answered, 'I heard thy sighs,
15   And all thy moans flew o'er my roof, but I have called them down.
    Wilt thou, O Queen, enter my house? 'Tis given thee to enter
    And to return. Fear nothing: enter with thy virgin feet.'

Plate 6 design. Above the text, to the right, stands Thel with, to her right, the lower part of a tree trunk. Her back is to the viewer, and her arms are raised to shoulder height expressing surprise. She looks down towards the human form of the worm, a baby lying cradled in a lily plant with long thin tendrils. Above them flies the human form of the cloud, naked except for a broad ribbon which loops round his body and flutters behind him. The design illustrates 5.30–6.1.

7.4 a crown ... away] See 1 Peter, 5.2–5: 'a crown of glory that fadeth not away' is given to those who 'feed the flock of God' and are 'clothed with humility'. Cf. the crown signifying virtue in Revelation, 3.11.

Plate 7 design. Below the text Thel sits with her head bowed and arms crossed on her knees. Before her lie the naked human forms of the worm (a baby with arms raised to express delight) and, with her back to the viewer, the 'matron' clay (apparently a young woman). To the right grows a large plant with pendulous blossoms, one of which hangs above Thel's head. The design illustrates 6.7–9.

[Plate 8]

IV

The eternal gates' terrific porter lifted the northern bar:
Thel entered in and saw the secrets of the land unknown.
She saw the couches of the dead, and where the fibrous roots
Of every heart on earth infixes deep its restless twists:
5   A land of sorrows and of tears, where never smile was seen.

She wandered in the land of clouds through valleys dark, list'ning
Dolours and lamentations; waiting oft beside a dewy grave
She stood in silence, list'ning to the voices of the ground,
Till to her own grave plot she came, and there she sat down,
10   And heard this voice of sorrow breathèd from the hollow pit:

'Why cannot the ear be closèd to its own destruction?
Or the glist'ning eye to the poison of a smile?
Why are the eyelids stored with arrows ready drawn,
Where a thousand fighting men in ambush lie?
15   Or an eye of gifts and graces, show'ring fruits and coinèd gold?

8.1 *terrific porter*] In the Neoplatonic reading (see following note) this is Pluto, god of the Underworld. But any important liminal gate may be expected to have a noteworthy porter (gate-keeper): see, for example, Spenser, *The Faerie Queene*, 3.6.31 ('Old Genius', porter at the gate of the Garden of Adonis).

8.1 *northern bar*] This may draw on a passage of the *Odyssey*, book 13, describing the two entries to the cave of Phorcys, one for the gods, the other (the northern entry) for human beings. The passage was famous for the symbolic reading of the Neoplatonist Porphyry, *De antro nympharum*, where the myth is interpreted as referring to the descent of the soul into the body. Blake could have known of this from Pope's discussion in his translation of the *Odyssey* (note to 13.124). Blake refers to the myth again in *Milton* (26.13–17) in a context of 'souls descending to the body' through 'two gates' – an analogy which gives some support to the Neoplatonic reading of *Thel* itself. (On the problems of this reading, see headnote.)

8.1 *bar*] barrier (*OED sb*[1] II, esp. 12 and 13a).

8.3 *the dead*] Often used by Blake to mean 'the spiritually dead': see, for example, *America*, 17.23, *The Book of Urizen*, 20.26.

8.6 *list'ning*] This transitive use (contrast line 8) was not archaic in the late eighteenth century (*OED v* 1a).

8.11–18] The voice from Thel's grave is trapped within pain at and mistrust of sense-experiences which give intimations of difficult – though perhaps also fulfilling – emotions. Cf. the somewhat similar (cancelled) lines on the senses as dangerous and deceitful in *Tiriel*, 365–8 (Bentley, *Writings*, 919; cf. note on Thel's motto which uses line 370). There is a similar, but more comprehending, lament written from the point of view of the fallen senses in *Milton* (f.19–37).

Why a tongue impressed with honey from every wind?
Why an ear a whirlpool fierce to draw creations in?
Why a nostril wide inhaling terror, trembling and affright?
Why a tender curb upon the youthful burning boy?
20   Why a little curtain of flesh on the bed of our desire?'

The virgin started from her seat, and with a shriek
Fled back unhindered till she came into the vales of Har.

The End

8.19–20 *Why . . . desire*] These two lines ask questions which abruptly invert the implications of what precedes them – and so may be taken as implying what is there (barely) suppressed. They were erased after printing and colouring in copies I and J.

8.20 *curtain of flesh*] The hymen.

Plate 8 design. Below the text three naked children ride on the back of a bridled serpent which has a protruding forked tongue and looped tail. The same design appears reversed in *America* (plate 13).

THE MARRIAGE OF HEAVEN AND HELL

The Marriage of Heaven and Hell is a manifesto – a comprehensive early statement of the attitudes and ideas that, with whatever developments and changes, were to occupy Blake for the next decade, and in some measure for the rest of his life. Almost certainly, however, Blake came at the work from a tangent, beginning it as a satire on the Swedish religious writer and mystic Emanuel Swedenborg (1688–1772).

In 1788 a New Jerusalem Church, with Swedenborg as its prophet, was established in Eastcheap, London. Blake and his wife attended its first General Conference in April 1789, and signed its Minute Book, though as sympathizers, not as members of the Church. What Blake admired in Swedenborg has been variously identified as both ethical and literary: that love was the key to releasing what Blake called 'the poetic genius' in all people, that sexual love was spiritual and need not necessarily be confined to marriage as conventionally understood; or Swedenborg's way of interpreting biblical materials so as to reveal meanings apparently contrary to official Christian teaching, and his way of presenting doctrines dramatically in terms of conversations with spirits. However, it appears from Blake's annotations of his extant copies of Swedenborg that after an initial enthusiasm he quickly began to see a more conservative side to this spiritual mentor, and – from what can be reconstructed of its debates – even more so to the London organization which claimed to base itself on Swedenborg's doctrines, which in 1789 expelled prominent members for radical sexual and political views.[1] Copies of three of Swedenborg's books with Blake's marginalia are extant (Bentley, *Writings*, 1349, 1388–1403). The annotations of *Divine Providence* (*c.* 1790) are hostile, at times denunciatory. Blake later took a view of Swedenborg which was only slightly more positive. In *Milton* he is the 'strongest of men, the Samson shorn by the churches' (*Milton*, 20.50), but shorn to the deeply conventional, 'Showing the transgressors in Hell, the proud warriors in Heaven, / Heaven as a punisher, and Hell as one under punishment' – that is, he has what are for Blake some of the usual delusions about Heaven and Hell. And while the catalogue of Blake's one exhibition (1809) contains an entry praising Swedenborg's works as 'well worthy the attention of poets and painters' and as 'foundations for grand things', the main point of the picture the entry accompanies is not to praise Swedenborg but to illustrate from his works a Blakean theme: learning is inferior to inspiration.[2] Swedenborg is important to Blake because his

---

[1] The main materials bearing on Blake's relation with Swedenborg are collected in Harvey Bellin and Darrell Ruhl (eds.), *Blake and Swedenborg: Opposition is True Friendship* (New York, 1985). See also E. P. Thompson, *Witness Against the Beast* (1993), chapter 8. The dates of Swedenborg's works given in the annotations are those of their first English translations.

[2] 'The Spiritual Preceptor', *A Descriptive Catalogue*; Bentley, *Writings*, 855–6. See also the ambivalent comments recorded from Blake's conversation in 1825 by Henry Crabb Robinson (Bentley, *Blake Records* (1969), 312–13), and the antagonistic comment recorded on Blake's 7th Dante design (*c.* 1824, Bentley, *Writings*, 1341).

failure is illustrative: it shows the usual degeneration of religious vision, the patter traced as archetypal in *The Marriage of Heaven and Hell* itself (plate 11).

Satire on Swedenborg stems from a view of Christianity in which Prophecy – OI and New Testament: Isaiah and Ezekiel as well as Jesus – is opposed to Law. On th view Christianity lies not in the observation of Mosaic Law but in the proper cultiva tion of human energies – cultivation for which the Prophets are models, energie which Mosaic Law actually inhibits. Properly understood, all religion is poetry – the perception of spiritual existence in metaphoric terms. The usual degeneration c religion lies in taking such metaphors as literal truth and appointing guardians a priesthood – to cultivate the error. Understanding this requires a new view o God: God too is a metaphor for extremes of human experience. The ancient poets inventors of Greek religion, testify to this in one way, Old Testament prophets ii another. The supreme exemplar of this view is Jesus, whose life is constructed t exhibit an almost systematic opposition to Mosaic Law (plates 23–24).

The Proverbs of Hell are the philosophical core of *Marriage*. They show hov the energies underlying a true religious consciousness are to be cultivated, praise uninhibited vigour of thought and action in all spheres, especially the sexual, and affirm individual uniqueness and the consequently relative nature of moral laws Their targets are orthodox Christianity, scientific rationalism, and philosophies which teach restraint or scepticism, philosophies which take a negative view of the passiona or imaginative. While some of the proverbs are straightforward in expression, their method is typically riddling, in accordance with Blake's principle that 'what is not too explicit [is] the fittest for instruction, because it rouses the faculties to act' (Letter of 23.8.1799; Bentley, *Writings*, 1526). The active involvement of the reader to discover meaning is part of Hell's educational method. The individual proverbs are open-ended, and this undercuts the usual proverb's bland and unBlakean assump- tion of generalizing authority. Similarly, while a few proverbs are grouped themat- ically, or by their rhetorical shape, the arrangement is largely irregular. There are consistent trains of imagery with evaluative implications: fountains, lions and eagles are noble; cisterns, foxes and crows are base. Beyond this, perimeters of appropriate possible meaning, insofar as they are Blake's, are described by the work as a whole. Parallels, contrasts and contexts are to be found by the individual reader, and so can be constructed variously. Accordingly, for S. Foster Damon 'Drive your cart and your plough over the bones of the dead' enjoins 'utilizing the graveyard as the most fertile soil'; it shows 'Blake's appreciation of the value of the past' (*William Blake: His Philosophy and Symbols* (1924), 319). For Harold Bloom it urges us 'to renew human life by a refreshment of sexuality, even at the cost of defying the codes of the past' (*Blake's Apocalypse* (1975), 85). Both readings seem to me surprising – Damon's fundamentally, Bloom's tangentially. Damon assumes that the only place worth ploughing in is a graveyard, Bloom that the only thing worth doing with a graveyard is to plough it. The first depends on arguments about Blake's possible relations to various traditions: it is the construction of a reader who knew Blake's work well and often showed himself a fine interpreter. The second seems to me more consonant with *Marriage* as a whole – though I regard the specific application to sexuality as Bloom's not Blake's. I take the proverb to be iconoclastic: new life can ɔe made to spring from the past only by a creative use of it which is not inhibited ɔy orthodox feelings of respect or reverence.[3]

Despite the doctrine *Marriage* enunciates that an interaction of contraries is ɹecessary to sustain the forward dynamic of existence, the work finally endorses ɩts devils. Through the voice of the devil Blake often speaks straight. He is of the Devil's party, and he knows it. Some critics are (as Blake has Isaiah say) 'not capable ɔf a firm persuasion'.[4] Certainly Blake is at times teasing – as when, in a vision coolly presented as though its status were unproblematic, visionaries asked about the status of their visions give most equivocal answers (plates 12–13); but the masks adopted, whether of playfulness or of blandly confident prophetic authority, are transparent disguises: they do not signify the final absence of implied authorial perspectives. The mighty devil who writes on the rock face with corroding fires is Blake etching the copper plates of an illuminated book (plates 6–7) – an identification with the devils that is variously repeated. In his account of the giants who formed the world, Blake endorses the proverbial wisdom of Hell (plate 16: 'the weak in courage is strong in cunning'). The harpist whose theme illustrates another hellish proverb points by his song one moral of Blake's conflict with the angel who reads Aristotle (plate 19). Proponents of irony and obliquity who will not accept that the 'I' of this episode is Blake can hardly deny that the precisely similar 'I' of the next, equally fantastic 'Memorable Fancy' (plates 21–24) is Blake, since he announces a forthcoming 'Bible of Hell' which all agree means some other of Blake's illuminated books. Moreover, the devils propound views known from other works to be Blake's (see, for example, note to 23.11 and 'The Everlasting Gospel'). And beyond any particular endorsements, the whole rhetorical and imaginative impact of the work is on the side of the devils. The proposed 'marriage' is not a match of equals. The angel who becomes the archetypal prophet Elijah and then a devil shows what is expected: conversion. Heaven joins Hell in marriage as constituted by the angelic party, an eighteenth-century union of dominant and dominated, but with the expected roles reversed.

The mode and structure of *Marriage* have been much discussed. Northrop Frye's suggestion about its form – 'Menippean satire'[5] – has been often repeated, though perhaps largely because it offers so uncategorical a category, mixing genres, tones and styles – poetry and prose, the comic and the serious, overt fiction and quasi-historical writing (letters, orations, philosophical discussions). Max Plowman early pointed out that, between the opening poem and the closing song, the intervening prose is divided into six sections by the placing of the major designs. Beyond these mild suggestions about mode and form it seems better to accept Michael Ferber's

---

[3] Cf. David Simpson on how other proverbs can be read in different ways: *Irony and Authority in Romantic Poetry* (London, 1979), 84–5.

[4] For a moderate version of this view see, for example, Harold Bloom, *Blake's Apocalypse* (1963), 69–98; and for a more extreme version Andrew M. Cooper, *Doubt and Identity in Romantic Poetry* (New Haven, CT, 1988), 41–53.

[5] *Anatomy of Criticism* (Princeton, NJ, 1957), 311–12, 365.

verdict that *Marriage* is 'about as heterogenous as one could imagine', and 'a struc-tureless structure'. More specific suggestions seem imposed rather than elicited.[6]

By examining various material features of the text, such as plate size and hand-writing, Joseph Viscomi has constructed a convincing chronology of its develop-ment.[7] In Viscomi's account, Blake began from plates 21–24 (possibly intending these as a separate anti-Swedenborgian pamphlet), then added plates 12–13 (the prophets' dinner party), 1–3 (basic positions *contra* Swedenborg), 5–6a (readings of *Paradise Lost* and Job), 11 (a genealogy of religions), 6b–10 (largely Proverbs of Hell), 14–15 (improving sensual enjoyment, engraving prophetic books), 16–20 (angel/devil dialogues), and finally plates 25–27 ('A Song of Liberty'). Where in this sequence plate 4 (the voice of the devil) was engraved cannot be determined – not earlier than two-thirds into the composition (perhaps after plate 15), possibly last. The traditional view has been that the work was composed over an extended period, *c.* 1790–93. Viscomi argues that the evidence for this is weak, and that the whole work was composed in 1790.[8] All copies have the same plates in the same order, except copy B which has an added frontispiece (see title-page design note) and copy G (*c.* 1818) in which the plates are in the order 1–11, 15, 14, 12, 13, 16–27.

Blake did not include *Marriage* in lists of works offered for sale in 1818 and 1827 (Bentley, *Writings*, 1648–9, 1668), but both these lists are responses to specific enquiries: they are not evidence for the view sometimes expressed that Blake repudi-ated the work in later life. As with many other early works most extant copies were printed by 1795, but two are late – copy G (*c.* 1818), and copy I, printed in the year of Blake's death.[9]

---

[6] Plowman, *The Poems and Prophecies of William Blake* (London, 1927), xxiii. Ferber, *The Poetry of William Blake* (1991), 89, 90. A full range of other suggestions is briefly surveyed in Morris Eaves, Robert N. Essick and Joseph Viscomi, *William Blake: The Early Illuminated Books* (1993), 117–18.

[7] 'The Evolution of *The Marriage of Heaven and Hell*', *Huntington Library Quarterly*, 58 (1997). Viscomi has also written on the Swedenborgian aspects of *Marriage* in Thomas Pfau and Robert F. Gleckner (eds.), *Lessons of Romanticism: A Critical Companion* (Durham, NC, 1998); and on its print-making imagery in Steve Clark and David Worrall (eds.), *Blake in the Nineties* (Basingstoke, 1999).

[8] 'Evolution', *passim* (esp. 285). Cf. Eaves, Essick and Viscomi, *The Early Illuminated Books* (1993), 113–16.

[9] Viscomi, *Blake and the Idea of the Book* (1993), 261. Viscomi discusses the letter sale lists and Blake's late printing sessions (chapters 33 and 35).

[Title-page]

The Marriage of Heaven and Hell

[Plate 2]

The Argument

Rintrah roars and shakes his fires in the burdened air;
Hungry clouds swag on the deep.

Once meek, and in a perilous path,
The just man kept his course along
5   The vale of death.
Roses are planted where thorns grow,
And on the barren heath
Sing the honey bees.

Then the perilous path was planted:
10   And a river and a spring
On every cliff and tomb;
And on the bleachèd bones
Red clay brought forth.

Title-page. Design. A cross-section of the earth. Above, on the earth's surface, framed by over-arching bare trees, are (left) a man and woman walking, engaged in conversation, and (right) a naked man kneeling before a figure lying on the ground. Below the earth's surface a man lying on a bank of clouds (right) embraces a woman lying in flames (left). Above them numerous small flying figures (mostly in couples) ascend towards the earth's surface in postures expressing exuberant joy. The clouds and flames suggest that the embrace represents the 'marriage' of the title. (In copy B only the title-page is followed by a frontispiece, the usually separate plate 'Our End is Come', dated '5 June 1793'. It is reproduced in Bentley, *Writings*, 163.)

2.1 *Rintrah*] A spirit of prophetic wrath. His nature here is defined by his action ('roars'), attributes ('fires'), and contexts ('burdened air' [i.e. full of signs]; the displacement of the just man). He reappears in more developed forms (consistent with his nature here) in Blake's later work, particularly *Milton*. The signs with which the air is burdened are apocalyptic: 'A Song of Liberty' suggests that their main manifestation is the French Revolution.

2.2 *swag*] Sink down, hang heavily.

2.5 *vale of death*] Cf. Psalm 23: 'though I walk through the valley of the shadow of death . . .'. In Bunyan's *Pilgrim's Progress* Christian journeys through a valley named from this psalm.

2.10–11 *river . . . cliff*] Cf. Exodus, 17.1–7 where Moses produces water from a rock for the Israelites to drink in the wilderness.

2.12 *the bleachèd bones*] See Ezekiel's vision of the valley filled with dry bones which are resurrected and covered in flesh (Ezekiel, 37.1–14).

2.13 *Red clay*] 'Adam' means in Hebrew 'red', and 'Adamah' 'red clay'. In his late (c. 1827) illuminated Genesis manuscript, in quoting the biblical text Blake consistently wrote 'Adamah' over, or in parentheses after, 'the ground'.

Till the villain left the paths of ease
15   To walk in perilous paths, and drive
The just man into barren climes.

Now the sneaking serpent walks
In mild humility,
And the just man rages in the wilds
20   Where lions roam.

Rintrah roars and shakes his fires in the burdened air;
Hungry clouds swag on the deep.

[Plate 3]

As a new Heaven is begun, and it is now thirty-three years since its advent, the eternal Hell revives. And lo! Swedenborg is the angel sitting at the tomb; his writings are the linen clothes folded up. Now is the

---

2.17 *serpent*] A standard type of hypocrisy following the biblical serpent's deception of Eve (Genesis, 3.1–6).

2.19 *the just . . . wilds*] Like such biblical prophets as Elijah or his New Testament counterpart, John the Baptist. Blake used as an epigraph to his tractate *All Religions Are One* (*c.* 1788) an adaptation of Isaiah 40.3, 'the voice of one crying in the wilderness', a phrase traditionally understood to prefigure the mission of John the Baptist. Cf. 3.1 (on Blake's self-identification as the new Messiah).

Plate 2 design. To the right of the text a woman standing under a tree reaches up to take a bunch of grapes from a young man clambering athletically in the tree dressed in a swirling robe. (Cf. 'The Echoing Green', *Songs of Innocence*, plate 2 design.) To the left, beneath the text, lie three naked figures in postures epitomizing inactive contrast with the athletic tree-climber.

3.1–2 *new Heaven . . . eternal Hell*] Blake announces a contrast between transitory ideas of the Good (Heaven) and a permanent reality which challenges such superficial notions (Hell).

3.1 *thirty-three years*] In copy F Blake has written above the first clause of this sentence '1790'. 1757 was both the year of Blake's birth and the year assigned by Swedenborg to a 'Last Judgement' (*A Treatise Concerning the Last Judgement*, 1788, sect. 45); thirty-three was the age traditionally assigned to Christ at his crucifixion and resurrection. Blake mocks Swedenborg and wrily assumes the identity of a new Messiah.

3.2 *advent*] Coming; the word is used specifically of the part of the church year, leading up to Christmas, which celebrates the birth of Jesus.

3.2–3 *angel . . . linen clothes*] Blake takes details from the resurrection of Christ as described in the gospels of Mark, Luke and John: see Mark, 16.5 (the single seated angel), Luke 24.12, and John 20.5–7 (the linen grave-clothes laid aside). Swedenborg is superseded: his writings are merely transitional.

ominion of Edom, and the return of Adam into Paradise; see Isaiah XXXIV
nd XXXV Chap.

Without contraries is no progression. Attraction and repulsion, reason
.nd energy, love and hate, are necessary to human existence.

From these contraries spring what the religious call Good and Evil. Good
s the passive that obeys reason. Evil is the active springing from energy.
Good is Heaven. Evil is Hell.

[Plate 4]

The Voice of the Devil

All Bibles or sacred codes have been the causes of the following errors:
1. That man has two real existing principles, viz, a body and a soul.

3.4 *Edom*] The country of Esau (Genesis, 32.3), who is tricked of his birthright (as elder)
by his brother Jacob (Genesis, 27). Their father, Isaac, grants Esau one blessing: 'it shall come
to pass when thou shalt have dominion that thou shalt break his yoke from off thy neck'
(Genesis, 27.40; this prophecy is fulfilled – though in a minor way only – at 2 Kings, 8.20).
Esau is a biblical example of the displaced 'just man' of the Argument (plate 2). Throughout
the Old Testament the Edomites are enemies of Israel, that is, of the orthodox party, those
who accept the Mosaic Law (see, for example, the denunciation of them in Ezekiel, 35; and
the vision of the destruction of Edom in Obadiah, 1–16). In terms of the contemporary polit-
ical perspectives invoked by 'A Song of Liberty' Edom is revolutionary France.

3.4 *return . . . Paradise*] Like 'the dominion of Edom', such a return (not prophesied in the Bible)
would reverse the course of actual Old Testament history and prophecy, restoring the situa-
tion which appertained before the Fall.

3.4–5 *Isaiah . . . Chap.*] Isaiah 34 prophesies the apocalyptic destruction of Idumea (Edom).
Isaiah 35 is one of the most famous Old Testament prophecies of a world redeemed from
suffering, a world the inhabitants of which 'shall obtain joy and gladness, and sorrow and
sighing shall flee away'.

3.8 *contraries*] Cf. the joint title-page of *Songs* (1794), 'showing the two contrary states of the
human soul'. Blake returns to the doctrine of contraries in *Milton* and *Jerusalem*, where he
adds the idea of a 'negation': 'Contraries are positives: a negation is not a contrary' (*Milton*,
plate 30); cf. *Jerusalem*, 10.7–16 and 17.29–47.

3.10 *Good . . . Evil*] Cf. Blake's marginalium to Lavater, *Aphorisms on Man*, 409: (Lavater) 'He
alone is good who, though possessed of energy, prefers virtue with the appearance of weak-
ness to the invitation of acting brilliantly ill.' (Blake) 'Noble! But mark: active evil is better
than passive good' (Bentley, *Writings*, 1369).

Plate 3 design. Above the text a naked female figure, with long hair streaming backwards be-
hind her and with arms and legs extended, bathes exultantly in flames (cf. *The Book of Urizen*,
plate 3 design). Below the text (left) a naked woman gives birth to a baby, the upper body of
which emerges with arms spread wide to greet the world; (right) a figure running towards the
right, with arms and legs outstretched, kisses a figure lying with arms also spread wide: cf. the
Notebook poem, 'Eternity', above, p. 154.

4.2 *two . . . soul*] Joseph Priestley, of whom Blake certainly knew and with whom he was
probably acquainted, likewise attacked the idea that the material and the spiritual can be
distinguished, in his *Disquisitions Relating to Matter and Spirit*, published by Joseph Johnson
(1777; 2nd edn., 1782). See Morton Paley, *Energy and the Imagination* (1970), 8–10.

2. That energy, called evil, is alone from the body; and that reason, called good, is alone from the soul.

5   3. That God will torment man in eternity for following his energies.

But the following contraries to these are true:

1. Man has no body distinct from his soul, for that called body is a portion of soul discerned by the five senses, the chief inlets of soul in this age.

2. Energy is the only life and is from the body; and reason is the bound
10 or outward circumference of energy.

3. Energy is eternal delight.

[Plate 5]

Those who restrain desire do so because theirs is weak enough to be restrained; and the restrainer or reason usurps its place and governs the unwilling.

And being restrained it by degrees becomes passive, till it is only the
5 shadow of desire.

The history of this is written in *Paradise Lost*, and the governor, or reason, is called Messiah.

And the original Archangel, or possessor of the command of the heavenly host, is called the Devil or Satan, and his children are called Sin and Death.
10   But in the Book of Job Milton's Messiah is called Satan.

For this history has been adopted by both parties.

It indeed appeared to Reason as if Desire was cast out, but the Devil's account is, that the Messiah fell and formed a heaven of what he stole from the abyss.

4.8 *in this age*] In this stage of the soul's immortal existence.

Plate 4 design. Underneath the text a naked (male?) figure (left), standing on the sea with the sun behind him, clasps a child with arms and legs outstretched as if leaping away from another naked male figure (right) backed by flames; this figure projects himself leftwards with outspread arms, but is restrained by a manacle round one ankle. Blake produced a version of this design in watercolour (*c.* 1790–93), and another version (reversed) in his series of Colour Prints of 1795 entitled 'The Good and Evil Angels' (Butlin, *Paintings and Drawings*, 257 and 323–4).

5.9 *his children . . . Death*] Sin is Satan's daughter, born from his head; Death is their child (*Paradise Lost*, 2.727–814).

5.10 *Book . . . Satan*] One of Messiah's roles in *Paradise Lost* is to act as God's 'vicegerent' in various capacities, including that of arraigning Adam and Eve for their sin (Book 10) – a role, Blake claims, comparable to that of Satan in the Book of Job, in which (as his name signifies) Satan is 'the Adversary' of Job (see Job, chapters 1 and 2; the Authorized Version marginal gloss to 1.7 explains Satan's name).

Plate 5 design. Above the text a naked man and a horse, with a sword, and what are perhaps intended to be a cloak and part of a chariot wheel, tumble head-downwards into flames – presumably a warrior from the losing side of the war in heaven falling into the abyss. Cf. 'A Song of Liberty', v. 15.

6.1 *the Messi- / ah fell*] As elsewhere in prose sections the new plate begins in the middle of a word.

THE MARRIAGE OF HEAVEN AND HELL

This is shewn in the Gospel, where he prays to the Father to send the Comforter, or Desire, that Reason may have ideas to build on, the Jehovah of the Bible being no other than he who dwells in flaming fire.

Know that after Christ's death he became Jehovah.

But in Milton the Father is Destiny, the Son a ratio of the five senses, and the Holy Ghost vacuum!

Note. The reason Milton wrote in fetters when he wrote of angels and God, and at liberty when of devils and Hell, is because he was a true poet and of the Devil's party without knowing it.

A Memorable Fancy

As I was walking among the fires of Hell, delighted with the enjoyments of genius, which to angels look like torment and insanity, I collected some of their proverbs, thinking that, as the sayings used in a nation mark its character, so the proverbs of Hell shew the nature of infernal wisdom better than any description of buildings or garments.

6.2–3 *the Comforter*] Identified by Christ with 'the Holy Ghost' and 'the Spirit of Truth', and promised by Christ to the disciples as the Father's gift after his death (John, 14.16 and 26, 15.26, 16.7). Blake's identification of the Comforter as Desire is in keeping with the surrounding unorthodox interpretations of Milton and the Bible.

6.4 *he who dwells*] It is clear from a gap in the text after 'he' that the plate has been emended at this point. Erdman reads the deleted text as 'the Devil who dwells' (*Complete Poetry and Prose*, 801).

6.5 *Know . . . Jehovah*] The later plates of *Marriage* set Jesus in opposition to the Law propounded by Jehovah (plate 23). Here Christ is to be identified with Jehovah revalued – as the (morally positive) Devil, or Desire.

6.6 *ratio*] Blake apparently uses the word loosely to mean 'knowledge as an (inevitably meagre) product'; the Son in Milton, Blake claims, is (unlike Milton's Devil) a construct of merely empirical knowledge with no vital imaginative existence.

6.8 *Note*] This epigrammatic expression of an 'against the grain' reading of *Paradise Lost*, postulating an unconscious Milton who subverts his own conscious intention, is comparable to that formulated at greater length by Shelley in his *Defence of Poetry* (c. 1820; *Shelley's Poetry and Prose*, ed. Donald H. Reiman and Sharon B. Powers (New York, 1977), 498–9).

6.11 *A Memorable Fancy*] The 'Memorable Fancies' of *Marriage* parody the 'Memorable Relations' of various Swedenborgian texts – brief narratives exemplifying ideas which are also described discursively.

6.13–15 *I collected . . . character*] Eaves, Essick and Viscomi (*William Blake: The Early Illuminated Books* (1993), 211) offer a parallel from the popular biblical commentator, Matthew Henry (*An Exposition of All the Books of the Old and New Testament*, 1725):

Much of the wisdom of the ancients has been handed down to posterity by proverbs, and some think we may judge the temper and character of a nation by the complexion of its vulgar proverbs . . . Yet there are many corrupt proverbs which tend to debauch men's minds and harden them in sin. The Devil has his proverbs, and the World and the Flesh have their proverbs, which reflect reproach on God and Religion, as Ezekiel 12.22 and 18.2.

An 8th edn. of *An Exposition* was published in 1772, and selections from Henry's notes were included in several eighteenth-century annotated Bibles.

When I came home, on the abyss of the five senses, where a flat-sided steep frowns over the present world, I saw a mighty devil folded in black clouds, hovering on the sides of the rock. With corroding fires he wrote the following sentence now perceived by the minds of men, and read by them on earth:

How do you know but ev'ry bird that cuts the airy way,
5   Is an immense world of delight, closed by your senses five?

Proverbs of Hell

In seed time learn, in harvest teach, in winter enjoy.
Drive your cart and your plough over the bones of the dead.
The road of excess leads to the palace of wisdom.
Prudence is a rich ugly old maid courted by Incapacity.

6.18–7.1 *mighty Devil . . . fires*] Since Blake used the 'corroding fires' of acid to bite his etched texts and designs on to copper plates it is possible to understand the 'mighty Devil' as Blake himself. Cf. 14.9–11.

Plate 6 design. This plate has only small interlinear designs, as do many others in *Marriage* (plates 7–9, 12–13, 17–19, 22–23, 25–27 – fourteen in all, just over half the total number).

7.1] The plate begins in the middle of the word 'cor/roding'.

7.4–5 *How . . . five?*] An echo of lines from Chatterton's *Bristowe Tragedie* (1768): 'How dydd I knowe that ev'ry darte / That cutte the airie waie / Myghte nott fynde passage toe my harte / And close myne eyes for aie?'. Blake admired Chatterton, whose pseudo-medieval 'Rowley' poems he considered authentic (Bentley, *Writings*, 1512).

7.6 *Proverbs of Hell*] The main point of reference is the largely conventional and prudential wisdom of the biblical Proverbs (one of which is loosely quoted on plate 23). Though Blake often contradicts the wisdom of the biblical Proverbs he uses the book's sometimes riddling manner and structure of non-logical juxtapositions. He also occasionally uses its forms, particularly the modes identified by the analyses of Bishop Robert Lowth in his *Lectures on the Sacred Poetry of the Hebrews*. This translation of Lowth's 1759 volumes (originally written in Latin) was published by Joseph Johnson in 1787. Lowth identified three forms of parallelism – synonymous, synthetic and antithetical. Synonymous: a second clause re-states a first in varied form; synthetic: a second clause presents an analogy to or elaboration of the first; antithetical: a second clause presents a contrary idea to the first – a form evidently suited to the ideal of progression by means of contraries announced on plate 3. For an account of Lowth and his importance, see Murray Roston, *Poet and Prophet: The Bible and the Growth of Romanticism* (London, 1965), and Stephen Prickett, *Words and The Word: Language, Poetics and Biblical Interpretation* (Cambridge, 1986, chapter 3). Collections of quasi-proverbial maxims were a popular form in the eighteenth century. Caspar Lavater's *Aphorisms on Man* (1788), which were translated by Blake's friend Fuseli, and which Blake himself annotated, are an example of the genre. The proverbs are numbered consecutively without reference to the division by plates.

2 *Drive . . . dead*] Cf. 'The Voice of the Ancient Bard', *Songs of Innocence*, line 9.

4 *Prudence . . . Incapacity*] Contrast the central ethos of the biblical Proverbs: 'I wisdom dwell with prudence' (8.12); 'The wise in heart shall be called prudent' (16.21).

He who desires but acts not breeds pestilence.
The cut worm forgives the plough.
Dip him in the river who loves water.
A fool sees not the same tree that a wise man sees.
He whose face gives no light shall never become a star.
Eternity is in love with the productions of Time.
The busy bee has no time for sorrow.
The hours of folly are measured by the clock, but of wisdom no clock
    can measure.
All wholesome food is caught without a net or a trap.
Bring out number, weight and measure in a year of dearth.
No bird soars too high if he soars with his own wings.
A dead body revenges not injuries.
The most sublime act is to set another before you.
If the fool would persist in his folly he would become wise.
Folly is the cloak of knavery.
Shame is pride's cloak.

[Plate 8]

Prisons are built with stones of Law, brothels with bricks of Religion.
The pride of the peacock is the glory of God.
The lust of the goat is the bounty of God.
The wrath of the lion is the wisdom of God.
The nakedness of woman is the work of God.
Excess of sorrow laughs. Excess of joy weeps.
The roaring of lions, the howling of wolves, the raging of the stormy sea,
    and the destructive sword, are portions of eternity too great for the eye
    of man.
The fox condemns the trap, not himself.
Joys impregnate. Sorrows bring forth.
Let man wear the fell of the lion, woman the fleece of the sheep.
The bird a nest, the spider a web, man friendship.

---

6 *The cut . . . plough*] A deleted stanza from 'The Fly' (Notebook, p. 101) reads: 'The cut worm / Forgives the plough / And dies in peace, / And so do thou'.

22–4 *pride . . . lust . . . wrath*] Pride, lechery and wrath are three of the traditional Christian 'seven deadly sins'; the peacock, goat and lion are their conventional symbols.

31 *The bird . . . friendship*] This form of tripartite juxtaposition occurs among the biblical proverbs: cf. for example 'A whip for the horse, a bridle for the ass, and a rod for the fool's back' (Proverbs, 26.3).

The selfish smiling fool and the sullen frowning fool shall be both
    thought wise, that they may be a rod.
What is now proved was once only imagined.
The rat, the mouse, the fox, the rabbit watch the roots; the lion, the
    tiger, the horse, the elephant, watch the fruits.
35 The cistern contains: the fountain overflows.
One thought fills immensity.
Always be ready to speak your mind, and a base man will avoid you.
Everything possible to be believed is an image of truth.
The eagle never lost so much time as when he submitted to learn of
    the crow.

[Plate 9]

40 The fox provides for himself, but God provides for the lion.
Think in the morning, act in the noon, eat in the evening, sleep in
    the night.
He who has suffered you to impose on him knows you.
As the plough follows words, so God rewards prayers.
The tigers of wrath are wiser than the horses of instruction.
45 Expect poison from the standing water.
You never know what is enough unless you know what is more than
    enough.
Listen to the fool's reproach! It is a kingly title!
The eyes of fire, the nostrils of air, the mouth of water, the beard of
    earth.
The weak in courage is strong in cunning.
The apple tree never asks the beech how he shall grow, nor the lion the
50   horse how he shall take his prey.

---

44 *tigers ... horses*] The symbolism of bold, independent creatures (lion, eagle, etc.) and cunning or conformist ones (fox, crow, etc.) is largely consistent throughout the proverbs. In 34, however, the horse is paired with the tiger (and cf. 'A Song of Liberty', v. 20), while in 50 the horse is contrasted with the lion, though in neutral terms (they properly have different natures: the lion does not seek advice from the horse, not because the horse is lesser but because it is other). Here the horse is lesser: its proper inherent wildness submits to being trained; the intractable tiger fulfils the inherent nature of its being.

45 *Expect ... water*] Cf. the theme of the harper, 19.6–7.

48 *fire ... air ... water ... earth*] The classical four elements of which all things are composed. Cf. the fourfold systematization of the whole human form of 61. In the present proverb the point lies not in the particular correspondences but in the way of seeing in terms of correspondences.

49 *The weak ... cunning*] Repeated on plate 16.

The thankful receiver bears a plentiful harvest.
If others had not been foolish we should be so.
The soul of sweet delight can never be defiled.
When thou seest an eagle thou seest a portion of genius: lift up thy
    head!
As the caterpillar chooses the fairest leaves to lay her eggs on, so the
    priest lays his curse on the fairest joys.
To create a little flower is the labour of ages.
Damn braces: bless relaxes.
The best wine is the oldest, the best water the newest.
Prayers plough not! Praises reap not!
Joys laugh not! Sorrows weep not!

[Plate 10]

The head Sublime, the heart Pathos, the genitals Beauty, the hands and
    feet Proportion.
As the air to a bird or the sea to a fish, so is contempt to the
    contemptible.
The crow wished everything was black, the owl that everything was
    white.
Exuberance is Beauty.
If the lion was advised by the fox he would be cunning.
Improvement makes straight roads, but the crooked roads without
    improvement are roads of genius.
Sooner murder an infant in its cradle than nurse unacted desires.
Where man is not nature is barren.
Truth can never be told so as to be understood and not be believed.
                        Enough! or too much.

---

51 *The thankful receiver*] Perhaps intended as a comment on the biblical stress on giving, as in Acts 20.35: 'Remember the words of the Lord Jesus, how he said, It is more blessed to give than to receive.'

53 *The soul . . . defiled*] Repeated in *America*, 10.14, and adapted in *Visions*, 4.9–10.

61 *Sublime . . . Pathos*] Principal terms of eigtheenth-century aesthetics, which (the proverb claims) are properly derived from the human form.

Plate 10 design. Below the text a naked, bat-winged devil kneels with a scroll unfurled across his legs, and behind him a small table. On either side a gowned human student sits writing, apparently transcribing from the devil's scroll. The devil turns towards the student on the left, who writes intently, while the student on the right peers across, apparently so as to catch advice being given. Both are presumably making their own collection of hellish wisdom (plate 6).

[Plate 11]

The ancient poets animated all sensible objects with gods or geniuses, calling them by the names and adorning them with the properties of woods, rivers, mountains, lakes, cities, nations, and whatever their enlarged and numerous senses could perceive.

5   And particularly they studied the genius of each city and country, placing it under its mental deity.

Till a system was formed, which some took advantage of and enslaved the vulgar by attempting to realize or abstract the mental deities from their objects: thus began priesthood.

10   Choosing forms of worship from poetic tales.

And at length they pronounced that the gods had ordered such things.

Thus men forgot that all deities reside in the human breast.

[Plate 12]

A Memorable Fancy

The prophets Isaiah and Ezekiel dined with me, and I asked them how they dared so roundly to assert that God spake to them; and whether they did not think at the time that they would be misunderstood, and so be the cause of imposition.

Plate 11. Eighteenth-century analogies can be adduced to this history of the origin of religion in myths and metaphors which project on to the exterior world faculties of the mind itself. Robert Essick cites passages in William Stukeley's *Stonehenge* (1740), Swedenborg's *True Christian Religion* (1781), and Richard Payne Knight's *Account of the Worship of Priapus* (1786) (*William Blake and the Language of Adam* (1989), 122). There is also an analogue in Swedenborg's *The Delights of Wisdom Concerning Conjugial Love* (1794, sect. 78; quoted in Eaves, Essick and Viscomi, *William Blake: The Early Illuminated Books* (1993), 213). Blake is unlikely to have known this passage when he completed *Marriage*, but the analogy may indicate that the line of thought was somewhat familiar in 'advanced' thinking about religion in the period. All of these analogues, however, deal with pagan religions – religions which, from a Christian viewpoint, can comfortably be seen as human projections. (Even in *The True Christian Religion* Swedenborg is specifically discussing 'the idolatries of the gentiles of old' [sect. 205].) Blake is unique in pitching the argument at a more general level – and later specifically applying it to Christianity (plates 12–13, 22–23).

11.12 *all deities . . . breast*] Cf. Blake's marginalium to Lavater's aphorism 554: 'Human nature is the image of God.' Cf. also his marginalia to aphorisms 549 (see note to 22.18–23.2 below) and 630 (Bentley, *Writings*, 1384–5).

Plate 11 design. Above the text the humanoid genii of various natural forms reveal themselves. To the right the infant spirit of a flower reaches up with outstretched arms towards the adolescent female form of some nearby vegetation. To their left is a tree stump with bearded face and the upper body of a dryad with long yellow hair who leaps, arms-raised, out of the ground. Below the text swim two water-genii, one a bearded head with arms spread sideways who has, in miniature, a looming aspect suggestive of Blake's mythic tyrant Urizen (see *Visions*, 8.3 note). The design above the text is included in *A Small Book of Designs* (1794 and 1796 copies). In the 1796 copy it is inscribed 'Death and Hell teem with life' (Butlin, *Paintings and Drawings*, 261.2).

Isaiah answered, 'I saw no God, nor heard any in a finite organical perception; but my senses discovered the infinite in everything, and as I was then persuaded, and remain confirmed, that the voice of honest indignation is the voice of God, I cared not for consequences but wrote.'

Then I asked, 'Does a firm persuasion that a thing is so, make it so?'

He replied, 'All poets believe that it does, and in ages of imagination this firm persuasion removed mountains; but many are not capable of a firm persuasion of anything.'

Then Ezekiel said, 'The philosophy of the east taught the first principles of human perception: some nations held one principle for the origin and some another. We of Israel taught that the Poetic Genius (as you now call it) was the first principle and all the others merely derivative, which was the cause of our despising the priests and philosophers of other countries, and prophesying that all gods would at last be proved to originate in ours, and to be the tributaries of the Poetic Genius. It was this that our great poet King David desired so fervently and invokes so pathetically, saying by this he conquers enemies and governs kingdoms. And we so loved our God that we cursed in his name all the deities of surrounding nations, and asserted that they had rebelled. From these opinions the vulgar came to think that all nations would at last be subject to the Jews.'

'This,' said he, 'like all firm persuasions, is come to pass, for all nations believe the Jews' code and worship the Jews' God, and what greater subjection can be?'

12.5 *I saw no God*] Isaiah endorses the argument of plate 11 that the idea of 'god' is a way of identifying human imaginative constructions.

12.11 *firm . . . mountains*] This proverbial idea draws on the words of Jesus after he has cursed a fig tree which immediately withers away: 'If ye have faith, and doubt not . . . if ye shall say unto this mountain, Be thou removed, and be thou cast into the sea; it shall be done' (Matthew, 21.21). Cf. Saint Paul, 1 Corinthians, 13.2: 'though I have all faith, so that I could remove mountains, and have not charity, I am nothing.'

12.15–16 *Poetic . . . principle*] Like Isaiah, Ezekiel endorses the argument of plate 11. That the human imagination is in some sense divine is a fundamental principle of Blake's work. The theme is central to the early tractate *All Religions Are One* (*c.* 1788), as it is to *Jerusalem* (1804–20), at the climax of which Los, the poetic imagination, is identified with Jesus. Cf. the marginalium to Swedenborg's *Divine Love* (*c.* 1788): 'the Poetic Genius . . . is the Lord'.

13.1 *all gods / would at last*] Plate 13 begins at this point.

13.2–3 *great . . . David*] King David was traditionally understood to be the author of the Psalms. The psalms often take the Lord's power as conqueror and governor as their subject, though the formulation here does not echo any specific psalm.

13.3 *pathetically*] passionately, vehemently.

13.5 *cursed*] Old Testament prophets frequently curse Israel's neighbours in God's name. Isaiah has a whole series of oracles against surrounding nations (chapters 13 to 23), as does Ezekiel (chapters 25 to 32).

I heard this with some wonder, and must confess my own conviction. After dinner I asked Isaiah to favour the world with his lost works. He said none of equal value was lost. Ezekiel said the same of his.

I also asked Isaiah what made him go naked and barefoot three years. He
15 answered, 'The same that made our friend Diogenes the Grecian.'

I then asked Ezekiel why he ate dung, and lay so long on his right and left side. He answered, 'The desire of raising other men into a perception of the infinite. This the North American tribes practise, and is he honest who resists his genius or conscience only for the sake of present ease or
20 gratification?'

[Plate 14]

The ancient tradition that the world will be consumed in fire at the end of six thousand years is true, as I have heard from Hell.

For the cherub with his flaming sword is hereby commanded to leave his guard at [the] Tree of Life, and when he does, the whole creation will be
5 consumed, and appear infinite and holy, whereas it now appears finite and corrupt.

13.14 *naked . . . years*] Isaiah, 20.2–6. One of many symbolic actions by which Isaiah, like other Old Testament prophets, enforces his warnings.

13.15 *Diogenes the Grecian*] Like the Old Testament prophets, the Cynic philosopher Diogenes (died *c.* 320 BC), one of the most famous dissidents of ancient culture, also engaged in symbolic actions, notably searching for an honest man through Athens in broad daylight with a lighted lantern. Isaiah is said to act under a direct command from God. In identifying his inspiration with that of Diogenes, Isaiah again affirms that 'the voice of God' and 'the voice of honest indignation' are one and the same.

13.16–17 *ate . . . side*] Ezekiel, chapter 4. As with Isaiah, Ezekiel's bizarre actions are symbolic warnings. Ezekiel does not in fact eat dung: he cooks with it (though he is described as eating dung by Swedenborg, *The True Christian Religion*, sect. 296, perhaps by a misunderstanding of Ezekiel 4.12). Ezekiel's divinely inspired action, as he recognizes (4.14), involves a violation of Mosaic Law (Deuteronomy, 14.21): cf. plate 23: 'no virtue can exist without breaking these ten commandments'.

13.18 *North . . . practise*] Like Isaiah in comparing his activities with those of Diogenes, Ezekiel implies that 'all religions . . . have one source, . . . the Poetic Genius' (*All Religions Are One*, plate 10). In his marginalia to Watson, Blake compares 'the accounts of North American savages (as they are called)' with the Iceland Edda and the *Iliad*: his argument is fragmentary, but he apparently means to assert, against exclusivist Christian claims, a knowledge of the divine in all three (Bentley, *Writings*, 1413). What accounts of North American tribes Blake read is not known.

14.1 *consumed in fire*] That the end of the world will be by fire is predicted in 2 Peter, 3.4–7.

14.2 *six thousand years*] The standard chronology, worked out by Bishop James Ussher in the 1650s, was often printed in eighteenth-century Bibles. It dates the Creation at 4004 BC. Since many New Testament texts, including words of Christ (Matthew, 24.29–35), predict the apocalypse as imminent, Ussher's chronology made the traditional supposition of the earth's 6,000-year duration appear more probable.

14.3–4 *cherub . . . Life*] This angelic guard is placed at Genesis, 3.24 (see design note).

This will come to pass by an improvement of sensual enjoyment.

But first the notion that man has a body distinct from his soul is to be expunged. This I shall do by printing in the infernal method, by corrosives, which in Hell are salutary and medicinal, melting apparent surfaces away, and displaying the infinite which was hid.

If the doors of perception were cleansed everything would appear to man as it is: infinite.

For man has closed himself up, till he sees all things through narrow chinks of his cavern.

[Plate 15]

A Memorable Fancy

I was in a printing house in Hell and saw the method in which knowledge is transmitted from generation to generation.

In the first chamber was a dragon-man, clearing away the rubbish from a cave's mouth. Within a number of dragons were hollowing the cave.

In the second chamber was a viper folding round the rock and the cave, and others adorning it with gold, silver and precious stones.

In the third chamber was an eagle with wings and feathers of air. He caused the inside of the cave to be infinite. Around were numbers of eagle-like men, who built palaces in the immense cliffs.

In the fourth chamber were lions of flaming fire raging around and melting the metals into living fluids.

In the fifth chamber were unnamed forms which cast the metals into the expanse.

14.9 *printing . . . corrosives*] Etching on metal and biting out the design using acids. Cf. 6.18–7.1 note.

Plate 14 design. Above the text lies a sleeping or dead naked man, seen in side view, head to the left, arms at his sides. Above him in flames, head to the viewer, hovers a long-haired woman with her arms outstretched horizontally. The design is included in *A Small Book of Designs* (1794 and 1796 copies). In the 1796 copy it is inscribed 'a flaming sword revolving every way' (Butlin, *Paintings and Drawings*, 261.3), from Genesis, 3.24: God 'placed at the east of the garden of Eden Cherubims, and a flaming sword which turned every way, to keep the way of the tree of life'.

15.1 *printing . . . Hell*] This printing house is primarily a workshop in which illuminated books such as *The Marriage of Heaven and Hell* itself are produced. It can also be taken loosely to suggest the human body with its five senses, inlets of knowledge which are cleansed by creative action such as Blake undertakes in writing, drawing and printing. Swedenborg discusses writing in heaven in *A Treatise Concerning Heaven and Hell* (1784), sects. 258–64.

15.12 *unnamed forms*] Possibly radical publishers who did not put their names to their publications for fear of prosecution. *Marriage* is one of only three of Blake's illuminated books in which his own name does not appear on the title-page as either author or printer. (The others are the early and experimental *All Religions Are One* and the late broadsheet *On Homer's Poetry* [and] *On Virgil*.)

There they were received by men who occupied the sixth chamber, and
15 took the forms of books and were arranged in libraries.

[Plate 16]

The giants who formed this world into its sensual existence and now seem
to live in it in chains are in truth the causes of its life and the sources of all
activity; but the chains are the cunning of weak and tame minds which
have power to resist energy. According to the proverb, 'The weak in cour-
5 age is strong in cunning.'

Thus one portion of being is the Prolific, the other the Devouring: to the
devourer it seems as if the producer was in his chains, but it is not so. He
only takes portions of existence and fancies that the whole.

But the Prolific would cease to be prolific unless the Devourer as a sea
10 received the excess of his delights.

Some will say, 'Is not God alone the Prolific?' I answer, 'God only acts
and is in existing beings or men.'

These two classes of men are always upon earth, and they should be en-
emies. Whoever tries to reconcile them seeks to destroy existence.

Religion is an endeavour to reconcile the two.

15.15 *took . . . libraries*] Often taken to be a sardonic comment on the mudane fate of inspired
work, though see Viscomi, 'The Lessons of Swedenborg' (footnote 7), in Pfau and Gleckner
(eds.), *Lessons of Romanticism* (1998), 173–212.

Plate 15 design. Below the text an eagle, with its head raised and wings spread as though
rising from the ground, grasps in its talons a coiling snake with open mouth and protruding
tongue. This may be understood as an emblem of dynamic conflict: see for example *Iliad*,
12.200ff., imitated in *Aeneid*, 11.751ff. Désirée Hirst explains it in more esoteric terms as an
alchemical symbol for 'the union of sulphur and mercury, matter and spirit' (*Hidden Riches*
(1964), 135).

16.1 *giants*] These antediluvians (17.7) – 'giants in the earth in those days' – appear in Gen-
esis, chapter 6.

16.2 *live . . . chains*] Echoing the famous opening sentence of Rousseau's *Social Contract* (1762):
'Man was born free, and everywhere he is in chains.'

16.4 *the proverb*] That is, the proverb of Hell; above, plate 9 (49).

16.6 *Prolific . . . Devouring*] Cf. the doctrine of contraries, plate 3.

Plate 16 design. Above the text a bearded old man, flanked on either side by two young men,
sits with his knees drawn up in front of him; all are gowned. The four young men sit with
their heads buried in huddled postures. These are apparently 'the giants who . . . seem to
live . . . in chains'. Blake used a similar design in *For Children: The Gates of Paradise* (1793),
plate 14, over the legend 'Does thy God, O priest, take such vengeance as this?' The
figures are specifically Ugolino and his sons and grandsons in prison – a subject drawing on
Dante, *Inferno* canto 32, and representing cruelty justified under a cloak of religion – a theme
consistent with the anti-clericalism of *Marriage*. (The design was printed in *A Small Book of
Designs*, 1794 copy, but without inscription.)

17.1 *Whoever tries / to reconcile*] Plate 17 begins at this point.

Note. Jesus Christ did not wish to unite but to separate them, as in the parable of sheep and goats. And he says, 'I came not to send peace but a sword.'

Messiah or Satan or Tempter was formerly thought to be one of the antediluvians who are our energies.

A Memorable Fancy

An Angel came to me and said, 'O pitiable, foolish young man! O horrible! O dreadful state! Consider the hot burning dungeon thou art preparing for thyself to all eternity, to which thou art going in such career.'

I said, 'Perhaps you will be willing to show me my eternal lot, and we will contemplate together upon it and see whether your lot or mine is most desirable.'

So he took me through a stable and through a church and down into the church vault, at the end of which was a mill: through the mill we went, and came to a cave. Down the winding cavern we groped our tedious way, till a void boundless as a nether sky appeared beneath us, and we held by the roots of trees and hung over this immensity. But I said, 'If you please, we will commit ourselves to this void, and see whether providence is here also. If you will not, I will.' But he answered, 'Do not presume, O young man, but as we here remain, behold thy lot, which will soon appear when the darkness passes away.'

17.4 *parable . . . goats*] Christ describes the division of the saved and the damned at the Last Judgement: 'Before him shall be gathered all nations: and he shall separate them one from another, as a shepherd divideth his sheep from the goats: And he shall set the sheep on his right hand, but the goats on the left' (Matthew, 25.32–3).

17.4–5 *I came . . . sword*] 'Think not that I come to send peace on earth: I came not to send peace, but a sword' (Jesus, in Matthew, 10.34).

17.6 *Messiah . . . Tempter*] For this view of the Messiah cf. the discussion of Job (plate 5) and note there. Satan is always the tempter, but he plays this role particularly in Matthew, 4.1–11 (where he is so called: v. 3), and Luke, 4.1–13. For the antdiluvians cf. 16.1 note.

17.9–11 *O pitiable . . . such career*] Several parts of this 'Memorable Fancy' parody Swedenborg's manner in his 'Memorable Relations'. Cf. *Conjugial Love*, sect. 477. A youth 'boasting of his scortations' (fornications) asks, 'What is more dismal than for a man to imprison his love, and to confine himself to one woman? And what is more delightful than to set the love at liberty?' Swedenborg has divine direction set him right: 'a certain angel looking down from heaven . . . said to him, come up hither, and I will show you to the life what heaven is, and what hell, and what the quality of this latter is to confirmed scortators.' The angel proceeds to open the young man's mental eyes to various visions of Hell.

17.16–17 *mill . . . cave*] Cf. Swedenborg's *The Apocalypse Revealed* (1791, sects. 791, 794) where the narrator descends through a mill to a house, and thence to a passage through a cavern. If Joseph Viscomi is right that *Marriage* was completed in 1790 (see headnote) Blake may nevertheless have known this closely analogous passage from the readings from Swedenborg which had a regular place in meetings of the New Church. Mills in Blake are commonly associated with abstract ratiocination, mechanical repetition, and slavery.

So I remained with him sitting in the twisted root of an oak. He was suspended in a fungus which hung with the head downward into the deep.

By degrees we beheld the infinite abyss, fiery as the smoke of a burning
5 city. Beneath us at an immense distance was the sun, black but shining. Round it were fiery tracks on which revolved vast spiders crawling after their prey, which flew or rather swum in the infinite deep, in the most terrific shapes of animals sprung from corruption; and the air was full of them, and seemed composed of them. These are Devils, and are called Powers of
10 the Air. I now asked my companion which was my eternal lot. He said, 'Between the black and white spiders.'

But now from between the black and white spiders a cloud and fire burst and rolled through the deep, black'ning all beneath, so that the nether deep grew black as a sea and rolled with a terrible noise. Beneath us was nothing
15 now to be seen but a black tempest, till, looking east between the clouds and the waves, we saw a cataract of blood mixed with fire, and not many stones' throw from us appeared and sunk again the scaly fold of a monstrous serpent. At last to the east, distant about three degrees, appeared a fiery crest above the waves. Slowly it reared like a ridge of golden rocks till
20 we discovered two globes of crimson fire from which the sea fled away in clouds of smoke; and now we saw it was the head of Leviathan. His forehead was divided into streaks of green and purple like those on a tiger's forehead. Soon we saw his mouth and red gills hang just above the raging foam tinging the black deep with beams of blood, advancing toward us with all the fury of a spiritual existence.

My friend the Angel climbed up from his station into the mill. I remained alone, and then this appearance was no more, but I found myself sitting
5 on a pleasant bank beside a river by moonlight hearing a harper who sung to the harp. And his theme was, 'The man who never alters his opinion is like standing water, and breeds reptiles of the mind.'

18.1 *the twisted / root of*] Plate 18 begins at this point.

18.18 *east . . . degrees*] Paris is about three degrees of longitude from London. What appears to the angel as a monster is the French Revolution.

18.21 *Leviathan*] A biblical sea-monster, identified as a serpent in Psalm 74 (vv. 13–14) and by Isaiah (27.1). In Job Leviathan provides awesome evidence of God's power (chapter 40). Though nothing in the description specifically recalls this, Blake may have intended this vision of Leviathan to suggest the various hellish apocalyptic beasts of Revelation, creatures bred in the angelic mind of St John of Patmos.

18.22 *tiger*] For the tiger as a symbol of untameable energy cf. the symbolism of the Proverbs of Hell and the Song of Experience (pp. 92–4). The tiger is specifically associated with revolutionary violence in *Europe* (18.7).

19.1 *advancing toward / us with*] Plate 19 begins at this point.

But I arose, and sought for the mill, and there I found my angel, who, surprised, asked me how I escaped.

I answered, 'All that we saw was owing to your metaphysics: for when you ran away, I found myself on a bank by moonlight hearing a harper. But now we have seen my eternal lot, shall I show you yours?' He laughed at my proposal, but I by force suddenly caught him in my arms, and flew westerly through the night, till we were elevated above the earth's shadow: then I flung myself with him directly into the body of the sun. Here I clothed myself in white, and taking in my hand Swedenborg's volumes sunk from the glorious clime, and passed all the planets till we came to Saturn. Here I stayed to rest, and then leaped into the void between Saturn and the fixed stars.

'Here' said I, 'is your lot, in this space, if space it may be called.' Soon we saw the stable and the church, and I took him to the altar and opened the Bible, and lo! it was a deep pit, into which I descended driving the Angel before me. Soon we saw seven houses of brick: one we entered. In it were a number of monkeys, baboons, and all of that species chained by the middle, grinning and snatching at one another, but withheld by the shortness of their chains. However, I saw that they sometimes grew numerous, and then the weak were caught by the strong and, with a grinning aspect, first coupled with and then devoured, by plucking off first one limb and then another till the body was left a helpless trunk. This, after grinning and kissing it with seeming fondness, they devoured too; and here and there I saw one savourily picking the flesh off of his own tail. As the stench terribly annoyed us both, we went into the mill, and I in my hand brought the skeleton of a body, which in the mill was Aristotle's *Analytics*.

19.14–19 *earth's shadow . . . Saturn . . . fixed stars*] The fixed stars are those which, unlike the planets, appear always to occupy the same position in the heavens: reference to them suggests the planetary spheres of pre-Copernican (Ptolemaic) astronomy. Accordingly Blake treats Saturn as the most remote planet, though Uranus was discovered in 1781 (see *Urizen*, 15.9–10 note).

19.15–16 *clothed . . . white*] The colour in which the elect are clothed in Revelation (7.9).

19.16 *taking . . . Swedenborg's volumes*] That is, to use them as ballast because of their weight.

19.23 *seven . . . brick*] Perhaps parodying the seven churches of Asia to which St John of Patmos addressed Revelation (1.4).

20.1 *were a / number of*] Plate 20 begins at this point.

20.1 *monkeys, baboons*] Blake presumably intends here a parody of the Christianity of the churches, implying that it is loving in profession, cruel and exploitative in practice.

20.10–11 *Aristotle's* Analytics] That is, Aristotle's two treatises on logic. Swedenborg took a positive view of Aristotle.

So the Angel said, 'Thy fantasy has imposed upon me, and thou oughtest to be ashamed.'

I answered, 'We impose on one another, and it is but lost time to con-
15 verse with you whose works are only Analytics.'

Opposition is true Friendship

[Plate 21]

I have always found that angels have the vanity to speak of themselves as the only wise. This they do with a confident insolence sprouting from systematic reasoning.

Thus Swedenborg boasts that what he writes is new; though it is only the
5 contents or index of already published books.

A man carried a monkey about for a show, and because he was a little wiser than the monkey, grew vain, and conceived himself as much wiser than seven men. It is so with Swedenborg: he shows the folly of churches and exposes hypocrites, till he imagines that all are religious, and himself the single one on earth that ever broke a net.

Now hear a plain fact: Swedenborg has not written one new truth. Now hear another: he has written all the old falsehoods.

And now hear the reason: he conversed with angels, who are all religious,
5 and conversed not with devils, who all hate religion, for he was incapable through his conceited notions.

Thus Swedenborg's writings are a recapitulation of all superficial opinions, and an analysis of the more sublime, but no further.

20.16 *Opposition . . . Friendship*] In context this can most immediately be taken as Blake's comment on his own satire on Swedenborg. (The sentence is fully visible only in copy B; usually it is at least partly obscured by the coloration.)

Plate 20 design. Below the text swims Leviathan, his body composed of three huge coils emerging from a rough sea; his head is raised above the water with mouth open, teeth visible and forked tongue protruding. The design is included in *A Small Book of Designs* (1794 and 1796 copies). In the 1796 copy it is inscribed 'O revolving serpent, O the ocean of Time and Space' (Butlin, *Paintings and Drawings*, 260.6 and *BIQ*, 26 (1992)).

Plate 21 design. Above the text a naked man with splayed legs sits looking upwards above what a skull lying beneath his left knee suggests is a grave. In copies E and F behind him is a pyramid, in copy D with a second to the left behind it. The design is re-worked in *America*, plate 8, and as the upper portion of the design 'Death's Door' for Blair's *The Grave* (1808). Blake also returned to the design for an experimental relief plate *c.*1805–22 (Robert Essick, *The Separate Plates of William Blake* (Oxford, 1983), XIV).

22.1 *the single / one*] Plate 22 begins at this point.

Have now another plain fact: any man of mechanical talents may, from the writings of Paracelsus or Jacob Behmen, produce ten thousand volumes of equal value with Swedenborg's, and from those of Dante or Shakespeare an infinite number.

But when he has done this, let him not say that he knows better than his master, for he only holds a candle in sunshine.

A Memorable Fancy

Once I saw a devil in a flame of fire who arose before an angel that sat on a cloud. And the devil uttered these words.

'The worship of God is: honouring his gifts in other men, each according to his genius, and loving the greatest men best. Those who envy or calumniate great men hate God, for there is no other God.'

The angel hearing this became almost blue, but mastering himself he grew yellow, and at last white-pink and smiling, and then replied:

22.10 *Paracelsus*] Philippus Aureolus Theophrastus Bombastus von Hohenheim (1493–1541), Swiss-German physician and alchemical philosopher. He rejected traditional education as offered in various European universities, and the authority of ancient writers on which such education was based, and drew on popular knowledge for his medical and scientific work.

22.10 *Jacob Behmen*] The usual eighteenth-century English spelling of the name of Jakob Boehme or Böhme, shoe-maker and philosophical mystic (1575–1624), who was himself influenced by Paracelsus and was, like him, a dissident. His unconventional combination of Renaissance nature mysticism and biblical theology was attacked and at times silenced by more orthodox theologians among his contemporaries. His works were published in English translation by William Law, 1764–81. In a poem in a letter to the sculptor John Flaxman (12.9.1800) Blake associated Paracelsus and Boehme as important influences on his thinking, apparently contemporaneously with the beginning of the American War of Independence, that is when Blake was in his early twenties (Bentley, *Writings*, 1537).

22.18–23.7 *The worship . . . nothings*] Again (cf. 17.9–11) parts of the 'Memorable Fancy' parallel a dialogue in *Conjugial Love* (sect. 82). Swedenborg is challenged on the doctrine of the Trinity: 'How can you demonstrate the first, that there is one God, in whom is a divine trinity, and that he is the Lord Jesus Christ?' He replies: 'I demonstrate it thus: Is not God one and individual? Is not there a trinity? If God be one and individual, is not he one person? If he be one person, is not the trinity in that person? That this God is the Lord Jesus Christ is evident from these considerations.' See 17.16–17 note on the New Church and readings from Swedenborg; but the resemblance here may simply indicate how accomplished was Blake's skill in writing Swedenborgian pastiche.

22.18–23.2 *The worship . . . no other God*] Cf. Blake's adaptation of Lavater's aphorism 549: 'He who loves the wisest and best of men loves the Father of men; for where is *the Father of men to be seen but in the most perfect of his children?*' Lavater had written 'He who hates . . . hates the Father.' Blake altered 'hates' to 'loves', underlined the clause printed here in italic, and added the marginal comment, 'This is true worship' (Bentley, *Writings*, 1378). Blake re-worked this paragraph of *Marriage* (with some re-statement and with significant changes) in *Jerusalem*, 91.7–12.

23.1 *loving the / greatest*] Plate 23 begins at this point.

143

5   'Thou idolater, is not God One? And is not he visible in Jesus Christ? And has not Jesus Christ given his sanction to the law of ten commandments; and are not all other men fools, sinners, and nothings?'

The devil answered, 'Bray a fool in a mortar with wheat, yet shall not his folly be beaten out of him: if Jesus Christ is the greatest man, you ought to
10   love him in the greatest degree. Now hear how he has given his sanction to the law of ten commandments. Did he not mock at the sabbath, and so mock the sabbath's God? Murder those who were murdered because of him? Turn away the law from the woman taken in adultery? Steal the labour of others to support him? Bear false witness when he omitted making a
15   defence before Pilate? Covet when he prayed for his disciples, and when he bid them shake off the dust of their feet against such as refused to lodge them? I tell you, no virtue can exist without breaking these ten commandments: Jesus was all virtue, and acted from impulse, not from rules.'

When he had so spoken I beheld the angel who stretched out his arms embracing the flame of fire, and he was consumed and arose as Elijah.

23.6–7 *given . . . commandments*] 'Think not that I am come to destroy the law, or the prophets: I am not come to destroy but to fulfil. For verily I say unto you, Till heaven and earth pass, one jot or one tittle shall in no wise pass from the law, till all be fulfilled' (Matthew, 5.17–18). Adherence to the Ten Commandments was enjoined among the resolutions recorded in the *Minutes* of the 1789 Conference of the Swedenborgian New Church which Blake signed (see headnote).

23.8–9 *Bray . . . out of him*] The devil quotes scripture for his own purposes – Proverbs, 27.22: 'Though thou shouldest bray [crush] a fool in a mortar among wheat with a pestle, yet will not his foolishness depart from him.'

23.11 *Mock at the sabbath*] On several occasions Jesus contravened Jewish sabbath regulations. See for example Mark, 2.18–28, where the Pharisees object to Jesus that on the sabbath his disciples do not fast: 'he said unto them, The sabbath was made for man, and not man for the sabbath. Therefore the Son of man is Lord also of the sabbath.' Cf. Luke, 6.1–11 – the same incident, followed by a controversy about healing on the sabbath. Here and in what follows the ways of interpreting Christ's actions as rejections of the Mosaic Law (Exodus, 20.1–17) are more or less tendentious. The orthodox view is that, insofar as Christ may appear to contravene any specific law, he does so to fulfil the underlying aims of the Law as a whole. Cf. 'The Everlasting Gospel', part d, 17–18, 43, and 47–8 (Bentley, *Writings*, 1057–8).

23.13 *Turn away . . . adultery*] John, 8.2–11. This passage was omitted from several early manuscripts of John's gospel, probably on the grounds that its apparent contradiction of Mosaic Law was controversial in the ancient world.

23.14–15 *Bear . . . Pilate*] Matthew, 27.14; Mark, 15.2–5.

23.16–17 *shake off . . . lodge them*] 'Whosoever shall not receive you, nor hear your words, when ye depart out of that house or city, shake off the dust of your feet' (Matthew, 10.14).

24.1 *from im / -pulse*] Plate 24 begins at this point.

24.3 *arose as Elijah*] Elijah is the Old Testament archetype of the prophet. As such he is a precursor of John the Baptist (Malachi, 4.5; Matthew, 11.7–15, and several subsequent New Testament texts), and appears with Moses (as complementary archetype, giver of the Law) at Christ's Transfiguration (Matthew, 17.3; Mark, 9.4; Luke, 9.30). Elijah did not die, but 'there appeared a chariot of fire, and horses of fire' in which he 'went up by a whirlwind into heaven' (2 Kings, 2.11).

Note. This Angel, who is now become a Devil, is my particular friend: we often read the Bible together in its infernal or diabolical sense, which the world shall have if they behave well.

I have also the Bible of Hell, which the world shall have whether they will or no.

One law for the lion and ox is oppression.

[Plate 25]

A Song of Liberty

1. The Eternal Female groaned! It was heard over all the earth.
2. Albion's coast is sick, silent; the American meadows faint!
3. Shadows of prophecy shiver along by the lakes and the rivers, and mutter across the ocean! France, rend down thy dungeon!

24.5 *infernal . . . sense*] Swedenborg and Swedenborgians claimed to present the Bible's internal sense'.

24.7 *the Bible of Hell*] Blake may have seen *The [First] Book of Urizen* (1794), *The Book of Ahania* (1795) and *The Book of Los* (1795) as this promised (or threatened) text. All were printed (like Bibles) in double columns and with numbered verses, and the first offers a counter-myth to the Creation story of Genesis (the First Book of Moses): see *The Book of Urizen*, headnote. 'The Bible of Hell' may also include 'A Song of Liberty', likewise divided into biblically numbered verses; and, if Joseph Viscomi is correct in supposing that plates 21–24 of *Marriage* were composed first (see headnote), the phrase may also refer to the Proverbs of Hell and other parts of *Marriage* itself. A lost drawing included a draft title-page inscribed 'The Bible of Hell, in nocturnal visions collected. Vol. 1. Lambeth' (Bentley, *Writings*, 1323, 1677, 1735).

24.9 *One law . . . oppression*] Cf. *Tiriel* (1789?), line 360, and *Visions*, 7.22.

Plate 24 design. Below the main text, above 'One law . . . is oppression', a naked crowned man with a huge beard stares out at the viewer with an expression of alarm or horror as he crawls from right to left on hands and knees. Behind him are what appear to be massive tree trunks. A version (reversed) included in the series of Colour Prints of 1795 identifies the figure as Nebuchadnezzar in his madness (Daniel, 4.28–33). However, nothing in *Marriage* enforces the Colour Print's identification. In 1790 an unidentified mad king might suggest George III, whose bout of insanity lasting from autumn 1788 to spring 1789 was public knowledge. (The design and the following line are not present in the early copy K.)

Plate 25 Title] 'A Song of Liberty' makes explicit the contemporary political significance of *Marriage*, which is largely left implicit in the main body of the work. It also relates *Marriage* to the mythic mode – and some of the specific mythic materials – of *America*. No extant copy of *Marriage* was issued without the 'Song'. There are two extant copies of the 'Song' alone (*Marriage* copies L and M): these were probably proofs not intended to be issued separately.

25.v.1 *Eternal Female*] Apparently a personification of forces of destiny, who is presumably groaning as she gives birth to Revolution (v. 7). She can be related to other women associated in Blake's early myth with Orc (see v. 7 note), the 'shadowy daughter of Urthona' in the Preludium to *America*, and Enitharmon as mother of Orc (*Urizen*, chapters 6–7). The epithet 'eternal' connects her with the revival of Hell announced in plate 3.

25.v.2 *Albion*] An ancient name for England.

25.v.3 *thy dungeon*] The Bastille, the state political prison in Paris, the sack of which on 14 July 1789 is usually seen as the initiating action of the French Revolution.

4. Golden Spain, burst the barriers of old Rome!

5. Cast thy keys, O Rome, into the deep down falling, even to eternity dow: falling,

6. And weep!

7. In her trembling hands she took the new-born terror howling.

8. On those infinite mountains of light now barred out by the Atlantic se the new-born fire stood before the starry king!

9. Flagged with grey-browed snows and thunderous visages, the jealous wing waved over the deep.

10. The speary hand burned aloft, unbuckled was the shield, forth wen the hand of jealousy among the flaming hair, and hurled the new-borr wonder through the starry night.

11. The fire, the fire, is falling!

12. Look up! look up! O citizen of London. Enlarge thy countenance. O Jew leave counting gold! Return to thy oil and wine. O African! black African Go, wingèd thought, widen his forehead.

13. The fiery limbs, the flaming hair, shot like the sinking sun into the western sea.

25.v.4 *Golden Spain*] 'Golden' because financed by plunder from the Americas.

25.v.4 *old Rome*] That is, the Catholic Church, allied, in Blake's view, to reactionary and oppressive political forces.

25.v.5 *thy keys*] Symbolic of the power of the Catholic Church, signifying the power supposedly given by Christ to St Peter over the eternal destiny of each individual soul (Matthew, 16.19).

25.v.6 *And weep*] Verse 6 originally continued 'and bow thy reverend locks' (copy L), but the words were removed from the copper plate. Blake perhaps meant to imitate what is famously the shortest verse in the New Testament: 'Jesus wept' (John, 11.35).

25.v.7 *the ... terror*] The figure in later works named Orc; cf. *America*, 3.1 note.

25.v.8 *infinite mountains ... Atlantic sea*] The mountains of the mythical utopian kingdom of Atlantis; see *America*, 12.6–8 note.

25.v.8 *the starry king*] The figure in later works named Urizen. For his snows and 'jealous wings' cf. *America*, 18.2–6.

25.v.9 *Flagged*] Perhaps based on the Spenserian 'flaggy' (applied to wings), meaning 'dropping, pendulous'.

25.v.10 *speary*] A Miltonic invented adjective; *OED* lists no comparable usage. Cf. v. 18, 'beamy'.

26.v.10 *flaming hair, and / hurled the*] Plate 26 begins at this point.

26.v.12 *oil and wine*] Characteristic agricultural products of Jewish civilization: the revolution will be appropriately served by occupations which are ennobling because essential to life (such as that of the farmer), not by those which are degrading because parasitic (such as that of the profiteering financial intermediary). Jews were thought of as especially associated with financiering because of a ban in traditional and Catholic Christianity (long-since lapsed by the late eighteenth century) on taking interest on money loaned.

4. Waked from his eternal sleep, the hoary element roaring fled away.

5. Down rushed beating his wings in vain the jealous king: his grey browed ounsellors, thunderous warriors, curled veterans, among helms, and shields, nd chariots, horses, elephants, banners, castles, slings and rocks,

6. Falling, rushing, ruining! buried in the ruins, on Urthona's dens.

17. All night beneath the ruins, then, their sullen flames faded, emerge round he gloomy king,

18. With thunder and fire: leading his starry hosts through the waste wilderness he promulgates his ten commands, glancing his beamy eyelids over the deep in dark dismay,

19. Where the son of fire in his eastern cloud, while the morning plumes her golden breast,

20. Spurning the clouds written with curses, stamps the stony law to dust, loosing the eternal horses from the dens of night, crying: 'Empire is no more! And now the Lion and Wolf shall cease.'

Chorus

Let the priests of the raven of dawn no longer, in deadly black, with hoarse note curse the sons of joy. Nor his accepted brethren whom, tyrant, he calls free, lay the bound or build the roof. Nor pale religious lechery call that virginity that wishes but acts not!

For every thing that lives is holy.

26.v.14 *hoary element*] That is, the sea, which Blake commonly associates with Urizen; cf. *Urizen*, plate 12; its departure is necessary as a prelude to the reappearance of the submerged Atlantis (v. 8 and note). In the apocalypse described in Revelation the sea disappears as 'a new heaven and a new earth' appear (21.1).

26.v.15–16 *Down rushed . . . ruining*] Cf. plate 5 design.

26.v.16 *ruining*] Falling headlong, going down with a crash (*OED*, ruin, *v* 5).

26.v.16 *Urthona's dens*] The earth; on Urthona see *America*, 3.1 note.

26.v.18 *leading . . . wilderness . . . ten commands*] The Urizen figure partly represents contemporary European kings, but he is also (as usual) associated with the Jehovah of the Old Testament – here leading the Israelites through the wilderness and formulating the Mosaic Law, as in Exodus, 13.20ff. and 20.1–17; cf. *America*, 10.3–4 and notes.

27.v.18 *wilderness / he promulgates*] Plate 27 begins at this point.

27.v.20 *stamps . . . to dust*] Cf. *America*, 10.5.   *Empire . . . cease*] Cf. *America*, 8.15.

27. Heading *Chorus*] This section is missing from the early copy M (now lost), and so was presumably added after the first engraving of the plate.

27.4 *bound*] brickwork in courses (*OED*, bond, *sb*[1] 13a; *OED* gives 'bound' as an alternative archaic spelling).

27.6 *every thing . . . holy*] This contradiction of the song of Moses of Revelation 15.3–4 – 'thou [God] only art holy' – is developed from Blake's annotation of Lavater's aphorism 309: 'hell is the being shut up in the possession of corporeal desires which shortly weary the man for *all life is holy*' (Bentley, *Writings*, 1364). The line is repeated in *Visions* (11.10), *America* (10.13), and *The Four Zoas* (34.79).

LYRICS FROM THE NOTEBOOK
(*c.* 1791–93)

Blake's Notebook, in which he made drawings and wrote poetry, prose and personal memoranda from the late 1780s until about 1820, had belonged to his brother Robert, of whom Blake was particularly fond. Robert died, after an illness during which Blake nursed him, in 1787. Blake later reported that Robert, after his death, taught him his technique of illuminated printing in a vision. Robert is depicted overwhelmed by a moment of visionary experience in one of the most dramatic designs of *Milton*, a design paralleled by another depicting Blake himself in a similar posture, which indicates what continuing spiritual communion Blake felt with his brother. Blake described this in a letter of 1800 to his patron William Hayley (Blake was writing to express his sympathy with Hayley whose son Thomas had just died):

> Thirteen years ago I lost a brother and with his spirit I converse daily and hourly in the spirit, and see him in my remembrance in the regions of my imagination. I hear his advice and even now write from his dictate.
>
> (Bentley, *Writings*, 1533–4)

Blake may have the regarded the book inherited from Robert as quasi-talismanic.

The Notebook contains, alongside drafts and fair copies of almost all the *Songs of Experience*, many lyrics written over the same period but not engraved which are on similar themes: many are concerned with religion and sexual repression, hypocrisy in sexual relationships, and the free love ethic most fully enunciated in *Visions of the Daughters of Albion*; a few deal with political subjects common to the *Songs* and Continental Prophecies (including *America*). In mode the poems range from quasi-private thoughts in verse and explicit moral epigrams to symbolic poems, the symbolism of which is open to varied interpretation. As in the *Songs*, the presence of rhyme, assonance, alliteration and other forms of verbal music means that these poems are often highly lyrical in effect. Many are akin to *Poetical Sketches* in their experiments with metrical form. A change of metre in mid-poem is a common feature which rarely occurs in the engraved work: this perhaps suggests that Blake himself regarded such formal freedom as aesthetically defective, though readers often find it legitimate and expressive.

The Notebook (often referred to as the 'Rossetti Manuscript' because from 1847 to 1882 it belonged to the painter and poet Dante Gabriel Rossetti, an early enthusiast for Blake's work) reveals more than any other document about Blake's working methods, at least with lyric poetry. Though he later described himself as writing a long poem (probably *Jerusalem*) 'from immediate dictation . . . without premeditation and even against my will', and as the secretary of spiritual beings (Bentley, *Writings*, 1572, 1575), the Notebook indicates methods of composition in lyric more consistent with the struggles of his later mythic figure of poetic creativity – Los, the

148

blacksmith. Since some of these poems were abandoned rather than finished, variants are given in the notes where they are especially interesting.

The order in which the poems are printed here largely follows that of Erdman, *Complete Poetry and Prose*. This aims as far as possible to be chronological – though Blake's use of the Notebook is too chaotic for any chronology to be more than tentative. There is a facsimile and transcript of the Notebook edited by David Erdman with the assistance of Donald K. Moore (Oxford, Clarendon Press, 1973; rev. edn., Redex Books, 1977).

*

> Never pain to tell thy love,
> Love that never told can be,
> For the gentle wind does move
> Silently, invisibly.
>
> 5   I told my love, I told my love,
> I told her all my heart.
> Trembling cold, in ghastly fears,
> Ah, she doth depart.
>
> Soon as she was gone from me
> 10   A traveller came by,
> Silently, invisibly:
> O, was no deny.

*

> I feared the fury of my wind
> Would blight all blossoms fair and true,
> And my sun it shined and shined,
> And my wind it never blew.
>
> 5   But a blossom fair or true
> Was not found on any tree,
> For all blossoms grew and grew
> Fruitless, false, though fair to see.

*

1–4] In the MS the whole first stanza is cancelled, though most editors accept it as part of the poem. (In the Notebook draft of 'Earth's Answer' in *Songs of Experience* Blake deleted a stanza which he later engraved.)

1 *pain*] MS cancelled reading: 'seek'.

4] Cf. 'To Nobodaddy', line 4.

12] MS cancelled reading: 'He took her with a sigh'.   *was*] Elliptical: 'there was'.
deny] refusal.

I saw a chapel all of gold
That none did dare to enter in,
And many weeping stood without,
Weeping, mourning, worshipping.

5   I saw a serpent rise between
The white pillars of the door,
And he forced and forced and forced:
Down the golden hinges tore,

And along the pavement sweet
10   Set with pearls and rubies bright
All his slimy length he drew,
Till upon the altar white

Vomiting his poison out
On the bread and on the wine.
15   So I turned into a sty,
And laid me down among the swine.

*

I laid me down upon a bank
Where love lay sleeping.
I heard among the rushes dank
Weeping, weeping.

5   Then I went to the heath and the wild,
To the thistles and thorns of the waste,
And they told me how they were beguiled,
Driven out and compelled to be chaste.

*

1] Cf. 'The Garden of Love', *Songs of Experience*.

13 *Vomiting*] The syntax is incomplete.

14 *bread . . . wine*] The elements of the communion service which symbolize the salvific body and blood of Christ.

15–16 *sty . . . swine*] The speaker behaves like the Prodigal Son of Christ's parable (Luke, 15.11–32): honest dirt is preferred to filth generated by unnatural cleanliness.

A Cradle Song

Sleep, sleep, beauty bright,
Dreaming o'er the joys of night.
Sleep, sleep: in thy sleep
Little sorrows sit and weep.

5   Sweet babe, in thy face
Soft desires I can trace,
Secret joys and secret smiles,
Little pretty infant wiles.

As thy softest limbs I feel
10   Smiles as of the morning steal
O'er thy cheek and o'er thy breast
When thy little heart does rest.

O, the cunning wiles that creep
In thy little heart asleep.
15   When thy little heart does wake,
Then the dreadful lightnings break

From thy cheek and from thy eye
O'er the youthful harvests nigh.
Infant wiles and infant smiles
20   Heaven and earth of peace beguiles.

*

I askèd a thief to steal me a peach;
He turnèd up his eyes.
I asked a lithe lady to lie her down;
'Holy and meek', she cries.

Title] A contrary to 'A Cradle Song' in *Songs of Innocence* on which it is closely modelled; 'Infant Sorrow' was the contrary actually engraved in *Songs of Experience*.

I askèd a thief] Blake later made a separate copy of this lyric which he signed, 'W. Blake / Lambeth / 1796'.

5   As soon as I went
                      An angel came.
                      He winked at the thief
                      And smiled at the dame,

                      And without one word said
10   Had a peach from the tree,
                      And still as a maid
                      Enjoyed the lady.

*

In a Myrtle Shade

Why should I be bound to thee,
O my lovely myrtle tree?
Love, free love, cannot be bound
To any tree that grows on ground.

5   O how sick and weary I
                      Underneath my myrtle lie,
                      Like to dung upon the ground,
                      Underneath my myrtle bound.

                      Oft my myrtle sighed in vain
10   To behold my heavy chain;
                      Oft my father saw us sigh
                      And laughed at our simplicity.

5–6] Written as a single line in the Notebook.

8–9] There is no break between the stanzas in the Notebook.

11 *still . . . maid*] That is, the woman hypocritically assumes a passive role. (This replaces the cancelled line, 'And twixt earnest and joke', which rhymed with cancelled 'spoke' in line 9.)

The myrtle is generally associated with Aphrodite (Venus), but Erdman does not allow that this should be considered a separate poem, and has excluded it from revisions of his *Complete Poetry and Prose*. He explains his view of the textual history of the development of these stanzas in his edition of the Notebook (pp. 67–9): there he does accept that, when Blake first wrote them, 'he may have thought of these . . . stanzas as the draft of a separate poem.'

Title *Myrtle*] *In a Myrtle Shade*] Blake perhaps chose it because of its opecific association with unhappy love in the Virgilian Underworld (*Aeneid*, VI. 440–76).

3 *free love*] Cf. 'Earth's Answer', *Songs of Experience*, line 25 note.

So I smote him, and his gore
Stained the roots my myrtle bore,
.5   But the time of youth is fled,
And grey hairs are on my head.

*

To my Myrtle

To a lovely myrtle bound,
Blossoms show'ring all around,
O how sick and weary I
Underneath my myrtle lie.
5   Why should I be bound to thee,
O my lovely myrtle tree?

*

O lapwing thou flyest around the heath,
Nor seest the net that is spread beneath.
Why dost thou not fly among the corn fields?
They cannot spread nets where a harvest yields.

*

[Experiment]

'Thou hast a lap full of seed,
And this is a fine country:
Why dost thou not cast thy seed,
And live in it merrily?'

15–16] Cf. 'The Angel', *Songs of Experience*, lines 15–16.

To my Myrtle] Many texts from the Notebook which editors print as complete poems are derived from drafts which have been considerably re-written, and several from drafts which are also incomplete (left, for example, with uncancelled alternatives). This poem is unique in its relation to the preceding one, of which it is a concentrated and re-organized revision. (In its draft form 'In a Myrtle Shade' also contains lines 1–2 above.)

Experiment] The title is applied to this poem only conjecturally (Erdman, *Complete Poetry and Prose*, 852): it comes from a pencilled memorandum which suggests that Blake was considering engraving five of these short lyrics on a single plate (Notebook, p. 101).

5   'Shall I cast it on the sand,
And turn it into fruitful land?
For on no other ground
Can I sow my seed
Without tearing up
10   Some stinking weed.'

*

Riches

The countless gold of a merry heart,
The rubies and pearls of a loving eye,
The indolent never can bring to the mart,
Nor the secret hoard up in his treasury.

*

If you trap the moment before it's ripe
The tears of repentance you'll certainly wipe,
But if once you let the ripe moment go
You can never wipe off the tears of woe.

*

Eternity

He who binds to himself a joy
Does the wingèd life destroy,
But he who kisses the joy as it flies
Lives in eternity's sunrise.

*

Silent, silent night,
Quench the holy light
Of thy torches bright,

7–10] Though written as printed, metrically these are (like lines 5–6) two lines of four feet.

Riches 1 *countless*] Of incalculable or infinite value.

Silent, Silent night, 3 thy torches] The stars.

For, possessed of day,
5   Thousand spirits stray
That sweet joys betray.

Why should joys be sweet
Usèd with deceit,
Nor with sorrows meet?

10   But an honest joy
Does itself destroy
For a harlot coy.

*

To Nobodaddy

Why art thou silent and invisible,
Father of Jealousy?
Why dost thou hide thyself in clouds
From every searching eye?

5   Why darkness and obscurity
In all thy words and laws,
That none dare eat the fruit but from
The wily serpent's jaws?
Or is it because secrecy
10   Gains females' loud applause?

*

6 *betray*] That is, 'spirits . . . betray . . . joys': potentially possessed of the spiritual light of sexual love, they betray this by corrupt feelings which impel them to enjoy it in secret.

9 *sorrows*] Urizen seeks for 'a joy without pain' (*The Book of Urizen*, 4.10).

Title *Nobodaddy*] Blake's coinage: perhaps 'nobody's daddy', the contrary of the Christian God as 'Father of all'; or 'nobody + daddy', the non-existent (being man-made) Heavenly Father.

2 *Father of Jealousy*] Cf. 'Earth's Answer', *Songs of Experience*, line 7 note, and *Visions*, 10.12 note.

7–8 *eat . . . jaws*] Referring to the fall of Eve, Genesis, 3.1–6. In his illustrations of *Paradise Lost* Blake depicts Eve as literally taking the fruit of the Tree of the Knowledge of Good and Evil into her mouth from the jaws of the serpent (Butlin, *Paintings and Drawings*, 536.9, and cf. the separate drawing, 589).

9–10] An afterthought, written as a single line and in pencil (lines 1–8 are in ink).

Are not the joys of morning sweeter
Than the joys of night?
And are the vig'rous joys of youth
Ashamèd of the light?

5   Let age and sickness silent rob
The vineyards in the night,
But those who burn with vig'rous youth
Pluck fruits before the light.

*

[How to know Love from Deceit]

Love to faults is always blind,
Always is to joy inclined,
Lawless, winged and unconfined,
And breaks all chains from every mind.

5   Deceit to secrecy confined,
Lawful, cautious and refined,
To everything but interest blind,
And forges fetters for the mind.

*

The Wild Flower's Song

As I wandered the forest
The green leaves among,
I heard a wild flower
Singing a song.

5   'I slept in the earth
In the silent night,
I murmured my fears,
And I felt delight.

Title *How to Know Love from Deceit*] Cancelled in the MS.

In the morning I went,
10   As rosy as morn,
        To seek for new joy,
        But I met with scorn.'

*

Soft Snow

I walkèd abroad in a snowy day,
I asked the soft snow with me to play:
She played and she melted in all her prime,
And the winter called it a dreadful crime.

*

Why should I care for the men of Thames,
Or the cheating waves of chartered streams,
Or shrink at the little blasts of fear
That the hireling blows into my ear?

5   Though born on the cheating banks of Thames,
        Though his waters bathed my infant limbs,
        The Ohio shall wash his stains from me.
        I was born a slave, but I go to be free.

*

Day

The sun arises in the east
Clothed in robes of blood and gold.
Swords and spears and wrath increased
All around his bosom rolled,
5   Crowned with warlike fires and raging desires.

Soft snow 4] The proverb of Hell, 'The cut worm forgives the plough' (*Marriage*, 8.6) implies a Blakean perspective on the winter's verdict. A cancelled version of this line interprets the symbolism: 'Ah, that sweet love should be thought a crime'. Cf. 'A Little Girl Lost', *Songs of Experience*, line 4.

Why should I care 2 *chartered*] Cf. 'London', *Songs of Experience*, line 1.

7–8 *Ohio . . . free*] English radicals emigrated to America during the 1790s to escape prosecution. E. P. Thompson (*The Making of the English Working Class*, Harmondsworth, 1963) gives a number of examples.

Day 1 *sun*] On different perceptions of the sun cf. *Visions*, 5.37 note.

*

The sword sung on the barren heath,
The sickle in the fruitful field;
The sword he sung a song of death,
But could not make the sickle yield.

*

Abstinence sows sand all over
The ruddy limbs and flaming hair,
But desire gratified
Plants fruits of life and beauty there.

*

An old maid early, e'er I knew
Aught but the love that on me grew,
And now I'm covered o'er and o'er,
And wish that I had been a whore.

5   O I cannot cannot find
The undaunted courage of a virgin mind,
For early I in love was crossed
Before my flower of love was lost.

*

The Fairy

'Come hither my sparrows,
My little arrows.

1–2 *sword . . . sickle*] This basic opposition of weapon and agricultural implement would reso-
nate for Blake with echoes of one of the most famous passages of Old Testament visionary
prophetic idealism: 'They shall beat their swords into ploughshares, and their spears into prun-
ing hooks; nation shall not lift up sword against nation, neither shall they learn war any more'
(Isaiah, 2.4, repeated in Micah [4.3], and echoed in Joel [3.10]).

An old maid early 3] Cf. the preceding poem, line 1–2.

6 *virgin mind*] Cf. *America*, 10.10–12.

Title *The Fairy*] Cancelled title: 'The Marriage Ring'. Cf. 'Hail matrimony, made of love', *An
Island in the Moon* (Bentley, *Writings*, 891–2).

If a tear or a smile
Will a man beguile,
5   If an amorous delay
Clouds a sunshiny day,
If the step of a foot
Strikes the heart to its root,
'Tis the marriage ring
10   Makes each fairy a king.'
So a fairy sung.
From the leaves I sprung,
He leaped from the spray
To flee away,
15   But in my hat caught
He soon shall be taught.
Let him laugh, let him cry,
He's my butterfly,
For I've pulled out the sting
20   Of the marriage ring.

*

Motto to the Songs of Innocence and of Experience

The good are attracted by men's perceptions
And think not for themselves,
Till experience teaches them to catch
And to cage the fairies and elves.

5   And then the knave begins to snarl,
And the hypocrite to howl,
And all his good friends show their private ends,
And the eagle is known from the owl.

*

Title *Motto . . . Experience*] This poem gives some index of how Blake viewed Innocence and
Experience, but he presumably judged that indication too partial for the poem to act as an
adequate introduction to the final collection as a whole – for example, in its account only of
the limitations of Innocence. See *Songs*, headnote.

'Let the brothels of Paris be opened
With many an alluring dance,
To awake the physicians through the city,'
Said the beautiful Queen of France.

5   Then Old Nobodaddy aloft
Farted and belched and coughed,
And said 'I love hanging and drawing and quartering
Every bit as well as war and slaughtering.'

Then he swore a great and solemn oath:
10   'To kill the people I am loath,
But if they rebel they must go to hell;
They shall have a priest and a passing bell.'

The King awoke on his couch of gold
As soon as he heard these tidings told:
15   'Arise and come both fife and drum,
And the famine shall eat both crust and crumb.'

Let the brothels of Paris be opened] The complex textual situation of this and the following poem are described by Erdman, *Complete Poetry and Prose*, 861–3. Blake finally cancelled the second and third stanzas of 'Let the brothels . . .', but see 'Never pain to tell thy love', lines 1–4 note. This and the following poem can be dated after 25 October 1792 when Lafayette's imprisonment in Austria was reported in the London *Times*.

3 *physicians*] Cancelled reading, 'pestilence': like other tyrannous figures in Blake the Queen aims to use disease as an instrument of social control (cf. *America*, 15.15).

4 *Queen of France*] Marie Antoinette (b. 1755), guillotined in October 1793, about a year after the probable date of composition.

5 *Old Nobodaddy*] Cf. 'To Nobodaddy', title, note.

8] This was followed by a cancelled couplet (of which lines 1 and 2 were written as two lines, bringing out the internal rhyme):

> Damn praying and singing / Unless they will bring in
> The blood of ten thousand by fighting or swinging.

12 *passing bell*] bell tolled at death to invite prayers for the dead or dying.

16 *famine*] This word was cancelled in the MS but not replaced.   *crust and crumb*] Perhaps proverbial; cf. *King Lear*, 1.4.180.

The Queen of France just touched this globe,
And the pestilence darted from her robe;
But our good Queen quite grows to the ground,
20   And a great many suckers grow all around.

*

Who will exchange his own fire side
For the stone of another's door?
Who will exchange his wheaten loaf
For the links of a dungeon floor?

5   Fayette beheld the King and Queen
In curses and iron bound,
But mute Fayette wept tear for tear,
And guarded them around.

---

17 *just touched this globe*] Blake apparently refers to one of the most famous (or notorious) passages of Edmund Burke's *Reflections on the Revolution in France* in which Burke recalled seeing Marie Antoinette in the early 1770s: 'surely never lighted on this orb, which she hardly seemed to touch, a more delightful vision' (*Reflections*, ed. Conor Cruise O'Brien (Harmondsworth, 1968), 169).

18] Followed by a cancelled couplet:

> But the bloodthirsty people across the water
> Will not submit to the gibbet and halter.

19 *our good Queen*] Queen Charlotte, wife of George III: corruption resulting from her inactivity is contrasted with the corrupt activity of her French counterpart.

20] This replaces the cancelled line, 'There is just such a tree at Java found', which explains Blake's image of flatterers as 'suckers' (cf. 'The Human Abstract', *Songs of Experience*, line 22 note).

Who will exchange his own fire side 4] Followed by two cancelled lines (the second referring to Marie Antoinette):

> Who will exchange his own heart's blood
> For the drops of a harlot's eye?

5 *Fayette*] Marie Joseph Paul Lafayette (1757–1834), French statesman who played an important part in both the American and French Revolutions. Blake's attitude to him is more explicit in a cancelled stanza:

> Fayette, Fayette thou'rt bought and sold
> For well I see thy tears
> Of pity are exchanged for those
> Of selfish slavish fears.

At first a leading figure in the revolution of 1789, Lafayette's compassion for the King and Queen in defeat gave rise to what were in Blake's view corrupt political compromises. When Lafayette fled to Austria in 1792, after a failed attempt to sustain a degree of monarchical power, he was at first imprisoned as a presumed revolutionary (cf. line 4).

O who would smile on the wintry seas

10 And pity the stormy roar?

Or who will exchange his new-born child

For the dog at the wintry door?

12] Cf. *The Book of Urizen*, 25.2 and plate 26 design.

VISIONS OF THE DAUGHTERS
OF ALBION

The main critical problem of *Visions* is how to relate to each other, and in what proportion to emphasize, its themes of sexual freedom, the position of women, slavery, and epistemology. Openness to love is set against the desire for power – epitomized by slavery and late eighteenth-century marital arrangements and sexual codes – and the rationalist understanding of mind with which Blake sees all the corruptions he attacks as ultimately involved. One perspective on these issues is provided by Blake's sources – in the poems of Ossian, in classical myth, and in contemporary writing on the position of women and on slavery.

The supposed translations of James Macpherson from the ancient Gaelic bard, Ossian, which began with *Fragments of Ancient Poetry* (1760), were still of controversial interest in the 1790s. Blake admired these poems and believed them genuinely ancient (Bentley, *Writings*, 1413, 1512), and he drew on them for the narrative of *Visions*. In Ossian's *Oithóna*, in the absence of her betrothed, Gaul, Oithóna is carried off to an island, raped and concealed in a cave by the chieftain, Dunrommath. Oithóna reveals her situation to Gaul in a dream. He and Dunrommath fight and Dunrommath is killed. Oithóna, seeing herself as dishonoured, commits suicide. The basic situation is described in an introductory argument. The poem itself begins when Gaul returns to Oithóna's country to find her absent, and consists largely of dialogues between the three main characters. Ossian is no more than a starting point. The perspective he offers is largely one of contrast. Blake borrows only the basic situation of three characters and a love rivalry, the action of rape, and the structure of a series of dialogues. Oithóna is a Lucrece figure: she sees the rape as a defilement which requires her death. Oothoon wholly rejects this ethic. Gaul is not trapped in the ideologies that torture Theotormon, and Blake's dialogues are concerned with issues and feelings which play no part in Ossian.

As with the story of Lyca ('The Little Girl Lost'), some critics see behind Oothoon the myth of the rape of Persephone by Dis and her imprisonment in the Underworld interpreted as describing the soul's descent into the world of generation.[1] Oothoon/Persephone brings to generation a memory of the values of the eternal world, particularly its view of the spiritual nature of love. Blake was familiar with this way of interpreting the Persephone myth, which he would have encountered in the works of his acquaintance, the Platonist Thomas Taylor. Blake was also a syncretic mythographer: the story of Oothoon is connected with the myth of Prometheus overtly in both text and designs of *Visions* (see 5.13 note and plate 6 design). The difficulty with reading *Visions* symbolically in relation to the myth of

---

[1] See George Mills Harper, *The Neoplatonism of William Blake* (1961), 256–62; and Kathleen Raine, *Blake and Tradition* (1968), vol. I, 166–79.

Persephone is that it is almost necessarily combined with a refusal to read it liter-
ally. The Platonic dialogues on which the view of love appropriate to such a sym-
bolic reading draws are (with the partial exception of the *Phaedrus*) determinedly
anti-physical: the view of love described by Diotima through the mouth of Socrates
in the *Symposium* is that love is concerned with spiritual beauty and so ultimately
leaves behind the physical. Blake's view of love is quite different. Blake celebrates
sexual desire, both in itself and as a key to the proper perception of other legitimate
creative joys and the understanding of various social and intellectual corruptions.
Conceived as other than a broadly analogical narrative, the myth of Persephone
deflects attention from these central themes.

More important than these ancient and pseudo-ancient influences in creating the
context in which Blake composed *Visions* was Mary Wollstonecraft's *A Vindication
of the Rights of Woman*. Blake may have known Wollstonecraft through the pub-
lisher Joseph Johnson. Blake did engraving work for Johnson, including illustra-
tions from his own designs for Wollstonecraft's *Original Stories from Real Life* (1788;
illustrated edition 1791). He probably also executed the (unsigned) engravings
from designs by others which accompanied her translation of Christian Gotthilf
Salzmann's *Elements of Morality* (1791). Johnson was to have been the publisher of
Blake's eventually unpublished poem *The French Revolution* (1791), and Johnson was
the publisher of *A Vindication* which appeared in 1792, the year before *Visions*. The
heroine of *Visions*, Oothoon, is the most positive and active of Blake's early female
characters, and since her exemplary history is witnessed by a chorus of 'enslaved'
Englishwomen, Blake's (possibly indirect) acquaintance with Mary Wollstonecraft
and his knowledge of *A Vindication* have both attracted discussion, as has his pre-
sumed knowledge of her private life – her relations with his close friend, the painter
Henry Fuseli, to whom Wollstonecraft proposed a highly unconventional domestic
relationship by which she was to co-habit with him and his wife in order to enjoy
daily his intellectual companionship.

Blake would have found much to assent to in *A Vindication*, particularly its basic
analysis of the supposedly innate character of woman as socially produced by an
oppressive male–female hierarchy. On the issue of sexuality, however, his views and
Wollstonecraft's as presented in *A Vindication* were different, as were their aims.
The proposal to Fuseli may have led Blake to think of Mary Wollstonecraft as a
woman intellectual attempting to live out experimental ideas about emotional rela-
tionships in an era of revolutionary social philosophies, and so a figure not unlike
Oothoon. But in *A Vindication* Wollstonecraft presents herself more convention-
ally, as a rationalist who – albeit in a paradoxically passionate idiom – sets reason in
opposition to 'the impulse of the heart' and 'the storms of passion'.[2] Wollstonecraft
wanted immediate attention and a practical response to radical but also pragmatic
proposals for the emancipation of women. *A Vindication*'s insistence on chastity –
by which Wollstonecraft meant sexuality within marriage divested of its usual
role-playing – would have evinced for Blake a puritanism bred in the norms of the

---

[2] *A Vindication of the Rights of Woman*, chapter 5, ed. Miriam Brody Kramnick (Harmondsworth,
1975), 217.

English dissenting tradition, too much accepting negative Christian attitudes to sexuality. Oothoon celebrates desire – not at all part of the agenda of *A Vindication*, which celebrates friendship. Blake's plea for the liberation of women has, therefore, little in common with the feminist discourses of his contemporaries. Nevertheless, *Visions*, and from it Blake's treatment of women in his poetry more generally, has been extensively discussed in a modern feminist context.[3] In this context it has recently become one of the most controversial and diversely interpreted of all Blake's illuminated books. Oothoon, it has usually been supposed, is in some degree a mouthpiece for Blakean values about sexual freedom,[4] and, arising from that, about the position of women in Blake's society and human freedom more generally. In reaction against criticism which celebrated the obvious senses of the work, negative estimates of Oothoon – as in some measure infected by the values she supposes herself to oppose, as failing to bring her radical agenda to fruition in action,[5] even as a sadomasochist and voyeur – became for a while almost standard. Some recent answers to these views from within feminist perspectives accept that there are complicating undercurrents to the work, but do not find that these wholly undermine the positive values Oothoon articulates.[6]

Another more direct and important contemporary influence on *Visions* is John Gabriel Stedman's *Narrative of a Five Years' Expedition against the Revolted Negroes of Surinam from the year 1772 to 1777*, published by Joseph Johnson in 1796. During 1791 and 1792, while working on *Visions*, Blake engraved sixteen plates for this book. Stedman had been a soldier who had helped to subdue a slave revolt, but he had been disgusted by the cruelties he saw. His book was written in part to expose these. Since the work has been published in a modern edition from Stedman's manuscript,[7] it is possible to see that the 1796 publication was bowdlerized so as to reduce the horrific nature of Stedman's accounts of oppression and torture. Blake came to know Stedman personally while working on the engravings, and so we may presume not only that Blake was familiar with the savage cruelties he illustrated but that he also heard from Stedman about the material suppressed in the original

---

[3] See, for example, Susan Fox, 'The Female as Metaphor in William Blake's Poetry', *Critical Enquiry*, 3 (1977), reprinted in Nelson Hilton (ed.), *Essential Articles for the Study of William Blake, 1970–84* (1986). Fox sees Oothoon almost entirely in positive terms.

[4] This view is attacked by Thomas Vogler in an essay in *Critical Paths: Blake and the Argument of Method*, ed. Dan Miller, Mark Bracher and Donald Ault (1987).

[5] This line of thought is expressed in moderate terms in Alicia Ostriker's 'Desire Gratified and Ungratified: William Blake and Sexuality', *BIQ*, 16 (1982–83), 148–55, reprinted in Hilton (ed.), *Essential Articles* (see note 3 above). A more general feminist and critical view of Blake is offered (in the same issue of *BIQ*, 156–65) by Anne K. Mellor, 'Blake's Portrayal of Women'. Mellor's polemic leads her here almost entirely to omit *Visions* from her argument. She returns to the subject, equally tendentiously, to consider *Visions*, in *The Huntington Library Quarterly*, 58 (1996), 345–71.

[6] See Harriet Kramer Linkin, 'Revisioning Blake's Oothoon', *BIQ*, 23 (1989–90), 184–94; and James A. W. Heffernan, 'Blake's Oothoon: the Dilemmas of Marginality', *Studies in Romanticism*, 30 (1991), 3–18.

[7] Ed. Richard and Sally Price (Baltimore, MD, 1988).

publication. The Society for the Abolition of the Slave Trade had been formed in 1787, and a bill for abolition of the British trade was discussed in Parliament between 1789 and 1793. The issue attracted controversial attention in both liberal and conservative political circles. Though *Visions* is primarily concerned with sexual freedom and the position of women, for Blake all freedoms were indivisible, and in *Visions* he presents the sexual codes of the demand for physical purity and the hierarchy of male over female – as did Wollstonecraft in *A Vindication* – as continuous with the violence and injustice of slavery, more widely acknowledged as illegitimate in his society.[8] Bromion is a violent man and a slave-owner, Oothoon is both a representative woman and 'the soft soul of America' – a character in a loose political allegory. Theotormon is incapable of responding positively to Oothoon's vision of freedom in sexual love and of rejecting Bromion's views, partly because he shares Bromion's Lockean – and on Blake's argument therefore passive – view of mind,[9] but also because his own sexual suppressions give him a covert sympathy for Bromion's domineering violence (5.6–10).

'Execution is the chariot of genius.' Or, more elaborately: 'I have heard many people say, "Give me the ideas: it is no matter what words you put them into" ... These people know enough of artifice, but nothing of art. Ideas cannot be given but in their minutely appropriate words' (Bentley, *Writings*, 1463, 1041–2). Blake constantly insisted that content was inseparable from form in art, and his life as a poet was, accordingly, one of constant experiment with form. In his later work he was in conflict with inherited ideas of narrative structure in epic, in his earlier work with the predominant eighteenth-century ideas of prosodic correctness. In both cases his aim was to find forms which were appropriate vehicles of his opposition to contemporary ideas of beauty and order while they embodied his feeling for the sublime and his libertarian ethics. *Visions* is one of the earliest works to use the seven-stress line which Blake developed more freely in his later engraved poetry. The patterns of stress in this line are more irregular than those of his lyric poetry, but this rhythmic freedom is complemented in *Visions* by the relative formality of rhetorical patterns which are often emphasized by the lineation, particularly where parallel structures begin successive lines. There are also rhetorical patterns – of a kind that were to become characteristic of Blake's later poetry – which, while still giving the verse a shapely emphasis, are irregular in relation to the lineation. At times these irregular patterns are juxtaposed with the more formal, so as to give an effect of formality climactically emerging from passionate irregularity, or, vice-versa, of irregularity breaking down the orderly emphasis of stricter patterns. Blake's ear had been trained on the prosodic freedom of Milton, and probably received some stimulus both from the metrically irregular pseudo-ancient 'Rowley' poems of Chatterton (which he professedly admired [Bentley, *Writings*, 1512]), and the

---

[8] For an account of this aspect of the work, see Erdman, *Prophet Against Empire*; and Erdman's 'William Blake's Vision of Slavery', *Journal of the Warburg and Courtauld Institutes*, 15 (1952), 242–52. Erdman misleads in presenting Stedman as an abolitionist: Stedman attacks the abuses of slavery but defends the institution.

[9] On the importance of Locke in the poem's arguments see notes to 5.31 and 7.15.

genuinely ancient ballads collected in Bishop Percy's *Reliques of Ancient English Poetry*.[10] Most important of all to Blake's sense of rhetoric and prosodic structure was the King James ('Authorized') Version of the Bible in which the Old Testament's characteristic patterns of repetition, to which the structural analyses of Bishop Robert Lowth had recently drawn attention,[11] are based on what is often poetry in the original Hebrew translated into rhythmical prose. This gives the poetry of *Visions* the character of what W. H. Auden defined all poetry as being – 'memorable speech',[12] a stylization of the spoken language, the spoken language passionately heightened by pattern, regular and irregular.

---

[10] Blake's copies of Chatterton's Rowley poems and Percy's *Reliques* are both extant: see G. E. Bentley, *Blake Books* (1977), 685, 691.

[11] Cf. *Marriage*, 7.6 note.

[12] Introduction to *The Poet's Tongue*, in *The English Auden: Poems, Essays and Dramatic Writings, 1927–1939*, ed. Edward Mendelson (London, 1977), 327.

3. *Visions of the Daughters of Albion*, Frontispiece
(Fitzwilliam Museum, Cambridge; original size: 11.6 × 16.8 cms)

Frontispiece [Plate 1]

Title-page [Plate 2]

Visions of the Daughters of Albion

The eye sees more than the heart knows

Printed by William Blake: 1793

Frontispiece.

Design (*Plate 3*). In a cave by the sea Bromion is bound back-to-back with Oothoon. He is chained by his ankles to the rock beneath and looks out to the left with an expression of terror, eyes staring and hair standing on end: like other tyrannous figures in Blake, this slave-owner suffers as a prisoner of the ideology which generates his oppressive behaviour. To the right Theotormon sits in a huddled posture, his head in his arms. All three are naked. The viewer looks from inside the cave outwards, towards the sun, which in many copies is painted so as to suggest its imperfect perception as described in the text (5.35–6). The design illustrates 5.5–7, and epitomizes the fundamental relation of the three characters. (This design was placed by Blake after the title-page in one copy. It is often said that it was also bound after the final plate, but this arrangement, which occurs in only one copy, was probably made after Blake's death: see Bentley, *Writings*, 697.)

Title-page.

Daughters of Albion] Albion is an ancient name for England. His daughters are Englishwomen, seen collectively in imagination.

The eye . . . knows] The motto postulates a gap between experience and understanding which can be referred to the work's discussions of the problematic relation of sense experience to knowledge (plates 6 and 7), and to the fact that Bromion and Theotormon fail to make sense of their own experience. Some commentators have proposed that Blake likewise confesses not fully to understand his own visions. Cf. Isaiah, 6.9 (God speaks): 'Go, and tell this people, Hear ye indeed, but understand not; and see ye indeed, but perceive not.' The words are famous, being echoed in each of the gospels, and in Acts and in Romans. God proposes to chastise those who refuse to understand because they are morally unwilling to do so, a line of thought that can be applied to Bromion and Theotormon.

Design. In the foreground a young woman (Oothoon) runs across the waves of a turbulent sea (cf. 3.14–15), fleeing from a bearded old man (Urizen) with huge spread wings who is surrounded by flames. To their left three figures dance in a ring in postures of exuberant delight under a rainbow. Above the ring of dancers are three figures slumped in postures expressing suffering and exhaustion. To the upper right a seated figure casts blights down the margin. (In a separate pencil drawing this figure is called 'the evil demon'.) The motto, and Blake's name as the printer, are at the bottom of the plate.

[Plate 3]

The Argument

I lovèd Theotormon,
And I was not ashamèd;
I trembled in my virgin fears
And I hid in Leutha's vale.

5   I pluckèd Leutha's flower,
And I rose up from the vale;
But the terrible thunders tore
My virgin mantle in twain.

[Plate 4]

Visions

Enslaved, the Daughters of Albion weep; a trembling lamentation
Upon their mountains, in their valleys sighs toward America.

For the soft soul of America, Oothoon, wandered in woe
Along the vales of Leutha, seeking flowers to comfort her.
5   And thus she spoke to the bright marigold of Leutha's vale:

3.1 *lovèd*] On Blake's distinction between syllabic 'ed' and non-syllabic "d' see Introduction (3), pp. 25–6.

3.1 *Theotormon*] The name suggests that he is tormented by his idea of god (*theos* in Greek), and perhaps also by his idea of law (*torah* in Hebrew). (Both are words Blake would know without any extensive knowledge of Greek or Hebrew.) There is a minor character called Torthóma in Ossian's 'Berrathon' (which also includes a reference to Lutha: see following note), and a place-name, Tromáthon, in *Oithóna*, which Macpherson derives from words meaning 'heavy or deep-sounding wave' (cf. 4.15 note).

3.4 *Leutha*] Lutha is a place-name (a valley, or sometimes a plain) in Ossian. Leutha recurs in several of Blake's later poems. The nearest contemporary use is in a cancelled plate of *America* (Bentley, *Writings*, 161), where it appears to be a world of oppression which revolutionary action shows to be ultimately unreal.

3.5 *flower*] A traditional symbol of love; cf. 'my flower of love' in the Notebook poem 'An old maid early' (p. 158).

3.8 *virgin mantle*] the hymen.

Plate 3 design. Oothoon, naked, with the rays of the rising sun behind her, touches her breasts and kisses the naked human form of the spirit of a heliotropic flower. The design illustrates 3.5 and 4.5–13. A gloss is also provided by the Notebook quatrain 'Eternity' (p. 154).

4.3 *soft . . . Oothoon*] The identification of Oothoon with America points to the political significance of the narrative: she is the New World of potential freedom assaulted by exploitation and moral schemes which stem from the Old World. 'Soft' implies that she is naturally gentle: she is turned into the fiery revolutionary of the later parts of the poem by abuse and

'Art thou a flower? Art thou a nymph? I see thee now a flower,
Now a nymph! I dare not pluck thee from thy dewy bed.'
The golden nymph replied, 'Pluck thou my flower, Oothoon
   the mild.
Another flower shall spring, because the soul of sweet delight
10   Can never pass away.' She ceased and closed her golden shrine.

Then Oothoon plucked the flower saying, 'I pluck thee from
   thy bed,
Sweet flower, and put thee here to glow between my breasts;
And thus I turn my face to where my whole soul seeks.'

Over the waves she went in winged exulting swift delight,
15   And over Theotormon's reign took her impetuous course.
Bromion rent her with his thunders. On his stormy bed
Lay the faint maid, and soon her woes appalled his
   thunders hoarse.

---

suffering. On Ossian's heroine, Oithóna, see headnote: Macpherson explains this name as meaning 'the virgin of the wave' (cf. plate 7 design). Erdman (*Prophet Against Empire*, 233) points out that there are African words in Stedman built around a reduplicated 'oo'. Catherine Blake's reference, after Blake's death, to 'a work called Outhoun' (Bentley, *Writings*, 1679) presumably indicates Blake's pronunciation (not the native American sounding 'Oöthoön'), and – unless it refers to a lost poem – may indicate that Blake referred to *Visions* by the name of its heroine.

4.5 *marigold*] Spelt by Blake 'Marygold', perhaps as a way of drawing attention to its human form. (Blake originally etched the 'M' lower case and changed it to a capital on the plate.) Blake may have associated the marigold with the heliotropic flower of the Clytie and Apollo myth (see note to 'Ah Sunflower', p. 95), and so thought of it as a flower the characteristic action of which 'says' 'I turn my face to where my whole soul seeks.'

4.6 *Art thou ... nymph*] Cf. plate 3 design and note. The marigold has a human significance open to the eye of vision and drawn out by the poem. Cf. *The Book of Thel*, in which Thel sees all her non-human interlocutors in human form, and specifically 6.2–3: 'Image of weakness, art thou but a worm? / I see thee like an infant wrappèd in the lily's leaf'; also Blake's letter-poem on levels of imaginative perception: 'For double the vision my eyes do see, / And a double vision is always with me: / With my inward eye 'tis an old man grey, / With my outward a thistle across my way' (22.11.1802, Bentley, *Writings*, 1564; cf. the same line of thought in the letter-poem of 2.10.1800, *Writings*, 1546).

4.8 *Pluck ... flower*] A traditional symbol of accepting sexual experience.

4.9–10 *the soul ... pass away*] Cf. *Marriage* plate 9 (53) and *America*, 10.14, 'the soul of sweet delight can never be defiled.'

4.15 *reign*] realm (*OED sb* 2a); 'Theotormon's reign' is the sea (with which Theotormon is constantly associated).

4.16 *Bromion*] The name suggests 'thunderer' (Greek, *bromos*, thunder; cf. 3.7 and 4.16–17), or perhaps 'roarer' (Greek, *bromios*, noisy). (Blake used the name again in later poems, but for a significantly different character.)

Bromion spoke: 'Behold this harlot here on Bromion's bed,
And let the jealous dolphins sport around the lovely maid.
20   Thy soft American plains are mine, and mine thy north and south.
Stamped with my signet are the swarthy children of the sun.
They are obedient, they resist not, they obey the scourge.
Their daughters worship terrors and obey the violent.

[Plate 5]

Now thou may'st marry Bromion's harlot, and protect the child
Of Bromion's rage that Oothoon shall put forth in nine
    moons' time.'

Then storms rent Theotormon's limbs; he rolled his waves around,
And folded his black jealous waters round the adulterate pair.
5   Bound back to back in Bromion's caves terror and meekness dwell.

At entrance Theotormon sits, wearing the threshold hard
With secret tears. Beneath him sound like waves on a desert shore
The voice of slaves beneath the sun, and children bought with
    money,
That shiver in religious caves beneath the burning fires
10   Of lust, that belch incessant from the summits of the earth.

4.19 *jealous dolphins*] Perhaps referring to the myth of Galatea, who was rescued by dolphins from rape by Polyphemus (Ovid, *Metamorphoses*, XIII). The dolphins are 'jealous' because they are unable to reach (or rescue) Oothoon: Bromion is asserting ownership (as in the following lines).

4.21 *Stamped . . . signet*] Referring to the practice of branding slaves.

4.23 *worship . . . violent*] Cf. 'harlot' (line 18): Bromion explains his own actions as a response to what women supposedly actually want. Blake re-used the line in *The Four Zoas* (68.26), giving it to Urizen (see 8.3 note), the archetype of which Bromion is the exemplar.

Plate 4 design. Above the 'V' of 'Visions' a naked woman plays a serpent-like horn and another rides on a cloud. To the right two naked men shoot with bows and arrows. Below, and towards the right of the title, a flying figure in a costume which ends in billowing draperies holds out what is perhaps a small dripping paint brush. Below the text Oothoon and Bromion lie sprawled in postures of exhaustion after the rape.

5.1 *child*] Pregnancy increased the value of a slave.

5.2 *rage*] Sexual passion (*OED sb* 6b).

5.5 *Bromion's caves*] Symbolic of his limited perceptions: cf. *Marriage*, plate 14: 'Man has closed himself up, till he sees all things through narrow chinks of his cavern.' Blake would know Plato's famous use of the cave as symbolic of limited human abilities to perceive the real (*Republic*, VII.1).

5.8–10 *slaves . . . religious caves . . . lust*] Repression generated by religious sexual codes is one cause of the oppression from which slaves and child-labourers suffer. Cf. the connection between sexual and political freedom implied by the myth of Orc in *America*.

Oothoon weeps not. She cannot weep, her tears are lockèd up;
But she can howl incessant, writhing her soft snowy limbs
And calling Theotormon's eagles to prey upon her flesh.

'I call with holy voice! Kings of the sounding air,
15   Rend away this defilèd bosom that I may reflect
The image of Theotormon on my pure transparent breast.'

The eagles at her call descend and rend their bleeding prey.
Theotormon severely smiles. Her soul reflects the smile,
As the clear spring mudded with feet of beasts grows pure and smiles.

20   The Daughters of Albion hear her woes and echo back her sighs.

'Why does my Theotormon sit weeping upon the threshold,
And Oothoon hovers by his side, persuading him in vain?
I cry, "Arise O Theotormon, for the village dog
Barks at the breaking day, the nightingale has done lamenting,
25   The lark does rustle in the ripe corn, and the eagle returns
From nightly prey and lifts his golden beak to the pure east,
Shaking the dust from his immortal pinions to awake
The sun that sleeps too long. Arise my Theotormon, I am pure,
Because the night is gone that closed me in its deadly black."
30   They told me that the night and day were all that I could see;
They told me that I had five senses to enclose me up,

5.13 *Theotormon's . . . flesh*] Oothoon's requested 'cleansing' resembles the punishment inflicted on Prometheus, archetype of rebellion against divine oppression. Cf. plate 6 design.

5.14 *sounding*] Resounding.

5.20 *The Daughters . . . sighs*] A choric line, repeated at 8.2 and 11.13, which marks the poem as divided into three sections: narrative, dialogues between the three main characters, statement by Oothoon.

5.31 *They told me . . . five senses*] The relation of thought to sense experience was a central topic of eighteenth-century epistemology. Blake opposed the argument of Locke, in his *Essay of Human Understanding*, that we have no innate ideas but that the mind is a *tabula rasa* (blank tablet) in which all ideas are built up from sense experience. Cf. 6.2–13 and 7.14–18 and notes. In the tractate *All Religions Are One* (c. 1788) Blake argues that 'Man's perceptions are not bound by organs of sense: he perceives more than sense (though ever so acute) can discover.' Similarly, *There is No Natural Religion* (c. 1788) is anti-Lockean in opposing to the part of the mind that reasons on the basis of sensation (the 'philosophic and experimental') the more fundamental innate imaginative capacities ('the poetic or prophetic character'). The argument against Locke's epistemology remained basic to Blake's work: in his annotations of Reynolds' *Discourses* (made c. 1808) he recorded that he read Locke's *Essay* as a young man and 'felt the same contempt and abhorrence [for it] then that I do now' (Bentley, *Writings*, 1497). (Blake's relation to Locke is discussed at length, and as a basic aspect of his outlook, in the first chapter of Northrop Frye's *Fearful Symmetry* (1947).) Oothoon's juxtaposition of apparently different subjects implies an analogy between sexual and intellectual oppression.

And they enclosed my infinite brain into a narrow circle,
And sunk my heart into the abyss, a red round globe hot
    burning,
Till all from life I was obliterated and erasèd.
35   Instead of morn arises a bright shadow, like an eye
In the eastern cloud, instead of night a sickly charnel-house,
That Theotormon hears me not. To him the night and morn
Are both alike: a night of sighs, a morning of fresh tears;

[Plate 6]

And none but Bromion can hear my lamentations.

With what sense is it that the chicken shuns the ravenous hawk?
With what sense does the tame pigeon measure out the expanse?
With what sense does the bee form cells? Have not the mouse
    and frog
5   Eyes and ears and sense of touch? Yet are their habitations
And their pursuits as different as their forms and as their joys.
Ask the wild ass why he refuses burdens, and the meek camel
Why he loves man: is it because of eye, ear, mouth or skin,
Or breathing nostrils? No, for these the wolf and tiger have.
10   Ask the blind worm the secrets of the grave, and why her spires
Love to curl round the bones of death; and ask the rav'nous snake
Where she get poison, and the winged eagle why he loves the sun;
And then tell me the thoughts of man that have been hid of old.

5.32–3 *they enclosed . . . hot burning*] Cf. the creation of the fallen Urizen, *The Book of Urizen*,
11.2–4, '. . . a red / Round globe, hot burning, deep, / Deep down in to the abyss', and the
consequent fall of humankind: 'The senses inward rushed, shrinking' (25.29).

5.35 *bright shadow*] That is, the sun. Far from sense experience giving rise to ideas, sense
experience takes its character from a person's mental set. As Blake put it succinctly, 'As a man
is, so he sees' (Letter, 23.8.1799; Bentley, *Writings*, 1527); and, specifically by reference to the
sun, 'The sun's light when he unfolds it / Depends on the organ that beholds it' (*For the Sexes:
the Gates of Paradise*, plate 1). Cf. the Notebook poem, 'Day' (below, p. 157), and *A Vision of
the Last Judgement*, Notebook, p. 95 (Bentley, *Writings*, 1027).

5.37 *That*] Because.

Plate 5 design. Between lines 16 and 17 a black slave, stretched out at full length on the ground,
attempts to raise himself with one arm. His pick-axe lies behind him against a fallen leafless
tree.

6.2–13 *With what sense . . . of old*] Oothoon argues that the different characters of creatures
with similar sense experience show that our conceptions of reality are not purely sense-based,
and that to realize this is the basis of true wisdom. Cf. 5.31 note.

Silent I hover all the night, and all day could be silent,
15 If Theotormon once would turn his lovèd eyes upon me.
How can I be defiled when I reflect thy image pure?
Sweetest the fruit that the worm feeds on, and the soul preyed
    on by woe,
The new-washed lamb tinged with the village smoke, and the
    bright swan
By the red earth of our immortal river. I bathe my wings
20 And I am white and pure to hover round Theotormon's breast.'

Then Theotormon broke his silence, and he answerèd,

'Tell me what is the night or day to one o'erflowed with woe?
Tell me what is a thought, and of what substance is it made?
Tell me what is a joy, and in what gardens do joys grow?
25 And in what rivers swim the sorrows, and upon what mountains

[Plate 7]

Wave shadows of discontent? And in what houses dwell
    the wretched
Drunken with woe, forgotten, and shut up from cold despair?

Tell me where dwell the thoughts forgotten till thou call
    them forth?
Tell me where dwell the joys of old, and where the ancient loves?
5 And when will they renew again and the night of oblivion past?

6.17–19 *Sweetest . . . river*] That is, Theotormon's ideal of 'purity' is mistaken: it contributes to fineness of being that one should have engaged with and be marked by experience.

6.19 *red earth*] Referring to the literal meaning in Hebrew of the name 'Adam' (who was formed from the earth). Cf. *Marriage*, 2.13 note.

6.22–7.11 *Tell me . . . the envier*] The posing of questions is an important mode of address for all three characters, but only Theotormon asks questions almost exclusively. Like the 'idiot questioner' of *Milton* he 'is always questioning / But never capable of answering' (43.12–13). Many of Theotormon's questions are framed in mistaken terms: he asks that mental and spiritual realities be made real to his senses.

Plate 6 design. Illustrates 5.12–17: Oothoon lies naked on a cloud; an eagle hovering above her with widely spread wings tears at her midriff.

7.2 *woe, forgotten, and*] Blake's punctuation is 'woe forgotten. and'. Keynes (*The Complete Writings of William Blake* (1957; rev. edn., 1966), 192) modernizes 'woe forgotten, and'; Stanley Gardner glosses 'having forgotten their misery in drink' (*William Blake: Selected Poems* (London, 1962), 163). However, since Blake's pointing is often not primarily syntactic, this sense is less probable.

7.5 *they*] That is, the thoughts, joys and loves of lines 3–4.   *past*] be past.

That I might traverse times and spaces far remote, and bring
Comforts into a present sorrow and a night of pain.
Where goest thou, O thought? To what remote land is thy flight?
If thou returnest to the present moment of affliction
Wilt thou bring comforts on thy wings, and dews and honey
10   and balm,
Or poison from the desert wilds, from the eyes of the envier?'

Then Bromion said, and shook the cavern with his lamentation,

'Thou knowest that the ancient trees seen by thine eyes have fruit,
But knowest thou that trees and fruits flourish upon the earth
15   To gratify senses unknown – trees, beasts and birds unknown,
Unknown, not unperceived, spread in the infinite microscope,
In places yet unvisited by the voyager, and in worlds
Over another kind of seas, and in atmospheres unknown?
Ah, are there other wars beside the wars of sword and fire?
20   And are there other sorrows beside the sorrows of poverty?
And are there other joys beside the joys of riches and ease?
And is there not one law for both the lion and the ox?
And is there not eternal fire, and eternal chains,
To bind the phantoms of existence from eternal life?'

25   Then Oothoon waited silent all the day and all the night,

---

7.14–18 *trees . . . unknown*] Bromion has in mind discoveries of scientific experimentation and contemporary geographical exploration (such as are reported in Stedman's *Surinam* [see headnote]).

7.15 *senses unknown*] Cf. 5.31 and 6.2–13 notes. The argument here concerns whether or not one might deduce additional senses from those already known. Locke discusses the issue (*Essay*, 2.2.3 and 2.9.8), denying the possibility. For Blake's view of this, see *There is No Natural Religion*, principles III–VI. Blake agrees with Locke but draws from this opposite conclusions: it is evidence that all knowledge cannot be based on sense experience. Though the following questions (lines 19–21) imply Bromion's materialism (he doubts whether there can be spiritual battles, joys and sorrows), nevertheless he also has intimations of knowledge beyond what is possible, in Blake's view, on Lockean premises.

7.22 *one law . . . ox*] Cf. *Marriage*, plate 24, 'One law for the lion and ox is oppression', and Blake's manuscript poem of *c*. 1789, *Tiriel* (Tiriel opposes the 'mistaken' laws of his father), 'Why is one law given to the lion and the patient ox?'.

Plate 7 design. Above the text Oothoon, outside Bromion's cave, her left leg attached by a manacle and chain to the ground, her hands together in a gesture expressing grief or supplication, floats in a large flame-like wave above Theotormon (cf. 4.3 note on Oothoon as 'the virgin of the wave'). He sits on the sea shore with his head sunk behind raised knees, apparently unaware of or ignoring her. To the right the sun rises behind the sea.

[Plate 8]

But when the morn arose her lamentation renewed.
The Daughters of Albion hear her woes and echo back her sighs.

'O Urizen, creator of men, mistaken demon of heaven,
Thy joys are tears, thy labour vain, to form men to thine image.
5   How can one joy absorb another? Are not different joys
Holy, eternal, infinite? And each joy is a love.

Does not the great mouth laugh at a gift, and the narrow
     eyelids mock
At the labour that is above payment? And wilt thou take the ape
For thy counsellor, or the dog for a schoolmaster to thy children?
10   Does he who contemns poverty, and he who turns with abhorrence
From usury, feel the same passion, or are they movèd alike?
How can the giver of gifts experience the delights of the merchant?
How the industrious citizen the pains of the husbandman?
How different far the fat-fed hireling with hollow drum,
15   Who buys whole cornfields into wastes, and sings upon the heath!
How different their eye and ear! How different the world to them!

8.3 *Urizen*] The first appearance in Blake's work of a major figure in his mythology, the arche-type of oppression, here associated with the God of the Pentateuch (see 8.4 and 10.12 and notes), and with a drive to produce uniformity at odds with the proper diversity of existence. The name may be formed from a play on 'horizon' and possibly its etymology from Greek *horizein*, 'to bound': Blake early on drew the character with the inscription 'who shall bind the Infinite?' (sketch for the frontispiece to *Europe*, Notebook, p. 96). Blake's pronunciation of the name is uncertain. It can be pronounced so as to suggest a play on 'reason' ('your reason' [but not mine]), but analysis of the metrical contexts in which the name occurs suggests that Blake himself accented it on the first syllable.

8.4 *form . . . image*] Cf. Genesis, 1.26–7, 'God said, 'Let us make man in our image, after our likeness . . . So God created man in his own image, in the image of God created he him'. ('Form' is also used of the creation of man, as at Genesis, 2.7.)

8.5–6 *How can . . . infinite*] Contrast Urizen's desire to enforce uniformity in *The Book of Urizen*, 4.34–40.

8.7–40] Oothoon argues: (1) against the Urizenic desire for uniformity, that different experi-ences of life inevitably lead to different visions and values; and (2) that the religion of the church is exploitative, and its sexual ethics give rise to cycles of oppression and unhappiness for both women and men. Cf. lines 27–31 note.

8.8–9 *the ape . . . thy children*] Cf. *The Four Zoas*, Night II (Enion speaks, lamenting enforced errors [see p. 248]): 'I have chosen the serpent for a counsellor, and the dog / For a schoolmas-ter to my children.'

8.14–15 *hireling . . . wastes*] His drum indicates that this hireling is a recruiting sergeant: he devastates agricultural production by depriving farms of labourers. (Blake gives an ideal view of the military versus the agricultural in 'The sword sung on the barren heath', Notebook, above, p. 158.)

With what sense does the parson claim the labour of the farmer?
What are his nets and gins and traps, and how does he
    surround him
With cold floods of abstraction, and with forests of solitude,
To build him castles and high spires where kings and priests
20   may dwell,
Till she who burns with youth, and knows no fixèd lot, is bound
In spells of law to one she loathes? And must she drag the chain
Of life in weary lust? Must chilling murderous thoughts obscure
The clear heaven of her eternal spring? To bear the wintry rage
25   Of a harsh terror driven to madness, bound to hold a rod
Over her shrinking shoulders all the day, and all the night
To turn the wheel of false desire, and longings that wake
    her womb
To the abhorrèd birth of cherubs in the human form,
That live a pestilence and die a meteor, and are no more?
30   Till the child dwell with one he hates, and do the deed he loathes,
And the impure scourge force his seed into its unripe birth
Ere yet his eyelids can behold the arrows of the day?

Does the whale worship at thy footsteps as the hungry dog?
Or does he scent the mountain prey because his nostrils wide
35   Draw in the ocean? Does his eye discern the flying cloud
As the raven's eye? Or does he measure the expanse like the
    vulture?
Does the still spider view the cliffs where eagles hide their young?

8.17 *the parson . . . the farmer*] Referring to the practice of tithing, whereby one tenth of the
produce of land and stock, or its monetary equivalent, was collected as a form of tax to sup-
port the established Church. Cf. the Notebook couplet, 'An Answer to the Parson': 'Why of
the sheep do you not learn peace? / Because I don't want you to sheer my fleece.'

8.18 *nets . . . traps*] Cf. *Marriage*, plate 7 (13): 'All wholesome food is caught without a net or a
trap', and *The Song of Los*, 4.1–2, where the 'nets and gins and traps to catch the joys of eter-
nity' include (as here) castles and churches ('high spires') – the allied oppressive powers of
church and state.

8.25 *rod*] Apparently meaning a yoke (see *OED sb*[1] III 8b), though the more usual sense of an
instrument of punishment (*OED sb*[1] 2a) is also invoked by 'shrinking'.

8.27–31 *turn the wheel . . . unripe birth*] The consequences of the oppression of women are passed
on down the generations: sex within a loveless marriage produces children who are corrupted
by that lovelessness, and who in turn pass on its brutal and oppressive ethos. The shift of
pronouns ('her womb . . . he hates') implies that the whole cycle of behaviour is oppressive to
men as well as women.

8.27 *wake her womb*] Michael Mason notes that in the sexual physiology of Blake's time the
whole reproductive apparatus of a woman was thought to participate in arousal and orgasm
(*Blake*. The Oxford Authors (1988), 551).

Or does the fly rejoice because the harvest is brought in?
Does not the eagle scorn the earth and despise the treasures beneath?
40 But the mole knoweth what is there, and the worm shall tell it thee.
Does not the worm erect a pillar in the mouldering churchyard,

[Plate 9]

And a palace of eternity in the jaws of the hungry grave?
Over his porch these words are written: "Take thy bliss, O Man!
And sweet shall be thy taste, and sweet thy infant joys renew!"

Infancy, fearless, lustful, happy; nestling for delight
5 In laps of pleasure! Innocence, honest, open, seeking
The vigorous joys of morning light, open to virgin bliss,
Who taught thee modesty, subtle modesty, child of night
    and sleep?
When thou awakest, wilt thou dissemble all thy secret joys?
Or wert thou not awake when all this mystery was disclosed?
10 Then com'st thou forth a modest virgin, knowing to dissemble,
With nets found under thy night pillow, to catch virgin joy
And brand it with the name of whore, and sell it in the night,
In silence, ev'n without a whisper, and in seeming sleep;
Religious dreams and holy vespers light thy smoky fires.
15 Once were thy fires lighted by the eyes of honest morn.

8.39–40 *eagle . . . mole*] Cf. Thel's motto: 'Does the eagle know what is in the pit? / Or wilt thou go ask the mole?'. Blake may have remembered Locke: 'the blindness of a mole is [not] an argument against the quicksightedness of the eagle' (*Essay*, 4.3.23. Locke's example in context does not, as might appear, support Blake's argument: Locke is discussing the 'want of simple ideas that other creatures in other parts of the universe may have').

8.41–9.1 *Does not . . . grave*] These lines are repeated with minor variations in *The Four Zoas* (108.11–12), but adapted to a quite different purpose.

Plate 8 design. Between lines 32 and 33 a narrow vignette shows a woman (perhaps Oothoon) seen from behind, lying at full length, with her head against a pillow and her lower body covered by a long dress or sheet. The design can be connected both with the preceding lines and with 9.10–11.

9.2–3 *Take . . . renew*] Cf. 4.9–10.

9.10 *modest . . . dissemble*] Cf. 'The Angel', *Songs of Experience*.

9.12 *sell . . . night*] Referring to prostitution which, as in *The Marriage of Heaven and Hell*, Blake connects (line 14) with Christian views of marriage and chastity. ('Prisons are built with stones of Law, brothels with bricks of Religion', *Marriage*, plate 8 (21).)

Plate 9 design. Below the text, to the left, Theotormon sits on a cloud, flagellating himself with a three-tailed whip in his left hand; his right arm over his head pulls his head back from the forehead in a frenzied gesture. To the right Oothoon strides away from him with her head bent in her hands. Both are naked.

And does my Theotormon seek this hypocrite modesty,
This knowing, artful, secret, fearful, cautious, trembling hypocrite?
Then is Oothoon a whore indeed, and all the virgin joys
Of life are harlots; and Theotormon is a sick man's dream,
20   And Oothoon is the crafty slave of selfish holiness.

But Oothoon is not so, a virgin filled with virgin fancies,
Open to joy and to delight wherever beauty appears.
If in the morning sun I find it, there my eyes are fixed

[Plate 10]

In happy copulation; if in evening mild, wearied with work,
Sit on a bank and draw the pleasures of this free-born joy.

The moment of desire! The moment of desire! The virgin
That pines for man shall awaken her womb to enormous joys
5   In the secret shadows of her chamber; the youth shut up from
The lustful joy shall forget to generate and create an
    amorous image
In the shadows of his curtains and in the folds of his silent pillow.
Are not these the places of religion, the rewards of continence,
The self-enjoyings of self-denial? Why dost thou seek religion?
10   Is it because acts are not lovely that thou seekest solitude,
Where the horrible darkness is impressèd with reflections of
    desire?

Father of Jealousy, be thou accursèd from the earth!
Why hast thou taught my Theotormon this accursèd thing,
Till beauty fades from off my shoulders, darkened and cast out,
15   A solitary shadow wailing on the margin of non-entity?

10.1 *copulation*] True visual pleasure can be an erotic sensation, and a form of union between subject and object.

10.3–7 *virgin . . . pillow*] Referring to female and male masturbation.

10.9 *thou*] Theotormon, but the sudden shift of addressee also has the effect of a direct appeal to the reader.

10.12 *Father of Jealousy*] Urizen. Cf. 'Earth's Answer', line 7 note: this title connects him with the God of the Pentateuch (and cf. 8.4 note).

10.15 *solitary shadow . . . non-entity*] Cf. the fate of Urizen's emanation, Ahania, both in *The Book of Ahania* ('I weep on the verge / Of non-entity' [5.53–4]) and in *The Four Zoas* (36.17). Both women attempt to express a sense of unreality and near-dissolution of the personality consequent on the non-fulfilment of love and desire.   *margin*] brink.

I cry, "Love! Love! Love! Happy, happy Love! Free as the
   mountain wind!"
Can that be Love that drinks another as a sponge drinks water,
That clouds with jealousy his nights, with weepings all the day,
To spin a web of age around him, grey and hoary, dark,
20 Till his eyes sicken at the fruit that hangs before his sight?
Such is self-love that envies all, a creeping skeleton
With lamplike eyes, watching around the frozen marriage bed.

But silken nets and traps of adamant will Oothoon spread,
And catch for thee girls of mild silver or of furious gold.
25 I'll lie beside thee on a bank and view their wanton play
In lovely copulation, bliss on bliss with Theotormon.
Red as the rosy morning, lustful as the first-born beam,
Oothoon shall view his dear delight, nor e'er with jealous cloud
Come in the heaven of generous love, nor selfish blightings
   bring.

30   Does the sun walk in glorious raiment on the secret floor

---

10.23 *nets and traps*] Cf. 8.18 note. That Oothoon also proposes to use nets and traps may bring into doubt what Blake has usually otherwise been understood to present as an ideal vision of freedom in love. Blake perhaps intended to show Oothoon reacting against Theotormon's failure to free himself from the values which threaten to destroy their love by going to the opposite extreme. As the Proverbs of Hell have it, 'You never know what is enough unless you know what is more than enough', and 'Enough! or too much' (*Marriage*, plate 9 (46), plate 10 (69)).

10.24–6 *catch . . . Theotormon*] An element of supposed voyeurism in this libertarian ideal has sometimes attracted adverse comment. It has also been argued that some closeness to a passage from Erasmus Darwin's 'The Loves of the Plants' (1791) – Part 2 of *The Botanic Garden*, Part 1 of which, 'The Economy of Vegetation', contains illustrations engraved by Blake – suggests that Blake may have thought of this libertarian ideal as modelled on natural processes. But the resemblance is slight: in Darwin's account of sexual reproduction in plants Venus catches lovers in a 'silken net' (4.405; but cf. 'Song' ['How sweet I roamed'], line 11). Blake's later articulations of a comparable view of multiple sexual relationships are apparently modelled on the actions of Old Testament patriarchs: see *Milton*, 32.17–18 and *Jerusalem*, 69.15 (in both a woman 'give[s] her maiden[s] to her husband'), and cf. Genesis, 16.2 (Abram, Sarai, and her maid, Hagar) and 30.4 (Jacob, Rachel, and her maid, Bilhah). In 1826 Blake told Crabb Robinson that the Bible advocated polygamy (Bentley, *Blake Records* (1969), 332).

Plate 10 design. Above the text three Daughters of Albion (with a fourth, much smaller, to the left) sit huddled together, two in slumped postures, one with her head raised and hair flying in the wind looking up and out of the picture. Blake colour-printed a separate copy of this design, without its poetic text, with the inscription 'Wait sisters, though all is lost' (*A Small Book of Designs* [second copy, 1796], Butlin, *Paintings and Drawings*, 261.7).

[Plate 11]

Where the cold miser spreads his gold? Or does the bright
   cloud drop
On his stone threshold? Does his eye behold the beam that brings
Expansion to the eye of pity? Or will he bind himself
Beside the ox to thy hard furrow? Does not that mild beam blot
5   The bat, the owl, the glowing tiger, and the king of night?
The sea-fowl takes the wintry blast for a cov'ring to her limbs,
And the wild snake the pestilence to adorn him with gems
   and gold.
And trees, and birds, and beasts, and men behold their eternal joy.
Arise you little glancing wings, and sing your infant joy!
10   Arise and drink your bliss. For every thing that lives is holy!'

Thus every morning wails Oothoon. But Theotormon sits
Upon the margined ocean conversing with shadows dire.

The Daughters of Albion hear her woes and echo back her sighs.

The End

11.9 *glancing*] darting.   *wings*] a synecdochism: 'birds'.

11.10 *every thing . . . holy*] A line repeated from *Marriage* ('A Song of Liberty'), and also used in *America* (10.13) and *The Four Zoas* (p. 34, which incorporates the rest of lines 9–10).

11.12 *margined*] bordered (by the sea shore).

Plate 11 design. Below the text three Daughters of Albion sit by the sea shore. Two cling to one another and look upwards, one has her head sunk in her knees, Oothoon, her arms spread wide and supported by a wreath of flame, floats above them with her face directed outwards to the reader.

AMERICA: A PROPHECY

Blake wrote four primarily political poems, *The French Revolution* (1791), *America* (1793), *Europe* (1794), and *The Song of Los* (1795). *The French Revolution* is an uncharacteristic work. Blake's only mature poem in letterpress, it is without designs; and it does not, as the later works do, combine history with myth. The three engraved poems are thoroughly characteristic. They increasingly subsume history into myth, and they constitute a single connected narrative. The light of social transformation, temporarily arrested in *America*, in *Europe* is passed to France. *The Song of Los* is in two sections which frame the other two works. 'Asia' (its second section) projects the narrative of world history into an ideal future. 'Africa' (its first section) epitomizes the spiritual history of the world up to the American Revolution – which is thus presented as marking a fundamental reversal in world history. This history is one of spiritual decay, the shrinking of humanity under the influence of its major philosophies and religions, particularly Judaic legalism, Greek abstraction, Christian passivity (as Blake here exceptionally represents it) and the militarism of Norse myth. This gradual loss of contact with the eternal reaches an epitome in the philosophy of Locke and its consequences in Newton which precipitate reversal – the emergence of Orc with which *America* begins.

Though Blake's illuminated works are often described as 'prophetic books', Blake himself described only *America* and *Europe* as 'prophecies'. He explained his meaning in doing so in an annotation of 1798 to Bishop Richard Watson's *Apology for the Bible*: 'Prophets in the modern sense of the word have never existed. Jonah was no prophet in the modern sense, for his prophecy of Nineveh failed. Every honest man is a prophet; he utters his opinion both of private and public matters. Thus: if you go on so, the result is so. He never says, "Such a thing shall happen, let you do what you will." A prophet is a seer, not an arbitrary dictator.' (Marginalia to Watson; Bentley, *Writings*, 1417–18.) *America* is a prophecy in the sense implied by this annotation: it is not a poetic account of the American Revolution or War of Independence (1776–83); it attempts to trace, using some of the particulars of that war, the ideal form of the issues implicit in it. Blake accepts the distinction of Aristotle's theory (*Poetics*, 9) and Shakespeare's practice between the historian and the poet, the historian tied to the uniqueness of fact, the poet shaping the unique into the typical. As Blake expressed it (describing one of the pictures from his one public exhibition of 1809), 'Mr B. has done as all the ancients did, and as all the moderns who are worthy of fame: given the historical fact in its poetical vigour so as it always happens' (*A Descriptive Catalogue*, V; Bentley, *Writings*, 851). Blake's concern is not with the contingencies of a particular corporeal war but with the permanent form of the spiritual conflicts of which that war was a shadow. As he expressed in the same 1809 account of his own work: 'his opinion who does not see spiritual agency is not worth any man's reading' (*A Descriptive Catalogue*, V; Bentley, *Writings*, 852).

Blake's method of eliciting the action of spiritual agency is to mix history and myth: the preludium to *America* pitches events entirely at a mythic level, and in the body of the work Blake moves between myth and history, arranging history to suit his sense of the distinction between what is permanent and what is adventitious, which means adjusting historical detail as necessary. It is interesting to observe the partial ways in which *America* is rooted in the actual, but criticism which attempts uniformly to read Blake's myths as covert historical allegory inverts the method of his work.[1] A clear distinction between the actual and the ideal in *America* may, moreover, be a false one if we imagine the point of view of Blake's contemporary reader. Some of the work falls clearly into the categories of actual or ideal history (any reader would recognize Washington as actual, the claim that 'the doors of marriage are open' [17.19] as ideal), but a certain amount does not. Especially in a period of difficult communications and considerable government control of information, facts on sensitive issues – the rate of desertions by troops in a war situation (17.4–5), or the extent of civil disturbance of an anti-government nature under reactionary monarchies (18.16–18) – will often be sparse. Where much of *America*'s material was to be placed on a spectrum from the actual to the ideal, Blake cannot have expected to be clear to his first readers.[2]

In attempting to trace spiritual agency Blake also presents contemporary events in terms partly suggested by biblical analogies. These heighten the poetry's imaginative resonance. They also often carry particular significances, either by their transformation of their sources or by their unusual interpretations of them. In *The Marriage of Heaven and Hell* Blake described himself as writing a 'Bible of Hell' (plate 24) which turned on its head usual understandings of the sacred text.[3] The reader of *Marriage* will readily understand why Orc can be associated with both Christ and Satan, why Albion's Angel should be associated with the Old Testament Jehovah. Blake's wider biblical references are of a piece with these central reinterpretations.

America is unusual among Blake's works of this type in that some workshop materials are extant, three (perhaps four) cancelled plates which were not printed as part of any surviving copy (Bentley, *Writings*, 152–3, 156–61). Two of these are earlier versions of plates 5 and 6; the third may have been intended to follow plate 6

---

[1] This is too much the method of David Erdman's *Prophet Against Empire*. The accurate basis of Erdman's work is that Blake is a socially conscious writer who needs to be understood partly in terms of his social context, of which Erdman gives a full and vivid account. But he too much presents Blake as writing covert allegory of actual people and events and so makes him seem a more obscure writer than he was. See notes to 13.3, 17.16 and 17.19. Detail about the people and events Blake refers to can be found in Lillian B. Miller, *'The Dye Is Now Cast': The Road to American Independence, 1774–1776* (Smithsonian Institution, Washington, DC, 1975).

[2] How Blake would know about the historical figures he names in *America*, and what he and contemporary readers might know about them, can be discovered from Solomon Lutnick, *The American Revolution and the British Press 1775–83* (Columbia, MO, 1967).

[3] Cf. 'The Everlasting Gospel', part e (below, pp. 352–3). On how Blake might have done that in *America*, see Leslie Tannenbaum, *Biblical Tradition in Blake's Early Prophecies* (1982), chapter 5. (In his invocations of the Song of Solomon and the Apocryphal books of Ezra in relation to *America* Tannenbaum arguably employs an unduly free notion of allusion.)

or plate 10; the fourth is a colour-printed design (with text covered by pigment) usually known as 'A Dream of Thiralatha', which can be only tentatively assigned to *America*. *America* is also the one of Blake's illuminated books from which a fragment of the original engraved copper plate survives, a small portion of cancelled plate a (Bentley, *Writings*, 154–5) which has been of importance in reconstructing Blake's methods of producing his illuminated books.[4] Most of the fourteen extant copies were printed as monochrome relief-etchings and were left uncoloured. The four extant coloured copies (A, K, M, and O) are very richly tinted, and are among the most visually beautiful of Blake's early productions.[5]

---

[4] The now generally accepted account of Blake's engraving and reproductive processes is that of Joseph Viscomi, *Blake and the Idea of the Book* (1993).

[5] The Tate/Princeton edition of the collected Illuminated Books (vol. 4, ed. Detlef Dörrbecker, 1995) reproduces a monochrome copy. Coloured copies have been reproduced in the Blake Electronic Archive (Copy A), in the Blake Trust/Trianon Press series of facsimiles (Copy M), ed. Geoffrey Keynes (1963) (see the bibliography for full details of each of these), and by Dover Books (Copy M; 1983).

4. *America: a Prophecy*, Frontispiece

(Copyright the British Museum, Department of Print and Drawings; original size: 17 × 23.5 cms)

Frontispiece [Plate 1]

Title-page [Plate 2]

America: a Prophecy

Lambeth. Printed by William Blake in the year 1793.

Preludium [Plate 3]

The shadowy daughter of Urthona stood before red Orc,
When fourteen suns had faintly journeyed o'er his dark abode.

Frontispiece Design. (*Plate 4*). Below a dark cloudy sky, to the left a colossal naked winged figure (Orc?) with copious curly hair sits by a breach in a massive stone wall. His face is buried between his knees and his wrists are shackled by his sides. In front of him lie the barrel of a cannon and the hilt of a sword. To the right, in front of the wall, on one of its fallen blocks, sits a haggard-looking woman with one child in her lap and one standing beside her with its head bowed into her lap. All three are naked. See Introduction (2), pp. 15–16.

Title-page. Design. In the upper part of the plate, below 'America' and above 'Prophecy', in a cloud, to the left sits a woman facing left and peering into a book. A boy standing in front of her also gazes into the book; a girl sitting behind her leans against her back and points down to the title word, 'Prophecy'. To the right sits a man in a huddled posture absorbed in reading. In front of him a naked woman leaps upwards in a posture suggesting flight; a naked standing figure leans against his back and points up to the title word, 'America'. In the lower part of the plate, under rain falling from the cloud surrounding the title, a woman kneels over the naked body of a man whom she kisses. He grips the hand of another corpse lying beneath his legs, chest downwards, head towards the viewer (and has perhaps another similarly positioned corpse under his upper body). The frontispiece and title-page adapt motifs from Blake's watercolour of 1784, 'A Breach in a City, the Morning after a Battle'.

3 *Preludium*] This title was printed from a small separate plate and does not appear in all copies.

3.1 *Urthona*] Later a central figure of Blake's myth, one of the four zoas or living creatures which are the basis of Blake's account of being, here Urthona is simply the father of the 'nameless female' and Orc's gaoler. The name is often taken as playing on 'earth-owner'. Blake's myth was only beginning to take characteristic shape in the works of the early 1790s, and it is a mistake to interpret figures in his early poetry in the supposed light of their later development.

3.1 *red*] Cf. 3.11 note.

3.1 *Orc*] In Blake's myth Orc is associated with revolution and with sexual desire. The name comes principally from Latin 'orcus', hell (considered, as in *Marriage*, as a place of healthy opposition to oppressive or lifeless conventions): cf. *Tiriel*, 215, 'as dark as vacant Orcus'. Since Orc is here associated with the whale, and is seen by his opponents as monstrous, the obselete 'orc', 'applied . . . to more than one vaguely identified ferocious sea-monster' (*OED* 1), may also be relevant (the word is used by Milton, *Paradise Lost*, 11.835); as may 'orchil', a red dye.

3.2 *fourteen*] On the one occasion when Blake gives Orc's age as fourteen (perhaps the intended sense here) the significance is that he has arrived at puberty and so become a fully sexual being (*The Four Zoas*, 60.6). Various historical senses have also been given to the number:

His food she brought in iron baskets, his drink in cups of iron.
Crowned with a helmet and dark hair the nameless female stood.
5   A quiver with its burning stores, a bow like that of night
When pestilence is shot from heaven: no other arms she need.
Invulnerable though naked, save where clouds roll round her loins
Their awful folds in the dark air, silent she stood as night,
For never from her iron tongue could voice or sound arise,
10   But dumb till that dread day when Orc assayed his fierce embrace.

'Dark virgin', said the hairy youth, 'thy father stern, abhorred,
Rivets my tenfold chains, while still on high my spirit soars:
Sometimes an eagle screaming in the sky, sometimes a lion
Stalking upon the mountains, and sometimes a whale I lash
15   The raging fathomless abyss, anon a serpent folding
Around the pillars of Urthona, and round thy dark limbs,
On the Canadian wilds I fold, feeble my spirit folds,

Erdman refers it to the time which passed between Rousseau's *Social Contract* (1762), which challenged all earlier accounts of the legal bases of political power and so supplied something of the intellectual foundation of the American as of the French Revolution, and the Declaration of Independence (1776) with which the American Revolution proper began (*Prophet Against Empire*, 258–9). It would be not untypical of Blake to combine a psychological and an historical sense; but see headnote, note 1.

3.4 *nameless female*] The gaoler's daughter of folktale who helps the prisoner, at first almost against her will, later as a convert to his cause. She can be understood, in Blake's loose allegory, as the natural world, a world of unrealized potential (virginal) which both resists and can become the ally of human transformative power. Her iron implements suggest the last and worst of the 'ages' of classical myth (golden, silver, bronze and iron), the age of war, cruelty and oppression. (See also 3.17 note and 4.10.)

3.8–10 *silent . . . dumb*] Cf. the proverb of Hell, 'Where man is not Nature is barren' (*Marriage*, plate 10 (68)).

3.11 *hairy*] Perhaps with reference to the dispossessed Esau, whose name means 'hairy' and who, like Orc, is red: 'red all over like a hairy garment' (Genesis, 25.25). Esau's given name, 'Edom' (Genesis, 25.30), which comes from the red pottage for which he sells his birthright, and which passes to his descendants, means 'red', as the Authorized Version marginal gloss to Genesis, 25.30 explains.

3.13–15 *eagle . . . lion . . . whale . . . serpent*] Creatures of the four elements, air, earth, water and (for Blake) fire. The eagle, lion and whale are evidently to be regarded as the most powerful or exalted creatures of their particular element (cf. the eagle and lion in the symbolism of the Proverbs of Hell in *Marriage*). The serpent was associated as a symbol with the American Revolution: the thirteen states were depicted as serpent fragments – dangerous when united – and a serpent appeared on a revolutionary flag (the 'Rattlesnake Flag') the usual legend of which was 'Don't Tread on Me'.

3.17 *Canadian wilds*] Like Oothoon in *Visions* (4.3) the shadowy female is associated with America (4.10). Blake thinks of the whole North American land mass as a single political space: Canada did not in fact join the revolution, but (in Blake's view) it should have done.

For chained beneath I rend these caverns. When thou bringest food
I howl my joy, and my red eyes seek to behold thy face –
20 In vain! These clouds roll to and fro and hide thee from my sight.'

[Plate 4]

Silent as despairing love, and strong as jealousy,
The hairy shoulders rend the links, free are the wrists of fire:
Round the terrific loins he seized the panting struggling womb.
It joyed: she put aside her clouds and smilèd her first-born smile,
5 As when a black cloud shows its lightnings to the silent deep.

Soon as she saw the terrible boy then burst the virgin cry:

'I know thee, I have found thee, and I will not let thee go.
Thou art the image of God who dwells in darkness of Africa,
And thou art fall'n to give me life in regions of dark death.
10 On my American plains I feel the struggling afflictions
Endured by roots that writhe their arms into the nether deep.

Plate 3 design. Above the text lies Orc, like Prometheus, chained to the rock, naked and shackled at the wrists and ankles, his arms spread horizontally as though crucified and his legs spread apart. In front of him stand a naked woman whose gesture (hands clasped to her head) expresses grief, and a naked man whose gesture (hands raised above his head) expresses horror. Both look towards Orc. (Blake used this design again in *The Four Zoas* [p. 62], but in a different context where the figures each have a specific identity not relevant here, and in a separate plate of 1812, 'The Chaining of Orc'; cf. *The Book of Urizen*, 20.21–3.) The shackled Orc re-sembles the black slave in 'the Execution of Breaking on the Rack' which Blake had recently engraved for John Gabriel Stedman's *Surinam* (see *Visions*, headnote). Cf. also *The Book of Urizen*, 20.23 note. A thick tree trunk to the left extends largely barren branches over all three figures. The roots of this tree extend down the left margin; below them sits a naked man with an expression that suggests dejection, his chin on his knees and arms round his legs. Underneath the text is a serpent, the body of which is curled in six loops.

4.1–2] These lines are repeated (still in relation to Orc) in *The Four Zoas*, 91.13, 17.

4.3–4 *he seized . . . It joyed*] Cf. *Visions*, 8.27 and note.

4.4 *smilèd*] On Blake's distinction between syllabic 'ed' and non-syllabic ''d' see Introduction (3), pp. 25–6.

4.7 *I have . . . thee go*] Cf. Song of Solomon, 3.4: 'I found him whom my soul loveth: I held him, and would not let him go.'

4.8 *Thou art . . . Africa*] Orc epitomizes what Blake saw as the divine potential in all human beings. In American terms to associate him with Africa is to connect him with black slaves, whom Blake would evidently see as a potentially revolutionary force (cf. plate 3 design note). He may have known that slaves who served in the revolutionary army were manumitted on enlistment or promised their freedom after the war, and that the army was, in some regi-ments, the first in modern times to be racially integrated. In *The Book of Urizen* Africa is iden-tified with Egypt, the Old Testament land of slavery and symbolically the state of fallen life which is a prelude to the spiritual Exodus or redemption.

> I see a serpent in Canada who courts me to his love;
> In Mexico an eagle, and a lion in Peru;
> I see a whale in the South Sea, drinking my soul away.
> 15   O, what limb-rending pains I feel! Thy fire and my frost
> Mingle in howling pains, in furrows by thy lightnings rent.
> This is eternal death, and this the torment long foretold.'

[Plate 5]

A Prophecy

> The Guardian Prince of Albion burns in his nightly tent.
> Sullen fires across the Atlantic glow to America's shore,
> Piercing the souls of warlike men, who rise in silent night.
> Washington, Franklin, Paine and Warren, Gates, Hancock and
> Greene
> 5   Meet on the coast glowing with blood from Albion's fiery Prince.

4.17 *the torment long foretold*] That is, the pains of childbearing foretold to Eve, Genesis, 3.16. The nameless female identifies her experience of radical transformation as like both death and birth.

4.17] Followed by four lines (below the design) which were masked in printing (or in one copy erased) in all but four copies, three of which are probably posthumous.

> The stern bard ceased, ashamed of his own song; enraged he swung
> His harp aloft sounding, then dashed its shining frame against
> A ruined pillar in glitt'ring fragments; silent he turned away,
> And wandered down the vales of Kent in sick and drear lamentings.

Blake regularly cancelled this apparent recantation.

Plate 4 design. Below the text a naked muscular youth (Orc) with flame-like hair forces his way upwards out of the earth (freeing himself from Urthona). Rising up the left margin grows a sapling round which a vine loops and then spirals to the top of the margin.

5.1] Repeated as the final line of 'Africa', the second part (after 'Asia') of *The Song of Los*, and so a link between Blake's poems on the four principal continents. On the link to *Europe* see 18.14 note. The first stage of *America*'s narrative (extending to plate 13) begins here: a confrontation between Orc and Albion's Angel.

5.1 *Prince of Albion*] Historically this is George III, who is mentioned by name in a cancelled plate (b.9; Bentley, *Writings*, 157); though see 6.12, where 'the King of England' is mentioned as a separate character. For 'Albion' cf. *Visions*, title, note.

5.4 *Washington . . . Greene*] George Washington (1732–99), principal military commander of the colonial forces during the Revolution and first President of the United States (1789; elected for a second term 1792–93, while Blake was writing *America*). Benjamin Franklin (1706–90), scientist, early advocate of the abolition of slavery, drafter and signatory of the Declaration of Independence, diplomat in London during the 1760s and in Paris from 1777 where he negotiated funds from, and a treaty with, France central to American success in the war. Tom Paine (1737–1809), a journalist and political writer whom Blake may have known personally; his *Common Sense* (1775) was the most important political pamphlet of the Revolution (Blake described it as a work which overthrew armies [Bentley, *Writings*, 1417]); his *The Rights of Man* (1791, published by Joseph Johnson [see *Visions*, headnote]) is the best-known of the various

Washington spoke: 'Friends of America, look over the Atlantic sea.
A bended bow is lifted in heaven, and a heavy iron chain
Descends link by link from Albion's cliffs across the sea to bind
Brothers and sons of America, till our faces pale and yellow,
10   Heads depressed, voices weak, eyes downcast, hands work-bruised,
Feet bleeding on the sultry sands, and the furrows of the whip
Descend to generations that in future times forget.'

The strong voice ceased, for a terrible blast swept over the heaving
   sea.
The eastern cloud rent: on his cliffs stood Albion's wrathful Prince.
15   A dragon form clashing his scales, at midnight he arose,
And flamed red meteors round the land of Albion beneath.
His voice, his locks, his awful shoulders, and his glowing eyes

[Plate 6]

Appear to the Americans upon the cloudy night.

Solemn heave the Atlantic waves between the gloomy nations,
Swelling, belching from its deeps red clouds and raging fires.
Albion is sick! America faints! Enraged the zenith grew.
5   As human blood shooting its veins all round the orbèd heaven
Red rose the clouds from the Atlantic in vast wheels of blood,
And in the red clouds rose a Wonder o'er the Atlantic sea:
Intense! Naked! A human fire fierce glowing, as the wedge

---

radical responses to Burke's *Reflections on the French Revolution* (1790). The remaining characters are of lesser importance. Joseph Warren (1741–75), associate of Samuel Adams (see 13.3 note) and one of the most important Patriot leaders in Massachusetts in the years leading to the Revolution, killed at Bunker Hill. Horatio Gates (1728–1806), adjutant general to Washington, who played an important role in the creation of the Continental (American) army and was its principal commander at Saratoga (1777), one of the most important battles of the war. John Hancock (1737–93), a central figure in Massachusetts political life and the first signatory of the Declaration of Independence. Nathanael Greene (1742–86), general in the Continental army and important associate of Washington, with a reputation as a military leader second only to him.

5.15 *A dragon form*] Cf. 9.5 note.

Plate 5 design. Above 'A Prophecy' (in huge capitals exuberantly decorated with swirls, plants and birds) a naked floating figure (Orc) rises, having broken his chains, fragments of which hang from his arms and legs. Between the first and second paragraphs a muscular naked flying man, his hair streaming forwards in the wind, blows a blast on a trumpet which shoots flames ahead of it and into the margin. The trumpet and context suggest an angel of the Apocalypse (Revelation, 8). At the lower left a naked man, woman and child run looking backwards towards flames behind them.

6.7 *a Wonder*] Orc.

Of iron heated in the furnace; his terrible limbs were fire
10   With myriads of cloudy terrors, banners dark and towers
Surrounded: heat but not light went through the murky
    atmosphere.

The King of England looking westward trembles at the vision.

[Plate 7]

Albion's Angel stood beside the Stone of Night and saw
The terror like a comet, or more like the planet red
That once enclosed the terrible wandering comets in its sphere.
Then, Mars, thou wast our centre, and the planets three flew round
5   Thy crimson disk: so ere the sun was rent from thy red sphere.

6.11 *heat . . . light*] As in *Paradise Lost*, where the flames of Hell give 'no light but rather darkness visible' (1.63). That Orc should be associated with Milton's Satan as well as with the Christ of the gospels (see 8.1–4 note) is consistent with Blake's against-the-grain reading of *Paradise Lost* (see *Marriage*, plate 6 and cf. 10.1 below).

Plate 6 design. The dragon form of Albion's Angel, with wings, human hands and a long curling tail, is shown flying towards the left between lines 1 and 2. His archetypal form, Urizen, plunges down the left margin; his extended left hand holds a sceptre, what may be the tablets of the Law, held under his right arm, protrude from behind his back, and his long robe billows behind him. These figures illustrate lines from cancelled plate b (following directly from 5.17): 'Reveal the dragon through the human, coursing swift as fire / To the close hall of council, where his angel form renews' (Bentley, *Writings* 156). Below the text a naked man clutching the sides of his head in his hands gazes to the left at a fallen tree trunk which Erdman (*Illuminated Blake* (1975), 142) sees as a beached sea monster (and so a form of Orc: cf. 3.14); to the right a crouching woman protectively embraces a standing child.

7.1 *Stone of Night*] Blake refers to the Stone of Night again in the closely related *Europe* (13.26; 14.1) where it is associated with ancient stone circles (which Blake connected with the Druids and so with religion degenerated into priestcraftly oppression), the human skull (symbolizing the closure of what should be open to perception of the infinite), and the Tablets of the Mosaic Law. Since Orc is arraigned as the 'trangressor of God's Law' (9.6), and explicitly opposes the Mosaic decalogue (10.3), this symbol of Albion's Angel's power is best associated here with the last of these, understood as a source of oppressive authority which implies a mistaken idea of God. Blake interpreted the Law not as fulfilled by Christ (as in Matthew, 5.17) but as abolished in him (as usually in the writings of Saint Paul: see, for example, 2 Corinthians 3 and Galatians 2–6). See 8.1–4 note on the association of Orc and Christ.

7.2 *comet*] Comets were traditionally regarded as heralding cataclysmic change and so were associated with war.

7.4–5 *Mars . . . disk*] This astronomical myth, in which three planets (Mercury, Venus and the Earth?) orbit Mars, is probably Blake's invention. Mars is traditionaly associated with war (cf. preceding note), though the association with Orc here may be taken as revaluing that. It would make Blakean sense of this enigmatic invention to understand the supposed prelapsarian position of the Orc-like red planet as suggesting the lost centrality of passional freedom which must now reassert itself by rebellion. (Other readings are suggested by R. and M. Baine, *English Language Notes*, 13 (1975–76) and Michael Ferber, *BIQ*, 15 (1981–82), who returns to the passage in *The Poetry of William Blake* (1991), 81–2.)

192

The spectre glowed, his horrid length staining the temple long
With beams of blood; and thus a voice came forth, and shook
    the temple:

[Plate 8]

'The morning comes, the night decays, the watchmen leave
    their stations;
The grave is burst, the spices shed, the linen wrappèd up;
The bones of death, the cov'ring clay, the sinews shrunk
    and dried,
Reviving shake, inspiring move, breathing, awakening,
Spring like redeemèd captives when their bonds and bars
5   are burst!
Let the slave grinding at the mill run out into the field;
Let him look up into the heavens and laugh in the bright air;
Let the enchainèd soul shut up in darkness and in sighing,
Whose face has never seen a smile in thirty weary years,
Rise and look out: his chains are loose, his dungeon doors are
10   open.
And let his wife and children return from the oppressor's scourge;
They look behind at every step and believe it is a dream,
Singing, "The sun has left his blackness, and has found a fresher
    morning,

Plate 7 design. A Judgement scene. Above the text, to the right a flying figure holds a flaming sword; to the left a flying figure holds a pair of balances, one scale of which drops downwards (raising the other accordingly); between them a figure stands on a bank of clouds holding another imprisoned on his shoulders. (The sword and balance – power and judgement – are traditional symbols of justice.) Below the text, in flames, one figure plummets down the left margin beneath the scales; in the centre a figure tumbles upside-down in a circle created by a hissing serpent (cf. 3.15) the coils of whose tail descend in decreasing loops beneath the figure. While this may be no more than an effect of imperfect foreshortening, some critics take this central lower figure to be decapitated, in which case the design connects the American Revolution with the French (cf. 18.15).

8.1–4] Orc announces a resurrection which is described in terms based on that of Christ: for the spices, see Mark, 16.1; Luke, 23.56–24.1; and John, 19.39–40; for the watchmen, see Matthew, 27.66; and for the linen, see Luke, 24.12 and John, 20.6–7. Blake also alludes to what is in a Christian reading the principal adumbration of Christ's resurrection in the Old Testament, God's bringing to life of the dry bones in Ezekiel, 37.1–10.

8.4 *inspiring*] breathing in a divine influence.

8.6 *slave . . . mill*] Blake's phraseology is both biblical and Miltonic: cf. Judges, 16.21 (Samson 'did grind in the prison house'); Matthew, 24.41 ('two women shall be grinding at the mill: the one shall be taken, and the other left'); and *Samson Agonistes*, line 41 ('Eyeless in Gaza at the mill with slaves').

8.6–14] Repeated in *The Four Zoas*, 134.18–24, 138.20–21.

And the fair moon rejoices in the clear and cloudless night:
15   For Empire is no more, and now the Lion and Wolf shall cease".'

[Plate 9]

In thunders ends the voice. Then Albion's Angel wrathful burnt
Beside the Stone of Night; and like the eternal Lion's howl
In famine and war replied, 'Art thou not Orc, who,
   serpent-formed,
Stands at the gate of Enitharmon to devour her children?
5   Blasphemous demon, Antichrist, hater of dignities,
Lover of wild rebellion, and trangressor of God's Law:
Why dost thou come to angels' eyes in this terrific form?'

8.15] Repeated from 'A Song of Liberty', v. 20 (*Marriage*, plate 26).

Plate 8 design. Above the text a naked man sits looking upwards above what a skull lying beside him suggests is a grave. Below the text is a thistle with a newt, frog and small serpent playing around it. The design above the text is varied from that of *Marriage*, plate 21, and was re-used above that of *America*, plate 14, in Blake's designs for Blair's *The Grave*, 1808 (as a resurrection figure in the design 'Death's Door').

9.4 *Stands . . . children*] Cf. Revelation, 12.1–4: 'And there appeared a great wonder in heaven; a woman clothed with the sun, and the moon under her feet, and upon her head a crown of twelve stars: And she being with child cried, travailing in birth, and pained to be delivered. And there appeared another wonder in heaven; and behold a great red dragon, having seven heads and ten horns . . . and the dragon stood before the woman which was ready to be delivered, for to devour her child as soon as it was born.' The dragon is Satan; the woman clothed with the sun gives birth to 'a man child who was to rule all nations', that is, Christ. Albion's Angel sees Orc in terms opposite to those suggested by the rest of the work.   *gate*] The birth channel.   *Enitharmon*] The emanation of Los, and a central figure in *Europe* (1794); this is her only mention in *America*.

9.5 *Antichrist*] The Dragon of Revelation, Satan. The term itself comes from the letters of John (1 John, 2.18, 22 and 2 John, 7). The Antichrist was a central figure in the mythology of radical Protestantism, and was identified with various corrupt political and spiritual-cumtemporal powers, especially the Papacy. Albion's Angel takes the form of the dragon himself (5.15) but adopts the myths about it in relation to his opponents.

9.7 *Why . . . form*] Contrast what is shown by the design, and cf. *Marriage*, plates 17–20, with its central idea, 'All that we saw was owing to your metaphysics' (the metaphysics of the angel, who sees what appears to the devil as tranquil beauty as though it were a scene of horror). Cf. *Visions*, 5.35 note.

Plate 9 design (*Plate 5*). Below the text a ram lies asleep. The head and shoulders of a sleeping boy are visible resting across the ram's back and his feet appear by the ram's head; a naked androgynous figure, seen from behind, lies asleep in the foreground (in some copies beside a stream). Up the left margin and above the text grows a delicate tree in which are perched two birds of paradise and a smaller crested bird. A bird and a butterfly fly upwards to the right; to the left catkins hang from the tree's thin boughs. In coloured copies the whole design is irradiated by a sunrise.

5. *America: a Prophecy*, Plate 9

(Yale Center for British Art, Paul Mellon Collection; original size: 16.5 × 23.2 cms)

[Plate 10]

The terror answered: 'I am Orc, wreathed round the accursèd tree:
The times are ended; shadows pass; the morning 'gins to break:
The fiery joy that Urizen perverted to ten commands,
What night he led the starry host through the wide wilderness,
5   That stony law I stamp to dust, and scatter religion abroad
To the four winds as a torn book, and none shall gather the leaves,
But they shall rot on desert sands, and consume in bottomless deeps,
To make the deserts blossom, and the deeps shrink to their fountains,
And to renew the fiery joy, and burst the stony roof;
10 That pale religious lechery, seeking virginity,
May find it in a harlot, and in coarse-clad honesty
The undefiled, though ravished in her cradle night and morn:
For every thing that lives is holy, life delights in life,
Because the soul of sweet delight can never be defiled.

10.1 *the accursèd tree*] The tree of the knowledge of good and evil: Genesis, 2.17. The rhetoric and frame of reference of Orc's apocalyptic proclamation is elaborately biblical. On Orc as Satan cf. 6.11 note.

10.2 *The times are ended*] Orc announces the Last Judgement. Like other Christian myths Blake understood this as having symbolic meanings: 'Whenever any individual rejects error and embraces truth a Last Judgement passes upon that individual' (Bentley, *Writings*, 1021–2). Orc announces the social equivalent of such an individual transformation.

10.3 *Urizen*] See *Visions*, 8.3 note.   *ten commands*] The Mosaic decalogue of Exodus, 20.1–17.

10.4 *What night*] When; a Latinism which Blake would know from Milton (*Lycidas*, 28; *Paradise Lost*, 1.36).

10.4 *he led . . . wilderness*] Referring to the journey of the Israelites, led by Jehovah in a pillar of cloud by day and a pillar of fire by night, from the slavery of Egypt to the freedom of the Promised Land. The biblical account of this journey begins at Exodus, 13.20. The Exodus was one of the most important events of Old Testament history. In Christian typology it came to symbolize both physical and spiritual transitions from oppression to freedom.

10.5 *stony . . . dust*] Cf. *Marriage*, 'A Song of Liberty', 20.

10.8 *the deserts . . . fountains*] Isaiah, 35.1: 'the desert shall rejoice and blossom as the rose'; and the thought (though not the phraseology) of the apocalyptic transformation of Revelation, 21.1: 'and there was no more sea'. Though there are no specific allusions in *America* to Isaiah 34, Blake may also have expected the reader to recall throughout its images of 'the day of the Lord's vengeance'. (Isaiah 34 and 35 are cited as of particular importance in *Marriage*, plate 3.)

10.9 *stony roof*] The skull.

10.10–12 *pale . . . morn*] Cf. *Visions*, 9.4–13 and *Marriage*, 'A Song of Liberty', chorus.

10.13 *For . . . holy*] Cf. *Visions*, 11.10 and note.

10.14] Cf. Proverbs of Hell, *Marriage*, plate 9 (53).

15   Fires enwrap the earthly globe, yet man is not consumed:
      Amidst the lustful fires he walks: his feet become like brass,
      His knees and thighs like silver, and his breast and head like gold.'

[Plate 11]

    'Sound, sound, my loud war-trumpets, and alarm my thirteen
        Angels!
    Loud howls the eternal Wolf! The eternal Lion lashes his tail!
    America is dark'nèd, and my punishing demons terrified
    Crouch howling before their caverns deep like skins dried in the
      wind.
5   They cannot smite the wheat, nor quench the fatness of the earth,
    They cannot smite with sorrows, nor subdue the plough and spade.
    They cannot wall the city, nor moat round the castle of princes.
    They cannot bring the stubbèd oak to overgrow the hills,
    For terrible men stand on the shores, and in their robes I see
    Children take shelter from the lightnings. There stands
10   Washington,
    And Paine and Warren, with their foreheads reared toward the east;
    But clouds obscure my agèd sight. A vision from afar!
    Sound, sound, my loud war-trumpets, and alarm my thirteen
        Angels:
    A vision from afar! Ah, rebel form that rent the ancient

10.15 *Fires . . . not consumed*] Cf. Daniel, 3.25–27, where the furnace intended to inflict a death sentence fails to consume the divinely protected companions of Daniel.

10.16–17 *his feet . . . gold*] Cf. Daniel 2.32 (Daniel describes to Nebuchadnezzar a figure the king saw in his dream): 'This image's head was of fine gold, his breast and his arms of silver, his belly and his thighs of brass'. This image also has legs of iron and feet of iron and clay: Orc cuts out what proves to be its fatal weakness, claiming that participation in Orcish flames has a quasi-alchemical purifying effect on mankind.

Plate 10 design. Above the text an old man, bearded and wearing a long gown (Urizen), sits in a cloud; his arms are spread in a gesture which suggests he is pressing downwards. Below the text billow waves of a stormy sea. See Introduction (2), pp. 16–17.

11.1 *Sound . . . Angels*] Albion's Angel speaks: this call to arms punctuates his speech (lines 13, 21 and 26). When he refers to the colonies as 'angels' he separates them morally and politically from Orc as he sees him. When they are called angels in the narrative (12.11 and elsewhere) no such separation is implied because the narrative does not accept Albion's Angel's view of Orc.

11.1 *thirteen*] The number of colonies under British rule which, after the Revolution, made up the United States.

11.2 *Loud . . . tail*] Repeated at line 27; for the wolf and lion cf. 8.15.

11.8 *stubbèd*] pollarded (*OED ppl.a.* 1a, citing this example).   *oak*] For the manufacture of warships.

15 Heavens, eternal Viper self-renewed, rolling in clouds,
    I see thee in thick clouds and darkness on America's shore
    Writhing in pangs of abhorrèd birth: red flames the crest rebellious
    And eyes of death; the harlot womb oft openèd in vain
    Heaves in enormous circles. Now the times are returned upon thee,
20 Devourer of thy parent. Now thy unutterable torment renews.
    Sound, sound, my loud war-trumpets, and alarm my thirteen Angels:
    Ah, terrible birth! A young one bursting! Where is the weeping
        mouth?
    And where the mother's milk? Instead those ever-hissing jaws
    And parchèd lips drop with fresh gore. Now roll thou in the clouds;
25 Thy mother lays her length outstretched upon the shore beneath.
    Sound, sound, my loud war-trumpets, and alarm my thirteen Angels:
    Loud howls the eternal Wolf! The eternal Lion lashes his tail!'

[Plate 12]

Thus wept the Angel voice, and as he wept the terrible blasts
Of trumpets blew a loud alarm across the Atlantic deep;
No trumpets answer; no reply of clarions or of fifes;
Silent the colonies remain and refuse the loud alarm.

5 On those vast shady hills between America and Albion's shore,
   Now barred out by the Atlantic sea (called Atlantean hills
   Because from their bright summits you may pass to the Golden
       World),

11.15 *self-renewed*] The serpent, 'from its annually renewing its external skin has from great antiquity, even as early as the fable of Prometheus, been esteemed an emblem of renovated youth' (Erasmus Darwin, *The Botanic Garden*, 2 vols. (London, 1789–91), additional notes, XXII (The Portland Vase), 55–6; on Blake and Darwin cf. *Visions*, 10.24–6 note). On Orc and Prometheus cf. plate 3 design note.

11.20 *Devourer . . . parent*] This can be given a political and a metaphysical sense: politically Britain is the 'parent' of the rebellious American colonies which are attacking her; metaphysically Orc is born into time and space but destroys them by giving access to the infinite.

Plate 11 design. Below the text a baby lies in a field of wheat apparently driven flat by a storm (see line 5) the effect of which is to make it bend protectively over the baby. Some critics see the baby as asleep ('the new-born . . . Orc' [Swinburne]); others – comparing *Songs of Experience*, 'Holy Thursday', and *Europe*, plate 9 – see it as dead. On each side of the baby grows a wild flower.

12.6–8 *Atlantean hills . . . emperies*] Blake draws here on a myth originating from Plato's *Timaeus* (20b–25b) and *Critias* in which Atlantis is a mountainous island-continent in the Atlantic, beyond the Straits of Gibraltar, that was swallowed up by the sea. The colloquy of ideal rebellion takes place in a mythical location uncontaminated by actual politics and embodying lost ideals of brotherhood and spiritual perception.

Thus wept the Angel voice & as he wept the terrible blasts
Of trumpets, blew a loud alarm across the Atlantic deep.
No trumpets answer; no reply of clarions or of fifes,
Silent the Colonies remain and refuse the loud alarm.

On those vast shady hills between America & Albions shore;
Now barrd out by the Atlantic sea: call'd Atlantean hills;
Because from their bright summits you may pass to the Golden world
An ancient palace, archetype of mighty Emperies.
Rears its immortal pinnacles, built in the forest of God
By Ariston the king of beauty for his stolen bride.

Here on their magic seats the thirteen Angels sat perturb'd
For clouds from the Atlantic hover oer the solemn roof.

6. *America: a Prophecy*, Plate 12

(Copyright the British Museum, Department of Print and Drawings; original size: 17 × 23.2 cms)

An ancient palace, archetype of mighty emperies,
Rears its immortal pinnacles, built in the forest of God
10   By Ariston, the king of Beauty, for his stolen bride.

Here on their magic seats the thirteen Angels sat perturbed,
For clouds from the Atlantic hover o'er the solemn roof.

[Plate 13]

Fiery the Angels rose, and as they rose deep thunder rolled
Around their shores, indignant burning with the fires of Orc.
And Boston's Angel cried aloud as they flew through the dark night.

He cried: 'Why trembles honesty, and like a murderer
5   Why seeks he refuge from the frowns of his immortal station?
Must the generous tremble and leave his joy to the idle, to the
       pestilence,
That mock him? Who commanded this? What God? What Angel?
To keep the gen'rous from experience till the ungenerous
Are unrestrained performers of the energies of nature;

12.8 *emperies*] Territories ruled by an absolute or powerful ruler (*OED sb* 2).

12.10 *Ariston . . . bride*] Ariston was a King of Sparta who, by a trick, stole the wife of his friend Agestus (Herodotus, *History*, 6.61ff.). Blake apparently confounds Ariston with the god Poseidon, ruler of Atlantis, who married the mortal Cleito (*Critias* 113c–d).

Plate 12 design (*Plate 6*). Below the text a naked, muscular, curly-haired youth (Orc), with his arms spread wide, wells up in flames. Cf. 10.15–16 and *Marriage*, plate 3 design. The flames rise up the left margin and appear between the paragraphs of the text. The design is the obverse of that on plate 10.

13.1 *Fiery the Angels rose*] The second stage of the poem's narrative begins here: a mytholo-gized version of the American Revolution.

13.3 *Boston's Angel*] Boston is probably identified as a model for the rebellion of others (14.1–3) because of its opposition to the Stamp Act (1765), because of the 'Boston Massacre' (1770), and above all because of the famous 'Tea Party' (1773; cf. 16.14, where the mariners of Boston 'unlade'). This piece of direct action in the struggle over taxation without representation from which the Revolution began triggered the first British armed action against the Colonies. Erdman (*Prophet Against Empire*, 26) identifies the Angel as Samuel Adams (1722–1803), the famous Boston Patriot often known as 'the Father of the Revolution', but it is better to think of the Angel as embodying the voice of the city as a whole rather than as standing for an individual whom Blake could have named (as he names others) had he wished.

13.8–9 *To keep . . . nature*] The generous are Orc-like beings, in the vocabulary of *Marriage* (plate 16) the 'Prolific'. Boston's Angel sees the Urizenic ('ungenerous') as having usurped their place and so limited their experience. Cf. the Argument of *Marriage* in which the villain displaces the just man. Blake's insistent repetition of 'generous/ungenerous/generosity' may indicate that, as well as the usual modern senses ('munificent' etc.), he has also in mind a play on obsolete senses (related to the etymology, from *genus*) 'appropriate to one of noble birth, courageous, magnanimous' (*OED*, generous, 2a).

10   Till pity is become a trade, and generosity a science
      That men get rich by, and the sandy desert is giv'n to the
          strong.
      What God is he writes laws of peace and clothes him in a
          tempest?
      What pitying Angel lusts for tears and fans himself with sighs?
      What crawling villain preaches abstinence and wraps himself
15   In fat of lambs? No more I follow, no more obedience pay!'

[Plate 14]

      So cried he, rending off his robe and throwing down his sceptre
      In sight of Albion's Guardian; and all the thirteen Angels
      Rent off their robes to the hungry wind, and threw their golden
          sceptres
      Down on the land of America. Indignant they descended
5   Headlong from out the heav'nly heights, descending swift as fires
      Over the land. Naked and flaming are their lineaments seen
      In the deep gloom. By Washington and Paine and Warren they
          stood,
      And the flame folded roaring fierce within the pitchy night
      Before the demon red, who burnt towards America,
10   In black smoke, thunders and loud winds, rejoicing in its terror,
      Breaking in smoky wreaths from the wild deep, and gath'ring
          thick
      In flames as of a furnace on the land from north to south.

13.15 *fat of lambs*] A biblical phrase (from Deuteronomy, 32.14) indicating the good life enjoyed by those whom Jehovah favours.

Plate 13 design. Between lines 3 and 4 a naked youth, who turns back to look behind him, rides through a cloudy night sky on the neck of a flying, bridled giant swan. Below the text three naked children ride on the back of a bridled serpent – indicating that this creature is not the dangerous devourer of children seen by Albion's Angel (9.4). (The lower part of the design is repeated [reversed] from *The Book of Thel*, plate 8.)

14.5 *Headlong . . . heights*] Blake may have recalled the descent of Milton's devils: 'Headlong themselves they threw / Down from the verge of Heaven' (*Paradise Lost*, 6.864–5). Cf. the Satanic associations of Orc, 6.11 and 10.1 notes.

Plate 14 design. Below the text a bearded and gowned old man leaning on a crutch, whose hair implies that he is being blown from behind by a strong wind, enters a door built with a surround of massive stones at the base of a huge tree. The trunk of the tree goes up the left margin and two branches extend over the text. The old man and door were also used in *For Children: The Gates of Paradise* (1793: plate 17, 'Death's Door') and in Blake's designs for Blair's *The Grave* (1808): cf. plate 8 design and note. Plates 8 and 14, like plates 10 and 12, form an antithetical pair.

[Plate 15]

What time the thirteen governors that England sent convene
In Bernard's house, the flames covered the land. They rouse,
   they cry;
Shaking their mental chains, they rush in fury to the sea
To quench their anguish; at the feet of Washington down fall'n,
5   They grovel on the sand and writhing lie, while all
The British soldiers through the thirteen states sent up a howl
Of anguish, threw their swords and muskets to the earth, and ran
From their encampments and dark castles, seeking where to hide
From the grim flames, and from the visions of Orc, in sight
10   Of Albion's Angel, who, enraged, his secret clouds opened
From north to south, and burnt outstretched on wings of wrath
   cov'ring
The eastern sky, spreading his awful wings across the heavens.
Beneath him rolled his num'rous hosts; all Albion's Angels camped
Darkened the Atlantic mountains, and their trumpets shook the
   valleys,
15   Armed with diseases of the earth to cast upon the abyss,
Their numbers forty millions, must'ring in the eastern sky.

[Plate 16]

In the flames stood and viewed the armies drawn out in the sky
Washington, Franklin, Paine and Warren, Allen, Gates and Lee,

---

15.1 *What time*] Cf. 10.4 note.

15.2 *Bernard's house*] Sir Francis Bernard (1712–79), Governor of Massachusetts 1760–69, had returned to England before the conflict began, but he was famously unpopular. His inclusion indicates either that Blake did not have a fully accurate knowledge of the relevant historical facts or (more probably, given the accuracy of other specific historical references) that he was prepared to arrange what he knew to suit his sense of revolution's ideal form. The following account of a sudden collapse of British power at the outset of the war is, in relation to the actual history of events, equally an arrangement of fact which amounts to a fiction.

Plate 15 design. Above the text an eagle with wings spread wide preys on the naked body of a woman cast up on the shore of a stormy sea. Below the text, in the sea, fish and sea-serpents attack the body of a drowned man.

16.2 *Allen . . . Lee*] General Ethan Allen (1738–89), military hero, leader of a militia of irregulars, the so-called 'Green Mountain Boys', which became a regiment of the Continental army; best known for *A Narrative of Colonel Ethan Allen's Captivity* (that is, by the British, from 1775 to 1778). Probably, since he is most mentioned in English newspapers (see Lutnick [note 2 of headnote above]), Charles Lee (1731–82), one of the earliest proponents of American independence who rose to become for a time in the early part of the war second in command to Washington. Possibly Richard Henry Lee (1732–94), principal author of *An Address to the Inhabitants of Great Britain* (1775).

And heard the voice of Albion's Angel give the thunderous command.
His plagues, obedient to this voice, flew forth out of their clouds,

5   Falling upon America, as a storm to cut them off,
As a blight cuts the tender corn when it begins to appear.
Dark is the heaven above, and cold and hard the earth beneath;
And as a plague-wind filled with insects cuts off man and beast,
And as a sea o'erwhelms a land in the day of an earthquake,

10   Fury! rage! madness! in a wind swept through America,
And the red flames of Orc that folded roaring fierce around
The angry shores, and the fierce rushing of th' inhabitants together.
The citizens of New York close their books and lock their chests;
The mariners of Boston drop their anchors and unlade;

15   The scribe of Pennsylvania casts his pen upon the earth;
The builder of Virginia throws his hammer down in fear.

Then had America been lost, o'erwhelmed by the Atlantic,
And earth had lost another portion of the infinite.
But all rush together in the night in wrath and raging fire.
The red fires raged! The plagues recoiled! Then rolled they back

20   with fury

[Plate 17]

On Albion's Angels. Then the pestilence began in streaks of red
Across the limbs of Albion's Guardian: the spotted plague smote
   Bristol's,

16.4 *plagues*] A form of affliction employed by Jehovah – with whom (through Urizen) Albion's Angel is associated (cf. 10.3 note) – most notably in Exodus, 7–11 (where one of the plagues is specifically a wind filled with insects: 10.12–15).

16.18 *another portion*] That is, besides Atlantis (12.6).

16.20 *The plagues recoiled*] Cf. biblical examples of the wicked punished by afflictions modelled on their own sins (as in the Lord's refrain in Ezekiel, 'I will recompense their way upon their head', 9.10, 11.21, 16.43, 22.31). Perhaps also referring to the folkloric idea that a curse which fails of its object rebounds on the person who made it (and cf. 'Mock on, mock on', lines 3–4 [below, p. 272]); and to the fact that the war gave rise to some political strain and instability in Britain, most obviously the fall of Lord North's ministry in 1782 following the defeat at Yorktown (see 18.14 note).

Plate 16 design. Between lines 9 and 10 a naked Sibyl-like figure, wearing a scarf over her head, sits beside an enormous tree trunk from which one barren branch extends across the design. She gestures towards, and a serpent between her legs hisses at, a boy who sits with his arms resting on two closed books and his hands raised in an attitude suggesting prayerful obedience. Below the text a small dragon-headed serpent belches out flames.

17.2–3 *Bristol . . . London*] Trade with America was important to both of these port cities.

And the leprosy London's spirit, sickening all their bands.
The millions sent up a howl of anguish and threw off their
    hammered mail,
And cast their swords and spears to earth, and stood a naked
5   multitude.
Albion's guardian writhèd in torment on the eastern sky,
Pale, quiv'ring toward the brain his glimmering eyes, teeth
    chattering,
Howling and shuddering, his legs quivering, convulsed each muscle
    and sinew;
Sick'ning lay London's guardian, and the ancient mitred York,
10   Their heads on snowy hills, their ensigns sick'ning in the sky.

The plagues creep on the burning winds driven by flames of Orc,
And by the fierce Americans rushing together in the night,
Driven o'er the guardians of Ireland and Scotland and Wales.
They, spotted with plagues, forsook the frontiers and their banners,
    seared
With fires of hell, deform their ancient heavens with shame and
15   woe.
Hid in his caves the Bard of Albion felt the enormous plagues,
And a cowl of flesh grew o'er his head, and scales on his back and
    ribs;
And rough with black scales all his Angels fright their ancient
    heavens.
The doors of marriage are open, and the priests in rustling scales

---

17.6 *Albion's . . . torment*] Possibly a reference to George III's intermittent bouts of insanity, though the attested onset of the king's illness did not begin until after the American war (in 1788).

17.9 *London . . . York*] London is the seat of court and parliament and so represents political power, but 'London's guardian' may also suggest either the Bishop of London or the Archbishop of Canterbury, primate of England, whose official residence is Lambeth Palace, near where Blake lived in London. York is 'mitred' because it is the second archdiocese of England (after Canterbury): York (and perhaps London) represents the state (Anglican) church.

17.16 *the Bard of Albion*] The writer of official poetry. The primary such writer at the period of the American war was William Whitehead (1715–85), poet-laureate from 1757. Widely agreed to be an inferior holder of his office, he was apostrophized by Churchill as 'Dulness and Method's darling Son', and condemned by Johnson (in Boswell's *Life*) because 'grand nonsense is insupportable'.

17.19 *doors . . . open*] Erdman (*Prophet Against Empire*, 62–3) records an actual problem of 1781 about the legality of marriages conducted in chapels, and a consequent bill, passed by the Commons but rejected by the Lords, to legalize purely civil marriage. But this bill, had it been passed, would by no means have brought about an end of marriage such as is required by Blake's revolutionary ideal of unregulated sexual relations.

20   Rush into reptile coverts, hiding from the fires of Orc
      That play around the golden roofs in wreaths of fierce desire,
      Leaving the females naked and glowing with the lusts of youth.

      For the female spirits of the dead pining in bonds of religion
      Run from their fetters reddening, and in long-drawn arches sitting
25   They feel the nerves of youth renew, and desires of ancient times
      Over their pale limbs as a vine when the tender grape appears.

[Plate 18]

      Over the hills, the vales, the cities, rage the red flames fierce;
      The heavens melted from north to south; and Urizen, who sat
      Above all heavens in thunders wrapped, emerged his leprous head
      From out his holy shrine, his tears in deluge piteous
5   Falling into the deep sublime. Flagged with grey-browed snows
      And thunderous visages, his jealous wings waved over the deep:
      Weeping in dismal howling woe he dark descended, howling
      Around the smitten bands, clothèd in tears and trembling
        shudd'ring cold.
      His storèd snows he pourèd forth, and his icy magazines
10   He opened on the deep, and on the Atlantic sea, white, shiv'ring.
      Leprous his limbs, all over white, and hoary was his visage.
      Weeping in dismal howlings before the stern Americans
      Hiding the demon red with clouds and cold mists from the earth:
      Till angels and weak men twelve years should govern o'er the
        strong:
      And then their end should come, when France received the
15   demon's light.

Plate 17 design. Below the text four women (three of them huddled together) crouch in flames; to the left is a (relatively) huge bunch of grapes (cf. line 26). One woman leaps upwards into the left margin in which a woman with a child standing next to her takes on root- and plant-like forms (a transformation which recalls the classical myth of Daphne fleeing Apollo). Above (in the upper left margin) a woman sits slumped beneath a sapling and an ascending flying bird.

18.3 *emerged*] Though the meaning is obvious this transitive use of 'emerge' is unusual; *OED* offers only one distant parallel (sense 3a).

18.14 *twelve years*] Perhaps the period from Yorktown, 1781, the decisive battle of the war so seen as marking its conclusion, to the execution of Louis XVI in 1793 – though line 15 suggests rather twelve years before the beginning of the French Revolution in 1789, and so 1777 and the battle of Saratoga (cf. 5.4 note).

18.15 *their end should come*] Cf. Blake's apocalyptic engraving of 1793, 'Our End is Come' (Bentley, *Writings*, 162–3), in which a king and two warriors are consumed in flames.

Stiff shudderings shook the heav'nly thrones! France, Spain and
    Italy
In terror viewed the bands of Albion, and the ancient guardians
Fainting upon the elements, smitten with their own plagues.
They slow advance to shut the five gates of their law-built heaven,
20 Fillèd with blasting fancies and with mildews of despair,
With fierce disease and lust, unable to stem the fires of Orc.
But the five gates were consumed, and their bolts and hinges
    melted,
And the fierce flames burnt round the heavens, and round the
    abodes of men.

Finis

18.19 *five gates*] The five senses. Cf. *Marriage*, plate 14, where the Apocalypse 'will come to pass by an improvement of sensual enjoyment.'

18.20 *blasting . . . mildews*] An ironic allusion to Deuteronomy, 28.22 where the Lord threatens those who do not keep his commandments with 'blasting, and with mildew . . . [which] shall pursue thee until thou perish.'

Plate 18 design. Above the text a giant-like woman kneels, doubled-over with her hands clasped just above her head in prayer. Her hair merges into a waterfall in front of her; behind her are four knotted tree-trunks with somewhat humanoid forms. Small figures (human-sized in relation to the trees) are placed around the giant-woman's body, including: behind her a man and woman who are perhaps making love; at her waist a piper sitting under a tree; on her back two figures, one of whom raises a hand in a gesture which suggests supplication; and on her head a single figure who sits reading. Below the text the word 'Finis' written on the body of a serpent is ornamented with entangled flowers including two very thorny roses.

THE BOOK OF URIZEN

Blake composed three illuminated books dealing with the myth of Urizen, *The [First] Book of Urizen* (1794), *The Book of Ahania* (1795), and *The Book of Los* (1795). All three are primarily religious works dealing with Blake's Creation myth and his account of the development of organized religion. All have texts divided into chapters with numbered verses, and each is written in double-columns – the usual method of printing the Bible, which each in some degree parodies. *The Book of Ahania* and *The Book of Los* are etched in simple intaglio, not the more decoratively exuberant relief-etching used for the other illuminated books; they have only opening and closing illuminations, and are visually the least elaborated of Blake's early illuminated works. Each exists in only a single complete copy. *The Book of Ahania* describes the rebellion and crucifixion on the Tree of Mystery of Urizen's son, Fuzon – an Orc-like figure, but one who begins his revolt with a certain family likeness to Authority. Insofar as *Ahania* is a political poem it does not retract the revolutionary stance of *America* but shows a different kind of revolution, one which begins with seeds of authoritarian character present in its beginnings. The poem is most notable, however, not for its political implications but for the beautiful closing lament of Ahania, Urizen's emanation (female aspect), the book's imaginative centre from whom, accordingly, it takes its title. *The Book of Los* gives an alternative account of the matter of *The Book of Urizen*'s central chapters – Los's creation of the fallen Urizen. All three works provided material for the poetic project which occupied Blake for roughly the following decade – the composition and constant re-working of *Vala, or The Four Zoas.*

   The Book of Urizen is apparently a first instalment of 'the Bible of Hell' promised in *The Marriage of Heaven and Hell* (plate 24): it is a parody of Genesis with its own myths of Creation, Fall, primal couple, primal conflict, giving of law, and exodus or escape from slavery.[1] We are not to be fundamentalist interpreters of this new Bible. Blake's accounts of origins are not presented as histories: they are myths which explain the nature of life as we find it.[2] The main point of Blake's reworking of the Genesis myths is consistent with the revaluation of good and evil announced in *The Marriage of Heaven and Hell* (plate 3): life is vitiated by Urizen's deluded struggles against the fluxile energies which he comes to conceive as 'sin'. As a number of studies have shown, Blake's myth and its implications have something in common

---

[1] Leslie Tannenbaum proposes a more specific parody, one which recognizes the two conceptions of God (Elohist and Yahwist) which the redactors of Genesis combined: *Biblical Tradition in Blake's Early Prophecies* (1982), chapter 8.

[2] On the centrality to Blake of the myth-making 'poetic character' and its importance to his attack on Enlightenment epistemology, see my *Blake's Heroic Argument* (1988), 57–64.

with the early Christian heresy, Gnosticism.[3] In Gnostic thought the world is not in its origins beneficent: Blake's account of Creation as a splitting off from a primal unity and fall into agonistic division is Gnostic. Like Blake, Gnosticism often identifies the demiurge who is the creator of this world with the Old Testament God, who is then understood as a being whose retributive Justice shows him completely at odds with the New Testament Son and his ethic of Mercy – a thoroughly Blakean idea, though one only implicit in Urizen's Jehovah-like errors in *The Book of Urizen*. In Gnosticism the awakening of the divine spark in each being, its ability to re-unite with the divine substance beyond the fallen world, is not through holiness but through knowledge – *gnosis*. As Blake puts it – in his most contentious vein:

> Men are admitted into Heaven not because they have curbed and governed their passions, or have no passions, but because they have cultivated their understandings. The treasures of Heaven are not negations of passion but realities of intellect, from which all the passions emanate uncurbed in their eternal glory. The fool shall not enter into Heaven let him be ever so holy. Holiness is not the price of entrance into Heaven. Those who are cast out are all those who, having no passions of their own because no intellect, have spent their lives in curbing and governing other people's by the various arts of poverty and cruelty of all kinds. Woe, woe, woe to you hypocrites.
>
> ('A Vision of the Last Judgement', Bentley, *Writings*, 1024)

Two distinct attitudes to the senses can be deduced from the Gnostic view of Creation and the soul's place in it, and while they are usually at odds both can be found in Blake. The ascetic Gnostic sees the senses as inadequate inlets of knowledge – a view implied by Los's creation of Urizen's fallen being, which largely consists of delimiting the senses. But Gnosticism has also an antinomian libertarian strand such as is found in the proverbs of *The Marriage of Heaven and Hell* and is implied by the attitude to the Decalogue in *The Book of Urizen*: since the Old Testament God is the fallen demiurge his laws are one form of the cosmic tyranny which attempts to keep the fallen spark fallen. Reunion with the primal unity will in part come about not by eschewing but by improving the action of the senses. Blake is often actuated by opposition; he is always selective. Nothing is taken wholesale; everything is transmuted. But in his dissident Christianity, as elsewhere, Blake was not the homespun philosopher T. S. Eliot took him to be.[4]

---

[3] Gnosticism is discussed in relation to Blake's work as a whole by A. D. Nuttall, *The Alternative Trinity: Gnostic Heresy in Marlowe, Milton, and Blake* (Clarendon Press, 1998), and in essays by Stuart Curran (*Blake Studies*, 4 (1972)) and Stuart Peterfreund (in Peterfreund (ed.), *Literature and Science: Theory and Practice*, Northeastern University Press, 1990); also with specific reference to *The Book of Urizen* in the facsimile edited by Clark Emery (University of Miami Press, 1966). Curran and Peterfreund both show how Blake might have encountered Gnostic ideas; and see Nuttall (1998), 216–23. A standard modern account of Gnosticism is that of Hans Jonas, *The Gnostic Religion* (1958), 2nd edn., Beacon Press (1963). The definitive translation of Gnostic scriptures (none of which could have been known to Blake) is James M. Robinson (ed.), *The Nag Hammadi Library in English* (1977), E. J. Brill, 4th edn., Leiden (1996).

[4] See his largely excellent essay on Blake (1920) reprinted in *Selected Essays* (1932), (3rd edn., 1951). On Jacob Boehme's possible influence on Blake's Christianity, see 18.7 note. For political readings of *The Book of Urizen*, in terms of the visual and verbal discourses of

Bibliographically *Urizen* is the most complex of Blake's illuminated books. Of the seven extant copies only two have the full twenty-eight plates and none has the same plates in the same order as any other. *Urizen* is, therefore, an unusually fluid text. This is partly because of another unusual feature of the work – the many full-plate designs (ten excluding the title-page) which can be inserted at different points without disrupting the narrative. The additional oddity that two chapters are headed 'IV' may mean that plates 8 and 10 were at some stage intended as alternatives, but five of the extant copies contain both plates. Plates 4 and 16, however, are missing from copies D, E, F, and J – that is the majority of copies – though plate 4 especially is crucial for any sense of Urizen as a heroic, Los-like creator, particularly because it is the only plate in which Urizen speaks. The exclusion of plate 4 may represent a deliberate critical decision on Blake's part, aiming to simplify the role of Urizen. It is, therefore, open to question whether we should read *Urizen* as Blake wrote and engraved it, or as, at least while it was new (*c.* 1794 to 1800), he collated and sold it – that is, without plate 4.[5] The last copy Blake made up, copy G (*c.* 1815), lacks plate 4, but the reasons for this are probably purely technical.[6] The clearest evidence we have about Blake's final intentions is a letter of 1818 offering a selection of his works for sale in which he describes *Urizen* as a work in twenty-eight plates. Accordingly the full text from the twenty-eight-plate version is given below. The order of plates adopted here is that of the Erdman and Bentley editions (but see plate 12 note). This is the ordering of copy D, in which the plates are numbered by Blake by hand, except that copy D lacks plates 4 and 16.[7]

contemporary radicalism, see David Worrall (ed.), *William Blake: The Urizen Books*, Tate Gallery/Princeton (1995) and Jon Mee, *Dangerous Enthusiasm: William Blake and the Culture of Radicalism in the 1790s* (1992): but the supposed points of connection are either unremarkable or tenuous.

[5] It seems likely that two separate copies of plate 4 (in fragmentary copies I and H) were intended for copies E and F of the whole work but were extracted or not collated by Blake. See Joseph Viscomi, *Blake and the Idea of the Book* (1993), 281.

[6] See Robert Essick, *Studies in Bibliography*, 39 (1986), 230–5.

[7] Details of the sequence of plates in each extant copy are given in David Worrall, *The Urizen Books* (see note 4), 144–9.

[Title-page]

The [First] Book of Urizen

Lambeth. Printed by Will Blake 1794.

[Plate 2]

Preludium to the [First] Book of Urizen

Of the primeval priest's assumed power,
When Eternals spurned back his religion,
And gave him a place in the north,
Obscure, shadowy, void, solitary.

5   Eternals, I hear your call gladly.
Dictate swift-wingèd words, and fear not
To unfold your dark visions of torment.

Title-page.

First] This word is erased in copy G. (It is also erased or masked by paint on plates 2 and 28 of copies A and G.) The full title refers to Genesis, 'The First Book of Moses'.

Urizen] Cf. *Visions*, 8.3 note.

Design. An old man (Urizen) with long, flowing hair and an immense beard which reaches to the ground sits cross-legged in front of a pair of stone tablets or tombstones under the framing trunk and drooping branches of a slender, leafless tree. His beard rests on a large open book. His eyes are closed, his right foot protrudes through his beard, and, with his arms resting on tablets to right and left, he writes with both hands simultaneously. The design is included in *A Small Book of Designs* (1796 copy) where it is inscribed 'Which is the way? The right or the left?'

2.1 *Of*] The usual epic opening, announcing the central subject, as in *Paradise Lost*: 'Of Man's first disobedience . . . '. Blake's statement of his subject is, unusually, not syntactically organized around a verb.

2.1 *priest's*] Urizen's central error is religious (cf. 25.22 and note); here, specifically the claim that the divine requires a mediator, and (as Blake saw it) all the corruptions that spring from that illegitimate claim to authority. On Blake and priesthood cf. *Marriage*, plate 11.

2.3 *north*] The place where Lucifer/Satan organizes his rebellion in *Paradise Lost* (5.755). Like Milton's Satan, Urizen causes a Fall which gives rise to Creation. Cf. 5.17 note.

2.6 *Dictate*] Cf. *Jerusalem* plate 3, 'When this verse was dictated to me . . .', and Blake's letter to Thomas Butts of 25.4.1803: 'I have written this poem [probably *The Four Zoas*] from immediate dictation . . . without premeditation and even against my will'. The claim that the poet is a medium for spiritual powers beyond the self is an ancient one. Cf. *Paradise Lost*, 9.21–3, on the 'celestial patroness' – Urania as Muse of Christian poetry – who 'dictates' the poem to Milton.

Plate 2 design (*Plate 7*). Above the text, which is surrounded with flame-like growths, the floating figure of a woman (Enitharmon?) is seen from behind with her head in profile. With her extended left hand she holds the right arm of a flying naked baby (Orc?) which looks out towards the reader. The woman's legs are parallel to her extended arm, the left fully visible, the right covered by a long billowing robe which she gathers slightly with her right hand below the waist. The design is included in *A Small Book of Designs* (1794 and 1796 copies). In the 1796 copy it is inscribed 'Teach these souls to fly'.

7. 'Preludium to the Book of Urizen', plate 2 from 'The First Book of Urizen', 1794 (colour-printed relief etching with ink and w/c); Yale Center for British Art, Paul Mellon Collection, USA/The Bridgeman Art Library. Original size: 10.3 × 16.8 cms

[Plate 3]

Chapter I

1. Lo, a shadow of horror is risen
In Eternity! Unknown, unprolific,
Self-closed, all-repelling: what Demon
Hath formed this abominable void,
5   This soul-shudd'ring vacuum? Some said
'It is Urizen'. But unknown, abstracted,
Brooding secret, the dark power hid.

2. Times on times he divided and measured
Space by space in his ninefold darkness,
10   Unseen, unknown! Changes appeared
In his desolate mountains, rifted furious
By the black winds of perturbation.

3. For he strove in battles dire,
In unseen conflictions with shapes,
15   Bred from his forsaken wilderness,
Of beast, bird, fish, serpent and element,
Combustion, blast, vapour and cloud.

4. Dark revolving in silent activity:
Unseen in tormenting passions;
20   An activity unknown and horrible;
A self-contemplating shadow,
In enormous labours occupied.

Chapter I. The beginnings of Urizen's self-separation and of his creation of time and space.

3.4 *void*] Contrast Genesis, 1.2, where 'void' is used to describe the state that precedes Creation.

3.7, 25 *Brooding*] Milton's word for the activity in Creation of the Holy Spirit, conceived (traditionally) as a dove: *Paradise Lost*, 1.21, 7.235. Urizen is related to both Milton's God as Creator and to his Satan (cf. 2.3 and 5.17 notes).

3.9 *ninefold*] Intense (darkness); three times three, a number which Blake often associates with negative forces.

3.11 *In his*] The reading of copy G; the engraved plate read 'Like' (which is printed uncorrected in all other copies).

3.18–19 *silent . . . Unseen*] Cf. 'To Nobodaddy', 'Why art thou silent and invisible / Father of Jealousy?'.

5. But Eternals beheld his vast forests.
Age on ages he lay, closed, unknown,
25   Brooding, shut in the deep; all avoid
The petrific abominable chaos.

6. His cold horrors silent, dark Urizen
Prepared: his ten thousands of thunders
Ranged in gloomed array stretch out across
30   The dread world, and the rolling of wheels
As of swelling seas sound in his clouds,
In his hills of stored snows, in his mountains
Of hail and ice; voices of terror
Are heard, like thunders of autumn,
35   When the cloud blazes over the harvests.

Chapter II

1. Earth was not: nor globes of attraction.
The will of the Immortal expanded
Or contracted his all-flexible senses.
Death was not, but eternal life sprung.

40   2. The sound of a trumpet the heavens
Awoke and vast clouds of blood rolled
Round the dim rocks of Urizen, so named
That solitary one in Immensity.

3. Shrill the trumpet: and myriads of Eternity

3.26 *petrific*] Having the quality of making something into (or as hard as) stone (*OED* 1); a Miltonic coinage (*Paradise Lost*, 10.294) referring to the activity of Death in solidifying through Chaos a bridge between the earth and hell.

3.28 *ten thousands of thunders*] The Son in *Paradise Lost* makes use of 'ten thousand thunders' during the war in heaven (6.835).

3.29 *gloomed*] Lowering, dark and threatening (*OED*, gloom, v^1 2a).

Chapter II. Urizen proclaims his laws.

3.36 *globes of attraction*] Heavenly bodies held in relation one to another by the forces of gravity. Eternity is non-Newtonian.

3.37 *the Immortal*] The Eternals, conceived, before Urizen's self-separation, as a single unified being.

3.40, 44 *trumpet*] Cf. Exodus 19.16 and 19, where the trumpet-calls herald the voice of God and the delivery to Moses of the Ten Commandments (cf. 4.32–3 and note).

3.44 *Shrill . . . Eternity*] This line is erased in copy A.

Plate 3 design. Above the text a naked male figure, his legs extended in a running or leaping posture, his back and head turned from the reader and his arms outstretched, is enveloped in flames. The design perhaps illustrates the life of Eternals, 'in unquenchable burnings' (line 13), or 3.44b, 5.1–2 (consecutive lines in the majority of copies). It is included in *A Small Book of Designs* (1796 copy) where it is inscribed (not by Blake) 'O flames of furious desire'. Cf. *Marriage*, plate 3 design.

[Plate 4]

Muster around the bleak deserts
Now filled with clouds, darkness and waters
That rolled perplexed, lab'ring, and uttered
Words articulate, bursting in thunders
5   That rolled on the tops of his mountains.

4. 'From the depths of dark solitude, from
The eternal abode in my holiness,
Hidden, set apart in my stern counsels,
Reserved for the days of futurity,

10   I have sought for a joy without pain,
For a solid without fluctuation.
Why will you die, O Eternals?
Why live in unquenchable burnings?

5. First I fought with the fire; consumed
15   Inwards, into a deep world within:
A void immense, wild, dark and deep,
Where nothing was: Nature's wide womb;
And self-balanced, stretched o'er the void,
I alone, even I! the winds merciless
20   Bound; but condensing, in torrents
They fall and fall; strong I repelled
The vast waves, and arose on the waters
A wide world of solid obstruction.

Plate 4. Omitted from copies D, E, F, G and J (but see Introduction on two separate copies [I and H] which may have been intended for copies E and F). Without plate 4 the designs for plates 5 and 12 (and possibly for plate 14) lack their explanatory texts.

4.10 *a joy without pain*] On the inseparability of joy and pain see 'Auguries of Innocence', 55–62.

4.11 *a solid without fluctuation*] James Basire, to whom Blake was apprenticed from 1772 to 1779, engraved illustrations of scientific work for the Royal Society's *Philosophical Transactions*. It is not possible to detect Blake's hand specifically in any of the 123 plates engraved in Basire's shop during his apprenticeship, but it is probable that Blake worked on many of these and derived from them some sense of contemporary scientific developments. See William S. Doxey, *Bulletin of the New York Public Library*, 72 (1968), 252–60. The phrase 'a solid without fluctuation' is used again twice in *The Book of Los* (4.4–5 and 9).

4.12 *Why . . . die*] Urizen speaks; contrast the narrative account, 3.39.

4.17 *Nature's wide womb*] Cf. Chaos, 'The womb of Nature', with which Satan battles in *Paradise Lost* (2.911).

4.22–3 *arose . . . obstruction*] A syntactic inversion: 'a wide world . . . arose on the waters'.

6. Here alone I in books formed of metals
25   Have written the secrets of wisdom,
The secrets of dark contemplation,
By fightings and conflicts dire,
With terrible monsters, sin-bred,
Which the bosoms of all inhabit;
30   Seven deadly sins of the soul.

7. Lo! I unfold my darkness: and on
This rock place with strong hand the book
Of eternal brass, written in my solitude.

8. Laws of peace, of love, of unity:
35   Of pity, compassion, forgiveness.
Let each choose one habitation:
His ancient infinite mansion:
One command, one joy, one desire,
One curse, one weight, one measure,
40   One King, one God, one Law.'

4.24 *metals*] Noting that this word is hyphenated and printed on two lines, Nelson Hilton argues that a pun is intended: 'I in books formed of me[-/tals]' (*Studies in Romanticism*, 24 (1985)). However one estimates the significance of this material feature of the text it is clear that it has, in part at least, a material cause: Blake's narrow double columns in this text several times force him to hyphenate and carry over syllables; cf. 'attrac-/tion' (3.36), 'Eter-/nity' (3.44), 'ra-/ging' (5.20), 'astonish-/ment' (8.1), 'sulphure-/ous' (8.3), 'cur-/tains' (19.2), 'ser-/pent' (10.26), 'mis-/chievous' (23.6), 'Reli-/gion' (25.22). Blake's illuminated books were themselves 'formed of metals' – engraved on copper plates.

4.28 *monsters, Sin-bred*] Urizen thinks of these as having an objective existence, but, like Milton's Satan, he has created both the monsters and the conception of sin (cf. *Paradise Lost*, 2.747–802).

4.29 *Which . . . inhabit*] Urizen promulgates the doctrine of Original Sin – that beings have an innate tendency to corruption and depravity.

4.30 *Seven . . . soul*] Seven is the conventional number of 'Deadly Sins' in the traditional Christian scheme of 'cardinal' sins – those entailing spiritual death (pride, avarice, lust, anger, gluttony, envy and sloth). This line is erased in copy C (line 49 is erased in copy A).

4.32–3 *book . . . brass*] Cf. the Mosaic decalogue, written by God on tablets of stone (Exodus, 24.12, 31.18).

4.39 *one weight, one measure*] Cf. *Marriage*, plate 7 (14), 'Bring out number, weight and measure in a year of dearth.'

4.40 *one God*] Cf. the first commandment of the Decalogue: 'Thou shalt have no other God before me' (Exodus, 20.3; Deut., 5.7).   *one Law*] Cf. *Marriage*, plate 24, 'One law for the lion and ox is oppression'.

Chapter III

1. The voice ended. They saw his pale visage
Emerge from the darkness; his hand
On the rock of eternity unclasping
The book of brass. Rage seized the strong,

45   2. Rage, fury, intense indignation,
In cataracts of fire, blood and gall,
In whirlwinds of sulphurous smoke,
And enormous forms of energy;
All the seven deadly sins of the soul

[Plate 5]

In living creations appeared
In the flames of eternal fury.

3. Sund'ring, dark'ning, thund'ring!
Rent away with a terrible crash
5   Eternity rolled wide apart,
Wide asunder rolling.
Mountainous all around,
Departing, departing, departing:
Leaving ruinous fragments of life,
10   Hanging, frowning cliffs, and all between
An ocean of voidness unfathomable.

4. The roaring fires ran o'er the heav'ns
In whirlwinds and cataracts of blood,
And o'er the dark deserts of Urizen
15   Fires pour through the void on all sides,
On Urizen's self-begotten armies.

5. But no light from the fires. All was darkness
In the flames of eternal fury.

Chapter III. The casting out from Eternity of Urizen and first establishing of his world.

4.49 *seven deadly sins*] That is, so-called by Urizen (line 30).

Plate 4 design. Below the text a naked man sits, his left leg crossed in front of him, his right leg out straight to his side, and with his head bowed in his hands, in what appears to be heavily falling rain (illustrating lines 20–1). The design is antithetical to that of the preceding plate.

5.16 *On . . . armies*] This line is erased in copy A.

5.17 *no . . . fires*] The hell of *Paradise Lost* is lit by flames from which comes 'no light, but rather darkness visible' (1.63). (The phrase is repeated in *The Book of Los*, 3.49.)

6. In fierce anguish and quenchless flames
20   To the deserts and rocks he ran raging
To hide, but he could not: combining,
He dug mountains and hills in vast strength,
He pilèd them in incessant labour,
In howlings and pangs and fierce madness,
25   Long periods in burning fires labouring,
Till hoary, and age-broke, and agèd,
In despair and the shadows of death.

7. And a roof, vast, petrific, around
On all sides he framed like a womb;
30   Where thousands of rivers in veins
Of blood pour down the mountains to cool
The eternal fires beating without
From Eternals; and like a black globe
Viewed by sons of Eternity, standing
35   On the shore of the infinite ocean,
Like a human heart struggling and beating,
The vast world of Urizen appeared.

8. And Los round the dark globe of Urizen
Kept watch for Eternals, to confine
40   The obscure separation alone;
For Eternity stood wide apart,

5.21 *combining*] Urizen retains the ability of Eternals to divide into many parts ('self-begotten armies') or to contract into a single being.

5.21–2 *hide . . . mountains and hills*] Cf. Luke, 23.30 and Revelation, 6.15–16, both apocalyptic scenes in which the wicked seek to escape retribution by calling on the mountains to fall on them and conceal them.

5.38 *Los*] Though Blake had used the name in earlier works, this is the first extended appearance of Los, who was to develop into one of the most important figures of Blake's mythology. His role here as blacksmith and 'Eternal Prophet' (10.15) is consistent with his later development. The name is often understood as an anagram of Sol (sun, with which, as the spirit of poetry, and so a Blakean Apollo, Los is often associated), and a pun on 'loss'.

Plate 5 design. Above the text an old man (Urizen) with flowing hair and beard (in some copies his head backed by a halo-like sun), and with his arms fully extended to left and right, opens a huge book (the 'text' of which is composed of somewhat shapeless coloured splotches). The design apparently illustrates 4.41–4. It is included in *A Small Book of Designs* (1794 and 1796 copies). In the 1796 copy it is inscribed 'The book of my remembrance'. (The phrase is based on Malachi 3.16: 'Then they that feared the Lord spake often one to another: and the Lord hearkened, and heard it, and a book of remembrance was written before him for them that feared the Lord, and that thought upon his name': God proposes to reward those who have kept the Law of Moses and punish those who have not.)

[Plate 6]

As the stars are apart from the earth.

9. Los wept howling around the dark Demon:
And cursing his lot; for in anguish
Urizen was rent from his side;
5 And a fathomless void for his feet;
And intense fires for his dwelling.

10. But Urizen laid in a stony sleep
Unorganized, rent from Eternity.

11. The Eternals said: 'What is this? Death?
10 Urizen is a clod of clay.'

[Plate 7]

12. Los howled in a dismal stupor,
Groaning! gnashing! groaning!
Till the wrenching apart was healèd.

13. But the wrenching of Urizen healed not.
5 Cold, featureless, flesh or clay,
Rifted with direful changes
He lay in a dreamless night.

14. Till Los roused his fires, affrighted
At the formless unmeasurable death.

6.4 *rent from his side*] In Eternity separate beings can also unite into a single being; cf. 5.21 note. Blake by no means insists on an allegorical reading, but Los's pains can be understood as those of the poetic or prophetic faculty (10.15) separated from the reason.

Plate 6 design. Below the text three naked figures, each with a serpent entwined around his body and legs, fall downwards into flames. The figures to the left (facing away from the reader) and right (facing towards the reader) hold their heads in their hands. The central figure (also facing the reader) has his arms extended as though in a inverted cruciform posture; his encircling serpent's upper body and head (with threatening open mouth) appear below his head. Between the three figures are two mysterious incompletely formed heads. (Copies D and J have only the central falling figure; the heads do not appear in these copies or in copy C.) The figures' postures, the serpents and flames imply that Urizen's Creation can be seen as a Satanic Fall (cf. 5.15–18 and 5.17 note).

Plate 7. Omitted from copy C. This, with the omission of the following plate, considerably reduces the role of Los.

7.8 *his*] All copies read (uncorrected) 'his his'.

Plate 7 design. Below the text a naked man kneels in flames; his mouth is wide open, his eyes stare with an expression of horror, and his arms are crossed just below his head so that each hand apparently holds the opposite ear. The design perhaps illustrates line 1. It is included in *A Small Book of Designs* (1794 copy).

[Plate 8]

Chapter IV[a]

1. Los, smitten with astonishment,
Frightened at the hurtling bones

2. And at the surging sulphureous
Perturbèd Immortal, mad-raging

5   3. In whirlwinds and pitch and nitre
Round the furious limbs of Los.

4. And Los formèd nets and gins
And threw the nets round about.

5. He watched in shudd'ring fear
10   The dark changes, and bound every change
With rivets of iron and brass.

6. And these were the changes of Urizen.

[Plate 9]

Plate 8. Omitted from copies C and J.

Chapter IV[a]. Los begins to give the fallen world form. (Why two chapters were headed 'Chapter IV' has not been satisfactorily explained. Plate 10 may have been designed as a replacement for plate 8. All but copies C and J, however, contain both.)

8.2 *Frightened*] Took fright.   *hurtling*] Clashing, clattering (*OED*, hurtle, *v* 4, 5); cf. 13.25 and *The Book of Los*, 5.15.

8.7 *gins*] traps, snares.

Plate 8 design. Below the text a human skeleton (Urizen) is seen in side view (cf. 10.33–41 and plate 11 design); it sits crouched in a (paradoxically) foetal posture, with its skull drawn down between the legs and held in its hands. The design is included in *A Small Book of Designs* (1794 copy).

Plate 9 design. This, the first of several full-page plates, shows a naked old man (Urizen), with flowing white beard, his hands on the ground supporting him, kneeling on one knee inside a cave. His head stooped between his shoulders suggests that the cave roof is pressing down on him. He should perhaps be understood as pushing forwards (cf. plate 10 design, and the similar captions added to the separate prints of both designs). This design is included in *A Small Book of Designs* (1796 copy) where it is inscribed 'Eternally I labour on'.

[Plate 10]

Chapter IV[b]

1. Ages on ages rolled over him!
In stony sleep ages rolled over him!
Like a dark waste stretching changeable,
By earthquakes riv'n, belching sullen fires,
5   On ages rolled ages in ghastly
Sick torment; around him in whirlwinds
Of darkness the Eternal Prophet howled
Beating still on his rivets of iron,
Pouring solder of iron; dividing
10   The horrible night into watches.

2. And Urizen (so his eternal name)
His prolific delight obscured more and more
In dark secrecy, hiding in surging
Sulphureous fluid his phantasies.
15   The Eternal Prophet heaved the dark bellows,
And turned restless the tongs; and the hammer
Incessant beat; forging chains new and new,
Numb'ring with links hours, days and years.

3. The eternal mind, bounded, began to roll
20   Eddies of wrath ceaseless round and round,
And the sulphureous foam surging thick
Settled, a lake, bright, and shining clear:
White as the snow on the mountains cold.

4. Forgetfulness, dumbness, necessity!
25   In chains of the mind lockèd up,
Like fetters of ice shrinking together
Disorganized, rent from Eternity,

Chapter IV[b]. Los fixes the form of Urizen.

10.7 *Eternal Prophet*] Los.

10.9, 30 *solder*] Blake's spelling, 'sodor', is not recorded by *OED*.

10.10 *watches*] periods. Time is an aspect of the fallen world; cf. line 18.

10.12 *prolific*] creative; cf. Blake's usage in *Marriage* (plate 16) in opposition to 'devouring'.

10.19–13.19] These lines are re-used (adapted) in *The Four Zoas*, Night IV (54.1–55.9); and (from line 25, and more radically adapted) in *Milton*, plate b.6–26.

Los beat on his fetters of iron;
And heated his furnaces and poured
30   Iron solder and solder of brass.

5. Restless turned the Immortal, enchained,
Heaving dolorous! anguished! unbearable,
Till a roof, shaggy, wild, enclosed
In an orb his fountain of thought.

35   6. In a horrible dreamful slumber,
Like the linkèd infernal chain,
A vast spine writhed in torment
Upon the winds; shooting pained
Ribs, like a bending cavern,
40   And bones of solidness froze
Over all his nerves of joy.
And a first age passèd over,
And a state of dismal woe.

[Plate 11]

7. From the caverns of his jointed spine
Down sunk with fright a red
Round globe, hot-burning, deep,
Deep down into the abyss:
5   Panting, conglobing, trembling,
Shooting out ten thousand branches
Around his solid bones.
And a second age passèd over,
And a state of dismal woe.

10.33 *a roof, shaggy*] That is, the head and hair; cf. *Europe*, 13.29.

10.42–13.19 *a first age . . . dismal woe*] This sequence parodies the seven days of Creation in Genesis, 1.1–2.3.

Plate 10 design. Above the text a naked man seen from behind, his left leg bent at the knee, his right leg pushing out behind, thrusts his way upwards through rocks. This design is included in *A Small Book of Designs* (1794 and 1796 copies). In the 1796 copy it is inscribed 'Does the soul labour thus in the caverns of the grave?'. A similar design of a figure pushing upwards through rocks, but seen from the front, depicts Earth (as one of the four elements) in *For Children: The Gates of Paradise*, 1793. The sketch for this design in Blake's Notebook (p. 93) is inscribed (from *Hamlet*) 'Rest, rest perturbed spirit'.

11.2–3 *Down . . . burning*] Adapted from *Visions*, 5.33; cf. 13.33–4.

11.3–6 *globe . . . branches*] That is, the heart and blood vessels.

10   8. In harrowing fear rolling round
            His nervous brain shot branches
            Round the branches of his heart
            On high into two little orbs;
            And fixèd in two little caves
15   Hiding carefully from the wind,
            His eyes beheld the deep.
            And a third age passèd over,
            And a state of dismal woe.

            9. The pangs of hope began,
20   In heavy pain striving, struggling.
            Two ears in close volutions
            From beneath his orbs of vision
            Shot spiring out, and petrifièd
            As they grew. And a fourth age passèd,
25   And a state of dismal woe.

            10. In ghastly torment sick,
            Hanging upon the wind,

                  [Plate 12]

11.11 *brain shot branches*] That is, the nervous system.

11.14 *two little caves*] Cf. *Marriage*, plate 14: 'Man has closed himself up, till he sees all things through narrow chinks of his cavern.' Los's giving form to Urizen largely consists of the fixing of the fallen senses – sight (16), hearing (21), smell (13.1), and taste (13.8). Contrast 3.37–8.

11.23 *petrifièd*] Took solid form. (Blake perhaps knew the anatomical term 'petrous', the unusually hard [stony] bone which forms a protective case for the inner ear.)

11.24 *passèd*] As in each other use of this choric line Blake would have presumably added 'over' had there been room to do so.

11.26–7 *In . . . wind*] Repeated (with minor variation) from *Europe*, 15.18.

Plate 11 design. Below the text are two male figures. To the left, surrounded by flames, with a heavy chain in front of his ankles, sits an emaciated, almost skeletal figure (Urizen; cf. plate 8). His knees are drawn up in front of his chest, his arms are by his sides, his hands on his knees, and his skull-like face is turned upwards. To the right, just beyond the flames, a muscular figure (Los) sits in a bizarrely contorted position with his knees in front of his chest and his shoulders pulled round so that both arms appear to the right of his legs. His head is thrown back with an expression suggesting agony or exhaustion, and in his right hand appears the end of a hammer. The design illustrates 13.20–7. It is included in *A Small Book of Designs* (1794 copy).

Plate 12 design (full-plate). A naked, full-bearded old man (Urizen), his legs drawn upwards towards his chest and his arms raised above his head, swims upwards in dark water shot through with wave patterns. The design illustrates 4.21–2. (Bentley (*Writings*, 245) places this design between plates 4 and 5, its position in copy C.) It is included in *A Small Book of Designs* (1796 copy) where it is inscribed (not in Blake's hand) 'I labour upwards into futurity. Blake'. (Though the inscription is not in Blake's hand the attribution may mean that this was Blake's title, originally inscribed below the design before it was trimmed.)

[Plate 13]

Two nostrils bent down to the deep.
And a fifth age passèd over,
And a state of dismal woe.

11. In ghastly torment sick,
5   Within his ribs bloated round,
A craving hungry cavern;
Thence arose his channelled throat,
And like a red flame a tongue
Of thirst and of hunger appeared.
10   And a sixth age passèd over,
And a state of dismal woe.

12. Enragèd and stifled with torment
He threw his right arm to the north,
His left arm to the south,
15   Shooting out in anguish deep,
And his feet stamped the nether abyss
In trembling and howling and dismay.
And a seventh age passèd over,
And a state of dismal woe.

Chapter V.

20   1. In terrors Los shrunk from his task:
His great hammer fell from his hand:
His fires beheld and, sickening,
Hid their strong limbs in smoke.
For with noises ruinous loud,
25   With hurtlings and clashings and groans
The Immortal endured his chains,
Though bound in a deadly sleep.

13.6 *craving hungry cavern*] The thorax (containing the stomach).

13.16–17 *his feet . . . dismay*] Re-used (adapted) in *The Book of Los*, 3.47–8.

Chapter V. The birth of Enitharmon (called Pity) and the final separation of Urizen's world from Eternity.

13.24 *ruinous*] Strictly 'resulting from a fall' (*OED* 4); Blake perhaps recalled *Paradise Lost*, 2.920–2, 'Nor was his ear less pealed / With noises loud and ruinous . . . / . . . than when Bellona storms.'

13.26 *The Immortal*] Urizen.

2. All the myriads of Eternity,
All the wisdom and joy of life,
30   Roll like a sea around him,
Except what his little orbs
Of sight by degrees unfold.

3. And now his eternal life
Like a dream was obliterated.

35   4. Shudd'ring, the Eternal Prophet smote
With a stroke, from his north to south region.
The bellows and hammer are silent now.
A nerveless silence his prophetic voice
Seized; a cold solitude and dark void
40   The Eternal Prophet and Urizen closed.

5. Ages on ages rolled over them,
Cut off from life and light, frozen
Into horrible forms of deformity.
Los suffered his fires to decay.
45   Then he looked back with anxious desire,
But the space undivided by existence
Struck horror into his soul.

6. Los wept, obscured with mourning:
His bosom earthquaked with sighs;
50   He saw Urizen deadly black,
In his chains bound, and Pity began,

13.33–4 *eternal life . . . obliterated*] Cf. *Visions*, 5.34 and *The Song of Los*, 4.3.

13.37–40] Los, 'the Eternal Prophet' (35), is antithetical to Urizen as 'primeval priest' (2.1). Nevertheless, the Fall of Los repeats that of Urizen: Los now comes to resemble Urizen. When the binding of Urizen is re-cast in *The Four Zoas* and *Milton* the consequent transformation of Los explicitly replicates that of Urizen: '[Los] became what he beheld' (*The Four Zoas*, 53.24, 55.49; *Milton*, b.29).

13.40 *closed*] Enclosed.

13.49 *earthquaked*] Blake's invention: *OED* does not record 'earthquake' as a verb.

13.51 *Pity*] Blake here implies some re-valuation of a long Christian tradition of social action based on compassion for the suffering (see for example the words of Christ in Matthew, 25.34–40), perhaps because its specific Enlightenment forms could be linked to conservative social philosophies: on Blake's view such compassion is sentimental self-indulgence, a comforting moral gloss which conceals exploitation, palliating consequences without remedying causes. Cf. 'The Human Abstract', *Songs of Experience*: 'Pity would be no more / If we did not make somebody poor.'

7. In anguish dividing and dividing,
For pity divides the soul.
In pangs eternity on eternity
55   Life in cataracts poured down his cliffs.
The void shrunk the lymph into nerves
Wand'ring wide on the bosom of night,
And left a round globe of blood
Trembling upon the void.

[Plate 14]

[Plate 15]

Thus the Eternal Prophet was divided
Before the death-image of Urizen,
For in changeable clouds and darkness,
In a winterly night beneath,
5   The abyss of Los stretched immense:
And now seen, now obscured, to the eyes
Of Eternals the visions remote
Of the dark separation appeared.
As glasses discover worlds

13.53 *pity divides the soul*] Repeated in *Milton*, 6.19.

13.56–9 *nerves . . . void*] Illustrated in the design of plate 17.

13.56 *lymph*] For Blake's medical knowledge cf. notes on 18.4 and 19.34–5. Blake may have been reading the compendium by the well-known physician John Brown, *Elements of Medicine*, published by Joseph Johnson in 1795, for which he engraved a frontispiece portrait.

13.58 *globe*] globule (but see also design, plate 17).

Plate 13 design. In the middle of the plate a female figure with her back to the reader and her long hair blown to the left floats in a night sky; with extended arms she holds apart two banks of clouds. She is perhaps Pity (later specifically female (19.1)), seen at her characteristic work of dividing, here on a universal scale. (The design is below lines 16 and 30: the double-column text reads from the left to right column above the design, then similarly below.)

Plate 14 design (full-plate). A counterpart to plate 12, this shows a naked muscular male figure balanced upside down on his hands, arms bent at the elbow, perhaps in water. His right leg is bent towards the reader, the left curves above it towards the left of the design; his hands rest on rocks, or perhaps on a bank of clouds (in which case the 'water' is filmy air). The muscularity of the figure suggests that this is Los; indications of a beard in some copies suggest that this is Urizen – or Los becoming Urizenic (as is clearly the case in plate 21). On the identity of the two protagonists at this point, see 13.37–40 note and notes on plate 16 and plate 21 designs. If this is Urizen, and the element is air, this may show him 'self-balanced, stretched o'er the void' binding the winds (4.18–20). (The plate is placed immediately after plate 4 in copy B.) The design is included in *A Large Book of Designs* (c. 1794).

15.9–10 *As glasses . . . space*] The 'glasses' are optical instruments such as the telescope. William Herschel discovered Uranus in 1781. The discovery is vividly described in John Bonnycastle's *Introduction to Astronomy*, published by Joseph Johnson in 1786.

10
> In the endless abyss of space,
> So the expanding eyes of Immortals
> Beheld the dark visions of Los,
> And the globe of life-blood trembling.

> [Plate 16]

> [Plate 17]

> [Plate 18]

> 8. The globe of life-blood trembled,
> Branching out into roots,
> Fibrous, writhing upon the winds;
> Fibres of blood, milk and tears,
5
> In pangs, eternity on eternity.
> At length in tears and cries embodied
> A female form trembling and pale
> Waves before his deathy face.

> 9. All Eternity shuddered at sight
10
> Of the first female now separate,
> Pale as a cloud of snow
> Waving before the face of Los.

Plate 15 design. Below the text are the upper bodies of three male figures. Beneath them is a portion of a dark globe. The figures to the left and right have full-flowing beards. The central figure, beardless and youthful, bends downwards and draws his left hand across the globe's surface in which his fingers leave a light-coloured trail. (Copy G has four figures, the fourth perhaps female.) The design illustrates lines 11–13, or possibly 5.33–4.

Plate 16 (included in only copies A, B, and G) design (full-plate). A naked man (Los?) with a frowning or anguished expression, his knees pulled up to his chest and hands held behind his head, squats in a burst of flames. The man has a beard in copy A, which associates him with Urizen: he is perhaps Los becoming Urizenic (cf. plate 21 design), though here the beard is long and full. Fire is the usual element of Los, but Urizen labours in fire at 5.25. The design completes what may be a sequence associated with the four elements: earth (plate 10), water (plate 12), air (plate 14) and (here) fire; cf. 23.11–18 and note.

Plate 17 design. A full-plate design showing an androgynous figure kneeling with head down and hands held against the sides of the face. Blood vessels are shown in the body, as in an anatomical illustration; these seem to emerge from the head, as if through strands of long hair, and connect with a globe of blood suspended beneath. The design illustrates 13.55–9 or 18.1–8. It is included in *A Small Book of Designs* (1794 copy).

18.4 *blood . . . tears*] Blake refers accurately to the three kinds of vessels anatomists had discovered in the body: veins and arteries, lacteals and lacrymals.

18.7 *A female form*] In the theology of Jacob Boehme the separation of the sexes is an aspect of the Fall. See Bryan Aubrey, *Watchmen of Eternity: Blake's Debt to Jacob Boehme* (Lanham, MD, 1986), 27. On Blake and Boehme more generally cf. *Marriage*, 22.10 note.

18.8 *deathy*] OED's first recorded use is 1796.

10. Wonder, awe, fear, astonishment,
Petrify the eternal myriads
15   At the first female form now separate.

[Plate 19]

They called her Pity, and fled.

11. 'Spread a tent with strong curtains around them;
Let cords and stakes bind in the Void
That Eternals may no more behold them.'

5   12. They began to weave curtains of darkness;
They erected large pillars round the Void,
With golden hooks fastened in the pillars;
With infinite labour the Eternals
A woof wove, and callèd it Science.

Chapter VI

10   1. But Los saw the Female and pitièd.
He embraced her; she wept, she refused.
In perverse and cruel delight
She fled from his arms, yet he followed.

2. Eternity shuddered when they saw
15   Man begetting his likeness
On his own divided image.

Plate 18 design. Below the text a muscular naked man with curly hair (Los) stands, feet apart and arms spread wide, amid flames. His right hand rests on what appears to be a round fragment of rock; his left hand clasps a huge hammer.

19.2–3 *tent . . . curtains . . . cords . . . stakes*] Cf. Isaiah, 54.2: 'Enlarge the place of thy tent, and let them stretch forth the curtains of thine habitations; spare not, lengthen thy cords, and strengthen thy stakes.'

19.6–7 *large pillars . . . golden hooks*] Blake recalls details from the building of the tabernacle which has pillars of wood with golden hooks for the curtains hung across the doors (Exodus, 26.31–7, 36.31–8).

19.9 *Science*] Knowledge; cf. *Ahania*. 6.36, and *The Four Zoas*, 51.30 and 139.10.

Chapter VI. The birth of Orc.

3. A time passèd over; the Eternals
Began to erect the tent;
When Enitharmon, sick,
20   Felt a worm within her womb.

4. Yet helpless it lay like a worm
In the trembling womb
To be moulded into existence.

5. All day the worm lay on her bosom,
25   All night within her womb
The worm lay, till it grew to a serpent,
With dolorous hissings and poisons
Round Enitharmon's loins folding.

6. Coiled within Enitharmon's womb
30   The serpent grew, casting its scales;
With sharp pangs the hissings began
To change to a grating cry;
Many sorrows and dismal throes,
Many forms of fish, bird and beast,
35   Brought forth an infant form
Where was a worm before.

7. The Eternals their tent finishèd,
Alarmed with these gloomy visions,
When Enitharmon groaning
40   Produced a man-child to the light.

19.19 *Enitharmon*] Los and Enitharmon are the Adam and Eve of this 'Bible of Hell'. Like Eve (Genesis, 2.21–2), Enitharmon is born from Los (15.1). Blake locates the primal conflict not between their children, two brothers (Cain and Abel, as in Genesis, 4.1–16), but between father and son (Chapter VII).

19.20, 36 *a worm*] The idea that man is a worm is biblical, as in Job, 25.6 ('man, that is a worm') or Psalm 22 (v.6), 'I am a worm, and no man'. Blake used Job, 17.14, 'I have said . . . to the worm, Thou art my mother and my sister' as the legend to plate 18 of *For Children: the Gates of Paradise*. Both Albrecht von Haller (*First Lines of Physiology*, trans. 1786) and Buffon (*Natural History*, trans. 1791) associate sperm with worms. Blake engraved a portrait of Haller for Thomas Henry's *Memoirs of Albert de Haller* published by Joseph Johnson in 1783.

19.26 *serpent*] Orc appears as Satan-as-serpent in *America*, though in a somewhat different context (see *America*, 9.3–10.1 and notes).

19.34–5 *Many forms . . . Infant form*] Blake apparently describes an early evolutionary idea: the phases of Orc's embryonic development resemble the series of inferior forms of animal species – a notion Blake might have derived from the surgeon and anatomist John Hunter (satirized as Jack Tearguts in *An Island in the Moon*). On Blake's knowledge of anatomy, see Carmen S. Kreiter, *Studies in Romanticism*, 4 (1965).

8. A shriek ran through Eternity,
And a paralytic stroke,
At the birth of the human shadow.

9. Delving earth in his resistless way,
45   Howling, the child with fierce flames
Issued from Enitharmon.

10. The Eternals closèd the tent;
They beat down the stakes; the cords

[Plate 20]

Stretched for a work of eternity;
No more Los beheld Eternity.

11. In his hands he seized the infant;
He bathèd him in springs of sorrow;
5   He gave him to Enitharmon.

Chapter VII

1. They namèd the child Orc; he grew
Fed with milk of Enitharmon.

2. Los awoke her; O sorrow and pain!
A tight'ning girdle grew
10   Around his bosom. In sobbings

19.44 *resistless*] Irresistible.

19.46 *Enitharmon*] Because the 'o' here is joined to the 'n' at the base some critics read this name as 'Enitharman' and suppose some orthographic play suggesting androgyny; but the letter is clearly differently formed from the 'a' in the previous syllable. Cf. Introduction (1), p. 8.

Plate 19 design. Above the text to the right a naked man (Los) kneels with his upper body bowed down and his head clasped in his hands. To the left a woman standing before him (Enitharmon) also clasps her head in her hands and twists her upper body to lean away from him. The design illustrates lines 11–13 (and cf. 18.10–12: 'the first female now separate . . . / Waving before the face of Los'). It is included in *A Small Book of Designs* (1794 copy).

Chapter VII. The Chain of Jealousy; the binding of Orc; Urizen is prompted to explore the abyss.

20.6 *Orc*] Cf. *America*, 3.1 note.

20.9 *girdle*] Any confining garment; in *The Four Zoas* this becomes 'a bloody cord'; the illustration here (plate 21) shows it as a metal band from which hangs an enormous chain (cf. lines 18–19).

20.10–20] Re-used (adapted) in *The Four Zoas*, 60.10–13, 16–18 (Night V, in which the whole myth of Los, Enitharmon, Orc and the Chain of Jealousy is further developed).

He burst the girdle in twain,
But still another girdle
Oppressed his bosom. In sobbings
Again he burst it. Again
15   Another girdle succeeds.
The girdle was formed by day;
By night was burst in twain.

3. These falling down on the rock
Into an iron chain,
20   In each other link by link locked.

4. They took Orc to the top of a mountain.
O how Enitharmon wept!
They chained his young limbs to the rock
With the Chain of Jealousy
25   Beneath Urizen's deathful shadow.

5. The dead heard the voice of the child
And began to awake from sleep.
All things heard the voice of the child
And began to awake to life.

30   6. And Urizen craving with hunger,
Stung with the odours of Nature,
Explored his dens around.

7. He formed a line and a plummet
To divide the abyss beneath.
35   He formed a dividing rule.

20.23 *chained . . . rock*] Blake knew the Icelandic *Edda* (Bentley, *Writings*, 1413) through Paul Henri Mallet's *Northern Antiquities* (1770), and may have drawn something of the 'girdle' of Los and the chaining of Orc from the Edda's account of the binding of Loki: 'The Gods made of his intestines [those of Loki's son Nari] cords for Loke, tying him down to three sharp stones . . . These cords were afterwards changed into chains of iron' (1809 edn., vol. 2, p. 115). Mallet specifically compares the myth of Prometheus: cf. *America*, plate 3 design. Given the context of a father's jealous fears, the fate of the infant Oedipus, exposed on a mountain with his feet pierced and tied together, is also relevant.

20.26 *dead*] That is, the spiritually dead.

8. He formèd scales to weigh;
He formèd massy weights;
He formèd a brazen quadrant;
He formèd golden compasses
40   And began to explore the abyss.
And he planted a garden of fruits.

9. But Los encircled Enitharmon
With fires of prophecy
From the sight of Urizen and Orc.

45   10. And she bore an enormous race.

Chapter VIII

1. Urizen explored his dens,
Mountain, moor, and wilderness,
With a globe of fire lighting his journey,
A fearful journey, annoyed
50   By cruel enormities, forms

[Plate 21]

20.39 *golden compasses*] From *Paradise Lost*, 7.225–7 (the Son's creation of the world): 'He took the golden compasses, prepared / In God's eternal store, to circumscribe / This universe and all created things.' The ultimate source is Proverbs, 8.27: 'He set a compass upon the face of the depth.' Cf. the frontispiece to *Europe* (where the golden compasses are wielded by Urizen), the design often referred to (though not by Blake) as 'The Ancient of Days'.

20.45 *enormous*] Monstrous, given to abnormal modes of action or being.

Chapter VIII. Urizen explores the abyss: his pity for its sufferings spawns the Net of Religion.

20.50 *enormities*] Abnormal beings.

Plate 20 design. Below the text a naked boy (a baby or young child) leaps in an exuberant posture, with head downwards and arms and legs spread wide, apparently free-falling in the middle of a burst of flames. The design gives a somewhat new view of the birth of Orc (19.44–6).

Plate 21 design (full-plate). The design shows a naked man, woman and child – evidently Los, Enitharmon and Orc. The now pubescent Orc, who is seen from behind with head bent back, embraces his mother. Los, identified by the huge hammer to his right on which he rests his right hand, now has a full beard. A metal band circles his breast from which a chain with large links falls to the ground. The design illustrates 20.8–20. It is included in *A Large Book of Designs* (c. 1794).

[Plate 22]

[Plate 23]

Of life on his forsaken mountains.

2. And his world teemed vast enormities,
Fright'ning; faithless; fawning
Portions of life; similitudes
Of a foot, or a hand, or a head,
Or a heart, or an eye, they swam, mischievous
Dread terrors! delighting in blood.

3. Most Urizen sickened to see
His eternal creations appear,
Sons and daughters of sorrow on mountains,
Weeping! wailing! First Thiriel appeared,
Astonished at his own existence,
Like a man from a cloud born; and Utha
From the waters emerging, laments!
Grodna rent the deep earth, howling
Amazed! his heavens immense cracks
Like the ground parched with heat; then Fuzon
Flamed out! first begotten, last born.
All his eternal sons; in like manner
His daughters, from green herbs and cattle,
From monsters and worms of the pit.

5

10

15

20

Plate 22 design (full-plate). An old man with flowing white beard (Urizen) sits, naked, with his legs pulled up against his chest, eyes closed, and head backed by a halo-like burst of light. His feet and hands (by his sides, and so adjacent to his feet) are shackled with enormous fetters. In copy G his eyes flow with tears (cf. 25.3). The design shows Urizen 'in chains of the mind lockèd up' (10.25; cf. 13.26–7; in the majority of copies this plate is placed earlier, often adjacent to plate 13). The plate is included in *A Small Book of Designs* (1796 copy) where it is inscribed 'Frozen doors to mock / The world, while they within torments uplock': Urizens are victims of their own oppressions.

23.4 *similitudes*] Perhaps suggesting the Platonic idea that the material world is modelled on, but reflects only imperfectly, an ideal world of perfect 'forms'; the fragments here are surreal and horrific.

23.11–18 *Thiriel . . . Flamed out*] The sons of Urizen represent the classical four elements – air (Thiriel), water (Utha), earth (Grodna) and fire (Fuzon). Their birth is illustrated by the full-page design, plate 24. Cf. plate 16 design note, and 3.16–17, where Urizen begins to give shape to his creation by battling with representative creatures of each element ('serpent', as commonly in Blake, for fire), and with the elements themselves ('blast' for the volcanic earth).

4. He, in darkness closed, viewed all his race,
And his soul sickened! He cursed
Both sons and daughters; for he saw
25   That no flesh nor spirit could keep
His iron laws one moment.

5. For he saw that life lived upon death.

[Plate 24]

[Plate 25]

The ox in the slaughterhouse moans,
The dog at the wintry door.
And he wept, and he callèd it Pity;
And his tears flowèd down on the winds.

23.23 *his soul sickened*] Contrast the initial response of Jehovah to his Creation: 'God saw every thing that he had made, and, behold, it was very good' (Genesis, 1.31). However, he too is grieved by later corruptions – as by the wickedness which provokes the Flood (Genesis, 6.5–7), or by the worshipping of the Golden Calf (Exodus, 32.7–10).

23.23–6 *he cursed . . . his iron laws*] Cf. Galatians, 3.10: 'Cursed is every one that continueth not in all things which are written in the book of the law to do them': Saint Paul's words can be understood as based on various Old Testament penalties denounced against those who break the law, for example, Deut., 11.26–8: 'Behold, I set before you this day a blessing and a curse . . . a curse if ye will not obey the commandments of the Lord your God'; cf. Deut., 28.15–19.

23.27 *life . . . death*] Repeated in *The Four Zoas*, 87.19.

Plate 23 design. Below the text a full-bearded old man wearing a long gown (Urizen) strides from left to right, his left hand raised in front of him with the palm vertical, his right carrying a globe which emits long, thin spike-like rays. Below his raised hand is the head (in profile), mane and left foreleg of a lion. The design illustrates 20.46–50. It is included in *A Small Book of Designs* (1794 copy).

Plate 24 design (full-plate). The design shows (parts of) four figures, the sons of Urizen representing the four elements (cf. 23.11–18 and note). At the top of the plate is Fuzon (Fire), a flying or diving head surrounded by flames with arms extended and somewhat raised, palms open; below him Thiriel (Air) – the only complete figure – is a naked form floating left to right in a cloud, arms bent and palms raised in front of his breast ('Astonished at his own existence'); below right Grodna (Earth), his upper body and raised right knee visible only, pushes himself out of the ground with his hands; below left Utha (Water) shows a lank-haired head but is otherwise submerged in his element. (Copies D and J show Thiriel and Utha only.) The lower half only, showing only Utha, is included in *A Small Book of Designs* (1794 copy).

25.2 *The Dog . . . door*] Repeated from 'Who will exchange his own fire side' (see above, p. 161); this and the preceding line are adapted in *The Four Zoas*, 36.4.

25.3 *Pity*] Cf. 19.1 and 13.51 note, and plate 22 design, copy G.

5   6. Cold he wandered on high, over their cities,
In weeping and pain and woe!
And wherever he wandered in sorrows
Upon the agèd heavens
A cold shadow followed behind him
10   Like a spider's web, moist, cold, and dim,
Drawing out from his sorrowing soul,
The dungeon-like heaven dividing
Wherever the footsteps of Urizen
Walked over the cities in sorrow.

15   7. Till a web dark and cold, throughout all
The tormented element stretched
From the sorrows of Urizen's soul;
And the web is a female in embryo.
None could break the web, no wings of fire,

20   8. So twisted the cords, and so knotted
The meshes: twisted like to the human brain.

        9. And all called it, the Net of Religion.

25.5 *cities*] Cf. the development of cities in Genesis – Babel (chapter 11), and Sodom and Gomorrah (chapters 18–19).

25.10 *Like a spider's web*] 'Comparing the first cause to a spider, they [the Brahmins] say the universe was produced by that insect spinning out of its own entrails and belly; so that it brough forth first the elements, and then the celestial globes, etc.' Joseph Priestley, *A Comparison of the Institutions of Moses with those of the Hindoo and other antient Nations*, 1799, p. 50. Blake knew Priestley through Joseph Johnson. Piloo Nanavutty (in Pinto, *The Divine Vision* (1957)) argues that the resemblance to Priestley's account of Hindu myth at this point may indicate that Blake had heard of this from him before *A Comparison* was published.

25.18 *And . . . embryo*] That is, the first beginnings of Urizen's religion lie in false pity (25.3–6), which Blake has earlier personified in Enitharmon (19.1). This line is erased in copy A.

25.21 *like . . . brain*] Cf. 'The Human Abstract', line 24 and plate 28 design note.

25.22 *The Net of Religion*] Representing not religion *per se*, but religion as it is usually found in the world: the Church, Blake's critique of which is developed throughout his work. It is in sum a version of religion in which inspiration is replaced by regulation and an inner spiritual life by the observance of exterior forms. As Blake expressed it: 'Would to God that all the Lord's people were prophets' (*Milton*, plate 2, quoting words of Moses in Numbers, 11.29); and 'the outward ceremony is Antichrist' (*Laocoön*; below, p. 362).

Chapter IX

1. Then the inhabitants of those cities
   Felt their nerves change into marrow,
25 And hardening bones began
   In swift diseases and torments,
   In throbbings and shootings and grindings
   Through all the coasts; till weakened
   The senses inward rushed, shrinking,
30 Beneath the dark net of infection.

2. Till the shrunken eyes, clouded over,
   Discerned not the woven hypocrisy,
   But the streaky slime in their heavens
   Brought together by narrowing perceptions
35 Appeared transparent air; for their eyes
   Grew small like the eyes of a man,
   And in reptile forms shrinking together
   Of seven feet stature they remained.

3. Six days they shrunk up from existence,
40 And on the seventh day they rested.
   And they blessed the seventh day, in sick hope:
   And forgot their eternal life.

4. And their thirty cities divided
   In form of a human heart.
45 No more could they rise at will
   In the infinite void, but bound down
   To earth by their narrowing perceptions

Chapter IX. The degeneration of life in Urizen's world, and the exodus led by Fuzon.

25.28–9 *weakened . . . shrinking*] Cf. Chapter IV[b], and esp. 11.14 note.

25.38 *seven feet stature*] Cf. Genesis, 6.4: 'There were giants in the earth in those days.'

25.39 *Six . . . existence*] A parody of the six days of Creation, bringing order to chaos and life out of nothing, as described in Genesis, chapter 1.

25.40–1 *seventh . . . hope*] Similarly parodic: cf. Genesis, 2.2–3: 'And on the seventh day God ended his work which he had made; and he rested on the seventh day from all his work which he had made. And God blessed the seventh day, and sanctified it.'

Plate 25 design. Above the text are three (in some copies four) women caught by coiling serpents, one a bat- or dragon-like form whose huge wings appear in the centre (and in some copies in the background). The women are presumably Urizen's daughters, born 'from green herbs and cattle, / From monsters and worms of the pit' (23.20–1).

[Plate 26]

[Plate 27]

[Plate 28]

They livèd a period of years
Then left a noisome body
To the jaws of devouring darkness.

5. And their children wept, and built
5   Tombs in the desolate places,
And formed laws of prudence, and called them
The eternal laws of God.

6. And the thirty cities remained
Surrounded by salt floods, now called
10   Africa: its name was then Egypt.

7. The remaining sons of Urizen
Beheld their brethren shrink together
Beneath the Net of Urizen.
Persuasion was in vain;
15   For the ears of the inhabitants
Were withered, and deafened, and cold:
And their eyes could not discern
Their brethren of other cities.

Plate 26 design (full-plate). A contemporary, non-mythic tableau: a child wearing a long gown with its hands clasped in an attitude of prayer stands in front of a large panelled door. Behind the child a dog sits stretched out at full length with its head raised as if howling. The design illustrates 25.2.

Plate 27 design (full-plate). A gigantic muscular figure (Urizen) seen from behind, wearing a more than full-length, flowing and billowing gown, strides away from the viewer with his hands raised beside his head, fingers spread and palms facing forwards – perhaps a conventional gesture expressing horror (cf. 23.8–9: the design is partly narrative, taking up from that of Urizen exploring his dens (plate 23, upon which, in copies C, G and J it follows immediately)). The figure's head is surrounded by, in some copies a grey cloud, in others a halo of light which may be the distant sun. The capacious gown suggests the 'cold shadow . . . / Like a spider's web, moist, cold, and dim, / Drawing out from [Urizen's] sorrowing soul' which becomes 'the Net of Religion' (25.9–11, 22). The design is included in *A Small Book of Designs* (1794 copy).

28.6–7 laws . . . God] The Mosaic decalogue; cf. 4.32–3 note: Urizen's Creation, as it degenerates, repeats elements of the original Fall (cf. 25.3 and 25.28–9 notes).

28.10 Egypt] The land of bondage for the Israelites, as described in Exodus, chapters 1 to 13.

28.17–18 their eyes . . . cities] These lines must first be taken as simply parallel to the two preceding lines, which bear no esoteric sense; they describe directly what Blake sees as a permanent

8. So Fuzon called all together
20   The remaining children of Urizen:
And they left the pendulous earth:
They callèd it Egypt, and left it.

9. And the salt ocean rollèd englobed.

The End of the [First] Book of Urizen

(though transformable) limitation of the fallen senses, on which see *Visions*, 5.31 note. Blake may also, however, have intended a wry allusion to contemporary politics: members of the radical workers' association, the London Corresponding Society, ceased to be able to communicate with members in other cities after the seizure of their papers and arrest of their leaders in spring 1794.

28.19 *Fuzon*] Here, briefly, a Moses-like leader who rejects the contraction of human possibilities endemic to Urizen's world and initiates a journey out of the land of slavery.

Plate 28 design. Below the text a full-bearded old man (Urizen), wearing a long gown from which his left foot protrudes, sits with arms raised horizontally, apparently caught in a net of thick ropes – the Net of Religion (cf. 25.18–22). Cf. the design of 'The Human Abstract', *Songs of Experience* (above, p. 99).

FROM
THE FOUR ZOAS

The Four Zoas, the Torments of Love and Jealousy in the Death and Judgement of Albion the Ancient Man is Blake's longest and most difficult work. It occupied him for some ten years, from about 1797 to 1807, and is both the summation of the first period of his writing and a preparation for the two long works – *Milton* and *Jerusalem* – on which he spent the last fifteen years of his writing life. During much of its composition the work was called *Vala, or the Death and Judgement of the Eternal Man: a Dream of Nine Nights*. The division of the poem into 'Nights' follows that of Edward Young's *The Complaint, or Night Thoughts* (1742–45), one of the most popular poems of the eighteenth century. Blake illustrated its complete text in 537 watercolours on which he began working in 1795 shortly before he began *Vala*. *The Four Zoas* was never finally revised, and exists in a unique manuscript from which it is not certain that Blake intended to engrave and print in his usual way. The beautiful copperplate hand in which the earliest-composed parts of the manuscript are written may indicate that a handwritten poem, illuminated with watercolours, was at first intended, and that the manuscript became more like a working draft – difficult to read and less finished in appearance – only with the later additions, deletions and transpositions. It is also possible that Blake had in view, for once, a more commercial production, letterpress framed by designs, as in the edition of Young's *Night Thoughts* on which he worked while beginning the poem, proof sheets of which were used for text in the later stages of composition – or that he entertained all of these ideas at different stages of the work's development.[1]

The central figure of *The Four Zoas*, the Eternal Man, is human and divine, male and female, the spirit and – on the assumption that the material is an emanation of the spiritual – the exterior world, whether of nature or society. In the later additions he is called Albion, father of the British people in Spenser and Milton. The poem is concerned with his disintegration, the horrific consequences of his internal self-division, and his eventual apocalyptic regeneration. The myth of his four elements draws on one of the most famous and astonishing passages of Old Testament prophecy, the vision of God of Ezekiel (Ezekiel, 1.4–28). These elements Blake called 'Zoas', taking the word from the New Testament Greek of Revelation (4.6–9),

---

[1] These views are variously assumed, argued for, or discussed by G. E. Bentley Jr. (facsimile, 1963), David Erdman (*The Library*, 5th series, 19 (1964)), and (in separate articles) by Paul Mann and Robert Essick (*BIQ*, 1985). It is not certain how the designs relate to the text. Several commentators suggest that Blake chose the *Night Thoughts* engravings on which many later parts of the poem are written for their appropriateness to his own text (see page 65 design note). Conversely Andrew Lincoln speculates that some of the drawings themselves may be independent of the text (*Spiritual History* (1995), appendix 1). My own annotations assume that the drawings and the text belong together, but that the *Night Thoughts* engravings, at least insofar as they appear in the present selection, have no special relevance.

where it is used of the four beings who surround the throne of God. The word 'Zoa' is used only in Blake's title, not in his poetic text, but its source is directly referred to in Night IX (123.38), where Blake translated it 'Lifes' (meaning 'living creatures', as in the Authorized Version Ezekiel; the AV Revelation has 'beasts'). Ezekiel's vision suggested the basic shape of the poem's myth, but it was a shape towards which Blake's mythology in the illuminated books of the early 1790s – the mythology of Orc, Urizen and Los–Enitharmon – was already leading him. In its immense elaboration of this mythology and its implications *The Four Zoas* registers important developments in Blake's outlook.

While he was working on *The Four Zoas*, in a letter to his friend and patron Thomas Butts, Blake offered a 'definition of the most sublime poetry': 'allegory addressed to the intellectual powers while it is altogether hidden from the corporeal understanding' (Bentley, *Writings*, 1575). *The Four Zoas* is such an allegory – that is, an allegory in which the personifications can only in limited ways be translated into abstract qualities of the kind often found in the allegory of Spenser or Bunyan. The Zoas at times offer such accounts of themselves or each other, as when Luvah identifies himself as 'love' and Urizen as 'faith and certainty' (27.14–15), but to think of a figure such as Urizen – now 'the Prince of Light' and now 'a shadow from man's wearied intellect', now an architect and now a farmer – as Faith (or as Reason, or any such quality) is more than a simplification: it falsifies. The following introductions and annotations do at times discuss or assume such allegorical translations of Blake's symbolic writing as points of departure or as one aspect of their meaning, but they are primarily concerned with helping the reader inhabit the work's particulars and feel their emotional and imaginative force. Only on this basis can allegory address what Blake called the intellectual powers – the whole thinking-feeling-imaginative being. Blake described *The Four Zoas* as 'a dream'. Its dreamlike qualities are primary. What the inhabitants of this dream are is what, in all their aspects, they say and do, what is said of them and how they are illustrated. The grand mythological beings are utterly human in their passions and confusions. Blake's drama of immortals is a mirror for mortals, but not one in which the identities admit of a key.[2]

From Night II (14.7–18.15):
At the Wedding Feast of Los and Enitharmon

Night I begins, in the usual epic manner, in the middle of the central action, with the fall of the Zoa Tharmas and his female aspect or counterpart (what Blake calls his emanation), Enion. Their fall is a consequence of other disruptions of Albion, of whom all the poem's characters are aspects. Several accounts of the Fall are given in the course of the poem: that Urizen suggested to Luvah that they enslave Albion

---

[2] Nevertheless the great systematizer of Blake, Northrop Frye, provides a chart of correspondences for each Zoa, though he confesses that some aspects 'have been added merely to complete the pattern, and a number are mere guesses' (*Fearful Symmetry* (1947), 277).

Night II] Because of contradictory uncancelled directions in the manuscript some editors, including Erdman, begin Night II after this point; but see Bentley, *Writings*, 1088.

while he slept (21.20); that Luvah began the conflict (10.11; 39.4), with the result that Albion gave all power to Urizen (23.5); that Albion was seduced by Luvah's emanation, Vala (59.1; 83.7; 84.16). All have in common that an imbalance in Albion's internal faculties in the form of a conflict between Urizen and Luvah/Vala is responsible for his collapse. The Zoas weary of the republic of co-operating contraries: each Zoa should be 'servant to the infinite and eternal of the human form' (126.17), but one faculty seeks to usurp illegitimate powers and govern the unwilling. Beyond this all accounts come from a particular, engaged perspective: each depends on the nature and situation of the observer; none is authoritative. The poem as a whole provides multifarious contexts for understanding how we are to place the fallen conceptions of its participants. As readers we may know more than a given character, but this usually means that we experience his or her confusions from a more comprehensive perspective, not that we can resolve them.

The result of the opening quarrel between Tharmas and Enion is a fixing of the main elements of the fallen condition. Central to this is conflict between the sexes – 'the torments of love and jealousy' of the work's later title. The wedding of the Zoa Los and his emanation Enitharmon in Night II epitomizes what is wrong. Its demons' song recounts a version of the primal battle between Urizen and Luvah, and shows a world antagonistic to natural creativity, careless of life, and delighting in violence which has taken its character from this conflict. The puzzled and sorrowful song of experience from the outcast Enion with which the demons' song is juxtaposed gives an alternative perspective on the wedding celebrations and foreshadows the great lament with which she ends Night II (pp. 248–50 below). But the world of time and space into which Albion has fallen is also a place of hope, though hope largely unseen by its inhabitants. The healing Daughters of Beulah are its guardians; it allows glimpses of full spiritual life, mainly through the activities of Los; and (as the end of the following passage shows) the divine, personified in the later additions by Jesus, is at work in it, labouring for an eventual restoration. Apparently a Hell of immutable suffering, the fallen world is finally a Purgatory of possible redemption.

*

[Page 14]

This the song sung at the feast of Los and Enitharmon.

'Ephraim called out to Zion, "Awake O brother mountain,
Let us refuse the plough and spade, the heavy roller and spikèd
10   Harrow. Burn all these cornfields. Throw down all these fences.
Fattened on human blood and drunk with wine of life is better far

---

14.7 *Los*] See *The Book of Urizen*, 5.38 note.

14.7 *Enitharmon*] See *The Book of Urizen*, 19.19 note.

14.8 *Ephraim . . . Zion*] The holy mountains of (respectively) the northern and southern kingdoms into which Israel was divided after the death of Solomon. By encouraging violence they act totally at variance with their proper nature as sacred places. Blake's Old Testament geography images Albion's interior life.

14.9–10 *plough . . . Harrow*] Symbols of creative activity: cf. 92.17 and 124.6 and notes.

Than all these labours of the harvest and the vintage. See, the river,
Red with the blood of men, swells lustful round my rocky knees.
My clouds are not the clouds of verdant fields and groves of fruit,
15   But clouds of human souls. My nostrils drink the lives of men."

The villages lament; they faint outstretched upon the plain.
Wailing runs round the valleys from the mill and from the barn.
But most the polished palaces, dark, silent, bow with dread,
Hiding their books and pictures underneath the dens of earth.

20   The cities send to one another saying, "My sons are mad
With wine of cruelty. Let us plait a scourge, O sister city."
Children are nourished for the slaughter: once the child was fed
With milk, but wherefore now are children fed with blood?

[Page 15]

The horse is of more value than the man. The tiger fierce
Laughs at the human form; the lion mocks and thirsts for blood.
They cry, "O spider, spread thy web! Enlarge thy bones and,
    filled
With marrow, sinews and flesh, exalt thyself: attain a voice.

Call to thy dark armed hosts, for all the sons of men muster
5   together
To desolate their cities! Man shall be no more! Awake, O hosts."
The bowstring sang upon the hills! Luvah and Vala ride
Triumphant in the bloody sky, and the human form is no more.

14.20 *cities*] These 'sisters' (line 21) are female counterparts to the 'brother' mountains (line 8).

Page 14 design. Below the text, to the right, are three female heads (sister cities?), apparently growing from a single torso. (Cf. the corrupt three-headed Hand in *Jerusalem* (plate 50), with 'three brains in contradictory counsel brooding incessantly' (70.5).) She (they) stretches out her right arm: above it loops what appears to be a serpent body; above its hand are two small figures, running, leaping, or flying.

15.7 *Luvah*] Luvah is associated with the loins and with sexual love and desire. He is the eternal form of the being whom, manifested in time, Blake usually refers to as Orc (see *America*, 3.1 note) – though occasionally Blake also uses the name Luvah for manifestations of his temporal being. Orc is born from Enitharmon in *The Book of Urizen*, Chapter VI.   *Vala*] The emanation of Luvah, the character after whom the whole work was originally titled; a central figure of destruction who works by seduction rather than force. One of her most important properties is her veil, which symbolizes her obscuring of spiritual realities. The first syllable of her name may be pronounced so as to bring out this 'veil' association.

The list'ning stars heard, and the first beam of the morning
   started back.
10   He cried out to his father, "Depart! Depart!", but sudden seized
And clad in steel, and his horse proudly neighed; he smelt
   the battle
Afar off. Rushing back, redd'ning with rage, the mighty father

Seized his bright sheephook studded with gems and gold; he
   swung it round
His head, shrill sounding in the sky. Down rushed the sun
   with noise
15   Of war. The mountains fled away; they sought a place beneath.
Vala remained in deserts of dark solitude. Nor sun nor moon

By night nor day to comfort her, she laboured in thick smoke.
Tharmas endured not: he fled howling. Then a barren waste
   sunk down,
Conglobing in the dark confusion. Meantime Los was born,
20   And thou, O Enitharmon! Hark, I hear the hammers of Los.

[Page 16]

They melt the bones of Vala and the bones of Luvah into wedges.
The innumerable sons and daughters of Luvah, closed in furnaces,
Melt into furrows. Winter blows his bellows: ice and snow
Tend the dire anvils. Mountains mourn, and rivers faint and fail.

15.10 *father*] Urizen (cf. *Visions*, 8.3 note), 'Prince of Light', and so the father of a sunbeam.

15.10–11 *but . . . neighed*] The incomplete syntax may have arisen because 'seized' in the manuscript is written over an erased word (or words) now illegible. (Bentley conjectures 'he was seized'.)

15.11–12 *he smelt . . . off*] From Job, 39.25.

15.18 *Tharmas*] One of the four Zoas, the only one who does not appear in the earlier prophecies, and the one whose function in the fourfold scheme is least amenable to allegorical translation. In his fallen state he is often associated with water and so with formlessness. The narrative of the poem begins with his fall and quarrel with his emanation Enion. That fall is now set in the context of events which provide a mythological explanation for it and show its consequences.

15.19 *Conglobing*] Gathering in a compact mass (from *Paradise Lost*, 7.292: 'uprolled / As drops of dust conglobing from the dry').

Page 15 design. Below the text, a bearded old man, drawn in profile, apparently twists the fibres of a thick rope which extends up the right margin behind him. (Cf. *The Book of Urizen*, plate 28 design, where Urizen's net is made of sturdy ropes.)

16.4–5 *Mountains . . . sand*] That is, the destruction called for on pages 14 and 15 has taken place – a prelude to the birth of Luvah in the form of the fettered Orc (cf. the preludium to *America*; Orc in *America* is seen by his opponents in similar terms, as a 'fierce terror' and 'fiend').

5   There is no city, nor cornfield, nor orchard! All is rock and sand.
       There is no sun, nor moon, nor star, but rugged wintry rocks
       Jostling together in the void, suspended by inward fires.
       Impatience now no longer can endure. Distracted Luvah,

       Bursting forth from the loins of Enitharmon, thou fierce terror,
10   Go howl in vain. Smite, smite his fetters; smite, O wintry hammers;
       Smite, Spectre of Urthona. Mock the fiend who drew us down
       From heavens of joy into this deep. Now rage, but rage in vain.'

       Thus sang the demons of the deep. The clarions of war blew loud.
       The feast redounds, and crowned with roses and the circling vine
15   The enormous bride and bridegroom sat. Beside them Urizen
       With faded radiance sighed, forgetful of the flowing wine,
       And of Ahania, his pure bride; but she was distant far.

       But Los and Enitharmon sat in discontent and scorn,
       Craving the more the more enjoying, drawing out sweet bliss
20   From all the turning wheels of heaven and the chariots of the slain.

       At distance far in night repelled, in direful hunger craving,
       Summers and winters round revolving in the frightful deep,

---

16.8–11 *Distracted . . . Urthona*] These lines foretell what takes place in Night V – the birth of
Orc to Enitharmon (58.16–18) and his being fettered by Los/Urthona (61.1–9). Cf. *The Book of
Urizen*, Chapters VI and VII.

16.11 *Spectre of Urthona*] Urthona is one of the four Zoas, the eternal form whose name in
time is Los. On the spectre, see 'My spectre around me', line 1 note.

16.11–12 *Mock . . . deep*] The demons assume that Luvah is responsible for the Fall (see Night
II headnote).

16.14 *redounds*] resounds (*OED v* 5a: last recorded use 1632).

16.17 *Ahania*] The emanation (female counterpart) of Urizen: like the other Zoas, Urizen's
identity is corrupted by his fragmentation.

16.18] This line is repeated from 13.19 (just before the beginning of the present extract).

Page 16 design. Behind the text is a full-page drawing of Christ. His arms are extended to
left and right: later similar designs (pages 106, 108) suggest he is parting clouds (of error – all
that separates us from the divine vision). Below the text his ankles become tongues of flame.
(This design was also used, without the flaming feet, on page 108, and in Blake's illustra-
tions for Young's *Night Thoughts*.) To the left a small figure (Vala?) looks at the flaming ankles
with hands raised in a gesture expressing astonishment. To both right and left is a large
bowed and kneeling angel (each with huge wings rising from its back). The feet illustrate
31.9–10 (a late addition to the page, spoken by Vala): 'I see Luvah not as of old; I only see
his feet / Like pillars of fire travelling through darkness and nonentity.' Like Orc in *America*,
Luvah is identified with Christ – in Luvah's case particularly Christ crucified (see below
92.13–14).

[Page 17]

Enion, blind and age-bent, wept upon the desolate wind.
'Why does the raven cry aloud and no eye pities her?
Why fall the sparrow and the robin in the foodless winter?
Faint, shivering, they sit on leafless bush, or frozen stone,

5   Wearièd with seeking food across the snowy waste; the little
Heart cold, and the little tongue consumed, that once in
      thoughtless joy
Gave songs of gratitude to waving cornfields round their nest.

Why howl the lion and the wolf? Why do they roam abroad?
Deluded by summer's heat they sport in enormous love,
10   And cast their young out to the hungry wilds and sandy deserts.

[Page 18]

Why is the sheep given to the knife? The lamb plays in the sun:
He starts; he hears the foot of man; he says, "Take thou my wool,
But spare my life," but he knows not that winter cometh fast.

The spider sits in his laboured web, eager watching for the fly;
5   Presently comes a famished bird and takes away the spider;
His web is left all desolate, that his little anxious heart
So careful wove, and spread it out with sighs and weariness.'

This was the lamentation of Enion round the golden feast.

Eternity groaned and was troubled at the image of eternal death
10   Without the body of man, an exudation from his sick'ning limbs.

17.1 *Enion*] The emanation of Tharmas (15.18).

17.2–3 *raven ... sparrow*] Blake may have had in mind biblical examples of God's care and compassion, or its absence – Job's questioning: 'Who provideth for the raven his food? When his young ones cry unto God, they wander for lack of meat' (Job, 38.41); and Jesus's reassurance: 'Are not two sparrows sold for a farthing? And one of them shall not fall on the ground without your Father' (Matthew, 10.29).

Page 17 design. Below the text floats a female figure (presumably Enion, weeping on the wind). Her legs, extending behind her to the right, are covered by a long gown. The figure has two (or perhaps three) faces – probably indicating only that Blake was trying out different possible dispositions of the head within the one sketch. (These are not independent heads, as those in the page 14 design clearly are.) The main face looks up towards the text, its long and dishevelled hair held wildly in raised hands.

18.8] The text of this Night originally ended at this point: lines 9–15 are a later addition.

18.10 *Without*] Outside; that is, in what Blake elsewhere calls 'the void outside of existence' (*Milton*, 43.37), the everyday world of error and illusion.

Now man was come to the palm tree, and to the oak of weeping,
Which stand upon the edge of Beulah; and he sunk down
From the supporting arms of the Eternal Saviour, who disposed
The pale limbs of his eternal individuality
15 Upon the Rock of Ages, watching over him with love and care.

*

From Night II (34.55–36.13):
Two Songs of Experience

Night II describes Urizen's building of what Blake calls the Mundane Shell (the fallen universe), and Luvah's being cast into the furnaces of affliction – the latter fundamental to a central subject of *The Four Zoas*: the fate of love in the fallen world, where it becomes an instrument of oppression. Enitharmon, here the active agent, announces her corrupt ethic in *Europe* (1794): 'Who shall I call? Who shall I send? / That woman, lovely woman, may have dominion? / . . . / Go tell the human race that woman's love is sin, / That an eternal life awaits the worms of sixty winters / In an allegorical abode where existence hath never come. / Forbid all joy, and from her childhood shall the little female / Spread nets in every secret path' (8.2–9).

18.11 *palm . . . oak*] Cf. *Jerusalem*, 59.6, where the oak of weeping is again referred to, and the palm is specifically 'the palm of suffering'. The Authorized Version's marginal gloss explains that Allon-bachuth (Genesis, 35.8), the name of the oak at Bethel beneath which is buried Deborah the nurse of Rebekah (the beloved wife of the patriarch Jacob), means 'oak of weeping'. W. H. Stevenson (*Complete Poems* (1989), 315) reports the suggestion of Michael Tolley that Blake associated this with the palm of a quite different Deborah, also at Bethel, Deborah the prophetess and judge (Judges, 4.5). This is in fact a connection not dependent on the accident of a common name: the AV marginal gloss of Judges 4.5 refers back to Genesis, 35.8; the link between the two places was made for Blake by the AV translators. Bethel is the site of Jacob's dream of angels descending to and ascending from the earth (Genesis, 28.10–22): it therefore provides an appropriate biblical analogue to the potentially liminal experiences of Beulah.

18.12 *Beulah*] Cf. 'The Crystal Cabinet', line 8 note.

18.15 *Rock of Ages*] The ideal church, embodying the presence of Christ in time. See Matthew, 16.18: 'Thou art Peter, and upon this rock I will build my church' (where there is a play on the Greek origin of the name, *petra*, a rock). The Authorized Version marginal gloss to Isaiah, 26.4 ('Trust ye in the Lord for ever; for in the Lord Jehovah is everlasting strength') explains that the Hebrew translated as 'everlasting strength' means literally 'rock of ages'. Lines 11–15 are repeated in essence (and in part verbally) in *Jerusalem*, 48.1–4.

Page 18 design. A figure in a long robe plunges down the page and across it to the right, its feet in the left margin by the upper lines of text, its torso partly obscured by the added lower text, its head below the text to the right and its arms extended forward. Below there is a slight sketch of a kneeling figure drawn to connect with the plunging figure's head and arms – perhaps an alternative version which avoids the clash of text and design. The figure perhaps represents the Saviour swooping to rescue the Eternal Man.

The metaphor of heaven ('an allegorical abode'), misrepresented as literal truth, is offered as a bribe to encourage sexual abstinence; the corruption of sexual feelings makes us willing to accept it. Enitharmon in *Europe* is continuous with Enitharmon in *The Four Zoas*, but now she both finds pleasure in and suffers from the cruelties of her 'philosophy' of love. The end of Enitharmon's song at her wedding feast is brilliantly seductive: she conceals techniques of dominance in a persuasive profession of loving responsiveness. It persuades Los. But it may also properly persuade the reader that Enitharmon is not so much in control of manipulative strategies as her song's fierce opening implies: she too is a victim of the corrupt emotional patterns of which she is an agent. Enitharmon's cruelty is juxtaposed with the compassion of Enion – the outsider who cannot be blind to suffering, and who registers it with an utterly unsentimental simplicity. Enion's echoes of Job indicate that, like his, her wisdom is derived from painful experience; and, like Job's, it challenges orthodoxies of religious comfort. Ahania, hearing the lament, models an ideal response: 'never from that moment could she rest upon her pillow.'

*

[Page 34]

55   Night passed, and Enitharmon, e'er the dawn, returned in bliss.
     She sang o'er Los, reviving him to life. His groans were terrible,
     But thus she sang. 'I seize the sphery harp, I strike the strings.

     At the first sound the golden sun arises from the deep,
     And shakes his awful hair.
60   The echo wakes the moon to unbind her silver locks.
     The golden sun bears on my song,
     And nine bright spheres of harmony rise round the fiery king.

     The joy of woman is the death of her most best belovèd,
     Who dies for love of her
65   In torments of fierce jealousy and pangs of adoration.
     The lovers' night bears on my song,
     And the nine spheres rejoice beneath my powerful control.

34.55] All of the lines printed here from page 34 are additions written below and to the left of the original text (which resumes at 35.1).

34.58–92] Enitharmon's song is formalized to an unusual degree when compared with most of the poem: its five-line stanzas regularly alternate seven-stress lines with lines of three and four stresses.

34.59 *awful*] awe-inspiring.

34.62 *nine . . . harmony*] The planetary spheres of pre-Copernican cosmology, the rotation of which was supposed to produce an ideally harmonious music (*OED*, sphere, *sb* 2a).   *the fiery king*] That is, the sun.

They sing unceasing to the notes of my immortal hand.
The solemn silent moon
70 Reverberates the living harmony upon my limbs.
The birds and beasts rejoice and play,
And every one seeks for his mate to prove his inmost joy.

Furious and terrible they sport, and rend the nether deep.
The deep lifts up his rugged head,
75 And, lost in infinite humming wings, vanishes with a cry.
The fading cry is ever dying,
The living voice is ever living in its inmost joy.

Arise you little glancing wings, and sing your infant joy,
Arise and drink your bliss,
80 For every thing that lives is holy, for the source of life
Descends to be a weeping babe,
For the earthworm renews the moisture of the sandy plain.

Now my left hand I stretch to earth beneath
And strike the terrible string.
85 I wake sweet joy in dens of sorrow, and I plant a smile
In forests of affliction,
And wake the bubbling springs of life in regions of dark
    death.

O I am weary: lay thine hand upon me or I faint,
I faint beneath these beams of thine,
90 For thou hast touched my five senses and they answered thee.
Now I am nothing and I sink,
And on the bed of silence sleep till thou awakest me.'

34.72 *prove*] have experience of (*OED v* 3).

34.78–80 *Arise . . . holy*] From *Visions*, 11.9–10, where the lines are spoken by Oothoon. That they are spoken here by Enitharmon may indicate that in her 'rapturous trance' she rediscovers vestiges of her unfallen nature; or that no idea, however fine in itself, is invulnerable to abuse by the corrupt: 'the wicked will turn it to wickedness, the righteous to righteousness' (*Jerusalem*, plate 27). Enitharmon can powerfully foster delusive hopes in Los by role-playng to him her prelapsarian identity.

34.80–1 *source . . . babe*] Enitharmon refers to the birth of the Christ-like Orc: cf. 16.4–5 note and page 16 design.

Thus sang the lovely one in rapturous delusive trance.
Los heard, reviving; he seized her in his arms. Delusive hopes
95 Kindling, she led him into shadows and thence fled, outstretched
Upon the immense like a bright rainbow, weeping, and smiling,
    and fading.

Thus lived Los, driving Enion far into the deathful infinite,
That he may also draw Ahania's spirit into her vortex.
Ah, happy blindness: Enion sees not the terrors of the uncertain.
Thus Enion wails from the dark deep; the golden heavens
100   tremble.

[Page 35]

'I am made to sow the thistle for wheat, the nettle for a nourishing
    dainty.
I have planted a false oath in the earth: it has brought forth a
    poison tree.
I have chosen the serpent for a counsellor, and the dog
For a schoolmaster to my children.
I have blotted out from light and living the dove and
5   nightingale,
And I have causèd the earthworm to beg from door to door.
I have taught the thief a secret path into the house of the just.
I have taught pale artifice to spread his nets upon the morning.
My heavens are brass, my earth is iron, my moon a clod of clay;
My sun a pestilence burning at noon, and a vapour of death
10   in night.

34.94–5 *Delusive . . . Kindling*] Blake has no punctuation. Some editors take the lines to refer to Los's effect on Enitharmon: 'he seized her in his arms, delusive hopes / Kindling.' The context implies rather that they refer to Enitharmon's effect on Los.

34.98 *vortex*] Situation into which people are drawn, or from which they cannot escape (*OED* 5c), used metaphorically for a personality or system of thought. Blake elsewhere uses the word with reference to a more technical sense derived from Cartesian cosmology which may also be relevant here: a body of cosmic matter rapidly carried round in a continuous whirl (*OED* 1a and b); see esp. *Milton*, 14.21–35.

35.1 *thistle for wheat*] Cf. Job, 31.40: 'Let thistles grow instead of wheat, and cockle instead of barley.' With this line we return to text written in the original copperplate script.

35.2 *a false oath . . . a poison tree*] Cf. the 'soft deceitful wiles' of 'A Poison Tree', *Songs of Experience*.

35.3–4 *I have chosen . . . children*] Adapted from *Visions*, 8.8–9.

35.9 *heavens . . . iron*] From Deuteronomy, 28.23: 'thy heaven that is over thy head shall be brass, and the earth that is under thee shall be iron'. (Leviticus 26.19 is similar but transposes the terms: heaven is iron, earth is brass.) The heavens should be golden (34.16).

What is the price of experience? Do men buy it for a song,
Or wisdom for a dance in the street? No: it is bought with the price
Of all that a man hath, his house, his wife, his children.
Wisdom is sold in the desolate market where none come to buy,
15   And in the withered field where the farmer ploughs for bread in vain.

It is an easy thing to triumph in the summer's sun,
And in the vintage, and to sing on the wagon loaded with corn;
It is an easy thing to talk of patience to the afflicted,
To speak the laws of prudence to the houseless wanderer,

[Page 36]

To listen to the hungry raven's cry in wintry season,
When the red blood is filled with wine, and with the marrow
   of lambs.

It is an easy thing to laugh at wrathful elements,
To hear the dog howl at the wintry door, the ox in the
   slaughterhouse moan,
5   To see a god on every wind, and a blessing on every blast,
To hear sounds of love in the thunder-storm that destroys our
   enemy's house,

35.11 *What . . . experience*] Cf. Job, 28.12–28, which begins, 'Where shall wisdom be found? and where is the place of understanding.'

35.18 *It is an easy thing*] Not an absolute statement, as the syntax might at first seem to imply, but dependent on 36.2: 'It is an easy thing to do X, Y and Z when . . .'. 36.3–7 is similarly dependent on 36.8.

Page 35 design. Erotic drawings in the manuscript have been damaged by erasure, sometimes combined with pencil additions to further obscure disapprobated material. It is not known when or by whom. This design is one to have so suffered. Below the text three naked women gaze at sturdy phallic growths (perhaps to be thought of as mandrakes) which one of them handles. The genital area of the woman to the right has been partially erased and scribbled over in pencil. In the left margin a woman approaches the central group carrying a basket on her head. She has apparently naked breasts but wears a garment with a row of buttons running down to the upper thigh below them. What her basket contains it is difficult to identify: Bentley sees the shapes conjecturally as fruit, Erdman as phallic totems obscured by added scribbles. To the right a squatting figure (the lower part of whose body has been erased and scribbled over) is watched by a standing naked girl with prominently drawn vulva who raises her hands in a gesture suggesting alarm about whatever has been obliterated. (The erotic drawings are concerned principally with the sufferings of Luvah in the furnaces of affliction – the torments experienced in the fallen world by the faculty he represents, love and desire.)

36.4 *dog . . . moan*] Adapted from *The Book of Urizen*, 25.1–2.

36.6 *enemy's*] The manuscript has 'enemies' and some editors take this as a plural; the following lines indicate that it should be understood as Blake's idiosyncratic spelling of a singular possessive form.

To rejoice in the blight that covers his field, and the sickness that
    cuts off his children,
While our olive and vine sing and laugh round our door, and our
    children bring fruits and flowers.

Then the groan and the dolour are quite forgotten, and the slave
    grinding at the mill,
And the captive in chains, and the poor in the prison, and the
10   soldier in the field
When the shattered bone hath laid him groaning among the
    happier dead.

It is an easy thing to rejoice in the tents of prosperity.
Thus could I sing, and thus rejoice; but it is not so with me.'

*

From Night V (63.23–65.12):
Urizen laments

Night III deals with the further fall of Urizen as a result of conflict with his emana-
tion, Ahania, and further disintegration of Tharmas and Enion. In Night IV Los (as
in *The Book of Urizen*) fixes Urizen's fallen state. At the beginning of Night V Los
'left the cold / Prince of Light [Urizen] bound in chains of intellect among the
furnaces; / But all the furnaces were out, and the bellows had ceased to blow.' The
main body of the Night's narrative is then concerned with the birth of Orc and his
binding with the chain of jealousy (again as in *The Book of Urizen*). In the following
lament, with which the Night ends, Urizen communes with himself in fear of Orc,
contrasting memories of prelapsarian happiness with his present condition, his
sorrow exacerbated by the memory of what is lost. Soliloquizing, Urizen does not
express his usual self-righteous aggressiveness: in formalized rhetoric which gives
his difficult attempt at honesty a dignified pathos he acknowledges his part in the
Eternal Man's Fall.

*

36.13 *but . . . me*] Cf. Job, 9.34–5: 'Let him [God] take his rod away from me . . . Then would
I speak, and not fear him; but it is not so with me.'

Page 36 design. A figure wearing a long robe, with hair blown back and arms bent in front
of its face, plunges down the left margin (perhaps Ahania as described in the lines that
immediately follow this extract, 'drawn through unbounded space / On to the margin of
nonentity.').

[Page 63]

The woes of Urizen shut up in the deep dens of Urthona.

'Ah, how shall Urizen the King submit to this dark mansion?
Ah, how is this? Once on the heights I stretched my throne
25   sublime.
The mountains of Urizen, once of silver, where the sons of
     wisdom dwelt,
And on whose tops the virgins sang, are rocks of desolation.

My fountains, once the haunt of swans, now breed the scaly
     tortoise;
The houses of my harpers are become a haunt of crows;
30   The gardens of wisdom are become a field of horrid graves,
And on the bones I drop my tears and water them in vain.

[Page 64]

Once how I walkèd from my palace in gardens of delight.
The sons of wisdom stood around, the harpers followed with
     harps;
Nine virgins clothed in light composed the song to their immortal
     voices,
And at my banquets of new wine my head was crowned with joy.

5   Then in my ivory pavilions I slumbered in the noon,
And walkèd in the silent night among sweet-smelling flowers,
Till on my silver bed I slept, and sweet dreams round me hovered.
But now my land is darkened, and my wise men are departed.

My songs are turnèd to cries of lamentation
10   Heard on my mountains, and deep sighs under my palace roofs,
Because the steeds of Urizen, once swifter than the light,
Were kept back from my lord, and from his chariot of mercies.

64.3 *Nine virgins*] Blake perhaps had in mind the tutelary spirits of the nine planetary spheres and their music (cf. 34.62 note); or the classical nine muses (who, among other things, preside over the creation of poetry and music).

64.12 *my lord*] The reference to Genesis (line 22) indicates that Blake intends here a divine creator, and (the context implies) one more legitimately conceived than the Old Testament demiurge whom Blake often satirizes through Urizen himself.

O, did I keep the horses of the day in silver pastures?
O, I refused the lord of day the horses of his prince.
15 O, did I close my treasuries with roofs of solid stone,
And darken all my palace walls with envyings and hate?

O fool, to think that I could hide from his all-piercing eyes
The gold and silver and costly stones, his holy workmanship.
O fool, could I forget the light that fillèd my bright spheres
20 Was a reflection of his face who called me from the deep?

I well remember, for I heard the mild and holy voice
Saying, "O light, spring up and shine," and I sprang up from
      the deep.
He gave me a silver sceptre, and crowned me with a golden crown,
And said, "Go forth and guide my son who wanders on the ocean."

25 I went not forth. I hid myself in black clouds of my wrath.
I called the stars around my feet in the night of councils dark.
The stars threw down their spears and fled naked away.
We fell. I seized thee, dark Urthona, in my left hand falling;

I seized thee, beauteous Luvah: thou art faded like a flower,
30 And like a lily is thy wife, Vala, withered by winds.
When thou didst bear the golden cup at the immortal tables
Thy children smote their fiery wings, crowned with the gold
      of heaven.

64.22 *O light . . . shine*] Cf. the divine fiat with which creation begins in Genesis, 1.3: 'Let there be light.'

64.24 *my son*] The Eternal Man, Albion, of whom the Zoas (including Urizen) are ultimately aspects.

64.26–8 *I called . . . We fell*] The principal analogue to Urizen is the Old Testament Jehovah, but he also resembles Milton's Satan. As 'Prince of Light' he recalls the unfallen Satan's identity as Lucifer; like Milton's Satan, he goes to plot his revolt in the north (21.23; cf. *Paradise Lost*, 5.755). And here his fall resembles that of Satan in his rejection of a divine command and calling of a rebellious secret council (cf. *Paradise Lost*, 5.743–907).

64.27 *The stars . . . away*] Cf. 'The Tiger', *Songs of Experience*, lines 17–18 and note.

64.31 *bear . . . tables*] Luvah is here specifically associated with the classical myth of Ganymede, cupbearer to Zeus; behind this lies a more general association elsewhere in the poem with wine and the god Dionysus.

Page 64 design. At the bottom of the page (partly covered by the last five lines of text) are three naked figures. One (male), squatting on his heels, pulls a net from the left corner of the page. Behind him a woman with prominent breasts leans backwards to kiss, and reaches

[Page 65]

Thy pure feet stepped on the steps divine, too pure for other feet,
And thy fair locks shadowed thine eyes from the divine effulgence.
Then thou didst keep with strong Urthona the living gates of
    Heaven,
But now thou art bound down with him even to the gates of Hell,

5   Because thou gavest Urizen the wine of the Almighty
For steeds of light, that they might run in thy golden chariot
    of pride.
I gave to thee the steeds, I poured the stolen wine,
And, drunken with the immortal draught, fell from my throne
    sublime.

I will arise, explore these dens, and find that deep pulsation
That shakes my caverns with strong shudders. Perhaps this is
10   the night
Of prophecy, and Luvah hath burst his way from Enitharmon.
When thought is closed in caves, then love shall show its root
    in deepest Hell.'

*

---

backwards to hold the penis of a man who embraces her from behind. Probably they represent the family group, Los, Enitharmon and Orc, with whose Oedipal conflicts most of Night V is concerned (see headnote): the net is perhaps a potential weapon, like that with which Vulcan, the smith of the gods, snared his wife Venus and her lover, Mars. (Orc is compared to Mars in *America* (7.2); Enitharmon, whose main aim is power for women by manipulation of the erotic, is depicted as a 'Venus pudica' earlier (page 32 design); Los is imaged as a blacksmith from *The Book of Urizen* onwards, and at 137.8 is specifically, like Vulcan, lame.)

65.5–8] One central element shared by different accounts of the Fall in the poem is that it arose from the Zoas usurping each other's functions: here Urizen reports an exchange of roles with Luvah.

65.9 *explore these dens*] Cf. *The Book of Urizen*, Chapter VIII.

65.9–10 *that deep . . . shudders*] Urizen hears the struggles of the chained Orc whose binding is described earlier in Night V.

65.11 *Luvah . . . Enitharmon*] Orc/Luvah is born from Enitharmon earlier in Night V (58.16–22).

65.12 *When thought . . . Hell*] Blake's epigrammatic manner, but used dramatically: Urizen summarizes his own situation and, on the basis of that particular limited perspective, surmises that love is diabolic in origin.

As elsewhere in *The Four Zoas*, the text of page 65 is written in the (blank) central text window of one of Blake's engravings for Young's *Night Thoughts* and has, therefore, no design of its own.

From Night VII (80.1–81.6):
The Conflicts of Urizen and Orc

In Night VI Urizen acts on his resolution to 'explore these dens' (65.9) to discover Orc: he is horrified at the chaos and suffering he finds. The confrontation between Urizen and Orc in Night VII typically combines history and myth. Los and Enitharmon mingle with social commentary which, whether or not specific in its contemporary reference (see 80.9–14 note), is recognizably analogous to some contemporary social philosophy and political action. Blake lived in a society in which the state church was an ally of a social order which, from the point of view of the church, was a necessary stay against sufferings consequent on social disorder, but which, from Blake's point of view, actively caused the remediable sufferings of poverty. Blake's rage against what he saw as the abuse of religion as a sanction for social injustice may be gauged from his annotations of Bishop Richard Watson's reply to Paine's *Age of Reason*. Among the bishop's publications Blake found listed a sermon on 'the wisdom and goodness of God in having made both rich and poor.' Blake's repudiation is itself based in religion: 'God made man happy and rich, but the subtle made the innocent poor. This must be a most wicked and blasphemous book' (Bentley, *Writings*, 1405). The bishop's idea of God is blasphemy. Urizen's manipulation of 'moral duty' for exploitative purposes is only more knowingly hypocritical. 'Pity would be no more / If we did not make somebody poor' ('The Human Abstract') is so acute because 'make' allows to peep out what it is vital (from the point of view of the speaker) to conceal: whether or not suffering can be justified by the compassion it generates, no compensatory virtue can justify the active creation of evils advantageous to their apologist. In the following passage Blake satirizes through Urizen charitable giving designed to conceal and maintain a fundamentally exploitative situation. The unusual absence of complicating perspectives perhaps also implies that charitable giving as a general principle of action may always be vitiated by some acquiescence in injustice which is to the giver's advantage.

What to reject here may be in action difficult, but morally it is uncomplicated. What to follow is more problematic: even Urizen's opponents now take something of their character from the effectiveness of his domination. Orc-Prometheus becomes a Christ figure crucified on Urizen's Tree of Mystery, and this is not necessarily inconsistent with his association with the serpent at the Tree of Knowledge – the rebellious opponent of the archetypal tyrant, Jehovah. But here the Orc-serpent is sinister: under the influence of his torturer he takes on Urizenic characteristics, 'turning affection into fury and thought into abstraction', and Urizen 'suffer[s] him to climb that he might draw all human forms / Into submission to his will.' Urizen, that is, plans to use the crucified Orc as, in Blake's view, the Church used the crucified Christ: as an instrument of oppression.

*

[Page 80]

And Urizen read in his book of brass in sounding tones.

'Listen, O daughters, to my voice. Listen to the words of wisdom.
So shall ye govern over all. Let moral duty tune your tongue,
But be your hearts harder than the nether millstone.

5   To bring the Shadow of Enitharmon beneath our wondrous tree,
That Los may evaporate like smoke and be no more,
Draw down Enitharmon to the Spectre of Urthona,
And let him have dominion over Los, the terrible shade.

Compel the poor to live upon a crust of bread by soft mild arts.
Smile when they frown, frown when they smile; and when a man
10   looks pale
With labour and abstinence, say he looks healthy and happy;
And when his children sicken let them die: there are enough
Born, even too many, and our earth will be overrun
Without these arts. If you would make the poor live with temper,
15   With pomp give every crust of bread you give; with gracious cunning
Magnify small gifts; reduce the man to want a gift, and then give
    with pomp.

80.1 *book of brass*] Urizen's books of brass and iron are among his constant properties (*Europe*, 14.3–5; *Urizen*, Chapter II, vv. 7–8; *Ahania*, Chapter III, vv. 3–4; *The Four Zoas*, 71.40–2). Their 'adamantine leaves' (*The Four Zoas*, 71.42) embody the harsh and uncompassionate nature of their doctrines.

80.2–9] Line 1 was originally followed by line 9; line 2 was added under line 1, line 3 under line 9, and lines 4–8 in the margin, following on from line 3. The logic of the speech suggests that Blake intended the original second line (here line 9) to lead into what is now line 10. In terms of subject lines 2–4 prepare for lines 9–21, lines 5–8 for lines 22–6.

80.3 *ye*] 'be' in the manuscript, but clearly in error.

80.5 *Shadow of Enitharmon*] A phantasmal residue of Enitharmon's nature, consequent on Urizen's influence; Los describes the transformation in a lament, 81.23–82.14.   *our wondrous tree*] Cf. *Songs of Experience*, 'The Human Abstract', line 22 note.

80.9–14 *Compel . . . arts*] Blake may have had in view the notorious ideas of Thomas Malthus's *Essay on the Principles of Population* (1798; rev. edns., 1803 and 1805). Malthus argued that war, disease, shortage of food and poverty were of value as oblique instruments of population control. David Erdman also plausibly connects this speech with Pitt's Brown Bread Bill of 1800, designed, in a situation of scarcity, to diminish consumption (*Prophet Against Empire*, 367–9). Blake depicted shortage of food as an instrument of tyranny, however, without either of these promptings in *The Song of Los* (1795): 'Shall not the king call for famine from the heath / . . . / To restrain, to dismay, to thin / The inhabitants of mountain and plain / . . . / To cut off the bread from the city, / That the remnant may learn to obey; / . . . / To teach mortal worms the path / That leads from the gates of the grave' (6.9–7.8). Cf. *America* where Boston's Angel arraigns the 'crawling villain [who] preaches abstinence and wraps himself / In fat of lambs' (13.14–15).

80.14 *temper*] composure (under the provocation of want); in effect, acceptance of their lot.

Say he smiles if you hear him sigh; if pale, say he is ruddy.
Preach temperance: say he is overgorged and drowns his wit
In strong drink, though you know that bread and water are all
20   He can afford. Flatter his wife, pity his children, till we can
Reduce all to our will, as spaniels are taught with art.

Lo, how the heart and brain are formèd in the breeding womb
Of Enitharmon, how it buds with life and forms the bones,
The little heart, the liver, and the red blood in its labyrinths.
25   By gratified desire, by strong devouring appetite, she fills
Los with ambitious fury, that his race shall all devour.'

Then Orc cried, 'Curse thy cold hypocrisy! Already round thy tree,
In scales that shine with gold and rubies, thou beginnest to weaken
My divided spirit. Like a worm I rise in peace, unbound
30   From wrath. Now when I rage my fetters bind me more.
O torment, O torment! A worm compelled. Am I a worm?
Is it in strong deceit that man is born? In strong deceit
Thou dost restrain my fury, that the worm may fold the tree.
Avaunt, cold hypocrite! I am chained, or thou couldst not use
    me thus.
The Man shall rage, bound with this chain; the worm in
35   silence creep.
Thou wilt not cease from rage, grey demon. Silence all thy storms.

80.18 *temperance*] Blake's views on the legitimate and humane pleasures of the ale-house may be deduced from 'The Little Vagabond', *Songs of Experience*.

80.23 *Enitharmon*] Here seen as the archetypal woman and so representing womankind generally; similarly with Los (line 26), where he represents all men. Urizen is horrified that there should be so much breeding (cf. lines 12–14).

80.25 *gratified desire*] Cf. the Notebook quatrain (from the early 1790s): 'What is it men in women do require? / The lineaments of gratified desire. / What is it women do in men require? / The linements of gratified desire.' Urizen is opposed to it.

80.26 *that ... devour*] That is, those who follow Los's example will (it appears to Urizen) destroy everything. Cf. lines 5–8: Urizen fears and hopes to destroy Los just as he fears and hopes to destroy Orc.

80.27–8 *round thy tree, / In scales*] For Orc/Luvah as a Christ figure cf. 92.13–14. For Orc's association with the serpent cf. *America*, notes to 6.11, 9.4 and plate 13, design. Fuzon – a rebellious son of Urizen somewhat analogous to Orc, who nevertheless begins with a family likeness to his father – is crucified on the Tree of Mystery in *The Book of Ahania* (1795), Chapter III.

80.31 *Am I a worm*] The worm is used in biblical professions of human worthlessness: Job, 25.6, 'man, that is a worm, and the son of man, which is a worm'; Psalm 22.6, 'I am a worm, and no man.'

80.33 *fold*] enfold.

Give me example of thy mildness, king of furious hail storms.
Art thou the cold attractive power that holds me in this chain?
I well remember how I stole thy light, and it became fire
40   Consuming. Thou know'st me now, O Urizen, Prince of Light,
And I know thee. Is this the triumph, this the godlike state
That lies beyond the bounds of science in the grey obscure?'

Terrified, Urizen heard Orc, now certain that he was Luvah,
And Orc began to organize a serpent body,
45   Despising Urizen's light, and turning it into flaming fire,
Receiving as a poisoned cup receives the heavenly wine,
And turning affection into fury and thought into abstraction,
A self-consuming dark devourer, rising into the heavens.

Urizen envious brooding sat, and saw the secret terror
50   Flame high in pride, and laugh to scorn the source of his deceit,
Nor knew the source of his own, but thought himself the sole
        author

[Page 81]

Of all his wandering experiments in the horrible abyss.
He knew that weakness stretches out in breadth and length;
        he knew
That wisdom reaches high and deep; and therefore he made Orc,
In serpent form compelled, stretch out and up the mysterious tree.
5   He suffered him to climb that he might draw all human forms
Into submission to his will; nor knew the dread result.

*

80.39 *stole . . . fire*] Cf. 10.13, where Luvah 'seized the horses of light, and rose into the chariot of day': 'it became fire / Consuming' relates Orc-Luvah to Phaëton, the son of Apollo who drove the chariot of the sun with disastrous results (Ovid, *Metamorphoses*, II). If Orc is seen simply as stealing fire (which these lines taken alone might suggest) he acts like Prometheus, as friend of humankind and opponent of tyrannous deities: cf. Orc as Prometheus in *America*, plate 3 design and note.

80.42 *science*] knowledge (as often in Blake).

Page 80 design. The page has been trimmed immediately below the text, thereby removing any design it might have contained. The text of page 81 is written on the central panel of a *Night Thoughts* engraving (cf. page 65 design note).

81.3–6 *he made . . . will*] Cf. John 3.14: 'As Moses lifted up the serpent in the wilderness [a reference to Numbers 21.9], even so must the Son of man be lifted up'; and John 12.32: 'I, if I be lifted up from the earth, will draw all men unto me.'

From Night VII (91.1–93.20):
The Triumph of Vala

The Zoas become ever more deeply corrupted by conflict and disintegration, and by the measures Urizen particularly takes in response to this. Urizen's world is a commercial empire built on exploitation of child and slave labour and ruled by money regardless of moral values. Its injustice is protected by war, and it feeds off the violence it fosters. Its religion appropriates and so keeps in check the genuine visions of prophecy and poetry, and it foments violence by repressing and so perverting sexual energy. There are counter-elements: early in Night VII the fractured aspects of Los reintegrate and begin to work together creatively. Love is the key to their recovery (90.65–8). But, as Urizen's world moves towards epitomizing error, Love is the principal victim: just as all the forms of human excellence exhibited by Christ have been distorted by violence since the beginning of time (92.15), so specifically have the affections connected with Luvah. Such violence arises from repressed or diverted sexual feeling which thus becomes the antithesis of its proper self. Urizen and Vala are the two main negative forces of the poem. Orc is a victim of each in a different way. In the following passage Vala is invoked and celebrated as delighting in violence: she uses sex to gain power, and enjoys the pain she inflicts – though sobered from this orgy of sadism she becomes a 'howling melancholy' (94.48). Blake interrupts the war songs with an account of typical machines and work practices of the Industrial Revolution, contrasting these with the tools, machines and work practices of the handicraft traditions which factory machinery and organization displaced: these did not dry up the spirit because their mode of action was analogous to non-mechanical human activities. Adam Smith described the division of labour in *The Wealth of Nations* (1766): it was common practice in many industries before the end of the century. Blake's objections are to long hours and low pay, but above all what he sees as the inhuman implications of the new types of machinery, and to production-line specialization (Adam Smith describes 'about 18 distinct operations' which go to the making of a pin) because this divorces the worker from a sense of creative relation to the product. The specifically military products, the account of the spiritual consequences of factory work, and the placing of the passage all connect industrialization with militarism.

*

[Page 91]

Now in the caverns of the grave and places of human seed

91.1] Blake's preferred decision (if he made one) about how to relate the two sections of the manuscript headed 'Night the Seventh' has been much discussed (see *BIQ*, 12 (1978)). The two sections have been conventionally identified as Nights VIIa and VIIb. Night VIIb begins

The nameless shadowy vortex stood before the face of Orc.
The Shadow reared her dismal head over the flaming youth
With sighs, and howling, and deep sobs. That he might lose
    his rage,
5   And with it lose himself in meekness, she embraced his fire.
As when the earthquake rouses from his den, his shoulders huge
Appear above the crumbling mountain; silence waits around him
A moment, then astounding horror belches from the centre;
The fiery dogs arise; the shoulders huge appear:
10   So Orc rolled round his clouds upon the deeps of dark Urthona.
Knowing the arts of Urizen were pity and meek affection,
And that by these arts the serpent form exuded from his limbs,
Silent as despairing love, and strong as jealousy –
Jealous that she was Vala now become Urizen's harlot,
And the harlot of Los, and the deluded harlot of the kings
15   of earth –
His soul was gnawn in sunder.
The hairy shoulders rend the links; free are the wrists of fire.
Red rage redounds. He roused his lions from his forests black.
They howl around the flaming youth, rending the nameless
    Shadow,
And running their immortal course, through solid darkness
20   borne.
Loud sounds the war song round red Orc in his fury,
And round the nameless Shadowy Female in her howling terror,
When all the elemental gods joined in the wondrous song.

---

at this point.   *the caverns . . . seed*] The omega and alpha of human life as constructed by the Fall – beyond death and before conception. Also the action is both in the world and in the body: the mythic personifications have both political and psychological meanings. (The line is repeated almost precisely from 44.3.)

91.2 *nameless shadowy vortex*] Vala (line 14). Though this paragraph repeats lines from the preludium to *America* (lines 91.13, 17; *America*, 4.1–2), and the shadowy female reappears from the preludiums to both *America* and *Europe* (in both of which, however, she is the daughter of Urthona-Enitharmon), the contexts are quite different: in *America* the woman is a loving gaoler who helps Orc to become free; here she is a would-be seductive oppressor.   *vortex*] Cf. 34.98 note.

91.9 *fiery dogs*] Meaning unknown. The word 'dogs' is clearly written, and Blake uses this phrase in connection with earthquakes in *Tiriel* (line 204).

91.11–12 *the arts . . . limbs*] Cf. the previous extract.

91.15 *harlot . . . earth*] This phrase connects Vala with the Scarlet Whore of Revelation, 17–18, who commits fornication with the kings of the earth (see esp. Revelation 18.3, 9).

91.18 *redounds*] Cf. 16.14 note.

91.21 *his fury*] A word or words has been erased between these two words; Erdman reads (conjecturally) 'triumphant', Bentley (conjecturally) 'blind f th'.

'Sound the war trumpet, terrific souls clad in attractive steel;
25 Sound the shrill fife, serpents of war. I hear the northern drum;
Awake, I hear the flappings of the folding banners.

The dragons of the north put on their armour.
Upon the eastern sea direct they take their course.
The glitt'ring of their horses' trapping stains the vault of night.'

30 'Stop we the rising of the glorious king. Spur, spur your clouds

[Page 92]

Of death. O northern drum, awake. O hand of iron, sound
The northern drum. Now give the charge, bravely obscured
With darts of wintry hail. Again the black bow draw;
Again the elemental strings to your right breasts draw,
5 And let the thund'ring drum speed on the arrows black.'

The arrows flew from cloudy bow all day, till blood
From east to west flowed like the human veins in rivers
Of life upon the plains of death and valleys of despair.

'Now sound the clarions of victory. Now strip the slain.
10 Clothe yourselves in golden arms, brothers of war.'
They sound the clarions strong; they chain the howling captives.

91.24–9] Blake's text is unpunctuated: the assigning of speeches is editorial. The speakers here apparently have a different relation to the north from the speakers of 92.1–2. They and the speakers of 91.30–92.5 are therefore presumably opposed – supporters respectively of Urizen and of Urthona-Los (see lines 25, 27 and 30 notes). But the parties not clearly differentiated: the war of Albion's Zoas is a civil war.

91.24 *terrific*] terrifying.

91.25 *serpents*] Bass wind instruments with a deep tone, in the eighteenth and early nineteenth centuries commonly used in military bands.

91.25, 27 *northern . . . north*] The north is Urthona's: see Night VI, 74.17.

91.30 *the glorious king*] Probably Urizen: the 'Prince of Light' is naturally associated with the sun and so with 'rising', and these lines are apparently sung by supporters of Urthona-Los. Erdman, however, identifies this 'glorious king' as Orc/Napoleonic France, and reads the passage in terms of European campaigns of 1799 (*Prophet Against Empire*, 325–8).

The text of pages 91 and 93 is written on the central panels of two *Night Thoughts* engravings (cf. page 65 design note).

92.2 *bravely*] excellently.

92.11–93.19] These lines reappear with minor revisions in *Jerusalem*, 65.6–55 where they are sung by 'the spectre sons of Albion round Luvah's stone of trial.'

92.11 *chain . . . captives*] Blake refers to the Druid practice of human sacrifice before a battle to entreat divine favour. He returns repeatedly to Druidic human sacrifice as epitomizing the deepest depravity in *Milton* and *Jerusalem*.

They give the oath of blood; they cast the lots into the helmet;
They vote the death of Luvah, and they nailed him to the tree.
They pierced him with a spear, and laid him in a sepulchre,
15 To die a death of six thousand years, bound round with desolation.
The sun was black, and the moon rolled a useless globe through
    heaven.

Then left the sons of Urizen the plough and harrow, the loom,
The hammer, and the chisel, and the rule and compasses.
They forged the sword, the chariot of war, the battle-axe,
20 The trumpet fitted to the battle, and the flute of summer;
And all the arts of life they changed into the arts of death.
The hour-glass contemned because its simple workmanship
Was as the workmanship of the ploughman, and the waterwheel,
That raises water into cisterns, broken and burned in fire,
Because its workmanship was like the workmanship of the
25   shepherd.
And in their stead intricate wheels invented, wheel without wheel,
To perplex youth in their outgoings, and to bind to labours
Of day and night the myriads of eternity; that they might file
And polish brass and iron hour after hour, laborious
    workmanship,
Kept ignorant of the use; that they might spend the days
30   of wisdom
In sorrowful drudgery to obtain a scanty pittance of bread;
In ignorance to view a small portion and think that all,
And call it 'Demonstration', blind to all the simple rules of life.

92.13–14 *nailed . . . sepulchre*] All three details relate Luvah's death to the crucifixion of Christ.

92.15 *six thousand years*] Cf. *Marriage*, 14.2 note: (approximately) the duration of the world from its supposed beginning in 4004 BC.

92.16 *sun . . . heaven*] As a result of the corruption of humanity on earth the heavens cease to be perceived imaginatively; cf. 'The Mental Traveller', lines 62–6, and *The French Revolution*, lines 211–14: 'When the heavens were sealed with a stone, and the terrible sun closed in an orb, and the moon / Rent from the nations . . . / The millions of spirits immortal were bound in the ruins of sulphur heaven / To wander enslaved.'

92.17–19 *plough . . . sword*] In deserting agricultural implements to manufacture weapons the sons of Urizen reverse the famous vision of peace in Isaiah 2.4, repeated in Micah, 4.3: 'they shall beat their swords into ploughshares, and their spears into pruninghooks; nation shall not lift up sword against nation, neither shall they learn war any more.' In Joel, 3.10 ploughshares are made into swords as a prelude to the final battle of the Apocalypse.

92.19 *forged*] made, constructed.

92.22 *contemned*] despised, viewed with contempt.

92.26 *without*] outside.

'Now, now the battle rages round thy tender limbs, O Vala.
35   Now smile among thy bitter tears; now put on all thy beauty.
Is not the wound of the sword sweet, and the broken bone
    delightful?
Wilt thou now smile among the slain, when the wounded groan
    in the field?

[Page 93]

Lift up thy blue eyes, Vala, and put on thy sapphire shoes,
O melancholy Magdalen. Behold the morning breaks:
Gird on thy flaming zone. Descend into the sepulchre.
Scatter the blood from thy golden brow, the tears from thy silver
    locks.
Shake off the waters from thy wings, and the dust from thy white
5   garments.

Remember all thy feignèd terrors on the secret couch,
When the sun rose in glowing morn with arms of mighty hosts
Marching to battle, who was wont to rise with Urizen's harps,
Girt as a sower with his seed to scatter life abroad.

92.34] The beginning of a war song sung by the 'demons of the deep' (93.20).

Page 92 design. Below the text a gowned (male?) figure sits, with his back to the viewer; the feather of a quill is visible in his right hand, and he is apparently writing in a book in front of him – perhaps writing the poem. A tiny figure floats above his head – perhaps a Muse, or a being such as the fairy who dictated *Europe* (plate 3). A naked woman (Vala?) kneels to his left.

93.2 *Magdalen*] Mary Magdalene was among the first of the followers of Jesus to go to the sepulchre after the resurrection (Matthew, 28.1; Mark, 16.1–2; Luke, 24.10; John, 20.1 – where, uniquely, she is alone). Vala is connected with her because Vala's counterpart Luvah is connected with the crucified Christ (91.13–14), and because of her weeping: Mary Magdalene epitomized the weeping penitent because she was traditionally associated with the prostitute who washes Jesus's feet with her tears in Luke 7.37–50. As 92.36–7 indicate, the demons are mocking: any penitence Vala may show they take to be hypocritical (cf. line 6).

93.3 *zone*] girdle, belt.

93.6 *secret couch*] Referring allusively to Vala's seduction of Urizen when she left Luvah and displaced Ahania. The following lines describe Urizen's consequent transformation.

93.7–9 *the sun ... abroad*] Cf. *Visions*, 5.35 note.

93.8 *rise ... harps*] Cf. Blake's letter to Hayley (27.1.04) on the poetry of Edward Marsh, 'like the sound of harps which I hear before the sun's rising' (Bentley, *Writings*, 1589).

Arise, O Vala, bring the bow of Urizen; bring the swift arrows
10   of light.
How raged the golden horses of Urizen, bound to the chariot
      of Love,
Compelled to leave the plough to the ox, to snuff up the winds
      of desolation,
To trample the cornfields in boastful neighings. This is no
      gentle harp;
This is no warbling brook, nor shadow of a myrtle tree;
15   But blood, and wounds, and dismal cries, and clarions of war,
And hearts laid open to the light by the broad grisly sword,
And bowels hidden in hammered steel ripped forth upon the
      ground.
Call forth thy smiles of soft deceit; call forth thy cloudy tears.
We hear thy sighs in trumpets shrill when morn shall blood
      renew.'

20   So sung the demons of the deep; the clarions of war blew loud.

*

From Night IX (124.6–126.17): Apocalypse

Night IX describes an apocalyptic transformation. The reversal is sudden, though there are signs of it in earlier parts of poem: the lower levels of Blake's spiritual geography still allow some access to higher states of being. The Saviour has lain the Eternal Man to rest on the Rock of Ages and promised a resurrection parallel to that of Lazarus (Nights I and IV); the separated Los and Enitharmon aspects of Urthona have reintegrated, and they retain contact with higher levels of being through art (Night VII); Los's forge and Enitharmon's looms work creatively for good (Night VIII). Night VIII, however, shows the fall at its deepest point, setting against these positive forces a new epitome of error, the combined male and female figure, Satan/ Rahab, which takes over from the partial, redeemable errors of Urizen and Vala. But this epitome, by showing error's clear form, prepares for its overthrow: even the

---

93.10 *bow . . . arrows*] Urizen, 'Prince of Light', is imagined in terms that recall the traditional properties of the classical sun god, Apollo.

93.11 *How raged . . . Love*] Referring to a version of the Fall of Albion: Luvah usurped the function of Urizen as god of the sun (cf. Night II headnote and 65.5–8 note).

negative works indirectly in a way that ultimately brings about good. And in Night VIII two other redemptive figures are also prominent – Jerusalem, a counterpart to Vala based on the biblical image of the ideal heavenly city; and Jesus, who takes over from Luvah as the being who bears the suffering corruption has made inevitable, but does so without engendering further cycles of retributive violence. This Jesus is ultimately not the historical character of Christian orthodoxy who performs a once for all act of redemption, but a mythic being who shows how selfless love can act to reintegrate every positive aspect of life.

The following passage from the apocalypse of Night IX is part of a much longer section which shows the Eternal Man's regeneration. Blake takes his images of the harvest and the winepress from biblical apocalyptic writing, particularly Isaiah 63 and Revelation 14. These texts show regeneration as a complete remaking to which, besides the obviously creative processes of ploughing and sowing, violent breakings down – treading the grapes, threshing the grain – are also a necessary preliminary. The final paragraph of the following extract (126.6–17) gives in brief a central theme of the whole work.

*

[Page 124]

    Then seized the sons of Urizen the plough. They polished it
    From rust of ages: all its ornaments of gold and silver and ivory
    Reshone across the field immense, where all the nations
    Darkened like mould in the divided fallows, where the weed
10   Triumphs in its own destruction. They took down the harness
    From the blue walls of heaven, starry-jingling, ornamented
    With beautiful art, the study of angels, the workmanship
      of demons
    When Heaven and Hell in emulation strove in sports of glory.

    The noise of rural work resounded through the heavens of heavens.
    The horse[s] neigh from the battle, the wild bulls from the
15   sultry waste,
    The tigers from the forests, and the lions from the sandy deserts.
    They sing, they seize the instruments of harmony, they throw away
    The spear, the bow, the gun, the mortar; they level the
      fortifications;
    They beat the iron engines of destruction into wedges;

124.6–7 *plough . . . silver*] Reversing the movement of 92.17. Cf. 'Auguries of Innocence', lines 101–2: 'When gold and gems adorn the plough / To peaceful arts shall Envy bow.'

124.12 *angels . . . demons*] Inclusive, a marriage of heaven and hell.

20   They give them to Urthona's sons. Ringing the hammers sound
       In dens of death, to forge the spade, the mattock and the axe,
       The heavy roller, to break the clods, to pass over the nations.

       The sons of Urizen shout: their father rose. The eternal horses
       Harnessed, they called to Urizen: the heavens movèd at their call.
       The limbs of Urizen shone with ardour. He laid his ha[n]d on
25   the plough,
       Through dismal darkness drave the plough of ages over cities
       And all their villages, over mountains and all their valleys,
       Over the graves and caverns of the dead, over the planets
       And over the void spaces, over sun and moon, and star and
         constellation.

30   Then Urizen commanded and they brought the seed of men:
       The trembling souls of all the dead stood before Urizen,
       Weak wailing in the troubled air, east, west, and north and south.

[Page 125]

       He turned the horses loose and laid his plough in the northern
         corner
       Of the wide universal field, then stepped forth into the immense.

       Then he began to sow the seed. He girded round his loins
       With a bright girdle, and his skirt filled with immortal souls.
5   Howling and wailing fly the souls from Urizen's strong hand.

124.20–2 *Ringing . . . roller*] Reversing the movement of 92.17–19 (see note there on Old Testament visions of peace and apocalypse).

124.23 *horses*] Restoring to Urizen the creatures wrongly taken over by Luvah: one of the actions by which the Zoas, usurping each other's functions, began the Fall. Cf. 65.5–8 note.

124.30 *seed of men*] After the ploughing comes the sowing. Blake principally has in mind the parable of the sower (Matthew, 13.3–8; Luke, 8.5–8), and the seed which falls on different kinds of soil (here kings and princes, for whom there is no place in the regenerated Albion, fall on unproductive ground: 125.11). He perhaps also had in view the exemplary ploughman-sower of Isaiah 28.23–9, and Saint Paul discussing the resurrection: 'That which thou sowest is not quickened except it die' (1 Corinthians, 15.36).

Page 124 design. Below the text a clothed man resting on a stick leans forward towards a naked woman seated in a lotus-flower. She looks towards him and her right hand is raised to touch his forehead. Behind the woman, more lightly sketched, is a figure standing in a long, shroud-like cloak. The figures perhaps represent 125.26–9: Ahania about to cast off her death clothes, and Ahania restored in majesty with Urizen about to respond. Or the woman may be Vala: cf. 64.30.

For from the hand of Urizen the myriads fall like stars
Into their own appointed places. Driven back by the winds,
The naked warriors rush together down to the sea shores:
They become like wintry flocks, like forests stripped of leaves.
10 The kings and princes of the earth cry with a feeble cry,
Driven on the unproducing sands and on the hardened rocks;
And all the while the flames of Orc follow the vent'rous feet
Of Urizen; and all the while the trump of Tharmas sounds.
Weeping and wailing fly the souls from Urizen's strong hand.
The daughters of Urizen stand with cups and measures of
15   foaming wine,
Immense upon the heavens, with bread and delicate repasts.

Then follows the golden harrow in the midst of mental fires,
To ravishing melody of flutes and harps, and softest voice.
The seed is harrowed in, while flames heat the black mould
    and cause
20 The human harvest to begin. Towards the south first sprang
The myriads, and in silent fear they look out from their graves.

Then Urizen sits down to rest, and all his wearied sons
Take their repose on beds: they drink, they sing, they view
    the flames
Of Orc in joy; they view the human harvest springing up.
25 A time they give to sweet repose till all the harvest is ripe.

And lo, like the harvest moon, Ahania cast off her death clothes.
She folded them up in care, in silence, and her bright'ning limbs
Bathed in the clear spring of the rock, then from her
    darksome cave
Issued in majesty divine. Urizen rose up from his couch
30 On wings of tenfold joy, clapping his hands, his feet, his
    radiant wings
In the immense, as when the sun dances upon the mountains,
A shout of jubilee in lovely notes responding from daughter
    to daughter,

125.20 *south*] The usual compass point of Urizen.

125.25 *the harvest is ripe*] Cf. Revelation 14.15: 'Another angel came out of the temple, crying with a loud voice to him that sat on the cloud, Thrust in thy sickle, and reap: for the time is come for thee to reap; for the harvest of the earth is ripe.'

From son to son, as if the stars beaming innumerable
Through night should sing, soft warbling, filling earth and heaven;
35   And bright Ahania took her seat by Urizen in songs and joy.

The Eternal Man also sat down upon the couches of Beulah,
Sorrowful that he could not put off his new-risen body
In mental flames. The flames refused: they drove him back
   to Beulah.
His body was redeemed to be permanent through mercy divine.

[Page 126]

And now fierce Orc had quite consumed himself in mental flames,
Expending all his energy against the fuel of fire.
The regenerate Man stooped his head over the universe, and in
His holy hands received the flaming demon and demoness of
   smoke,
5   And gave them to Urizen's hands. The immortal frowned, saying:

'Luvah and Vala, henceforth you are servants: obey and live.
You shall forget your former state: return, O Love, in peace
Into your place, the place of seed, not in the brain or heart.
If gods combine against Man, setting their dominion above
10   The human form divine – thrown down from their high station
In the eternal heavens of human imagination, buried beneath
In dark oblivion with incessant pangs, ages on ages,
In enmity and war first weakened – then in stern repentance,

125.33–4 *stars . . . heaven*] A variation on the supposed music of the planetary spheres; cf. 34.62 note.

125.36 *Beulah*] Cf. The Ballads Manuscript, 'The Crystal Cabinet', line 8 note.

125.39 *body . . . divine*] Albion's regeneration is, like the Christian final resurrection (as in the Apostles' Creed), bodily as well as spiritual.

The text of page 125 is written on the central panel of a *Night Thoughts* engraving (cf. page 65 design note).

126.4 *demon . . . smoke*] That is, Orc-Luvah and Vala (line 6).

126.9–17 *If gods . . . form*] Cf. *A Descriptive Catalogue*, III: 'Visions of these eternal principles or characters of human life appear to poets in all ages: the Grecian gods were the ancient Cherubim of Phoenicia; but the Greeks, and since them the Moderns, have neglected to subdue the gods of Priam. These gods are visions of the eternal attributes or divine names which, when erected into gods, become destructive to humanity. They ought to be the servants and not the masters of man, or of society. They ought to be made to sacrifice to man, and not man compelled to sacrifice to them: for when separated from man, or humanity, who is Jesus the Saviour, the vine of eternity, they are thieves and rebels, they are destroyers' (Bentley, *Writings*, 839–40).

They must renew their brightness, and their disorganized functions
15 Again reorganize, till they resume the image of the human,
Cooperating in the bliss of man, obeying his will,
Servants to the infinite and eternal of the human form.'

126.14–15 *disorganized . . . reorganize*] Cf. to Butts, 10.1.02, where Blake writes of himself as one 'organized by Divine Providence for spiritual communion' (Bentley, *Writings*, 1558).

Page 126 design. There are three (or perhaps four) separate drawings. Below the text to the left strides a small figure with arms extended behind and before, carrying what appears to be a shepherd's crook (? Tharmas as shepherd: see 137.9–10). Behind him are shapes which may represent boulders or distant hills. He walks towards a relatively enormous figure (perhaps a separate drawing) only the upper half of whose body is visible (rear view) rising out of the ground – perhaps the reviving Albion. In the left margin is an incomplete sketch of a naked man seen from the side, his arms raised at an angle which suggests crucifixion. Over the text is a large and very roughly drawn figure with legs apart in a leaping or running posture, arms thrown in the air, and prominent goggle-like eyes. This last figure is difficult to interpret in relation to the text, and is not certainly by Blake (see Max Plowman, *TLS*, 1.4.1926).

LATER LYRICS, FROM THE NOTEBOOK (C. 1803–7) AND FROM THE BALLADS ('PICKERING') MANUSCRIPT

From the Notebook (c. 1803–7)

Though the following lyric uses the conceptions of spectre and emanation from Blake's later myth, its intelligibility is not dependent on knowledge of the myth. The relevant elements of the characters of spectre and emanation are articulated within the poem itself. The dialogue presents fragments of the divided psyche as lovers quarrelling in a potentially endless round of mutual accusation and self-exculpation, the opposite of that 'mutual forgiveness' which Blake put at the head of *The Gates of Paradise* (Bentley, *Writings*, 645). The poem underwent elaborate revision. In his facsimile of the Notebook (1973; rev. edn., 1977) Erdman distinguishes nine stages of revision and expansion. The full text, with deletions, is given in Bentley, *Writings*, 921–4. The manuscript is without punctuation: the assigning of speakers is editorial.

> My spectre around me night and day
> Like a wild beast guards my way;
> My emanation far within
> Weeps incessantly for my sin.
>
> 5   A fathomless and boundless deep,
> There we wander, there we weep.
> On the hungry craving wind
> My spectre follows thee behind.

---

1 *spectre*] In the fallen and divided human being of Blake's later myth the spectre is male and typically is aggressive, rationalistic and accusing: it keeps the personality internally divided and separate from sympathetic identification with others. See for example *Milton*, 42.34–7 and *Jerusalem*, 74.10–13.

3 *emanation*] The emanation is the spectre's female counterpart in the divided human being: the sense of sin and guilt are her typical weapons in the struggle for dominance with the spectre.

4] Two stanzas, part of the poem as first drafted, were cancelled at this point.

8 *thee*] The emanation.

He scents thy footsteps in the snow
10   Wheresoever thou dost go,
Through the wintry hail and rain:
'When wilt thou return again?

Dost thou not in pride and scorn
Fill with tempests all my morn,
15   And with jealousies and fears
Fill my pleasant nights with tears?

Seven of my sweet loves thy knife
Has bereavèd of their life;
Their marble tombs I built with tears,
20   And with cold and shuddering fears.

Seven more loves weep night and day
Round the tombs where my loves lay,
And seven more loves attend each night
Around my couch with torches bright.

25   And seven more loves in my bed
Crown with wine my mournful head,
Pitying and forgiving all
Thy transgressions great and small.

When wilt thou return and view
30   My loves, and them to life renew?
When wilt thou return and live?
When wilt thou pity as I forgive?'

'Never, never I return;
Still for victory I burn!
35   Living thee alone I'll have,
And when dead I'll be thy grave.

12] The spectre speaks.

17 *Seven*] Used conventionally (typically in ballads) to express an indefinite large number (*OED* 1d).

22 *lay*] lie.

29, 31, 33 *return*] revert to a previous state (*OED v*¹ 4a).

33] The emanation speaks.

Through the Heav'n and Earth and Hell
Thou shalt never, never quell;
I will fly and thou pursue,
40   Night and morn the flight renew.'

'Till I turn from female love
And root up the infernal grove
I shall never worthy be
To step into eternity,

45   And to end thy cruel mocks,
Annihilate thee on the rocks,
And another form create
To be subservient to my fate.

Let us agree to give up love,
50   And root up the infernal grove;
Then shall we return and see
The worlds of happy eternity,

And throughout all eternity
I forgive you, you forgive me.
55   As our dear Redeemer said,
"This the wine and this the bread."

O'er my sins thou sit and moan:
Hast thou no sins of thy own?
O'er my sins thou sit and weep,
60   And lull thy own sins fast asleep.'

'What transgressions I commit
Are for thy transgressions fit;
They thy harlots, thou their slave,
And my bed becomes their grave.'

---

38 *quell*] put an end to (my opposition); the intransitive use required by the rhyme is highly unusual.

41] The spectre speaks, rejecting (as 'female love') the relationship of contest and possessiveness threatened by the emanation. (Initially the line began 'Till thou'.)

43 *I shall*] Initially 'Thou shalt'.

53–72] The final stanzas are in pencil, and the first two are numbered '1' and '2', perhaps as if to begin a new poem. They are often separated from the main body of the poem by the editorial heading 'Postscript'.

56 *wine . . . bread*] Cf. 'I saw a chapel all of gold', Notebook, line 14 note.

61] The emanation speaks.

65   'Poor pale pitiable form
     That I follow in a storm,
     Iron tears and groans of lead
     Bind around my aching head;

     And let us go to the highest downs
70   With many pleasing wiles.
     The woman that does not love your frowns
     Will never embrace your smiles.'

         *

     Mock on, mock on, Voltaire, Rousseau,
     Mock on, mock on, 'tis all in vain!
     You throw the sand against the wind,
     And the wind blows it back again.

5   And every sand becomes a gem
     Reflected in the beams divine;
     Blown back they blind the mocking eye,
     But still in Israel's paths they shine.

65] The spectre speaks.

67–70 *Iron tears . . . pleasing wiles*] Ironic acceptance of what the emanation offers, before the final (unironic) general reflection.

69–72] The rhythm and rhyme patterns change for the final stanza.

69 *highest*] Erdman's reading. Bentley reads 'high'; Keynes records the word as illegible.

71–2 *The woman . . . smiles*] Cf. *Jerusalem*, 95.24: 'She who adores not your frowns will only loathe your smiles.' Keynes (*Complete Writings* (1957; rev. edn., 1966), 417) reads 'embrace' as 'endure' (almost certainly wrongly).

1 *Mock on*] Cf. Job to his 'comforters' (21.3): 'Suffer me that I may speak; and after that I have spoken, mock on.' *Voltaire, Rousseau*] Voltaire (1694–1778), one of the greatest writers of the Enlightenment, a campaigner against injustice and tyranny, especially forms showing religious prejudice. Jean-Jacques Rousseau (1712–78), philosopher, writer and political theorist whose work influenced the French Revolution and many writers of the Romantic period. From Blake's point of view both were rationalists in philosophy and Deists in religion. On his attitude to Voltaire as sceptic cf. 'The Everlasting Gospel', fragment h (Bentley, *Writings*, 1062). Voltaire and Rousseau are associated with the Spectre as a destructive rationalistic power in *Jerusalem* (54.18), and are attacked at length in the preface to chapter 3 (plate 52).

5 *sand . . . gem*] The 'same' object appears radically different depending on whether it is seen from a mechanistic or imaginative perspective. Cf. *Visions*, 5.35 note. On a grain of sand seen from different perspectives, as 'sin', or as 'Oothoon's palace' (a place of fulfilled sexual love), see *Jerusalem*, 41.15–20.

8 *Israel's . . . shine*] That is, they help the chosen people of God to find their way through the wilderness, from slavery to freedom; crossing the Red Sea is the first step in their escape (see Exodus, 14). For Blake, to clarify or epitomize error (as, unintentionally, do Voltaire, Rousseau, Democritus and Newton) is to assist the realization of truth: *Milton*, 6.47–8; *Jerusalem*, 9.29–30. Cf. *Europe*, 16.5, where Newton brings about the apocalypse by blowing the last trumpet.

The atoms of Democritus
10 And Newton's particles of light
Are sands upon the Red Sea shore
Where Israel's tents do shine so bright.

Morning

Blake deals in *Milton* with a 'science of wrath' (7.46) – a cleansing anger purified of egotism, for which Christ's cleansing of the Temple is the ultimate model (Matthew, 21.12–13; Mark, 11.15–17; Luke, 19.45–6; John, 2.14–17). Such anger, this lyric suggests, is not incompatible with mercy, and its expression obviates the desire for violence.

To find the western path
Right through the gates of Wrath
I urge my way.
Sweet Mercy leads me on
5 With soft repentant moan;
I see the break of day.

The war of swords and spears
Melted by dewy tears
Exhales on high.
10 The sun is freed from fears,
And with soft grateful tears
Ascends the sky.

From the Ballads ('Pickering') Manuscript

The Ballads Manuscript is unique in being a collection of Blake's later lyrics. Unlike the Notebook it contains no drafts or sketches. The poems are written in Blake's

---

9 *Democritus*] Greek (*c.* 460–370 BC), the first materialist philosopher: he argued that the physical world was composed of atoms in constant motion, and was therefore a purely mechanical system without intelligent cause or purpose.

10 *Newton's . . . light*] Newton (with Bacon and Locke) is a central figure of error in Blake because of what Blake took to be his view of the universe as a giant mechanism. Newton understood light to be composed (like solid matter) of minute material particles, but particles in motion.

1 *western*] In the symbolism of Blake's later books the west symbolizes positive values – freedom and imagination. *Jerusalem*, plate 54 has a diagram locating Wrath in the west (opposite Pity in the east).

7–8 *war . . . Melted*] For the Old Testament visions of renewal behind this phrasing, see *The Four Zoas*, 92.17–19 and note.

clearest hand, almost without corrections. The manuscript takes its traditional name from the publisher, Basil Montague Pickering (1836–78), who bought it in 1866. It is now in the Pierpont Morgan Library, New York, which has published a facsimile, introduced by Charles Ryskamp (1972). The poems are mostly ballad-like in their simplicity. Their subjects are various – sexual relationships, politics, the nature of visionary experience; likewise their forms – couplets, and stanzas with different rhyme-patterns and line-lengths.

The Smile

There is a smile of love,
And there is a smile of deceit,
And there is a smile of smiles
In which these two smiles meet.

5   And there is a frown of hate,
And there is a frown of disdain,
And there is a frown of frowns
Which you strive to forget in vain,

For it sticks in the heart's deep core,
10   And it sticks in the deep back bone,
And no smile that ever was smiled,
But only one smile alone,

That betwixt the cradle and grave
It only once smiled can be,
15   But when it once is smiled
There's an end to all misery.

*

The Golden Net

Three virgins at the break of day:
'Whither, young man, whither away?

11–16] The syntax is irregular but the sense is clear: there is a smile of smiles which can counteract the frown of frowns: love, not hatred, is ultimately the more powerful force.

The Golden Net] There is a draft of this poem in Blake's Notebook which contains several different readings, none of which were transferred to the Ballads Manuscript version. The Notebook version is given in Bentley, *Writings*, 932–3.

Title] The phrase 'a golden net of Providence' occurs in Edward Young's *Night Thoughts* which Blake illustrated in the late 1790s (Night IX, line 1402, design 488; Blake shows Christ's disciples as 'fishers of men'). But the net in Blake's poem is far from benign: it suggests the obsessional illusions of love, the frustration of desire, and the imprisoning pains these generate.

Alas for woe! Alas for woe!'
They cry, and tears for ever flow.
5   The one was clothed in flames of fire,
The other clothed in iron wire,
The other clothed in tears and sighs,
Dazzling bright before my eyes.
They bore a net of golden twine
10   To hang upon the branches fine.
Pitying I wept to see the woe
That Love and Beauty undergo.
To be consumed in burning fires,
And in ungratified desires,
15   And in tears clothed night and day
Melted all my soul away.
When they saw my tears, a smile
That did Heaven itself beguile
Bore the golden net aloft
20   As on downy pinions soft,
Over the morning of my day.
Underneath the net I stray,
Now entreating Burning Fire,
Now entreating Iron Wire,
25   Now entreating Tears and Sighs.
O when will the morning rise?

*

The Mental Traveller

This poem is the most discussed of Blake's later lyrics. Several critics survey the inadequacies of previous accounts, and one may conclude that, though the poem suggests an allegorical mode, its personifications cannot be consistently translated into conceptual terms. The world of the poem is recognizably the world we know but estranged because the speaker is not accustomed to its norms. Its symbolically suggestive beings – the potentially rebellious boy, Christ-Prometheus, the constricting and sadistic old woman – are apparently locked into cyclical patterns in which sexual and social relationships are dependent on exploitation and suffering. Whether it is implied that any development of the cycles – the birth of the female babe, or a perception of the world humanized by love (89–93) – might offer some potential

---

11 *Pitying*] For pity as a negative, incapacitating emotion cf. *Milton*, 6.19–20: 'pity divides the soul / And man unmans.'

20 *As*] Elliptical: as if it were.

escape from cyclicality critics have not agreed. 'The Mental Traveller' is the lyric most obviously related to the myths of Blake's prophetic books – particularly to Orc as a youthful male figure embodying revolt, and to Vala as a female figure embodying constriction. The events of the poem can also be compared with the narratives of the prophetic books at various points (see notes). These analogies are suggestive, but should not be treated as interpretative keys.

> I travelled through a land of men,
> A land of men and women too,
> And heard and saw such dreadful things
> As cold earth-wanderers never knew.
>
> 5 For there the babe is born in joy
> That was begotten in dire woe,
> Just as we reap in joy the fruit
> Which we in bitter tears did sow.
>
> And if the babe is born a boy
> 10 He's given to a woman old
> Who nails him down upon a rock,
> Catches his shrieks in cups of gold.
>
> She binds iron thorns around his head,
> She pierces both his hands and feet,
> 15 She cuts his heart out at his side,
> To make it feel both cold and heat.

7–8 *reap . . . sow*] The lines echo Psalm 126, v. 5: 'They that sow in tears shall reap in joy'; and cf. 'Auguries of Innocence', 67–70.

11 *nails him*] The babe resembles Orc (chained to a rock: cf. line 23) as he appears in *America*, plate 3 design, and in *The Book of Urizen*, chapter VII, v. 4, and so also Prometheus, Loki and Oedipus (see notes to *America*, plate 3 and *The Book of Urizen*, 20.23). Morton Paley also compares a passage from Thomas Taylor's translation of Plato's *Phaedo* on the sufferings inherent in corporeal existence: 'Every pleasure and pain, as if armed with a nail, rivets the soul to the body, and causes it to become corporeal' (*Energy and the Imagination* (1970), 125).

12 *Catches . . . gold*] The blood of Christ on the cross is often depicted as caught by angels in golden chalices: this image of compassion is here perverted into one where the victim's suffering gives pleasure.

13–15 *thorns . . . side*] The babe resembles the crucified Christ, with crown of thorns, and pierced through hands and feet where he was nailed to the cross. Christ was also pierced through his side (John, 19.34).

Her fingers number every nerve,
Just as a miser counts his gold;
She lives upon his shrieks and cries,
20   And she grows young as he grows old.

Till he becomes a bleeding youth,
And she becomes a virgin bright;
Then he rends up his manacles,
And binds her down for his delight.

25   He plants himself in all her nerves,
Just as a husbandman his mould,
And she becomes his dwelling place,
And garden fruitful seventyfold.

An agèd shadow soon he fades,
30   Wand'ring round an earthly cot
Full fillèd all with gems and gold
Which he by industry had got.

And these are the gems of the human soul,
The rubies and pearls of a love-sick eye,
35   The countless gold of the aching heart,
The martyr's groan and the lover's sigh.

They are his meat, they are his drink;
He feeds the beggar and the poor,
And the wayfaring traveller:
40   Forever open is his door.

His grief is their eternal joy;
They make the roofs and walls to ring;
Till from the fire on the hearth
A little female babe does spring.

---

17 *number . . . nerve*] Cf. *The Four Zoas*, 4.30–1: 'Why wilt thou examine every little fibre of my soul, / Spreading them out before the sun like stalks of flax to dry?' The lines are repeated (by a different speaker) in *Jerusalem*, 22.20–1.

21–4] The action here corresponds especially closely to that of Orc in the praeludium to *America*.

33–6] Cf. 'Riches', above p. 154.

45	And she is all of solid fire
	And gems and gold, that none his hand
	Dares stretch to touch her baby form,
	Or wrap her in his swaddling-band.

	But she comes to the man she loves,
50	If young or old, or rich or poor;
	They soon drive out the agèd host,
	A beggar at another's door.

	He wanders weeping far away,
	Until some other take him in;
55	Oft blind and age-bent, sore distressed,
	Until he can a maiden win.

	And to allay his freezing age
	The poor man takes her in his arms;
	The cottage fades before his sight,
60	The garden and its lovely charms.

	The guests are scattered through the land,
	For the eye altering alters all;
	The senses roll themselves in fear,
	And the flat earth becomes a ball.

65	The stars, sun, moon, all shrink away,
	A desert vast without a bound,
	And nothing left to eat or drink,
	And a dark desert all around.

	The honey of her infant lips,
70	The bread and wine of her sweet smile,
	The wild game of her roving eye,
	Does him to infancy beguile;

---

62 *the eye . . . alters all*] Cf. 'Mock on, mock on', line 5 note.

64 *flat . . . ball*] That is, perception is governed by abstract knowledge, not by experience. For an account of a properly humanized perception of the earth as flat, contrasted with 'that false appearance . . . of a globe rolling through voidness', see *Milton*, 28.4–26.

65 *The stars . . . shrink away*] Cf. *Jerusalem*, plate 24, design, where the heavens are still inscribed on Albion's (Everyman's) limbs; and contrast plate 27: 'the starry heavens are fled from the mighty limbs of Albion': in his fallen state Albion perceives the heavens as remote and mechanical, not as something to be understood in terms of analogy with the human.

70 *bread and wine*] Cf. Notebook, 'I saw a chapel all of gold', line 14 note.

For as he eats and drinks he grows
Younger and younger every day;
75   And on the desert wild they both
Wander in terror and dismay.

Like the wild stag she flees away,
Her fear plants many a thicket wild,
While he pursues her night and day,
80   By various arts of love beguiled;

By various arts of love and hate,
Till the wide desert planted o'er
With labyrinths of wayward love,
Where roams the lion, wolf, and boar;

85   Till he becomes a wayward babe,
And she a weeping woman old.
Then many a lover wanders here;
The sun and stars are nearer rolled,

The trees bring forth sweet ecstasy
90   To all who in the desert roam,
Till many a city there is built,
And many a pleasant shepherd's home.

But when they find the frowning babe
Terror strikes through the region wide;
95   They cry, 'The babe, the babe is born!'
And flee away on every side.

For who dare touch the frowning form,
His arm is withered to its root.
Lions, boars, wolves, all howling flee,
100   And every tree does shed its fruit.

And none can touch that frowning form,
Except it be a woman old;
She nails him down upon the rock,
And all is done as I have told.

*

The Land of Dreams

'Awake, awake, my little boy;
Thou wast thy mother's only joy.
Why dost thou weep in thy gentle sleep?
Awake, thy father does thee keep.'

5   'O what land is the Land of Dreams?
What are its mountains and what are its streams?
O father, I saw my mother there
Among the lilies by waters fair,

Among the lambs, clothèd in white,
10   She walked with her Thomas in sweet delight.
I wept for joy; like a dove I mourn;
O when shall I again return?'

'Dear child, I also by pleasant streams
Have wandered all night in the Land of Dreams,
15   But though calm and warm the waters wide,
I could not get to the other side.'

'Father, O Father, what do we here
In this land of unbelief and fear?
The Land of Dreams is better far,
20   Above the light of the morning star.'

*

Mary

Sweet Mary the first time she ever was there
Came into the ballroom among the fair;
The young men and maidens around her throng,
And these are the words upon every tongue:

5   'An Angel is here from the heavenly climes,
Or again does return the golden times.
Her eyes outshine every brilliant ray;
She opens her lips, 'tis the month of May!'

Mary] 6 *return . . . times*] Cf. 'A Little Girl Lost', *Songs of Experience*, line 5 note.

Mary moves in soft beauty and conscious delight
10   To augment with sweet smiles all the joys of the night,
Nor once blushes to own to the rest of the fair
That sweet love and beauty are worthy our care.

In the morning the villagers rose with delight,
And repeated with pleasure the joys of the night;
15   And Mary arose among friends to be free,
But no friend from henceforward thou, Mary, shalt see.

Some said she was proud, some called her a whore,
And some when she passèd by shut to the door.
A damp cold came o'er her, her blushes all fled,
20   Her lilies and roses are blighted and shed.

'O why was I born with a different face?
Why was I not born like this envious race?
Why did Heaven adorn me with bountiful hand,
And then set me down in an envious land?

25   To be weak as a lamb and smooth as a dove,
And not to raise envy is called Christian love;
But if you raise envy your merit's to blame
For planting such spite in the weak and the tame.

I will humble my beauty, I will not dress fine,
30   I will keep from the ball, and my eyes shall not shine;
And if any girl's lover forsakes her for me
I'll refuse him my hand and from envy be free.'

She went out in morning attired plain and neat;
'Proud Mary's gone mad!' said the child in the street.
35   She went out in morning in plain neat attire,
And came home in evening bespattered with mire.

She trembled and wept sitting on the bed side,
She forgot it was night and she trembled and cried;
She forgot it was night, she forgot it was morn,
40   Her soft memory imprinted with faces of scorn.

---

14 *repeated*] talked again about.

15 *free*] sociable and unreserved (*OED a* 23).

21 *O why . . . face*] Blake used this line of himself in a letter to Thomas Butts of 16.8.03, following it with a slight adaptation of the next line: 'Why was I not born like the rest of my race?'.

With faces of scorn and with eyes of disdain,
Like foul fiends inhabiting Mary's mild brain,
She remembers no face like the human divine:
All faces have envy, sweet Mary, but thine.

45   And thine is a face of sweet love in despair,
And thine is a face of mild sorrow and care,
And thine is a face of wild terror and fear
That shall never be quiet till laid on its bier.

*

The Crystal Cabinet

As in 'The Golden Net', love betrays the speaker to delights which are ultimately constricting and illusory. The speaker struggles to reach fulfilment by means of these beautiful illusions, but his misplaced intensity shatters him and the object of his love.

The maiden caught me in the wild
Where I was dancing merrily;
She put me in her cabinet,
And locked me up with a golden key.

5   This cabinet is formed of gold.
And pearl and crystal shining bright,
And within it opens into a world
And a little lovely moony night.

Another England there I saw,
10   Another London with its Tower,
Another Thames and other hills,
And another pleasant Surrey bower.

---

43 *human divine*] Cf. 'The Divine Image', *Songs of Innocence*, line 11: 'Love [has] the human form divine.' Blake may here have recalled *Paradise Lost*, 3.44, 'human face divine.'

4 *locked . . . key*] Cf. the 'golden cage' and general situation of 'How sweet I roamed' (*Poetical Sketches*, p. 45); also 'matrimony's golden cage' in the song from *An Island in the Moon* (not printed in this selection), 'Hail matrimony, made of love.'

8 *moony*] In Blake's later myth the moon is associated with the state of rest and love called Beulah: see *Milton*, 30.1–31.7. In the metaphorical geography of this myth Beulah is below the paradisal state of Eden but above that of ordinary consciousness, the world of Generation. It can be either positive or negative depending on the point of view from which it is seen.

12 *Surrey bower*] Lambeth, where Blake lived from 1790 to 1800, being south of the River Thames, was in Surrey.

Another maiden like herself,
Translucent, lovely, shining clear,
15 Threefold, each in the other closed:
O what a pleasant trembling fear!

O what a smile! A threefold smile
Filled me that like a flame I burned.
I bent to kiss the lovely maid
20 And found a threefold kiss returned.

I strove to seize the inmost form
With ardour fierce and hands of flame,
But burst the crystal cabinet,
And like a weeping babe became.

25 A weeping babe upon the wild,
And weeping woman pale reclined,
And in the outward air again
I filled with woes the passing wind.

*

The Grey Monk

This poem exists in three versions. The first version is a draft in the Notebook (p. 8) of fourteen stanzas with some alternatives and additions. The present nine stanzas are drawn from these, but substantially re-ordered (Notebook stanzas 5, 4, 6–10, 14, 11). The third version is a poem of seven stanzas which comes at the end of the preface 'To the Deists' which precedes chapter 3 of *Jerusalem*. That preface glosses the poem's Christian pacifism both in the religious and philosophical positions it attacks and in its positive view, that 'the glory of Christianity is to conquer by forgiveness.' The *Jerusalem* version too is made up from stanzas drafted in the Notebook, but largely different ones: the Ballads Manuscript and *Jerusalem* versions have only two stanzas in common (stanzas 2 and 7 below).

15, 17, 20 *threefold*] Cf. the letter-poem to Blake's patron, Thomas Butts, 22.11.02, lines 83–8: 'Now I a fourfold vision see, / And a fourfold vision is given to me. / 'Tis fourfold in my supreme delight, / And threefold in soft Beulah's night, / And twofold always. May God us keep / From single vision and Newton's sleep.' Here Blake stresses the incompleteness of the threefold: mistaking it for some final reality ('the inmost form') leads to disaster.

15 *each . . . closed*] The world inside the cabinet reflects the outer world, and so itself contains a reflecting cabinet; as in a mirror reflected in a mirror, the reflections regress infinitely, and so there can be no final 'inmost form'.

24 *weeping babe*] Cf. 'The Mental Traveller', esp. lines 85–6.

'I die, I die,' the mother said,
'My children die for lack of bread.
What more has the merciless tyrant said?'
The monk sat down on the stony bed.

5   The blood red ran from the grey monk's side,
His hands and feet were wounded wide,
His body bent, his arms and knees
Like to the roots of ancient trees.

His eye was dry, no tear could flow,
10   A hollow groan first spoke his woe,
He trembled and shuddered upon the bed;
At length with a feeble cry he said,

'When God commanded this hand to write
In the studious hours of deep midnight,
15   He told me the writing I wrote should prove
The bane of all that on earth I loved.

My brother starved between two walls,
His children's cry my soul appals;
I mocked at the rack and griding chain;
20   My bent body mocks their torturing pain.

Thy father drew his sword in the north,
With his thousands strong he marchèd forth;
Thy brother has armed himself in steel
To avenge the wrongs thy children feel.

25   But vain the sword and vain the bow:
They never can work war's overthrow.
The hermit's prayer and the widow's tear
Alone can free the world from fear.

For a tear is an intellectual thing,
30   And a sigh is the sword of an angel king,

---

19 *griding*] piercing, wounding.

29 *intellectual*] Blake gives the word a very wide meaning: arising from the whole reasoning, feeling and imaginative being. Cf. *Jerusalem*, 91.9–10: 'there is no other / God than that God who is the intellectual fountain of humanity.'

And the bitter groan of the martyr's woe
Is an arrow from the Almighty's bow.'

The hand of vengeance found the bed
To which the purple tyrant fled;
35   The iron hand crushed the tyrant's head,
And became a tyrant in his stead.

*

Auguries of Innocence

After the opening quatrain the form of the aphoristic couplet is the same through-
out this poem, but the poem's themes are highly various – the natural as an image
of the spiritual world, cruelty to animals and other social evils as indices of spiritual
sickness, the error of scepticism which doubts whatever is not susceptible of material
demonstration, the indissolubility of sorrow and joy. The variousness of theme is
made more problematic by the couplets' sometimes haphazard arrangement: for
example, lines 97–102 on the evils of empire and militarism connect with lines 77–
8 and interrupt a sequence on the error of materialist scepticism (lines 85–96, 103–
10). And the poetic quality is as various as the subject-matter. Some couplets are
flat moral statement, others have great vividness of metaphor and a riddling and
provocative openness to readerly interpretation similar to that of the Proverbs of
Hell. The variousness of theme has given rise to editorial rearrangements, by John
Sampson in his early Oxford (selected) edition of the *Poetical Works* (1914, 175–8),
and by David Erdman (with the assistance of John Grant; *Complete Poetry and Prose*,
493–6). Erdman's rearrangement is a piece of exploratory criticism: it 'is not pre-
sented as in any sense an improvement upon the text but as a thematic analysis of
it' (*Complete Poetry and Prose*, 860). The different editorial arrangements suggest that,
as with the Proverbs of Hell, valid connections can be made differently by different
competent readers.

To see a world in a grain of sand,
And a heaven in a wild flower,
Hold infinity in the palm of your hand,
And eternity in an hour.
5   A robin redbreast in a cage

Auguries of Innocence] Many critics accept W. B. Yeats's conjecture that the title refers, at least
primarily, to the opening quatrain. There is, however, no break in the manuscript after line 4.

1 *grain of sand*] Cf. 'Mock on, mock on', line 5 note; also Blake's poem in a letter to Thomas
Butts, 2.10.1800 (Bentley, *Writings*, 1546–7).

3 *Hold*] An elliptical infinitive parallel to 'To see'; lines 1–4 are syntacically incomplete.

Puts all Heaven in a rage;
A dove-house filled with doves and pigeons
Shudders Hell through all its regions.
A dog starved at his master's gate
10   Predicts the ruin of the state;
A horse misused upon the road
Calls to Heaven for human blood;
Each outcry of the hunted hare
A fibre from the brain does tear;
15   A skylark wounded in the wing,
A cherubim does cease to sing.
The game cock clipped and armed for fight
Does the rising sun affright.
Every wolf's and lion's howl
20   Raises from Hell a human soul.
The wild deer wandering here and there
Keeps the human soul from care.
The lamb misused breeds public strife,
And yet forgives the butcher's knife.
25   The bat that flits at close of eve
Has left the brain that won't believe.
The owl that calls upon the night
Speaks the unbeliever's fright.
He who shall hurt the little wren
30   Shall never be beloved by men.
He who the ox to wrath has moved
Shall never be by woman loved.

19–20 *Every . . . soul*] Like many couplets this is riddling and can be understood in more than one way. Elsewhere Blake uses the lion and the wolf together as symbols of imperial predatoriness (*Marriage*, 'A Song of Liberty', v. 20; *America*, 8.15); line 20 might then mean 'releases a wicked spirit (to do harm)', and the parallel between lines 20 and 22 indicate an antithesis between howling wolves and lions and wandering deer. But howling might also be understood as a proper activity for wolves and lions as free creatures, with line 20 meaning 'releases a captive being', and the parallel between lines 20 and 22 indicating correspondence.

24 *forgives*] Cf. the proverb of Hell, 'The cut worm forgives the plough.'

26 *believe*] '"Belief" does not consist of subscribing to a set of doctrinal articles, but of joining in the general affirmation by which the universe exists' (John Beer, *Blake's Humanism* (1968), 198). Cf. lines 107–10.

29–30 *He who . . . men*] John Adlard (*The Sports of Cruelty* (1972)) compares a Cornish rhyme, 'Hurt a robin or a wran, / Never prosper, boy or man.'

31–2 *He . . . loved*] 'It was a common custom in the East End of London, on which evidence was given before a Parliamentary Committee in 1828, to turn an ox loose in the street, bait it to madness, and hunt it to death.' Mona Wilson, *Life of William Blake* (1971 edn.), 188.

The wanton boy that kills the fly
Shall feel the spider's enmity.
35 He who torments the chafer's spright
Weaves a bower in endless night.
The caterpillar on the leaf
Repeats to thee thy mother's grief.
Kill not the moth nor butterfly,
40 For the Last Judgement draweth nigh.
He who shall train the horse to war
Shall never pass the polar bar.
The beggar's dog and widow's cat –
Feed them and thou wilt grow fat.
45 The gnat that sings his summer's song
Poison gets from Slander's tongue.
The poison of the snake and newt
Is the sweat of Envy's foot.
The poison of the honey bee
50 Is the artist's jealousy.
The prince's robes and beggar's rags
Are toadstools on the miser's bags.
A truth that's told with bad intent
Beats all the lies you can invent.
55 It is right it should be so:
Man was made for joy and woe,
And when this we rightly know
Through the world we safely go.
Joy and woe are woven fine,

---

33 *wanton . . . fly*] Blake recalls the phraseology of *King Lear*, 4.1.37–8.

35 *chafer*] A form of beetle, the cockchafer: Blake refers to the practice of impaling them to watch them spin and buzz.   *spright*] spirit.

37–8 *The caterpillar . . . grief*] Cf. *The Gates of Paradise*, 'The Keys to the Gates', 1–2, where the lines are repeated with the alteration in line 2, 'Reminds thee of'.

42 *Shall . . . bar*] Shall never transcend a purely earthly consciousness. Cf. the 'northern bar' of *The Book of Thel*, 8.1 and note.

45 *gnat . . . song*] Blake perhaps had in mind Aesop's fable of the ant and the grasshopper: the grasshopper generously sings all summer but is abused for imprudence by the ant. Blake compares his own methods of indirect instruction with Aesop's in his letter to Dr Trusler of 23.8.1799.

46, 47, 49 *Poison*] The gnat, snake, newt and bee are poisonous in that they bite or sting. The lines imply that even apparently natural facts about the world may be products of spiritual corruption and so transformable.

55–62] The Sampson and Erdman rearrangements agree in re-ordering these lines so that 55–8 follow 59–62; line 55, 'It is right . . .', is thereby given a more straightforward referent.

60   A clothing for the soul divine.
                     Under every grief and pine
                     Runs a joy with silken twine.
                     The babe is more than swaddling bands.
                     Throughout all these human lands

65   Tools were made, and born were hands,
                     Every farmer understands.
                     Every tear from every eye
                     Becomes a babe in eternity;
                     This is caught by females bright

70   And returned to its own delight.
                     The bleat, the bark, bellow and roar,
                     Are waves that beat on Heaven's shore.
                     The babe that weeps the rod beneath
                     Writes 'revenge' in realms of death.

75   The beggar's rags fluttering in air
                     Does to rags the Heavens tear.
                     The soldier armed with sword and gun
                     Palsied strikes the summer's sun.
                     The poor man's farthing is worth more

80   Than all the gold on Afric's shore.
                     One mite wrung from the lab'rer's hands
                     Shall buy and sell the miser's lands,
                     Or, if protected from on high,
                     Does that whole nation sell and buy.

85   He who mocks the infant's faith
                     Shall be mocked in age and death.
                     He who shall teach the child to doubt
                     The rotting grave shall ne'er get out.
                     He who respects the infant's faith

90   Triumphs over Hell and death.
                     The child's toys and the old man's reasons
                     Are the fruits of the two seasons.
                     The questioner who sits so sly
                     Shall never know how to reply.

95   He who replies to words of doubt
                     Doth put the light of knowledge out.

---

61 *pine*] suffering.

67–70] Cf. 'The Mental Traveller', lines 7–8 and note.

93–4 *The questioner . . . reply*] Cf. *Milton*, 43.12–13 on 'the idiot questioner, who is always questioning / But never capable of answering.'

The strongest poison ever known
Came from Caesar's laurel crown.
Nought can deform the human race
100   Like to the armour's iron brace.
When gold and gems adorn the plough
To peaceful arts shall Envy bow.
A riddle, or the cricket's cry,
Is to doubt a fit reply.
105   The emmet's inch and eagle's mile
Make lame philosophy to smile.
He who doubts from what he sees
Will ne'er believe, do what you please.
If the sun and moon should doubt
110   They'd immediately go out.
To be in a passion you good may do,
But no good if a passion is in you.
The whore and gambler by the state
Licensed build the nation's fate.
115   The harlot's cry from street to street
Shall weave Old England's winding sheet.
The winner's shout, the loser's curse,
Dance before dead England's hearse.
Every night and every morn
120   Some to misery are born;
Every morn and every night
Some are born to sweet delight.
Some are born to sweet delight,
Some are born to endless night.
125   We are led to believe a lie
When we see not through the eye,

97–8 *strongest . . . laurel*] Blake's metaphoric indictment of the evils of imperial military power has a literal truth: the violent toxicity of laurel (from which hydrocyanic or prussic acid is produced) was discovered in the early eighteenth century.

105 *emmet*] ant.

111 *you good may do*] That is, 'may do you good'. The couplet contrasts the possibly beneficial effect of giving anger scope with the malign effect of suppressing it (and so becoming possessed by it). Cf. 'A Poison Tree', *Songs of Experience*, and 'Morning' (above, p. 273).

125–8] Cf. 'The Everlasting Gospel', fragment k, 99–102.

126 *When . . . eye*] The line originally read 'When we see with, not through the eye'. Cf. 'I question not my corporeal or vegetative eye any more than I would question a window concerning a sight. I look through it and not with it' ('A Vision of the Last Judgement'; Bentley, *Writings*, 1027).

Which was born in a night to perish in a night
When the soul slept in beams of light.
God appears and God is light
130   To those poor souls who dwell in night,
But does a human form display
To those who dwell in realms of day.

*

William Bond

I wonder whether the girls are mad,
And I wonder whether they mean to kill,
And I wonder if William Bond will die,
For assuredly he is very ill.

5   He went to church in a May morning
Attended by fairies, one, two and three,
But the angels of Providence drove them away,
And he returned home in misery.

He went not out to the field nor fold,
10   He went not out to the village nor town,
But he came home in a black, black cloud,
And took to his bed and there lay down.

And an angel of Providence at his feet,
And an angel of Providence at his head,
15   And in the midst a black, black cloud,
And in the midst the sick man on his bed.

---

127 *Which . . . night*] Cf. Jonah's gourd, 'which came up in a night, and perished in a night' (Jonah, 4.10).

129–32] Cf. *Marriage*, plates 22 and 23, and 'The Everlasting Gospel', fragment k, 75–6 (Bentley, *Writings*, 1068).

William Bond 1–4] A typical ballad opening: Blake would have found such openings in Percy's *Reliques of Ancient English Poetry* (1765), but he may also have been prompted by Wordsworth and Coleridge's *Lyrical Ballads* (1798, 2nd edn., 1800).

5 *morning*] The metrical pattern would require an unnatural stress on the second syllable which mimics a feature of genuinely ancient ballads brought about by shifts of pronunciation. Cf. line 45, 'sunshine', where again the stress falls on the second syllable, and line 22, where the unnatural stress suggested by the metrical pattern is emphasized by the rhyme 'Mary' / 'be'.

7 *angels of Providence*] Apparently sinister figures, opposed to the fairies who finally defeat them (lines 41–4). The angels are associated with the church, the fairies with the ethic that the church nominally exists to promote (lines 49–52).

And on his right hand was Mary Green,
And on his left hand was his sister Jane,
And their tears fell through the black, black cloud
20   To drive away the sick man's pain.

'O William, if thou dost another love,
Dost another love better than poor Mary,
Go and take that other to be thy wife,
And Mary Green shall her servant be.'

25   'Yes Mary, I do another love,
Another I love far better than thee,
And another I will have for my wife.
Then what have I to do with thee?

For thou art melancholy-pale,
30   And on thy head is the cold moon's shine,
But she is ruddy and bright as day,
And the sun beams dazzle from her eyne.'

Mary trembled and Mary chilled,
And Mary fell down on the right hand floor,
35   That William Bond and his sister Jane
Scarce could recover Mary more.

When Mary woke and found her laid
On the right hand of her William dear,
On the right hand of his lovèd bed,
40   And saw her William Bond so near,

The fairies that fled from William Bond
Dancèd around her shining head;
They dancèd over the pillow white,
And the angels of Providence left the bed.

---

28 *Then . . . thee*] Cf. 'To Tirzah', *Songs of Experience*, lines 4, 16 and note.
30 *moon*] Cf. 'The Crystal Cabinet', line 8 note.
32 *eyne*] Eyes; an archaic, ballad-style word.

45   'I thought love lived in the hot sunshine,
            But O, he lives in the moony light;
            I thought to find love in the heat of day,
            But sweet love is the comforter of night.'

            Seek love in the pity of others' woe,
50   In the gentle relief of another's care,
            In the darkness of night and the winter's snow,
            In the naked and outcast, seek love there.

45, 49] The quotation marks are editorial: the stanza is best thought of as spoken by William Bond since it was he who made the error it acknowledges and retracts, and without such an acknowledgement there is no implied conclusion to the narrative. The narrator then draws the more general moral conclusion in the final stanza. (Some editors plausibly punctuate the final stanza as though it too were spoken by William Bond. Some editors give both stanzas to the narrator.)

49–50] Cf. 'On Another's Sorrow', *Songs of Innocence*, lines 1–4.

FROM
MILTON

The subject of *Milton* is the awakening of the imagination – Milton's, Blake's and the reader's – to its full human-divine potential. The poem is also an analysis of the evils of ordinary life which thwart and limit such an awakening, particularly the errors at the centres of spiritual life, in religion and in art, to which, according to Blake, John Milton showed himself subject in *Paradise Lost*. The aim of *Milton* is to enact the liberation of the individual human imagination from the consequences of the fallen intellect.

Blake's enacting of his subject, his uncompromising association of form and content, is part of the work's difficulty. *Milton* records, with all its contributing factors, a single moment of transcendent awareness, and all its events are presented as taking place simultaneously in that moment of pure being. Part of Milton's error had been to suppose he could embody a new ethic in a form designed to extol the heroic mode he aimed to displace. Blake could not deliver Milton from error in the residual Homerics of Miltonic form. There is, therefore, in *Milton* no narrative line in any normal sense; the 'same' character may have several modes of being which are presented as separate selves; 'different' characters who represent the same fundamental states of being may merge into one another. Underlying these difficulties, however, is a broadly clear structure of two books which deal with associated events – the descent from eternity of Milton, and the parallel descent of his 'emanation' (female aspect or counterpart), Ololon. The first movement of Book I, the Bard's Song, falls into two parts, both of which involve reworkings of *Paradise Lost*: a new account of the Creation and Fall, and a quarrel that epitomizes the nature of the fallen world. It gives a new view of Satan, who is identified with the law-giving God of orthodox Christianity; and a new view of sin, not as violation of a code but as imaginative failure. The moral for Milton is that 'he became what he beheld': in the fallen world the imagination is dragged down by its surroundings. But the Bard's Song does not only condemn Milton: it also shows why what is truly imaginative in his work is of permanent value. Taken together these negatives and positives prompt the second action of Book I, Milton's descent and wrestling with Urizen – the rehumanizing of the intellect by the imagination, the mind's grappling to create the fullest possible self in intellectual and social contexts that seek constantly to confine or corrupt it. Book II presents the other essential aspects of the redemptive process, Milton's union with Ololon and his confrontation with Satan which completes the defeat of superseded values which *Paradise Lost* failed to accomplish.

It is for Blake an ordinary but tragic fact of life that we commonly live by superficial levels of being, the products of forces which have a more or less limited relation to each individual's deepest possibilities and needs. Only when our deepest thoughts and feelings are touched do we come into contact with the more fundamental levels of being from which we are usually alienated, levels which lead us to reflect on ordinary consciousness as dream-like or unreal. Blake presents in *Milton* a variety of experiences that give access to, or intimations of, these finally more real levels of being, in religion, in art, and unusually (as in the second and third fragments below) in the natural world. The value of an experience of the kind Blake's Milton undertakes is that through such a cleansing of the spirit we can escape from powerfully moulding but essentially superficial 'states' of being (as Blake calls them) to discover those elements of the self that are inalienable, by which we can fulfil the life that is properly ours. It is to this issue that Milton's climactic final speech (the last fragment below) is addressed.

From the Preface [Plate 1]: 'And did those feet?'

The first two stanzas of this famous lyric ask questions – in effect, was there a golden age of Christian freedom before fallen history? The questions are not open: 'and' implies astonishment, as though responding with assent, but to a previous assertion so astounding that simple conviction is not at first possible. The third and fourth stanzas then call forth individual actions based on the assent underlying the amazement of the opening questions: what was once must be again. The openness of Blake's imagery in the final stanzas means that the poem can express idealistic conviction from a great variety of viewpoints: in the setting by Sir Hubert Parry the poem appears in numerous hymnals (including the current Anglican standard, *The New English Hymnal*), has become an unofficial anthem of the British Labour Party and the British Women's Institute, and was used by the Women's Suffrage Movement in Britian in the early part of this century; it appears in a not clearly defined context of national celebration (alongside Thomas Arne's setting of 'Rule, Britannia') at the Last Night of the BBC Promenade Concerts, as also in the different context of important soccer matches, such as the Football Association Cup Final. It is ironic that the Preface from which this lyric is taken occurs in only the first two of the four copies of *Milton* that Blake printed (copies A and B, printed on paper watermarked 1808), since 'And did those feet?' is perhaps – its whole text as distinct from its title and a few phrases – the most widely known poem in England. (Northrop Frye draws the lyric into a wider discussion of a 'popular' quality in Blake's work in 'Blake after Two Centuries', *University of Toronto Quarterly*, 27 (1957), 10–21; reprinted in Frye's *Fables of Identity: Studies in Poetic Mythology* (New York, 1963).) The lyric is followed in the Preface to *Milton* by a quotation from Numbers (11.29): 'Would to God that all the Lord's people were prophets' – words spoken by Moses, but in their new context implying Blake's desire that the first-person pronouns of his lyric might express, as the poem's wide use suggests it has, the individual reader's desire to shape a better future.

[Plate 1]

And did those feet in ancient time
Walk upon England's mountains green?
And was the holy Lamb of God
On England's pleasant pastures seen?

5   And did the countenance divine
Shine forth upon our clouded hills?
And was Jerusalem builded here
Among these dark Satanic mills?

Bring me my bow of burning gold;
10   Bring me my arrows of desire;

1.1–4 *And . . . seen*] The feet are those of Jesus, the divine and the human in one being. Blake may have known the legend recorded by William of Malmesbury that the first Christian missionaries to Britain found a church already built by God (though the first translation of William's *De gestis regum anglorum* was not published until 1815). (On the legend that Jesus's disciple, Joseph of Arimathea, came to Britain, see 'The Everlasting Gospel', m.1 note). The specific mention of 'feet' reflects Isaiah's prophecy of the messenger of salvation: 'How beautiful upon the mountains are the feet of him that bringeth good tidings' (52.7; quoted in Nahum, 1.15, and Romans, 10.15).

1.3 *Lamb of God*] Cf. 'The Lamb', *Songs of Innocence*, line 14 note.

1.7 *Jerusalem*] The ideal city, the utopian community described in visionary terms in Revelation chapter 21. Cf. 'The fields from Islington to Marybone', *Jerusalem*, plate 27, and 'England, awake!', *Jerusalem*, plate 77 (pp. 309–13, 324–5), both of which elaborate a positive answer to Blake's question.

1.8 *Among*] That is, where these 'mills' are now found: can that ideal possibility really have existed when it has been so displaced by its antithesis?   *dark . . . mills*] Both factories, with their new machinery (cf. *The Four Zoas*, 91.1–93.20, headnote), and mechanical operations of the mind and resultant views of the world which Blake often presented in terms of mills (for example, *There is No Natural Religion*, b6). Blake speaks of himself as having been 'a slave bound in a mill' in a letter to William Hayley (23.10.1804; Bentley, *Writings*, 1613), with a probable reminiscence of the literal and spiritual captivity of Milton's Samson (*Samson Agonistes*, 43: 'Eyeless in Gaza at the mill with slaves').

1.9 *bow . . . gold*] This suggests primarily the bow of Apollo, the god of poetry. Like Blake's archetypal poet, Los, Apollo is a sun-god; he is depicted with a burning, sun-like bow, symbolic of the powers of poetry, in Blake's illustrations of Gray ('The Progress of Poesy', plate 6; cf. the bow of Christ, whom Blake also associates with Los (*Jerusalem*, 96.7), casting the fallen angels out of Heaven in Blake's illustrations of *Paradise Lost*: Butlin, *Paintings and Drawings*, 529.7 and 536.7). Cf. also the letter-poem to Thomas Butts (22.11.1802): 'Los flamed in my path and the sun was hot / With the bows of my mind and the arrows of thought. / My bow-string fierce with ardour breathes; / My arrows glow in their golden sheaves.' (Bentley, *Writings*, 1566.)

1.10 *arrows of desire*] This makes clear that the weapons are metaphoric (and cf. lines 13 and 14 and notes). The Preface to which the lyric acts as a conclusion is an attack on those 'who would if they could forever depress mental and prolong corporeal war.' The phrase 'arrows of desire' may evoke the archer Eros, god of love, though it is the intensity of the desire rather than its nature that can be thought of as sexual: Blake's utopian community would include sexual freedom, but the openness of his imagery in this lyric does not insist on that specific ideal.

Bring me my spear; O clouds, unfold:
Bring me my chariot of fire!

I will not cease from mental fight,
Nor shall my sword sleep in my hand,
15   Till we have built Jerusalem
In England's green and pleasant land.

*

From Books I and II (25.66–26.12; 31.28–63): The Divine in Nature

Blake is not a poet of nature. As he wrote in annotating Wordsworth, 'Natural objects always did and now do weaken, deaden and obliterate imagination in me. Wordsworth must know that what he writes valuable is not to be found in Nature' (Bentley, *Writings*, 1511). Blake does not entertain Wordsworth's characteristic doubt about 'what [we] half create / And what perceive' ('Tintern Abbey', 107–8), about where the active principle lies in the relations between Nature and mind. Even in passages such as those that follow, it is not Nature that provokes the imaginative response but the imaginative response that transforms the natural objects: the constellations, the flies and the trees – the material, animal and vegetable worlds – are 'children of Los': that is, they are recognized not as things simply described, but as imaginative human realizations. 'The eye altering alters all': without imaginative perception the stars shrink away leaving 'a dark desert all around' ('The Mental Traveller', 62–8). Blake's incarnations of visionary moments are followed by an extrapolation about their nature and value.

There is a moment in each day that Satan cannot find,
Nor can his watch-fiends find it, but the industrious find
This moment and it multiply; and when it once is found
It renovates every moment of the day if rightly placèd.
(35.42–5)

1.12 *chariot of fire*] Elijah, the archetypal prophet, is taken up into heaven in a chariot of fire (2 Kings, 2.11; cf. 'The Everlasting Gospel', i.34 note). Angels also appear in 'chariots of fire' to aid Elijah's successor, Elisha (2 Kings, 6.17). Blake describes 'contemplative thought' in terms of a 'fiery chariot' in 'A Vision of the Last Judgement' (Bentley, *Writings*, 1018).

1.13 *mental fight*] Cf. 'The Grey Monk', lines 25–32 (where intellectual and spiritual conflicts are also presented in terms of swords, arrows and bows). On spiritual warfare in Blake, see Michael Ferber, 'Blake and the Two Swords', in Clark and Worrall (eds.), *Blake in the Nineties* (1999).

1.14 *sword*] Cf. Saint Paul's use of military metaphors in spiritual conflicts: 'Above all, taking the shield of faith, wherewith ye shall be able to quench all the fiery darts of the wicked. And take the helmet of salvation, and the sword of the Spirit, which is the word of God' (Ephesians, 6.16–17).

These moments are comparable with Wordsworth's 'spots of time' (*The Prelude*, 1805, 11.208), those influxes of extraordinary consciousness around which *The Prelude* is organized because they are fundamental to Wordsworth's sense of life. Whatever the spiritual preparation that allows one to receive them, for Wordsworth such moments are given. For Blake they can be cultivated by the industrious, and occur not a few times in a whole life but potentially 'in each day'. As the fairy who 'dictates' *Europe* has it, they are moments in which we see 'all alive / The world, where every particle of dust breathes forth its joy' (*Europe*, 3.17–18).

The first of the following extracts is taken from the conclusion to Book I which describes the creative work of Los in the individual, in nature and in society. The second is taken from the descent of Ololon in Book II where the heightened imaginative perceptions personified by Los are again crucial. The prosaic rhythms of the verse, Blake's restraint in refusing to evoke wonder and awe with any obvious elevation of verbal music, means that attention is convincingly on the subject, not the medium. Beautifully crafted though it is, in its understatement the poetry appears pellucid. As another prosaic poet of visionary moments has it, 'the poetry does not matter' (T. S. Eliot, *Four Quartets*, 'East Coker', II).

[Plate 25]

Thou seest the constellations in the deep and wondrous night:
They rise in order and continue their immortal courses
Upon the mountains and in vales with harp and heavenly song,
With flute and clarion, with cups and measures filled with
    foaming wine.
70   Glitt'ring the streams reflect the vision of beatitude,
And the calm ocean joys beneath and smooths his awful waves:

[Plate 26]

These are the sons of Los, and these the labourers of the vintage.
Thou seest the gorgeous clothèd flies that dance and sport in
    summer
Upon the sunny brooks and meadows: every one the dance
Knows in its intricate mazes of delight artful to weave,
5   Each one to sound his instruments of music in the dance,
To touch each other and recede, to cross and change and return:
These are the children of Los. Thou seest the trees on mountains:
The wind blows heavy, loud they thunder through the
    darksome sky,
Uttering prophecies and speaking instructive words to the sons

---

25.66 *Thou seest*] The direct address to the reader, here and at 31.28 and 31.46, is unusual and marks these separate passages as related, as they are also by subject and treatment.
25.71 *awful*] Cf. *The Four Zoas*, 34.59 note.

10   Of men: these are the sons of Los, these the visions of eternity;
But we see only as it were the hem of their garments
When with our vegetable eyes we view these wondrous visions.

*

[Plate 31]

Thou hearest the nightingale begin the song of spring:
The lark sitting upon his earthy bed, just as the morn
Appears, listens silent, then springing from the waving
30   cornfield loud
He leads the choir of day: trill, trill, trill, trill,
Mounting upon the wings of light into the great expanse,
Re-echoing against the lovely blue and shining heavenly shell.
His little throat labours with inspiration; every feather
35   On throat and breast and wings vibrates with the effluence divine.
All nature listens silent to him, and the awful sun
Stands still upon the mountain looking on this little bird
With eyes of soft humility and wonder, love and awe.
Then loud from their green covert all the birds begin their song:
40   The thrush, the linnet and the goldfinch, robin and the wren
Awake the sun from his sweet reverie upon the mountain;
The nightingale again assays his song, and through the day
And through the night warbles luxuriant, every bird of song

26.11 *hem . . . garments*] The phrase 'hem of his [Christ's] garment' is twice used in Matthew (9.20, 14.36) where miracles are performed by Christ's divine power being infused through, as it were, the most attenuated contact.

26.12 *When . . . vegetable . . . view*] 'Vegetable' means vegetative, without intellectual or imaginative activity. On this kind of passive vision see 43.23–4 below, and cf. 'Auguries of Innocence', line 126 note. Contrast Blake's comment to Rev. Dr Trusler (letter, 23.8.1799): 'to the eyes of the man of imagination nature is imagination itself' (Bentley, *Writings*, 1527).

31.28 *spring*] the first sign of day (*OED sb*[1] 5a).

31.29 *lark*] Analogies can be cited in Milton (*L'Allegro*, 41–4, and *Paradise Regained*, 2.279–81), but neither is verbally close: the lines draw on imaginative observation rather than reading. Of the poetic analogies, that from *L'Allegro* is the more interesting, since Blake later (*c*. 1816) illustrated the lines with a human lark such as the lark of *Milton* becomes or is found to be (36.12: 'the lark is a mighty angel'; Butlin, *Paintings and Drawings*, 543.2). As representative elements of the imaginative experience of the natural world, the lark and the wild thyme (line 51) are present in the final synoptic moment of vision (44.29–30). Just as the lark is discovered to be an angel, so the wild thyme becomes 'Los's messenger to Eden, a mighty demon' (35.54).

Attending his loud harmony with admiration and love.
45   This is a vision of the lamentation of Beulah over Ololon.

Thou perceivest the flowers put forth their precious odours,
And none can tell how from so small a centre comes such sweets,
Forgetting that within that centre eternity expands
Its ever-during doors that Og and Anak fiercely guard.
50   First, ere the morning breaks, joy opens in the flowery bosoms,
Joy even to tears, which the sun rising dries. First the wild
    thyme,
And meadow-sweet downy and soft, waving among the reeds,
Light springing on the air, lead the sweet dance: they wake
The honeysuckle sleeping on the oak: the flaunting beauty
55   Revels along upon the wind; the whitethorn, lovely may,
Opens her many lovely eyes. Listening the rose still sleeps:
None dare to wake her; soon she bursts her crimson-curtained
    bed
And comes forth in the majesty of beauty. Every flower –
The pink, the jessamine, the wallflower, the carnation,
60   The jonquil, the mild lily – opes her heavens. Every tree
And flower and herb soon fill the air with an innumerable dance,
Yet all in order sweet and lovely: men are sick with love.
Such is a vision of the lamentation of Beulah over Ololon.

*

31.44 *Attending*] listening to (the transitive use is archaic: *OED v* 1).

31.45, 63 *lamentation*] A surprising term in this context of joy, beauty and love: Blake presumably means that what appears as positive even to an imaginative perception in the world of generation may appear quite differently to the higher level of being represented by Beulah.

31.45 *Beulah*] Cf. 'The Crystal Cabinet', line 8 note.   *Ololon*] The emanation (female aspect or counterpart) of Milton; the name is possibly derived from English 'ululation', a cry of lamentation (with which Ololon is often associated), though it may also be derived from various Greek roots beginning 'olol . . .' associated with cries of joy, or cries to the gods.

31.49 *ever-during*] From *Paradise Lost*, 7.206, where it is used of the gates of Heaven.   *Og and Anak*] Kings of the heathen tribes defeated by the Israelites in their conquest of Canaan, the land promised by God, after their liberation from the slavery of Egypt (Numbers, 13 and 21): enemies, therefore, of spiritual vision.

31.55 *the whitethorn . . . may*] Blake remembers a phrase from the cancelled first line of the Notebook version of his lyric, 'The Golden Net' (Bentely, *Writings*, 932–3).

31.61 *innumerable*] The use with a singular substantive is archaic (the sense is as with a plural: 'innumerable dances').

31.62 *sick with love*] From the Song of Solomon, 2.5: 'I am sick of love' (where 'of' means 'with').

From Book II (42.28–43.28):
To bathe in the Waters of Life

This final extract is one of the great summary doctrinal statements on the intellectual, spiritual and creative life in Blake's later poetry. Blake grapples in *Milton* with the problems all individuals face of discovering and developing their own creativity. As the *Laocoön* and other late works make clear, the arts had for Blake a quasi-religious function: they are 'powers of conversing with paradise' ('A Vision of the Last Judgement'; Bentley, *Writings*, E, 559). One great human imperative is therefore to do one's duty by one's own creative potential. As Blake has it in the introduction to the final chapter of *Jerusalem*:

> Let every Christian, as much as in him lies, engage himself openly and publicly before all the world in some mental pursuit for the building up of Jerusalem.
>
> (plate 77)

Milton's great statement of how so to engage oneself, what to seek and what to avoid, invokes what may seem from a postmodern viewpoint an aspect of Romantic ideology – an opposition between an immortal spirit and a false body, an indestructible authentic self which can be found beneath the layers of accretion imposed by civilization. Whether Blake entirely endorses his prophetic speaker, and, if so, whether it is Blake or his postmodern commentators who are deluded, is for each reader to consider, and cannot be entirely decided when this fragment is read out of its context. But clearly Blake's character speaks with unqualified conviction against precisely the infinitely perspectivist doubts which much postmodern commentary finds in Blake's work.

[Plate 42]

But turning toward Ololon in terrible majesty Milton
Replied: 'Obey thou the words of the inspired man.
30   All that can be annihilated must be annihilated,
That the children of Jerusalem may be savèd from slavery.
There is a negation, and there is a contrary.
The negation must be destroyed to redeem the contraries.

42.30 *All . . . annihilated*] Because anything that can be destroyed (which must, on Blake's view, be material or a form of error) is ultimately not real (that is, spiritual or a form of truth). Cf. *Milton*, e.36 ('Whatever can be created can be annihilated'), and *Laocoön* [1]. (Blake etched 'All that can be ann be annihilated . . .'.)

42.33 *negation . . . contraries*] Blake introduces this reworking of his idea of a dynamic opposition of contraries from *The Marriage of Heaven and Hell* (plate 3) at the beginning of Book II of *Milton*: 'Contraries are positives. A negation is not a contrary.' That is, there are forms of opposition which are not creative and which actually prevent dynamic opposites from interacting one with another (line 34). The idea is further developed in *Jerusalem*, 10.7–16.

The negation is the spectre, the reasoning power in man.
35 This is a false body, an incrustation over my immortal
Spirit, a selfhood, which must be put off and annihilated alway,
To cleanse the face of my spirit by self-examination.

[Plate 43]

To bathe in the waters of life, to wash off the not-human,
I come in self-annihilation and the grandeur of inspiration,
To cast off rational demonstration by faith in the Saviour;
To cast off the rotten rags of memory by inspiration;
5 To cast off Bacon, Locke and Newton from Albion's covering;
To take off his filthy garments, and clothe him with imagination;
To cast aside from poetry all that is not inspiration,
That it no longer shall dare to mock with the aspersion of madness
Cast on the inspirèd by the tame high-finisher of paltry blots
10 Indefinite, or paltry rhymes, or paltry harmonies,
Who creeps into state government like a caterpillar to destroy;
To cast off the idiot questioner, who is always questioning
But never capable of answering, who sits with a sly grin
Silent plotting when to question, like a thief in a cave,

42.34 *spectre*] See 'My spectre around me', line 1 note.

Plate 42 design. Below the text, among the twisted trunks of leafless trees, to the left a serpent with two open-mouthed heads (one serpentine, the other that of a dog or wolf), apparently hisses and howls at a naked man to the right. Kneeling on one knee, he pushes against one of the trunks as though to flatten the monster or keep it at bay. The design relates to 43.17–18, or to lines immediately preceding those with which the extract above begins in which Milton is opposed by Rahab-Babylon.

43.5 *Bacon . . . Newton*] On Bacon and Newton see 'The Everlasting Gospel', k.37 note; on Locke see *Visions*, 5.31 note.

43.8 *aspersion of madness*] This aspersion was cast on Blake himself from the earliest accounts and critiques: see for example G. E. Bentley Jr., *William Blake: The Critical Heritage* (1975), Chapters 5 and 14. Andrew M. Cooper attempts an interpretation of Blake's supposed 'madness' in the light of modern social and psychoanalytic theories of subjectivity: *ELH*, 57 (1990), 585–642.

43.9–10 *paltry blots / Indefinite*] A major strand in Blake's criticism of visual art is the importance of clear outline and an associated attack on painters such as Titian and Rubens, Rembrandt and Reynolds, for employing chiaroscuro and other 'painterly' techniques in the use of tone and colour. Similarly, Blake practised engraving techniques which emphasize clear outlines, and attacked techniques (such as dot and lozenge) which he saw as the engraver's equivalent of chiaroscuro. These methods in visual art he sometimes linked to a use of abstract philosophical language in poetry: see 'Public Address', Bentley, *Writings*, 1033–42. Morris Eaves explores Blake's views in an art-historical context in *William Blake's Theory of Art* (1982), Chapter 1.

43.12 *idiot questioner*] Cf. 'Auguries of Innocence', lines 93–4.

43.14 *like . . . cave*] As in *Europe*, plate 4 design, and Blake's watercolour 'Malevolence' (1799; Butlin, *Paintings and Drawings*, 341).

Who publishes doubt and calls it knowledge, whose science is
15   despair,
Whose pretence to knowledge is envy, whose whole science is
To destroy the wisdom of ages to gratify ravenous envy,
That rages round him like a wolf day and night without rest.
He smiles with condescension; he talks of benevolence and virtue;
And those who act with benevolence and virtue they murder time
20   on time.
These are the destroyers of Jerusalem, these are the murderers
Of Jesus, who deny the faith and mock at eternal life;
Who pretend to poetry that they may destroy imagination
By imitation of nature's images drawn from remembrance;
25   These are the sexual garments, the abomination of desolation,
Hiding the human lineaments as with an ark and curtains
Which Jesus rent, and now shall wholly purge away with fire,
Till generation is swallowed up in regeneration.'

43.15 *doubt*] Cf. 'Auguries of Innocence', lines 85–8 and 107–10.

43.23 *pretend . . . imagination*] Cf. the attack in *Jerusalem* on 'A pretence of art to destroy art; a pretence of liberty / To destroy liberty; a pretence of religion to destroy religion' (43[38]. 35–6).

43.25 *sexual garments*] Delusions, aspects of life which seem to fallen consciousness inherent in its very nature but are in fact transformable. Blake's eternal beings are androgynous; division into sexes is one of the first manifestations of the Fall: see *The Book of Urizen*, Chapter V. Sexual differentiation is therefore a 'garment' in the sense that it is not part of a person's ultimate reality: it must finally be put off.   *abomination of desolation*] False religion. The phrase 'abomination that maketh desolate' first occurs among the prophecies of Daniel (11.31), where it apparently describes Roman (pagan) displacement of Jewish worship. The phrase is repeated by Christ (in the form used here by Blake), with the same implications (and in both cases with reference to Daniel): Matthew, 24.15; Mark, 13.14.

43.26–7 *ark . . . rent*] The ark, which contained God's covenant with his people, was kept in a tabernacle edged by curtains and was itself hidden by a veil (Exodus, 26, especially verses 31–4). This veil is rent when Christ dies on the cross (Matthew, 27.51; Mark, 15.38; Luke, 23.45): this is understood in Christian tradition as symbolizing the end of the old covenant.

43.27 *purge . . . fire*] As at the Last Judgement, an aspect of Christian eschatology which Blake interpreted symbolically: 'Whenever any individual rejects error and embraces truth a Last Judgement passes upon that individual' (Bentley, *Writings*, 1021–2).

43.28 *generation*] The world as we know it.   *swallowed up*] Blake recalls a famous phrase from Isaiah (25.8; echoed by Saint Paul: 1 Corinthians, 15.54): God 'will swallow up death in victory.'

Plate 43 design. Above the text six naked women float in a dance-like formation with their legs sideways and their hands joined in an interlocking pattern above their heads. They perhaps represent the three wives and three daughters of John Milton, and so a form of his emanation, Ololon (cf. 16.1–2 and plate 16 design).

FROM
JERUSALEM

Spiritual life-in-death and its causes; the struggle against this in religion, art, and politics; life as it might become, and how it can be transformed – these are, in outline, the subjects of *Jerusalem*. It is the summation of Blake's work in the form of the illuminated book, the drawing together of his poetry and painting's lifelong exultation (as he called it) in immortal thoughts (Bentley, *Writings*, 847). Blake stresses this drawing together by quoting in *Jerusalem* from earlier works – from *The Marriage of Heaven and Hell* and *Songs of Experience*, from *The Four Zoas* and *Milton*, and by naming as the places of *Jerusalem*'s conception, gestation and creation Felpham, South Molton Street, and Lambeth (38(34).40–2). Nothing specifically written for *Jerusalem* was even conceived in Lambeth, but by his work there Blake was attempting to do what Los is praised for, keeping the divine vision in time of trouble (30(44).15). By invoking work of the Lambeth period as part of his preparation for *Jerusalem* Blake indicates that his last illuminated book carries forward the project begun with his earliest experiments in illuminated printing thirty years earlier.

Beside this continuity there is considerable development, even from *The Four Zoas* and *Milton*, both almost certainly unfinished when *Jerusalem* was begun, perhaps shortly after Blake returned to London from Felpham in 1803. The self-quotation is never transcription: there is always change. There are also changes to the structures of myth taken from earlier works. Though the myth of the Zoas is worked into *Jerusalem*,[1] among its personifications only Los and Vala are of central importance, and the role of Vala particularly is somewhat changed: she is not now the emanation of Luvah but has a shifting role as his daughter or lover, as the wife of Albion, or (with Jerusalem herself) as his emanation. Jesus, worked into *The Four Zoas* only late in its composition, is in *Jerusalem* a central figure. In this way *Jerusalem* is connected with other late works – 'The Everlasting Gospel', *The Ghost of Abel*, and the *Laocoön*. Blake indicates the direction his view of Jesus will take by his Chapter 1 epigraph (in Greek), 'Jesus alone'. This refers the reader to two episodes from the gospels, the Transfiguration (Matthew, 17; Mark, 9; Luke, 9) and the story of the woman taken in adultery (John, 8). The first shows the most extreme possibilities of vision and human transformation, the second Jesus's ethic of unconditional forgiveness, turning aside the Mosaic Law, and opposing Pharisaic righteousness. Both episodes indicate essential elements of one of *Jerusalem*'s central concerns: Blake's account of Christianity.

The mode of *Jerusalem* is largely non-narrative. Blake sees 'the past, present and future existing all at once' (15.8), that is, he sees in the present archetypal elements which connect it with the past, and he sees their implied future: in his naturalistic sense of prophecy, 'if you go on so, the result is so' (marginalia to Watson; Bentley,

---

[1] On this myth, see the headnote to *The Four Zoas*, above pp. 238–9.

Writings, 1417). Sequential structure would be at odds with this simultaneity of view: Blake does not necessarily distinguish myth, legend, history and prophecy: what could or should have been, what was, what is, and what can be perceived by the imagination as implicit in all of these, are treated as having the same reality. Blake passes freely between them. *Jerusalem* has discernible sections which can be focused in terms of dominant issues, but many of these also contain heterogeneous materials, the connections between which may be fundamental but are sometimes less than obvious. The personal urgency of Blake's speaking voice is important to the work's tone: 'This theme calls me in sleep' (4.3); 'Trembling I sit day and night . . . I rest not from my great task' (5.16–17). Time and again Blake tugs the reader from the sleep of ordinary life to share his horror at what threatens to overwhelm a properly human existence.

Two incidents from Blake's life provided some material for *Jerusalem*: his arrest and trial for treason in 1803–4 on the accusation of a soldier, John Scolfield; and the attacks in *The Examiner* (a liberal journal run by the brothers Hunt) on his designs for Robert Blair's *The Grave* (1808) and his exhibition of 1809.[2] Distressing as these incidents undoubtedly were for Blake they might seem almost gifts for Blakean treatment: the artist harried by the soldier ('Bacon calls intellectual arts unmanly . . . so they are for kings and wars, and shall in the end annihilate them'); the true artist hindered by the second-rate from reaching a public and earning a living ('such artists as Reynolds are at all times hired by the Satans for the depression of art: a pretence of art to destroy art').[3] In fact the use Blake made of them in *Jerusalem* is limited to identities for the fallen sons of Albion. The incidents are among the most vivid and well-documented of Blake's life, but they are of relatively minor importance for understanding *Jerusalem*.

Blake produced only five complete copies of *Jerusalem*, the two earliest on paper watermarked 1818–19–20; he also produced one coloured copy of Chapter 1 only (watermarked 1818). The one complete copy which he coloured – one of the most remarkable works of its age, and perhaps in Blake's own estimate his most important single work, the production of which took at least fifteen years – remained unsold at his death. The five complete copies have two different orders of plates in Chapter 2. The order followed here is that of the minority of copies (D and E; not Blake's first and last ordering, copies A, C and F): this is the order of the complete coloured copy, the order followed in G. E. Bentley's edition of the *Writings*. Alternative plate numberings are given in parentheses.

From Chapter 1 (24.12–25.16):
Albion in Error

Chapter 1 deals with two principal issues: first the corruption of Albion in all his forms as forgiveness, love and faith are undermined by law, conflict and materialist

---

[2] The circumstances of Blake's arrest and trial are documented in Bentley, *Blake Records* (1988), 122–49; on the *Examiner* attacks, see *Blake Records*, 195–9 and 215–18.

[3] Marginalia to Bacon (Bentley, *Writings*, 1440); marginalia to Reynolds (Bentley, *Writings*, 1460).

philosophies; and second the struggle of Los (and Blake) to resist this corruption, by battling with the negative forces in Los himself personified by his Spectre, and by building Golgonooza, the city of art and humane manufactures.

The final section of the chapter, from which the following extract is taken, concerns the relations of Albion, Vala (here manifested as Babylon) and Jerusalem. Albion is corrupted by a false conception of Christianity as a religion of righteousness, judgement and atonement, and by the consequent notion that love is sin. His speeches are not expositions of doctrine but dramatic utterances which show him veering back and forth between different states of consciousness, trapped in his own fallen condition, an incoherent mixture of valid perception and error. Though Albion realizes his errors, he finds the truths that he in a sense knows – for example, that the moral law is an instrument of cruelty – not consistently thinkable. Questions which would lead to truth but which remain unanswered are the resource of his evasions. He can find no way out for himself because, in this moral, emotional and intellectual chaos, he is not capable of understanding his situation, or consistently acknowledging what he knows. It is a brilliant study in what Jean-Paul Sartre calls 'bad faith' which shows Blake's sense of what life amounts to without the unselfish love and friendship and the free imaginative and intellectual activities epitomized by Jerusalem and Los. The inhabitants of Beulah, watchers from outside the clash of perspectives within Albion, respond with a doctrinal statement which resolves his debates.

[Plate 24]

'O what is life and what is man? O what is death? Wherefore
Are you, my children, natives in the grave to where I go?
Or are you born to feed the hungry ravenings of destruction,
To be the sport of accident, to waste in wrath and love a weary
Life, in brooding cares and anxious labours that prove but chaff?
O Jerusalem, Jerusalem, I have forsaken thy courts,
Thy pillars of ivory and gold, thy curtains of silk and fine
Linen, thy pavements of precious stones, thy walls of pearl
And gold, thy gates of thanksgiving, thy windows of praise,
Thy clouds of blessing, thy cherubims of tender mercy,
Stretching their wings sublime over the little ones of Albion.
O human imagination, O divine body I have crucifièd!
I have turnèd my back upon thee into the wastes of moral law:

24.12] Albion speaks.

24.17 *O Jerusalem, Jerusalem*] Verbally this recalls Christ's lamentation over the city (Matthew, 23.37; Luke, 13.34), but the contexts are quite different: Christ laments the city's errors, Albion his own errors in relation to the city and what it represents. The description of Jerusalem draws on Revelation, Chapter 21.

24.23 *crucifièd*] See Introduction (3), pp. 25–6, on Blake's orthographic distinction between syllabic and non-syllabic pronuciation of 'ed'. (In the following lyric, where the regular metrical pattern can act as a test, the distinction is maintained with complete consistency.)

25 There Babylon is builded in the waste, founded in human desolation.
 O Babylon, thy watchman stands over thee in the night;
 Thy severe judge all the day long proves thee, O Babylon,
 With provings of destruction, with giving thee thy heart's desire.
 But Albion is cast forth to the potter, his children to the builders
30 To build Babylon, because they have forsaken Jerusalem.
 The walls of Babylon are souls of men, her gates the groans
 Of nations; her towers are the miseries of once happy families;
 Her streets are pavèd with destruction, her houses built with death,
 Her palaces with Hell and the grave; her synagogues with torments
35 Of ever-hardening despair, squared and polished with cruel skill.
 Yet thou wast lovely as the summer cloud upon my hills
 When Jerusalem was thy heart's desire in times of youth and love.
 Thy sons came to Jerusalem with gifts, she sent them away
 With blessings on their hands and on their feet, blessings of gold
40 And pearl and diamond. Thy daughters sang in her courts;
 They came up to Jerusalem; they walkèd before Albion.
 In the exchanges of London every nation walked,
 And London walked in every nation, mutual in love and harmony.
 Albion covered the whole earth, England encompassed the nations,
45 Mutual each within other's bosom in visions of regeneration.
 Jerusalem covered the Atlantic mountains and the Erythrean,
 From bright Japan and China to Hesperia, France and England.

24.25 *Babylon*] The Old Testament city epitomizing the captivity and oppression of the Jews after the sack of Jerusalem and destruction of the Temple in 588 BC (2 Chronicles 36.17–21; Jeremiah, 36.1–9, 52.1–30). The city is the antithesis of the visionary utopian Jerusalem of Revelation, 21; the description here contrasts with that of Jerusalem, lines 17–22.

24.26 *watchman*] A biblical figure, the guardian of the city; in Ezekiel the watchman becomes a figure for the prophet (33.6).

24.27 *proves*] puts to the test.

24.28 *provings of destruction*] tests that are destructive.

24.29 *cast . . . potter*] The potter is used as a type of God as creator by Isaiah (64.8), Jeremiah (18.2–6), and Saint Paul (Romans, 9.21). The image can be benign, but the context here suggests that Blake has in mind a process of creation which involves destruction and suffering (kneading, firing), and perhaps the inhuman rigidity of the product (fired clay).

24.34 *synagogues*] Any place of worship (*OED* 3b).

24.42 *exchanges of London*] The actual exchanges of London are mercantile and financial: Blake thinks of commerce in the ideal city as the material expression of spiritual co-operative interchange. Cf. 27.85–8.

24.45 *Mutual . . . bosom*] Cf. 88.3–5: 'When in eternity man converses with man, they enter / Into each other's bosom (which are universes of delight) / In mutual interchange.'

24.46 *covered . . . mountains*] In legendary pre-history: see *America*, 12.6–8 note. *Erythrean*] The Red Sea, seen as the extreme opposite of the Atlantic: Jerusalem covered the whole earth.

24.47 *Hesperia*] Italy.

Mount Zion lifted his head in every nation under heaven:
And the Mount of Olives was beheld over the whole earth:
The footsteps of the Lamb of God were there. But now no more,
No more shall I behold him: he is closed in Luvah's sepulchre.
Yet why these smitings of Luvah, the gentlest, mildest Zoa?
If God was merciful this could not be. O Lamb of God,
Thou art a delusion, and Jerusalem is my sin! O my children,
I have educated you in the crucifying cruelties of demonstration
Till you have assumed the providence of God and slain your father.
Dost thou appear before me who liest dead in Luvah's sepulchre?
Dost thou forgive me, thou who wast dead and art alive?
Look not so merciful upon me, O thou slain Lamb of God.
I die, I die in thy arms, though hope is banished from me.'

Thund'ring the veil rushes from his hand, vegetating knot by
Knot, day by day, night by night. Loud roll the indignant Atlantic
Waves and the Erythrean, turning up the bottoms of the deeps.

24.48 *Mount Zion*] Cf. *The Four Zoas*, 14.8 note.

24.49 *Mount of Olives*] Like Mount Zion, a holy place, to the west and just outside the walls of ancient Jerusalem: Christ went there to pray ('as he was wont') on the night before the arrest and trial which led to his crucifixion (Luke, 22.39).

24.50 *footsteps*] Cf. *Milton*, 'And did those feet?', 1.1–4 note.   *Lamb of God*] Cf. 'The Lamb', *Songs of Innocence*, line 14 note.

24.51 *closed . . . sepulchre*] On Luvah, the zoa associated in Blake's myth with sexual love and desire, see *The Four Zoas*, 15.7 note. In the turmoil created by Albion's fall, the Luvah aspect (the emotional life) is presented as analoguous to Christ in his sufferings, crucifixion and burial (cf. 25.6–7).

24.52 *smitings*] With boils (21.4): Albion's sufferings are several times imaged in terms derived from the trials of Job (see Job, 3.8).

24.55 *demonstration*] A crucial term in Locke's account of the reasoning mind: see *An Essay Concerning Human Understanding*, IV.2. On Blake and Locke, cf. *Visions*, 5.31 note; on 'demonstration' cf. also *The Four Zoas*, 92.33.

24.57 *Dost . . . sepulchre*] That is, 'Dost thou who liest dead . . . appear before me?'

24.59 *Look . . . me*] In a situation which Albion regards as one of sin and punishment (lines 53–4) it is clear from the context that mercy is antithetical to his expectations. Some commentators point up this antithesis by relating the line to the despairing cry of Marlowe's Faustus: 'My God, my God, look not so fierce on me' (5.2.120), which Blake might have known from Charles Lamb's *Specimens of English Dramatic Poets* (1808).

24.61 *the veil*] The veil of Vala (cf. *The Four Zoas*, 15.7 note), who is the antithesis of Jerusalem: earlier in his speech Albion describes it as 'the veil of moral virtue, woven for cruel laws' (cf. plate 28), and sees it as 'a law, a terror, and a curse' (23.22, 32); the design of plate 32 (46) shows its sinister enwreathing folds in contrast to the naked freedom of Jerusalem and her children.

Plate 24 design. Above the text a boat shaped like a crescent moon is tossed on a stormy, rain-swept sea; in it floats a being with arms or wings spread towards the points of the crescent (and a head looking towards the viewer in two copies) – perhaps an ark symbolizing hope

[Plate 25]

And there was heard a great lamenting in Beulah. All the regions
Of Beulah were movèd as the tender bowels are movèd, and they said:
'Why did you take vengeance, O ye sons of the mighty Albion,
Planting these oaken groves, erecting these dragon temples?
5   Injury the Lord heals, but vengeance cannot be healèd.
As the sons of Albion have done to Luvah, so they have in him
Done to the divine Lord and Saviour, who suffers with those that suffer;
For not one sparrow can suffer and the whole universe not suffer also
In all its regions, and its Father and Saviour not pity and weep.
10   But vengeance is the destroyer of grace and repentance in the bosom
Of the injurer, in which the Divine Lamb is cruelly slain.
Descend, O Lamb of God, and take away the imputation of sin
By the creation of states and the deliverance of individuals
    evermore. Amen.'

Thus wept they in Beulah over the four regions of Albion.
15   But many doubted and despaired, and imputed sin and righteousness
To individuals and not to states; and these slept in Ulro.

*

in Albion's troubles (see Genesis, 6–8). Immediately above line 12 figures apparently being created out of the earth ('natives of the grave'), crawl along on their knees in a chain, holding hands. A naked female figure (Vala?) kneels beside lines 15–23 in a posture suggesting sexual provocation.

25.1 *Beulah*] Cf. 'The Crystal Cabinet', line 8 note.

25.4 *oaken groves . . . dragon temples*] Druid places of worship. The antiquarian William Stukeley (1687–1765) argued that the stone circle at Avebury, supposedly built by the druids, was serpent-shaped (*Abury*, 1743) – an interpretation which Blake uses in his depiction of Urizenic cruelty in *Europe* (plate 13).

25.8–9 *sparrow . . . weep*] 'Are not two sparrows sold for a farthing? and one of them shall not fall on the ground without your Father' (Matthew, 10.29).

25.13 *states*] Blake first developed his distinction between transitory states through which each individual passes and the individual's essential being in the late additions to *Milton* (plate e: Bentley, *Writings*, 388–9). Cf. *Jerusalem*, 49.65–75, where the distinction is described as 'the only means to forgiveness of enemies' – that is, it is crucial to Blake's late interpretation of the gospel of Jesus as essentially about forgiveness: see *Laocoön* [31] and note.

25.16 *Ulro*] The lowest level of existence in Blake's fourfold scheme (Ulro, Generation, Beulah, Eden).

Plate 25 design. Below the text Albion, naked except for a pair of skin-like breeches, and with the sun, moon and stars painted on his body, kneels with his head thrown back in a posture suggesting agony. He is surrounded by three naked women, one of whom holds a long blood vessel apparently extracted from his navel. The woman above Albion has her arms spread wide, and from her arms and hands descend filaments similar to the blood vessel. The sun,

From Chapter 2 (plate 27):
Jerusalem Lost

The main subject of Chapter 2 is the opposition between on the one hand mercy, and on the other justice and atonement – the virtue of Jesus set against the ethical demands of Christianity. The preface, like the *Milton* lyric, 'And did those feet?', is concerned with the spiritual identity of Britain and Israel. Its beautiful and impassioned lyric echoes passages in Chapter 1 on the building of Golgonooza, and parallels Jerusalem and London as places of love and co-operation between nations; it also contains premonitions of Chapter 2 concerned with the constraints of family love and the evil of the Napoleonic wars. The lyric's passion comes from the direct personal tone of Blake's utterance. In Chapter 1 – registering his inadequacy and need for spiritual support – Blake implies that he is a builder of Jerusalem, as the poem urges us all to be (plate 77). Here Blake admits that he has been a builder of Babylon. The violence of history is a product of inadequate ideologies and oppressive social structures; but it is also a product of individual spiritual failure, whence the need for a 'friend of sinners' (plate 3), and Blake's fervent plea to that friend, 'Come to my arms . . .'. We are all implicated: we have all to struggle with ourselves as well as with society. The poem juxtaposes the two struggles. Both are aspects of one effort – to rehabilitate Jerusalem, to resurrect Albion, to rehumanize ourselves.

[Plate 27]

The fields from Islington to Marybone,
To Primrose Hill and Saint John's Wood
Were builded over with pillars of gold,
And there Jerusalem's pillars stood.

5   Her little ones ran on the fields,
The Lamb of God among them seen,
And fair Jerusalem his bride,
Among the little meadows green.

---

moon and stars on Albion's body indicate that his perception of the universe is still a human construction of a kind which ceases when his fall is complete (see 27.5, 70.32 and 75.27, all variants of 'now the starry heavens are fled from the mighty limbs of Albion'); cf. 'The Mental Traveller', line 65 note.

27.1–2 *Islington . . . Wood*] All the locations mentioned in this lyric are shown in the map of Blake's London in Bentley, *Writings*, 1823. The four places mentioned in lines 1–2 are in what is now inner north London ('Marybone' is modern Marylebone) north of Oxford Street. In the early nineteenth century (as the references to ponds for bathing and Willan's farm imply) they were more rural.

27.4 *Jerusalem's pillars stood*] Cf. *Milton*, 'And did those feet?', lines 1–4 and 7 notes.

27.6 *Lamb of God*] Cf. 'The Lamb', *Songs of Innocence*, line 14 note.

27.7 *Jerusalem his bride*] The Jerusalem of Revelation is 'prepared as a bride adorned for her husband' (21.2; cf. 22.17).

Pancras and Kentish Town repose
10   Among her golden pillars high,
Among her golden arches which
Shine upon the starry sky.

The Jew's Harp House and the Green Man,
The ponds where boys to bathe delight,
15   The fields of cows by Willan's farm,
Shine in Jerusalem's pleasant sight.

She walks upon our meadows green;
The Lamb of God walks by her side;
And every English child is seen,
20   Children of Jesus and his bride,

Forgiving trespasses and sins,
Lest Babylon with cruel Og,
With moral and self-righteous law
Should crucify in Satan's synagogue.

25   What are those golden builders doing
Near mournful ever-weeping Paddington,

27.9 *Pancras . . . Town*] Between Islington (to the east) and Primrose Hill.

27.13, 15 *Jew's Harp House . . . Green Man . . . Willan's farm*] All between Primrose Hill (to the north) and Marybone, within easy walking distance of Blake's childhood home in Broad Street and his residence while working on *Jerusalem* in South Molton Street. The Jew's Harp House was a tea garden in Marybone Fields, and the Green Man a pie-house. A contemporary drawing of Willan's farm is reproduced in Paul Miner, 'William Blake's London Residences', *Bulletin of the New York Public Library*, 62 (1958), 535–50.

27.21 *forgiving trespasses*] Referring to the so-called 'Lord's Prayer' (Matthew, 6.9–13; Luke, 11.2–4) in the Book of Common Prayer phraseology (more widely known than that of the Authorized Version): 'Forgive us our trespasses as we forgive those who trespass against us.'

27.22 *Babylon*] Cf. 24.25 note.   *Og*] Cf. *Milton*, 31.49 note.

27.24 *Satan's synagogue*] In Revelation, 2.9 'the synagogue of Satan' means those opposed to true religion; the phrase was conventional for any religious group to which the user was opposed (*OED*, synagogue, 2a). Blake means all supposedly Christian churches because they continue to think in terms of the Mosaic Law which, in his view, Christ abrogated.

27.25 *golden builders*] They are building Golgonooza, the ideal city of art and humane manufactures in Blake's myth, as 12.25–44 (where lines 25–6 are repeated) makes clear. Blake may also have had in mind ideal versions of actual contemporary development of London during the period of the Peace of Amiens (after 1803: see Chronology), particularly the creation by the architect and city planner John Nash of Regent's Park and Regent Street, begun in 1811.

27.26 *mournful . . . Paddington*] Paddington is to the west of Marybone, 'mournful' because it is near the site of public executions, Tyburn. Erdman (*Prophet Against Empire*, 473) records that in 1811 building development in the area revealed a cache of Tyburn burials.

Standing above that mighty ruin
Where Satan the first victory won;

Where Albion slept beneath the fatal tree,
30 And the druid's golden knife
Rioted in human gore,
In offerings of human life?

They groaned aloud on London Stone,
They groaned aloud on Tyburn's brook;
35 Albion gave his deadly groan,
And all the Atlantic mountains shook.

Albion's spectre from his loins
Tore forth in all the pomp of war,
Satan his name: in flames of fire
40 He stretched his druid pillars far.

Jerusalem fell from Lambeth's vale,
Down through Poplar and old Bow,
Through Maldon and across the sea,
In war and howling, death and woe.

27.27–8 *that . . . won*] Satan's first victory was to engineer the Fall of Man (Genesis, 3); 'that mighty ruin' is, therefore, the Garden of Eden: as with the ever-present Jerusalem, Blake treats the myth of the Fall as a reality immediately underlying contemporary life. The biblical Fall leds to the primal accusation of sin, which underlies the cruelty of judicial punishments and priestly sacrifices.

27.29 *the fatal tree*] The tree of the Knowledge of Good and Evil (Genesis, 3.3); again Blake treats biblical and British myths syncretically.

27.30–2 *druid's . . . life*] Cf. *The Four Zoas*, 92.11 note.

27.33 *London Stone*] An ancient execution site, near the Tower of London.

27.34 *Tyburn's brook*] The main site of public executions until 1783, in upper Oxford Street (near modern Marble Arch).

27.36 *Atlantic mountains*] Cf. *America*, 12.6–8 note.

27.37 *spectre*] Cf. 'My spectre around me', line 1 note.

27.41 *Lambeth*] Where Blake lived in the 1790s, just south of the Thames.

27.42 *Poplar . . . Bow*] North of the river, and to the east of all the locations so far mentioned.

27.43 *Maldon*] North of London, one of the nearest points of access to the sea, on the Essex (east) coast.

45   The Rhine was red with human blood;
     The Danube rolled a purple tide;
      On the Euphrates Satan stood,
     And over Asia stretched his pride.

     He withered up sweet Zion's hill
50   From every nation of the earth;
      He withered up Jerusalem's gates,
     And in a dark land gave her birth.

     He withered up the human form
     By laws of sacrifice for sin,
55   Till it became a mortal worm,
     But O, translucent all within.

     The Divine Vision still was seen,
     Still was the human form divine,
      Weeping in weak and mortal clay;
60   O Jesus, still the form was thine;

     And thine the human face, and thine
     The human hands and feet and breath,
      Entering through the gates of birth,
     And passing through the gates of death.

65   And O thou Lamb of God, whom I
     Slew in my dark self-righteous pride,
      Art thou returned to Albion's land,
     And is Jerusalem thy bride?

     Come to my arms and never more
70   Depart, but dwell for ever here:
      Create my spirit to thy love;
     Subdue my spectre to thy fear.

27.45–7 *Rhine . . . Danube . . . Euphrates*] The Rhine and Danube suggest the contemporary Napoleonic wars, but (as with London Stone and Tyburn) Blake immediately juxtaposes different periods: the Euphrates is one of the great rivers of ancient Mesopotamia.

27.49 *Zion's hill*] Cf. *The Four Zoas*, 14.8 note.

27.53–5 *He withered . . . worm*] Cf. *The Book of Urizen*, Chapter IX.

27.64 *gates of death*] The phrase is biblical: Job, 38.17, Psalms, 9.13 and 107.18.

Spectre of Albion, warlike fiend,
In clouds of blood and ruin rolled,
75   I here reclaim thee as my own,
My selfhood, Satan, armed in gold.

Is this thy soft family love,
Thy cruel patriarchal pride:
Planting thy family alone,
80   Destroying all the world beside?

A man's worst enemies are those
Of his own house and family;
And he who makes his law a curse
By his own law shall surely die.

85   In my exchanges every land
Shall walk, and mine in every land
Mutual shall build Jerusalem,
Both heart in heart and hand in hand.

*

From Chapter 2 (28.1–27):
Sin and Atonement

The main action of Chapter 2 shows Albion becoming ever more subject to Vala and attempting to give himself up wholly to his Spectre – an act that would confirm his fallen condition. The Chapter opens with a splendid condensation of the main elements of his corrupt state – his hatred of love as sin and his need for what is fixed – the Law and its accompanying righteousness, which Blake images in physical terms – rocks, snow and ice – and the eerily animate tree of endlessly

---

27.81–2 *A man's . . . family*] 'A man's foes shall be they of his own household' (Matthew, 10.36). Christ argues that family affections may be at odds with what should be the more fundamental loyalty, to himself. Blake takes the words out of context to give them a different sense (which his re-working of the lines makes clearer): family affections should be a step towards a sense of universal brotherhood, and it is only when they are corrupted by a false interpretation of Christianity that this is not so: 'The time will come when a man's worst enemies / Shall be those of his own house and family, in a religion / Of Generation, to destroy by sin and atonement happy Jerusalem' (46(41).25–7).

27.83–4 *he who . . . die*] Echoing biblical parallels such as Revelation, 13.10: 'He that leadeth into captivity shall go into captivity: he that killeth with the sword must be killed with the sword' (cf. Genesis, 9.6; Matthew, 26.52).

27.85 *exchanges*] Cf. 24.42 note.

proliferating error. The consequence of the Mosaic Law, which postulates a God for whom justice is primary and is opposed to mercy, is the atonement interpretation of the crucifixion on which Albion models his own cruel 'justice'. Blake comments by juxtaposing a radiant illustration of the friendship and love which Albion condemns.

[Plate 28]

Every ornament of perfection, and every labour of love,
In all the Garden of Eden, and in all the golden mountains
Was become an envièd horror, and a remembrance of jealousy;
And every act a crime, and Albion the punisher and judge.

5   And Albion spoke from his secret seat, and said:

'All these ornaments are crimes; they are made by the labours
Of loves, of unnatural consanguinities and friendships
Horrid to think of when enquirèd deeply into; and all
These hills and valleys are accursèd witnesses of sin.
10   I therefore condense them into solid rocks, steadfast,
A foundation and certainty and demonstrative truth,
That man be separate from man: and here I plant my seat.'

Cold snows drifted around him; ice covered his loins around.
He sat by Tyburn's brook, and underneath his heel shot up
15   A deadly tree: he named it Moral Virtue, and the Law
Of God who dwells in chaos hidden from the human sight.

The tree spread over him its cold shadows (Albion groaned).
They bent down, they felt the earth and, again enrooting,
Shot into many a tree, an endless labyrinth of woe.

28.2 *the golden mountains*] Of Atlantis: see *America*, 12.6–8 note.

28.7 *consanguinities*] Figurative: spiritual affinities (*OED* 3).   *friendships*] The nature of friendship is a major theme of *Jerusalem*, from the frontispiece announcement, 'Half friendship is the bitterest enmity', to Los's searching Albion's bosom 'in all the terrors of friendship' (31(45).4), to the selflessness shown by Jesus 'in the likeness and similitude of Los, [Albion's] friend' (96.22).

28.9 *sin*] Cf. *Laocoön* [30] and note, and *Jerusalem*, 41(37).15–20; also to Crabb Robinson (17.12.1825): 'What are called the vices in the natural world are the highest sublimities in the spiritual world' (*Blake Records* (1969), 316).

28.14 *Tyburn's brook*] See 27.34 note. Cf. *Marriage*, plate 8, proverb 21: 'Prisons are built with stones of law . . .'; and the marginalium to Watson: 'All penal laws court transgression and therefore are cruelty and murder' (Bentley, *Writings*, 1419).

28.15–19 *tree . . . woe*] Cf. 'The Human Abstract', *Songs of Experience*, line 22 note.

28.16 *God . . . sight*] See 91.7–12: God is within, not without. Cf. *Milton*, 'Seek not thy heavenly father then beyond the skies: / There chaos dwells, and ancient night' (18.32–3).

Jerusalem.
Chap. 2.

Every ornament of perfection, and every labour of love,
In all the Garden of Eden, & in all the golden mountains
Was become an envied horror, and a remembrance of jealousy:
And every Act a Crime, and Albion the punisher & judge.

And Albion spoke from his secret seat and said

All these ornaments are crimes, they are made by the labours
Of loves: of unnatural consanguinities, and friendships
Horrid to think of when enquired deeply into; and all
These hills & valleys are accursed witnesses of Sin
I therefore condense them into solid rocks, stedfast!
A foundation and certainty and demonstrative truth:
That Man be separate from Man, & here I plant my seat.

Cold snows drifted around him: ice covered his loins around.
He sat by Tyburns brook, and underneath his heel, shot up!
A deadly Tree, he namd it Moral Virtue, and the Law
Of God who dwells in Chaos hidden from the human sight.

The Tree spread over him its cold shadows, (Albion groand)
They bent down, they felt the earth, and again enrooting
Shot into many a Tree! an endless labyrinth of woe!

From willing sacrifice of Self, to sacrifice of (miscalld) Enemies
For Atonement: Albion began to erect twelve Altars,
Of rough unhewn rocks, before the Potters Furnace,
He namd them Justice, and Truth. And Albions Sons
Must have become the first Victims, being the first transgressors
But they fled to the mountains to seek ransom: building A Strong
Fortification against the Divine Humanity and Mercy,
In Shame & Jealousy to annihilate Jerusalem.

8. *Jerusalem*, Plate 28

(Yale Center for British Art, Paul Mellon Collection; original size: 15.8 × 22.2 cms)

20   From willing sacrifice of self to sacrifice of (miscalled) enemies
     For atonement, Albion began to erect twelve altars
     Of rough unhewn rocks before the potter's furnace.
     He named them Justice and Truth. And Albion's sons
     Must have become the first victims, being the first transgressors;
25   But they fled to the mountains to seek ransom, building a strong
     Fortification against the Divine Humanity and Mercy,
     In shame and jealousy to annihilate Jerusalem.

*

From Chapter 2 (30(44).21–31(45).38):
Los Explores London

Los here confronts the problem of how to act against the evils which vitiate Albion's
existence. Anger and force are counter-productive. Eternal beings can accept 'wounds

---

28.20 *From*] Turning from.   *willing . . . self*] Cf. the proverb of Hell, 'The most sublime act
is to set another before you', and below, 96.20–8.

28.21 *atonement*] Expiation. The word also invokes a specific understanding of the cruci-
fixion of Christ as atoning for the sin of Adam and Eve in eating from the tree of knowledge
by which 'original sin' (a propensity to sin inherent in human nature) was entailed on their
posterity. Cf. Los at 39(35).25–6: 'Must the wise die for an atonement? Does mercy endure
atonement? / No: it is moral severity, and destroys mercy in its victim.' Blake is in tune here
with late eighteenth-century Christian radicalism: Joseph Priestley attacked the doctrine of
the atonement in his *History of the Corruptions of Christianity* (1782), and the young Coleridge
called it 'perhaps the most irrational and gloomy superstition that has ever degraded the
human mind' (*Lectures on Revealed Religion*, 1795, V). The doctrine is diametrically opposite to
Blake's idea of the gospel of Jesus as proclaiming forgiveness unconditionally.

28.21–2 *altars . . . rocks*] Drawing on Joshua, 8.30–2, where, following the directions of
Mosaic Law, Joshua builds 'an altar of whole stones, over which no man hath lift up any
iron . . . And he wrote there upon the stones a copy of the law of Moses.' Blake would regard
it as indicative of the true nature of Joshua's piety that it follows immediately on his massacre
of all the inhabitants of the city of Ai and the hanging of their king: see his comment in the
marginalia to Watson, 'To me, who believe the Bible and profess myself a Christian, a defence
of the wickedness of the Israelites in murdering so many thousands under pretence of a
command from God is altogether abominable and blasphemous' (Bentley, *Writings*, 1409–10).

28.22 *the potter's furnace*] Cf. 24.29 note.

28.23 *Justice*] In *Milton* (28.48–9) justice, which in Christian tradition is one of the four Car-
dinal Virtues, is one of 'the four iron pillars of Satan's throne . . . / . . . the four pillars of tyranny.'

28.24 *Must have*] would certainly have.

Plate 28 design (*Plate 8*). Above the text two beings whose sex cannot be determined are seated
in an enormous water-lily, with a background of calm water. They embrace and kiss, with
arms around each other's body and head, radiant examples of the 'consanguinities and friend-
ships' which Albion finds 'unnatural' and 'horrid to think of when enquirèd deeply into.'
Two proof impression of earlier states of the plate show that Blake at first conceived of the
figures as with their legs entwined, apparently making love.

316

of love' and live 'Mutual in one another's love and wrath . . . as one man' (38(34).14–17), but a being deeply lost in error cannot understand that the opposition of a friend stems from love: such a being ceases to have any experience of the perspective from which friends resist his or her delusions. Opposition therefore generates resistance, which hardens into hatred and destructive feeling. The Zoas describe the dilemma: 'If we are wrathful, Albion will destroy Jerusalem . . . / If we are merciful, ourselves must suffer destruction' (43(38).8–9). The activities of Los and of Jesus in the work as a whole – for example, here, but especially in the final section – embody Blake's resolution.

As Los walks through London he sees what Blake attacked in *Songs of Experience*, a social system which permits the sufferings of poverty, which (quoting from the political satire of *The Four Zoas*) he emphasizes is man-made. Los is in early nineteenth-century London, but all tyrannies are one: Blake sees London in terms of the biblical archetype of tyranny, Egypt. Its brick-making provides a vivid image of careless brutality: combined with the rigid geometry of the pyramids it expresses a death-exalting power that destroys the variousness of living experience with which such power is at odds.

[Plate 30(44)]

And Los prayèd and said, 'O Divine Saviour, arise
Upon the mountains of Albion as in ancient time. Behold,
The cities of Albion seek thy face; London groans in pain
From hill to hill, and the Thames laments along the valleys.
The little villages of Middlesex and Surrey hunger and thirst;
The twenty-eight cities of Albion stretch their hands to thee
Because of the oppressors of Albion in every city and village.
They mock at the labourer's limbs; they mock at his starved children.
They buy his daughters that they may have power to sell his sons.
They compel the poor to live upon a crust of bread by soft mild arts;
They reduce the man to want, then give with pomp and ceremony.
The praise of Jehovah is chaunted from lips of hunger and thirst.

30.21–2 *arise . . . time*] Cf. *Milton*, 'And did those feet?', lines 1–4 and note.

30.25 *Middlesex and Surrey*] Southern counties of England bordering on London.

30.26 *twenty-eight cities*] Number symbolism is prominent in several parts of *Jerusalem*: numbers which are multiples of four (such as twenty-eight) are associated with good qualities (the main elements of Golgonooza, for example, are fourfold); numbers which are multiples of three (such as twenty-seven) are associated with imperfection or error (see, for example, on Beulah, 'The Crystal Cabinet', line 8 note). Albion's cities (with their cathedrals) are among his fellow-sufferers, friends and helpers.

30.30–1 *They compel . . . ceremony*] Adapted from *The Four Zoas*, 80.9, 16.

30.32 *The praise . . . thirst*] Cf. 'Holy Thursday', *Songs of Experience*; 'chaunted' (chanted) was probably archaic by the early nineteenth century, but Blake apparently uses it deliberately since he repeats the form at 56.2.

Humanity knows not of sex: wherefore are sexes in Beulah?
In Beulah the female lets down her beautiful tabernacle,
35   Which the male enters magnificent between her cherubim,
And becomes one with her, mingling, condensing in self-love
The rocky law of condemnation and double Generation and death.
Albion hath entered the loins, the place of the Last Judgement,
And Luvah hath drawn the curtains around Albion in Vala's bosom.
40   The dead awake to Generation. Arise O Lord, and rend the veil!'

So Los in lamentations followed Albion. Albion covered

[Plate 31(45)]

His western heaven with rocky clouds of death and despair.

Fearing that Albion should turn his back against the Divine Vision,
Los took his globe of fire to search the interiors of Albion's

---

30.33 *Humanity . . . Beulah*] Cf. *Milton*, 43.25 note.

30.34–5 *In Beulah . . . cherubim*] Blake here images love-making in terms of entry into the most holy place in the tabernacle in Jewish worship. The holy of holies contained the ark of the covenant and the mercy seat, covered by two cherubim; the whole was screened off by a veil (Exodus, 25.16–22, 26.33–4). It was entered only once a year, and only by the high priest after elaborate purification: Blake takes it therefore to epitomize restriction and secrecy. On Beulah, see 'The Crystal Cabinet', line 8 note. Contrast Blake's account of love-making in Eden, based on the total interpenetration of Milton's angels (*Paradise Lost*, 8.620–9): 'Embraces are comminglings from the head even to the feet, / And not a pompous high priest entering by a secret place' (*Jerusalem*, 69.43–4).

30.36–7 *condensing . . . death*] A problematic passage: Blake perhaps means that a conventional male-dominated view of sexual love centred on genital penetration does not lead to an adequate emotional and spiritual union, and without this the selfishness and egotism potential in sexual feeling can intensify the worst aspects of fallen creation. 'Magnificent' (line 35) implies what D. H. Lawrence called 'phallic pride', but here with satirical intention. 'Generation' is 'double' because it has two aspects: as well as the negatives which associate it with death and the accusations, condemnations and failures of love of the Mosaic Law (see, for example, 46(32).27) it is also potentially 'holy Generation, image of regeneration' (7.65).

30.39–40 *curtains . . . veil*] Cf. *Milton*, 43.26–7 note.

Plate 30 (44) design. Above the text Los sits with this hands held out to receive the winged flying figures of Enitharmon and the Spectre. (The design illustrates the passage of text directly preceding the selection above.)

31.3–4 *Los . . . Bosom*] This is illustrated in the frontispiece to the whole work which shows Los, in contemporary dress of a night watchman, stepping through a half-open door carrying a globe-shaped lantern. A proof copy of the plate includes the text, ' "Half friendship is the bitterest enmity," said Los, / As he entered the Door of Death for Albion's sake inspired' (Bentley, *Writings*, 418): cf. 28.7 note. Los's investigations are both psychological (lines 10, 21) and social (lines 14ff.); cf. 38.29–33, where Blake explicitly elaborates the social/psychological parallels: 'I behold London, a human awful wonder of God. / He says, '. . . / My streets are my ideas of imagination, / . . . / My houses are thoughts, my inhabitants affections, / The children of my thoughts . . .'.

Bosom in all the terrors of friendship, entering the caves
Of despair and death to search the tempters out, walking among
Albion's rocks and precipices, caves of solitude and dark despair,
And saw every minute particular of Albion degraded and murdered,
But saw not by whom: they were hidden within in the minute
    particulars
Of which they had possessed themselves. And there they take up
The articulations of a man's soul, and laughing throw it down
Into the frame, then knock it out upon the plank, and souls are
    baked
In bricks to build the pyramids of Heber and Terah. But Los
Searched in vain: closed from the minutia he walked, difficult.
He came down from Highgate through Hackney and Holloway
    towards London,
Till he came to old Stratford, and thence to Stepney and the Isle
Of Leutha's Dogs, thence through the narrows of the river's side,
And saw every minute particular, the jewels of Albion, running
    down
The kennels of the streets and lanes as if they were abhorred.
Every universal form was become barren mountains of moral
Virtue, and every minute particular hardened into grains of sand:
And all the tendernesses of the soul cast forth as filth and mire
Among the winding places of deep contemplation intricate

31.7, 17 *minute particular*] Attention to the particular (to which Blake often refers with the intensification 'minute') is central to Blake's epistemology and his aesthetics: see, for example, the marginalia to Reynolds, 'What is general knowledge? Is there such a thing? All knowledge is particular' (Bentley, *Writings*, 1473); and below, 91.20–30. At line 17 Blake uses the phrase to refer to children playing in insanitary slum conditions, and so implies that the moral duty of social reform is of a piece with his epistemological and aesthetic imperatives.

31.12 *pyramids*] Symbols of tyranny and oppression because the main labour of the Israelites during the period of slavery in Egypt: see especially Exodus, 1.14 and 5.5–19.   *Heber and Terah*] Both are mentioned in Genesis, 11 (verses 17 and 24) as among the ancestors of the patriarch Abraham; neither has anything to do with building pyramids.

31.14 *Highgate . . . Hackney . . . Holloway*] Areas of what was in Blake's day outer London, somewhat to the north of St Pancras and Kentish town (27.9); Hackney is to the east: Los descends circuitously.

31.15–16 *Stratford . . . Dogs*] Los is now east of Hackney and coming down towards the Thames on a straight southward path. The so-called 'Isle' of Dogs is a peninsula created by a bow-shaped bend in the river just south of Poplar. On Leutha see *Visions*, 3.4 note: if Blake had some meaning in attaching Leutha to the Isle of Dogs beyond that of miscellaneously connecting London with his own mythology it may be because the Isle of Dogs was an area known for prostitution.

31.18 *kennels*] surface street-drains.

31.20 *grains of sand*] Cf. 'Auguries of Innocence', line 1 and 'Mock on, mock on', line 5 and notes.

To where the Tower of London frowned dreadful over Jerusalem,
A building of Luvah builded in Jerusalem's eastern gate to be
25   His secluded court: thence to Bethlehem, where was builded
Dens of despair in the house of bread. Enquiring in vain
Of stones and rocks he took his way, for human form was none.
And thus he spoke, looking on Albion's city with many tears:

'What shall I do? What could I do? If I could find these criminals
30   I could not dare to take vengeance, for all things are so constructed
And builded by the divine hand that the sinner shall always escape,
And he who takes vengeance alone is the criminal of providence.
If I should dare to lay my finger on a grain of sand
In way of vengeance, I punish the already punished. O whom
35   Should I pity if I pity not the sinner who is gone astray?
O Albion, if thou takest vengeance, if thou revengest thy wrongs,
Thou art for ever lost! What can I do to hinder the sons
Of Albion from taking vengeance – or how shall I them persuade?'

*

From Chapter 4 (plate 77):
True Christianity

The main subjects of Chapter 4 are the false religions epitomized by the Cover-
ing Cherub (see 96.17 note), and the true religion which Albion discovers in his
awakening and reunion with Jesus. The structure is simple: deepening error leads
to apocalyptic reversal. The preface invokes biblical texts in submerged quotation

---

31.23 *Tower*] An ancient fortress used in earlier periods as a gaol for aristocratic or otherwise
important prisoners, to the west of the Isle of Dogs: Los is moving back towards central Lon-
don. In calling the Tower a building of Luvah Blake implies that its functions arise from the
corruption of the passions.

31.25 *Bethlehem*] Bedlam (the Bethlehem Royal Hospital, formerly the priory of St Mary of
Bethlehem) was the London lunatic asylum. It was situated in Moorfields, just north of the
Tower, until 1815, thereafter in a new building in St George's Fields near Lambeth (Blake's
home in the 1790s) which was being built while Blake was working on *Jerusalem*. Bethlehem
means in Hebrew 'house of bread'.

31.32 *criminal of providence*] Blake implies a fundamentally optimistic view: divine providence
works in history benevolently; the individual's task is to understand how to co-operate with
this, and not counter to it by stimulating cycles of violent reaction.

Plate 31(45) design. Below the text to the left a naked woman lying face downwards holds a
spindle in her right hand and reaches with her left between her legs to hold a net which
encloses another naked woman to the right. (In the text following the extract (31(45).48–9)
Jerusalem hears Vala's 'shuttles sing in the sky, and round my limbs / I feel the iron threads of
love and jealousy and despair.')

to expound true Christianity (often opposed by Christians) and denounce false religions (often propounded by Christians). True Christianity is the cultivation of imagination and intellect. False religion is that of Caiaphas and Saul: the accusation of sin and pride in righteousness, both of which lead to persecution and cruelty. 'Put off holiness / And put on intellect', Los tells his Spectre (91.55–6). It is the preface in a slogan.

[Plate 77]

To the Christians

Devils are false religions.

'Saul, Saul, why persecutest thou me?'

> I give you the end of a golden string:
> Only wind it into a ball.
> It will lead you in at Heaven's gate,
> Built in Jerusalem's wall.

We are told to abstain from fleshly desires that we may lose no time from the work of the Lord. Every moment lost is a moment that cannot be redeemed: every pleasure that intermingles with the duty of our station is a folly unredeemable, and is planted like the seed of a wild flower among our wheat.
5 All the tortures of repentance are tortures of self-reproach on account of

---

Headings.

Saul ... me] The words spoken by Christ to Saint Paul (whose Hebrew name was Saul) on the road to Damascus in a vision by which he was converted and became a Christian (Acts, 9.4). Blake implies that those who consider themselves Christians are in fact in the condition of Saul before his conversion (when he was a Pharisee and active anti-Christian persecutor), and need to be transformed if they are to become true followers of Jesus.

I give you ... Jerusalem's wall] This quatrain was drafted in Blake's Notebook (p. 46), apparently independently of its context in *Jerusalem* (Bentley, *Writings*, 954).

Prose.

77.1 *We are told*] While the first three sentences of this paragraph can be given positive Blakean senses, a directive to 'abstain from fleshly desires' especially suggests a doctrine of conventional Christian chastity, and that Blake intends the reader to interpret understanding a contrast between 'we are told' and 'I know' (see also the following notes on 'All the tortures ...', and 'the struggles ...').

77.4 *a wild ... wheat*] Referring to the parable of the wheat and the tares (weeds): Matthew, 13.24–30.

77.5–6 *All the tortures ... enemy*] Compare Blake's letter to Thomas Butts (both similar and different) on the theme of the self-reproach of artists or intellectuals who 'refuse to do spiritual acts because of natural fears or natural desires' (10.1.1802: here too (see below) Blake invokes the parable of the talents; Bentley, *Writings*, 1558).

our leaving the divine harvest to the enemy, the struggles of entanglement with incoherent roots. I know of no other Christianity and of no other Gospel than the liberty both of body and mind to exercise the divine arts of imagination: imagination, the real and eternal world of which this
10 vegetable universe is but a faint shadow, and in which we shall live in our eternal or imaginative bodies when these vegetable mortal bodies are no more. The apostles knew of no other gospel. What were all their spiritual gifts? What is the divine spirit? Is the Holy Ghost any other than an intellectual fountain? What is the harvest of the gospel and its labours? What is
15 that talent which it is a curse to hide? What are the treasures of Heaven which we are to lay up for ourselves? Are they any other than mental studies and performances? What are all the gifts of the gospel? Are they not all mental gifts? Is God a spirit who must be worshipped in spirit and in truth, and are not the gifts of the Spirit everything to man? O ye religious, dis-
20 countenance everyone among you who shall pretend to despise art and science! I call upon you in the name of Jesus! What is the life of man but art and science? Is it meat and drink? Is not the body more than raiment? What is mortality but the things relating to the body, which dies? What is immortality but the things relating to the spirit, which lives eternally? What
25 is the joy of Heaven but improvement in the things of the spirit? What are the pains of Hell but ignorance, bodily lust, idleness and devastation of the things of the spirit? Answer this to yourselves, and expel from among you

---

77.6–7 *the struggles . . . roots*] This may mean to repudiate the accusation levelled in the first part of the sentence: in effect, one should not reproach oneself for not undertaking spiritual struggles with materials that can only lead to uncreative results (in Blake's terms, with negations, not with contraries: cf. *Milton*, 42.33 and note).

77.14 *harvest . . . labours*] Referring to Matthew, 9.37–8: 'The harvest truly is plenteous, but the labourers are few; Pray ye therefore the Lord of the harvest, that he will send forth labourers into his harvest.' Cf. Luke, 10.2.

77.15 *talent . . . hide*] Referring to the parable of the talents: Matthew, 25.14–30 (but echoing Milton's reference to it, 'that one talent which is death to hide', in the sonnet 'When I consider how my light is spent').

77.15–16 *treasures . . . ourselves*] From Matthew, 6.19–21: '. . . lay up for yourselves treasures in heaven . . . for where your treasure is there will your heart be also', part of Christ's so-called 'sermon on the mount' (from which two of the following references are also taken).

77.17 *gifts of the gospel*] Referring to Matthew, 7.6–12, on 'good gifts' that 'your Father which is in heaven' gives to those who ask.

77.18 *God . . . truth*] 'God is a Spirit: and they that worship him must worship him in spirit and in truth' (John, 4.24).

77.20 *pretend*] profess, claim (archaic).

77.21 *science*] Here used both the usual modern sense and the predominant sense of Blake's period, 'knowledge' (of all kinds): cf. *Laocoön* [6] and note.

77.22 *the body . . . raiment*] 'Is not the life more than meat, and the body than raiment?' (Matthew, 6.25; cf. Luke, 12.23).

those who pretend to despise the labours of art and science, which alone are the labours of the Gospel. Is not this plain and manifest to the thought? Can you think at all and not pronounce heartily that to labour in knowledge is to build up Jerusalem, and to despise knowledge is to despise Jerusalem and her builders? And remember, he who despises and mocks a mental gift in another, calling it pride and selfishness and sin, mocks Jesus, the giver of every mental gift, which always appear to the ignorance-loving hypocrite as sins. But that which is a sin in the sight of cruel man is not so in the sight of our kind God. Let every Christian as much as in him lies engage himself openly and publicly before all the world in some mental pursuit for the building up of Jerusalem.

> I stood among my valleys of the south
> And saw a flame of fire, even as a wheel
> Of fire surrounding all the heavens: it went
> From west to east against the current of
> 5   Creation and devoured all things in its loud
> Fury and thundering course round heaven and earth.
> By it the sun was rolled into an orb;
> By it the moon faded into a globe
> Travelling through the night; for from its dire
> 10   And restless fury man himself shrunk up
> Into a little root a fathom long.
> And I askèd a watcher and a holy one
> Its name. He answered, 'It is the wheel of religion.'
> I wept and said, 'Is this the law of Jesus,
> 15   This terrible devouring sword turning every way?'

Verse paragraph. This is written in two columns, the second beginning at line 19.

1 *south*] In the design of plate 54 'Desire' (Luvah) is placed in the south, opposite 'Reason' (Urizen) in the north. Blake associates Jesus with Luvah: cf. 24.51 note.

2 *fire . . . wheel*] This most obviously suggests Ezekiel's vision of God, on which Blake based his myth of four zoas and which prominently includes both fire and wheels (though not in combination): see Ezekiel, chapter 1. Blake's watercolour of the subject does in fact make the wheels themselves appear fiery (Butlin, *Paintings and Drawings*, 468). This wheel 'against the current of / Creation' would be its parodic opposite, a false religion in the guise of the true.

7–9 *sun . . . night*] Cf. plate 25 design note.

10–11 *man . . . long*] Cf. *The Book of Urizen*, 25.37–9.

12 *watcher . . . holy one*] The phrase occurs in the context of visionary experience in Daniel, chapter 4 (verses 13, 17 and 23).

15 *sword . . . way*] Referring to the sword of the Cherubims who keep guard over the Tree of Life after Adam and Eve are expelled from Eden, 'a flaming sword which turned every way' (Genesis, 3.24): it suggests the character of a God of judgement and wrath.

He answered, 'Jesus died because he strove
Against the current of this wheel: its name
Is Caiaphas, the dark preacher of death,
Of sin, of sorrow, and of punishment,
20   Opposing Nature. It is Natural Religion,
But Jesus is the bright preacher of life,
Creating Nature from this fiery law,
By self-denial and forgiveness of sin.
Go therefore, cast out devils in Christ's name:
25   Heal thou the sick of spiritual disease;
Pity the evil, for thou art not sent
To smite with terror and with punishments
Those that are sick, like to the Pharisees,
Crucifying and encompassing sea and land
30   For proselytes to tyranny and wrath.
But to the publicans and harlots go,
Teach them true happiness, but let no curse
Go forth out of thy mouth to blight their peace:
For Hell is opened to Heaven; thine eyes beheld
35   The dungeons burst and the prisoners set free.'

England, awake, awake, awake!
   Jerusalem thy sister calls.
Why wilt thou sleep the sleep of death,
   And close her from thy ancient walls?

---

18 *Caiaphas*] Cf. 'The Everlasting Gospel', k.29 note.

22 *Creating Nature*] It is not usual to find the natural world described by Blake as a divine creation (cf. *Milton*, 25.66–26.12 and 31.28–62, headnote), but Blake does several times in *Jerusalem* present Creation as an act of divine mercy: see 56.8, 'This world is all a cradle for the errèd wandering phantom', and cf. 13.44–5 and 59.8–9.   *from*] out of.

23 *self-denial*] On what Blake means by denial of self as it is exhibited by Jesus and as a model for the life of those who wish to follow his example, see 96.8–28.

24–31] Cf. Christ's directions to the apostles in Matthew, 10.1, 8.

24 *devils*] Cf. the epigraph: 'Devils are false religions.'

28 *Those . . . sick*] Referring to Matthew, 9.12: 'They that be whole need not a physician, but they that are sick.'

31 *publicans*] In Christ's Israel, under Roman occupation, a tax-collector, thence an outcast and 'sinner'. Christ and his disciples are on various occasions accused by the Pharisees of consorting with 'publicans and sinners' (Matthew, 9.11, 11.19; Luke, 5.30).

Lyric. Cf. *Milton*, 'And did those feet?', the final line of which is specifically recalled by the final line of this poem: the *Milton* lyric expresses determination to re-create a vanished Eden; this lyric asserts its present reality. (The first two stanzas are written in adjacent columns and the third is centred below them.)

5   Thy hills and valleys felt her feet
          Gently upon their bosoms move;
       Thy gates beheld sweet Zion's ways:
       Then was a time of joy and love.

       And now the time returns again,
10   Our souls exult, and London's towers
       Receive the Lamb of God to dwell
       In England's green and pleasant bowers.

*

From Chapter 4 (91.1–57):
Los and his Spectre

Los's exposition of the true religion of Jesus – before the apocalyptic finale shows it in action – is one of the key speeches of *Jerusalem*. It corresponds in importance to the climactic disquisition and denunciation of *Milton* (pp. 300–302), to which it is also similar in tone. Los restates and rephrases some of the central theses from *The Marriage of Heaven and Hell* on the nature of God, and repudiates all the principal sacraments of ecclesiastical tradition, even those with a biblical sanction – though he immediately rehabilitates the idea of sacramentality outside the context of ritual and tradition when he insists that we 'see the Divinity in his children', that is, through a material mediation. Religion is one central issue: friendship is the other. The two are continuous. Friendship, in the grand sense that the selflessness of Jesus will exemplify, is the first step towards the love of God, and the last. There is no passing from mortal to immortal, only intensification: 'One first, in friendship and love, then a divine family, and in the midst / Jesus.' When Los wields his hammer against the Spectre art begins to transform rationalist world-views and their consequences: Albion's apocalyptic renewal is imminent.

[Plate 91]

'It is easier to forgive an enemy than to forgive a friend.
The man who permits you to injure him deserves your vengeance:

---

10 *towers*] Editors disagree, but the original can be read as having a full stop after this word. If this punctuation were understood as carrying its modern force (as Blake's punctuation often does not) then 'London's towers' would depend on 'exult', and 'Receive' would be an imperative.

Plate 77 design. Above the prose text, to the right, a child holds the end of a string which goes beneath the first quatrain and rises up into the far left corner of the plate; the two opening sentences are below the string, to the left of the quatrain.

91.1 *It is . . . friend*] Cf. Psalm 55.12–14: 'It was not an enemy that reproached me; then I could have borne it . . . But it was thou . . . mine acquaintance. We took sweet counsel together.' Also Psalm 41.9.

He also will receive it. Go, Spectre, obey my most secret desire,
Which thou knowest without my speaking. Go to these fiends of
   righteousness:
5   Tell them to obey their humanities, and not pretend holiness
When they are murderers, as far as my hammer and anvil permit.
Go, tell them that the worship of God is honouring his gifts
In other men, and loving the greatest men best, each according
To his genius, which is the Holy Ghost in man. There is no other
10   God than that God who is the intellectual fountain of humanity.
He who envies or calumniates, which is murder and cruelty,
Murders the holy one. Go, tell them this, and overthrow their cup,
Their bread, their altar table, their incense and their oath,
Their marriage and their baptism, their burial and consecration.
15   I have tried to make friends by corporeal gifts but have only
Made enemies: I never made friends but by spiritual gifts,
By severe contentions of friendship and the burning fire of thought.
He who would see the Divinity must see him in his children,
One first, in friendship and love, then a divine family, and in the midst

---

91.6 *as far . . . permit*] The punctuation of this clause is problematic: Blake has no punctuation after 'permit' but a colon after 'murderers'. However, he frequently omits syntactically necessary punctuation, or allows the line-ending to act as punctuation, and in its three other appearances on this plate (lines 4, 12 and 55) 'Go' begins a syntactic unit. It seems probable, therefore, that this clause should be connected with what precedes it. The hammer and anvil are usual symbols of Los's creative power. Los means that his creative activities set limits to the destructiveness of his opponents.

91.7–12 *the worship . . . holy one*] Adapted from *Marriage*, plates 22–3.

91.10 *intellectual fountain*] Cf. 77.13–14.

91.12–14 *cup . . . consecration*] Referring to at least three of the traditional sacraments: marriage, baptism, and the eucharist or holy communion (the cup of wine and the bread symbolizing the blood and body of Jesus). 'Consecration' could mean the giving of a sacramental character to the eucharistic elements, but (given that the lines read as a list of sacraments) Blake more probably intends the sacrament of ordination ('consecration' is especially used of the ordination of bishops, to which Blake might especially object as an office not recognized by Protestants). The broadly catholic church traditionally identifies seven sacraments, of which two are recognized even by most Protestant sects as necessary to salvation because they are dominical, that is, instituted by Jesus and so carrying biblical authority. The overthrow of all sacraments proposed by Los is an extreme Protestant position. Cf. *Laocoön* [20]: 'The outward ceremony is Antichrist.'

91.13 *incense*] In a Christian context, in Blake's time used in worship only by the Roman Catholic Church.

91.15–16 *friends . . . enemies*] Cf. 30(44).10: 'corporeal friends are spiritual enemies', and Blake's letter to Thomas Butts of 25.4.1803 on his patron, William Hayley, as a corporeal friend and spiritual enemy (Bentley, *Writings*, 1572).

91.17 *contentions of friendship*] Cf. the account of intellectual debate in Eden: 'our wars are wars of life and wounds of love, / With intellectual spears and long-wingèd arrows of thought: / Mutual in one another's love and wrath all-renewing / We live as one man' (38(34).14–15).

Jesus will appear. So he who wishes to see a vision, a perfect whole,
Must see it in its minute particulars, organizèd, and not as thou,
O fiend of righteousness, pretendest. Thine is a disorganizèd
And snowy cloud, brooder of tempests and destructive war.
You smile with pomp and rigour; you talk of benevolence and virtue:
I act with benevolence and virtue and get murdered time after time.
You accumulate particulars and murder by analyzing, that you
May take the aggregate; and you call the aggregate moral law,
And you call that swelled and bloated form a minute particular.
But general forms have their vitality in particulars, and every
Particular is a man, a divine member of the divine Jesus.'

So Los crièd at his anvil, in the horrible darkness weeping.

The Spectre builded stupendous works, taking the starry heavens
Like to a curtain and folding them according to his will;
Repeating the Smaragdine Table of Hermes to draw Los down
Into the indefinite, refusing to believe without demonstration.
Los reads the stars of Albion; the Spectre reads the voids
Between the stars, among the arches of Albion's tomb sublime:
Rolling the sea in rocky paths, forming Leviathan

91.22 *fiend of righteousness*] The Spectre.   *Thine*] That is, your idea of the Divinity.

91.24–5] Adapted from *Milton*, 43.19–20.

91.27 *aggregate moral law*] Blake's argument is that all moral laws are inherently general (an aggregate), and so can never properly apply to any case of moral judgement, which is inherently particular.

91.32–3 *heavens . . . curtain*] Cf. the praise of God's greatness in Psalm 104: 'who stretchest out the heavens like a curtain.' Similar echoes from this Psalm are put into the mouth of Urizen in *The Four Zoas* (42.22, 95.20).

91.34 *Smaragdine . . . Hermes*] The Smaragdine (Emerald) Tablet of the legendary sage, Hermes Trismegistus (thrice-greatest), was a basic work of alchemical philosophy. Its use by the Spectre against Los implies an antipathetic view of at least one important document of occultism, though the apparent identification of it as rationalistic (line 35) also suggests that Blake knew little about it. It is printed in S. Foster Damon, *A Blake Dictionary* (1965/1988), 182–3.

91.36 *reads the stars*] In 1807 Blake wrote to the *Monthly Magazine* protesting against the reported arrest of an astrologer who had been entrapped into providing a horoscope by agents of the Society for the Suppression of Vice. Blake defended astrology: 'The man who can read the stars often is oppressed by their influence, no less than the Newtonian, who reads not and cannot read, is oppressed by his own reasonings and experiments' (14.10.1807; Bentley, *Writings*, 1636). For the 'stars of Albion' see plate 25 design note.

91.38–9 *Leviathan . . . Behemoth*] These biblical monsters are adduced as examples of God's power as Creator in Job (chapters 40 and 41). 'The Spiritual Form of Nelson Guiding Leviathan' and 'The Spiritual Form of Pitt Guiding Behemoth', mythological depictions of contemporary wars by sea and wars by land, were included in Blake's exhibition of 1809: see *A Descriptive Catalogue*, I and II (Bentley, *Writings*, 828–9).

And Behemoth, the war by sea enormous and the war
40 By land astounding, erecting pillars in the deepest Hell
To reach the heavenly arches. Los beheld undaunted, furious
His heaved hammer; he swung it round and at one blow,
In unpitying ruin driving down the pyramids of pride,
Smiting the Spectre on his anvil, and the integuments of his eye
45 And ear unbinding in dire pain, with many blows
Of strict severity self-subduing, and with many tears labouring.

Then he sent forth the Spectre. All his pyramids were grains
Of sand, and his pillars dust on the fly's wing, and his starry
Heavens a moth of gold and silver mocking his anxious grasp.
50 Thus Los altered his Spectre, and every ratio of his reason
He altered time after time, with dire pain and many tears,
Till he had completely divided him into a separate space.

Terrified Los sat to behold trembling and weeping and howling.
'I care not whether a man is good or evil; all that I care
55 Is whether he is a wise man or a fool. Go, put off holiness
And put on intellect, or my thund'rous hammer shall drive thee
To wrath which thou condemnest, till thou obey my voice.'

*

91.43 *pyramids*] Cf. 31(45).12 note.

91.44 *his eye*] That is, the Spectre's.

91.44–5 *eye . . . ear*] See *The Book of Urizen*, Chapter IV[b], verses 8 and 9 on the creation of the fallen eye and ear, and why they therefore need unbinding in such pain.

91.46 *self-subduing*] The Spectre, we are reminded, is an aspect of Los himself.

91.47–9 *All . . . grasp*] The true nature of what the Spectre tries to control is evanescent and beautiful, antithetical to his perception of it. On 'a grain of sand' and this same issue cf. 'Mock on, mock on', line 5 and note, and Blake's poem in a letter to Thomas Butts, 2.10.1800 (Bentley, *Writings*, 1546–7).

91.50 *ratio*] An abstract idea arrived at by systematic reasoning; cf. *Marriage*, 6.6 note.

91.54–6 *I care not . . . intellect*] Cf. 'A Vision of the Last Judgement': 'Men are admitted into Heaven not because they have curbed and governed their passions or have no passions, but because they have cultivated their understandings. The treasures of Heaven are not negations of passion but realities of intellect, from which all the passions emanate uncurbed in their eternal glory. The fool shall not enter into Heaven, let him be ever so holy. Holiness is not the price of entrance into Heaven' (Bentley, *Writings*, 1024).

Plate 91 design. Below the text a naked man (Albion) lies with his head thrown back and knees drawn towards him. Filaments that suggest blood vessels extend from his body to connect with, on the left a Solomon's seal (a six-pointed star made of a double triangle), and on the right an ear of wheat – symbols which it has been suggested are intended to represent the Old Testament and the New (because in the parable of the sower (Matthew, 13; Mark, 4; Luke, 8) the seed represents the word of God).

From Chapter 4 (96.3–99.5):
Apocalypse

Jesus, now identified with Los, demonstrates selfless friendship, and Albion is inspired by this to his own act of loving self-sacrifice. Though what usually exemplifies the selfless love of Jesus, the crucifixion, is a presence (it is illustrated in the design with which the Chapter begins) it is not mentioned at this point. Blake evades the usual theological implications, particularly about the uniqueness of Christ: Albion's response makes it clear that Jesus's action is precisely not unique: it is a model for the reader. Unselfish love generates love.

The final images of *Jerusalem* are of Albion's restored state. Conversation in paradise is analogous to Blake's work in its ideal form. Visionary and dramatic, varying in style according to the subject, it helps to shape the world in a more human way: it is differently perceived by different hearers who, like the ideal reader, actively participate in a continuing process. Such conversation is a work of the creative art of heightened living. Its context and complement is the moral stance of true Christianity, unconditional forgiveness, and, in social and personal politics, the end of oppression. Blake's Eden is the reverse of Christianity's usual static and aristocratic conception of heaven: it is a perpetually dynamic republic.

[Plate 96]

Then Jesus appearèd standing by Albion as the Good Shepherd
By the lost sheep that he hath found; and Albion knew that it
Was the Lord, the universal humanity; and Albion saw his form,
A man; and they conversèd as man with man, in ages of eternity.
And the divine appearance was the likeness and similitude of Los.

Albion said, 'O Lord, what can I do? My selfhood cruel
Marches against thee deceitful from Sinai and from Edom
Into the wilderness of Judah to meet thee in his pride.
I behold the visions of my deadly sleep of six thousand years
Dazzling around thy skirts like a serpent of precious stones and gold.
I know it is my self, O my divine creator and redeemer.'

96.3 *Good Shepherd*] From John, 10.11 (Christ speaks): 'I am the good shepherd: the good shepherd giveth his life for the sheep.'

96.4 *the lost sheep*] See the parable in Matthew, 18.12–14, and Luke, 15.3–7.

96.9 *Sinai . . . Edom*] On Sinai see 'The Everlasting Gospel', f.17 note; on Edom see *Marriage*, 3.4 note: together the descendants of Jacob (Sinai) and Esau (Edom).

96.11 *six thousand years*] Cf. *Marriage*, 14.2 note.

96.13 *self*] Selfhood: an aspect of Albion that is equivalent to the Spectre in relation to Los, a personification of all that is fallen and negative, his personal version of what is epitomized by the Covering Cherub.

Jesus replied, 'Fear not Albion: unless I die thou canst not live,
15   But if I die I shall arise again, and thou with me.
This is friendship and brotherhood: without it man is not.'

So Jesus spoke. The Covering Cherub coming on in darkness
Overshadowed them; and Jesus said, 'Thus do men in eternity
One for another, to put off by forgiveness every sin.'

20   Albion replied, 'Cannot man exist without mysterious
Offering of self for another? Is this friendship and brotherhood?
I see thee in the likeness and similitude of Los my friend.'

Jesus said, 'Wouldest thou love one who never died
For thee, or ever die for one who had not died for thee?
25   And if God dieth not for man, and giveth not himself
Eternally for man, man could not exist: for man is love,
As God is love. Every kindness to another is a little death
In the divine image, nor can man exist but by brotherhood.'

So saying, the cloud overshadowing divided them asunder.
30   Albion stood in terror, not for himself but for his friend
Divine; and self was lost in the contemplation of faith,
And wonder at the divine mercy, and at Los's sublime honour.

'Do I sleep amidst danger to friends? O my cities and counties
Do you sleep? Rouse up, rouse up! Eternal death is abroad.'

96.17 *Covering Cherub*] This symbolic figure of evil is based on Ezekiel's denunciation of the Prince of Tyre, as the despoiler of Jerusalem, and for his arrogance amounting to an assumption of godhead (Ezekiel, chapters 26–28; the phrase itself occurs at 28.16). The Prince of Tyre was understood in Christian tradition as Satan. Blake also draws on the cherubim which cover the mercy seat above the ark of the covenant, which he saw (with other aspects of how the ark was ritually set apart) as indicative of secrecy and exclusivity, hence false religion. Cf. *Milton*, 43.26–7 note, on the veil covering the ark. Blake's two main accounts of the Cherub are in *Milton*, 37.8–60 and *Jerusalem*, 89.9–62 (where the account is pointedly antithetical to that of *Jerusalem*, 86.1–32). In *Jerusalem* the Cherub contains 'a reflection / Of Eden all perverted' (89.14–15): it is a false vision of central issues – of God, as law-giving and violent; of religion, as priestcraftly and hierarchical; and of Jerusalem herself, as Rahab – oppression and violence in place of liberty and love.

96.26–7 *man . . . love*] Cf. 1 John, 4.16: 'God is love; and he that dwelleth in love dwelleth in God, and God in him,' quoted by Blake in his marginalia to Lavater (Bentley, *Writings*, 1384).

96.27–8 *kindness . . . image*] Cf. Christ on acts of compassion and charity: 'Inasmuch as ye have done it unto one of the least of these my brethren, ye have done it unto me' (Matthew, 25.40); 'death / In' means 'giving of self in the manner of.'

96.29 *So saying, the cloud . . .*] As Jesus said this the cloud (the Covering Cherub) . . .

So Albion spoke, and threw himself into the furnaces of affliction.
All was a vision, all a dream: the furnaces became
Fountains of living waters flowing from the humanity divine;
And all the cities of Albion rose from their slumbers, and all
The sons and daughters of Albion on soft clouds waking from sleep.
Soon all around remote the heavens burnt with flaming fires,
And Urizen and Luvah and Tharmas and Urthona arose into
Albion's bosom. Then Albion stood before Jesus in the clouds
Of Heaven, fourfold among the visions of God in eternity.

[Plate 97]

'Awake, awake, Jerusalem, O lovely emanation of Albion!
Awake and overspread all nations as in ancient time.
For lo, the night of death is past, and the eternal day
Appears upon our hills. Awake, Jerusalem, and come away.'

So spake the vision of Albion, and in him so spake in my hearing
The universal Father. Then Albion stretched his hand into infinitude,
And took his bow. Fourfold the vision, for bright beaming Urizen
Laid his hand on the south and took a breathing bow of carvèd gold.
Luvah his hand stretched to the east and bore a silver bow, bright,
    shining.
Tharmas westward a bow of brass, pure, flaming, richly wrought.
Urthona northward in thick storms a bow of iron terrible,
    thundering.

96.37 *Fountains ... waters*] The phrase is biblical, but a composite made up from different sources: Christ tells a woman of Samaria that he is able to give her 'living water', and 'a well of water springing up into everlasting life' (John, 4.10, 14); in Revelation he promises 'I will give unto him that is athirst of the fountain of the water of life freely' (21.6).

96.43 *fourfold*] Cf. 30.26 note.

Plate 96 design. For technical reasons (Blake had previously used the copper plate for an advertisement which he had to cover) the design is placed to the right of the text, extending from the top of the page to line 25 (lines 1–25 are all turned over). It shows a bearded patriarchal figure in a long robe embracing a naked woman, illustrating 96.2: 'England, who is Britannia, entered Albion's bosom rejoicing.'

97.2 *Awake ... time*] Cf. plate 77, lyric.

97.5 *in my hearing*] Blake insists on the reality of the transcendental experience he recounts.

97.7 *bow*] This first appears at 95.13, where it initiates the realignment of the fallen zoas. In being gold, silver, brass and iron the bow draws together the four prehistoric ages of classical myth. Like other aspects of regenerated humanity the bow is androgynous (line 12) as a symbol of its inclusiveness. Cf. *Milton*, 1.9 note: there, as the mythic property of Apollo the bow suggests imagination; as of Eros, love; and as of Christ, both. For the parodic antithesis of Albion's bow, see the 'black bow' of Satan (plate 52, lyric, line 17), and the triple bow of Satan's watch-fiend (plate 39 design).

And the bow is a male and female, and the quiver of the arrows
  of love
Are the children of this bow, a bow of mercy and loving-kindness,
  laying
Open the hidden heart in wars of mutual benevolence, wars of love.
15 And the hand of man grasps firm between the male and female loves.
And he clothèd himself in bow and arrows in awful state, fourfold
In the midst of his twenty-eight cities, each with his bow breathing.

[Plate 98]

Then each an arrow flaming from his quiver fitted carefully.
They drew fourfold the unreprovable string, bending through the
  wide heavens
The hornèd bow fourfold. Loud sounding flew the flaming arrow
  fourfold;

Murmuring the bowstring breathes with ardour. Clouds roll round
  the horns
5 Of the wide bow; loud sounding winds sport on the mountain's brows.
The druid Spectre was annihilate, loud thund'ring, rejoicing terrific,
  vanishing,
Fourfold annihilation; and at the clangour of the arrows of intellect
The innumerable chariots of the Almighty appeared in Heaven,
And Bacon and Newton and Locke, and Milton and Shakespeare
  and Chaucer,

97.13–14 *laying . . . heart*] Cf. 'the spiritual sword / That lays open the hidden heart' (9.18–19).

97.14 *wars of love*] Cf. 91.17 note.

97.17 *twenty-eight*] Cf. 30.26 note.

Plate 97 design. Below the text a naked man (Los) pictured from behind (on whom can be seen the waist- and thigh-bands of otherwise transparent breeches) strides towards the edge of a cliff. The right arm held above his head, and the fact that only his toes touch the ground, may suggest that his great stride is a dance-step. A crescent moon and a star show that it is night, but he carries in his left hand a sun-like globe, rays from which illuminate most of the design – a mythologized version of plate 1: Los as a watchman in contemporary dress, carrying a globe-shaped lamp.

98.7 *intellect*] 'The Grey Monk', line 29 note.

98.9 *Bacon . . . Locke*] See *Visions*, 5.31 note, and 'The Everlasting Gospel', k.37 note. In *Milton* they are to be cast off (43.5): that these previous epitomes of the fallen intellect are now transformed is symptomatic of the inclusive nature of Albion's resurrection.   *Milton . . . Chaucer*] 'Milton loved me in childhood and showed me his face . . . Shakespeare in riper years gave me his hand' (letter to Flaxman of 12.9.1800; Bentley, *Writings*, 1537) and Blake's many illustrations of both poets (Butlin, *Paintings and Drawings*, 527–49); for Blake's admiration of Chaucer see his accounts of his 'Canterbury Pilgrims' watercolour and engraving (*A Descriptive Catalogure*, I, and Bentley, *Writings*, 863–6).

A sun of blood-red wrath surrounding heaven on all sides around,
Glorious, incomprehensible by mortal man; and each chariot was
   sexual, threefold.

And every man stood fourfold. Each four faces had: one to the west,
One toward the east, one to the south, one to the north; the horses
   fourfold.
And the dim chaos brightened beneath, above, around, eyèd as the
   peacock,
According to the human nerves of sensation, the four rivers of the
   water of life.

South stood the nerves of the eye; east in rivers of bliss the nerves
   of the
Expansive nostrils; west flowed the parent sense, the tongue; north
   stood
The labyrinthine ear; circumscribing and circumcising the
   excrementitious
Husk and covering, into vacuum evaporating, revealing the linea-
   ments of man;
Driving outward the body of death in an eternal death and
   resurrection,
Awaking it to life among the flowers of Beulah, rejoicing in unity
In the four senses, in the outline, the circumference and form,
   for ever
In forgiveness of sins, which is self-annihilation. It is the covenant
   of Jehovah.

The four living creatures, chariots of humanity divine,
   incomprehensible,
In beautiful paradises expand. These are the four rivers of paradise,
And the four faces of humanity, fronting the four cardinal points
Of Heaven; going forward, forward, irresistible from eternity to
   eternity.

98.11–12 *threefold . . . fourfold*] See 30.26 note.

98.15 *four . . . life*] Cf. 'a pure river of water of life' (Revelation, 22.1), and the four rivers of
Eden (Genesis, 2.10–14).

98.18 *circumcising*] Following biblical usage (for example, Deuteronomy, 10.16; Colossians,
2.11) the word is often employed by Blake in a metaphoric sense, as here, where a literal cut-
ting away also implies a spiritual purification. Cf. *Laocoön*, [28] note.   *excrementitious*] of
the nature of an outgrowth, not essential to the being.

And they conversèd together in visionary forms dramatic which
    bright
Redounded from their tongues in thunderous majesty, in visions,
30   In new expanses, creating exemplars of memory and of intellect,
Creating space, creating time, according to the wonders divine
Of human imagination, throughout all the three regions immense
Of childhood, manhood, and old age; and the all-tremendous
    unfathomable non-ens
Of death was seen in regenerations, terrific or complacent, varying
According to the subject of discourse; and every word and every
35   character
Was human, according to the expansion or contraction, the
    translucence or
Opaqueness of nervous fibres: such was the variation of time and
    space,
Which vary according as the organs of perception vary. And they
    walkèd
To and fro in eternity as one man, reflecting each in each, and
    clearly seen
And seeing, according to fitness and order. And I heard Jehovah
40   speak
Terrific from his holy place, and saw the words of the mutual
    covenant divine
On chariots of gold and jewels, with living creatures starry and
    flaming

98.30 *exemplars of memory*] Blake usually sets memory in opposition to inspiration (see, for example, his use of Milton on 'Memory and her Siren daughters': marginalia to Reynolds; Bentley, *Writings*, 1469). Here he apparently means that we need reminders of the fallen state, 'that we may foresee and avoid' (92.19).

98.33 *non-ens*] non-being.

98.34 *complacent*] delightful; terrific and complacent point to modes of feeling related respectively to the two great eighteenth-century categories of the aesthetic, the sublime and the beautiful. Cf. lines 6 and 41.

98.36 *Was human*] Everything is now understood as not an objective exterior reality (and so fixed), but a construction of human perceptions (and so transformable). Cf. plate 25 design and note, and 99.1–2.

98.37–8 *variation . . . vary*] Cf. 'The Mental Traveller', line 65 note, and 34(30).55–6: 'If perceptive organs vary, objects of perception seem to vary: / If the perceptive organs close, their objects seem to close also.'

98.39–40 *clearly . . . seeing*] Blake may have had in mind Saint Paul's famous account of full knowledge in Paradise, 1 Corinthians, 13.12: 'For now we see through a glass, darkly; but then face to face: now I know in part; but then shall I know even as also I am known.'

With every colour: lion, tiger, horse, elephant, eagle, dove, fly,
worm,
And the all-wondrous serpent clothèd in gems and rich array,
humanize
In the forgiveness of sins according to the covenant of Jehovah.
They cry:

'Where is the covenant of Priam, the moral virtues of the heathen?
Where is the tree of good and evil that rooted beneath the cruel
heel
Of Albion's Spectre, the patriarch druid? Where are all his human
sacrifices
For sin, in war and in the druid temples of the accuser of sin,
beneath
The oak groves of Albion that covered the whole earth, beneath
his Spectre?
Where are the kingdoms of the world and all their glory that grew
on desolation,
The fruit of Albion's poverty-tree, when the triple-headed
Gog-Magog giant

98.44 *serpent*] Who provided the first ground of the accusation of sin in the Christian myth of the origin of evil (Genesis, chapter 3).

98.46 *Where is . . . ?*] They are nowhere: based on error and illusion, these things have now disappeared.   *covenant of Priam*] The opposite of 'the covenant of Jehovah . . . the mutual covenant divine', the central element of which is forgiveness of sins (lines 23, 41, 45; cf. *The Ghost of Abel*, line 48). In *Milton* John Milton returns to earth because 'the nations still / Follow after the detestable gods of Priam' (12.14–15), that is they accept a falsification of Christianity, distorted by classical presuppositions which are fundamentally militaristic.

98.47–8 *tree . . . Spectre*] Cf. 28.15–19 and note.

98.48 *sacrifices*] The plate reads 'sacrifice', but the word goes to the right margin, and there are traces of a final 's' beneath the marginal decoration.

98.51 *kingdoms . . . glory*] These are offered to Christ as one aspect of his temptation by Satan in the wilderness (Matthew, 4.8; Luke, 4.5–6). Blake's phraseology is from *Paradise Regained*, 4.89.

98.52 *triple-headed Gog-Magog*] Gog and Magog were the last survivors of a mythical race of giants who inhabited ancient Britain. Two statues popularly known as Gog and Magog stood outside the Guildhall, London, centre of the city's commercial life. Blake synthesizes British and biblical myth. Ezekiel is directed to prophesy against 'Gog, the land of Magog' (Ezekiel, 38.2: Blake refers to this passage in identifying Gog and Magog in his Last Judgement picture: Bentley, *Writings*, 1016). They reappear in Revelation (20.8) as nations to be gathered by Satan into the final battle against God. Blake turns these into a single being, triple-headed to ally it with other opponents of the fourfold in *Jerusalem*, the triple bow of Satan's watch-fiend (plate 39), the triple accuser (plate 93), and above all the leader of Albion's fallen sons, the triple-headed Hand (plate 50).

Of Albion taxèd the nations into desolation and then gave the
spectrous oath?'

Such is the cry from all the earth from the living creatures of
the earth,
And from the great city of Golgonooza in the shadowy
55   Generation,

And from the thirty-two nations of the earth among the living
creatures,

[Plate 99]

All human forms identifièd, even tree, metal, earth and stone,
all
Human forms identifièd, living, going forth and returning
wearièd
Into the planetary lives of years, months, days and hours;
reposing

98.53 *taxèd the nations*] This epitomizes the illegitimate powers of empire: cf. *Laocoön* [15] and note. At the time of *Jerusalem* taxes had been increased in recent British history to prosecute wars to which Blake was opposed, against the American colonists, and against Revolutionary and Napoleonic France.   *the spectrous oath*] One example of such an oath would be that demanded by the Test and Corporation Acts: these enforced what was in Blake's view a false religion by requiring a profession of allegiance to the Thirty-nine Articles of the Anglican Church as a condition for holding public office or graduating from Oxford and Cambridge (then the only two universities in England).

98.55 *Golgonooza*] Cf. 27.25 note.

98.56 *thirty-two*] These are listed on plate 72.

Plate 98 design. Above the text a serpent with mouth open and forked tongue protruding wriggles in many coils from right to left: see line 44. Between lines 55 and 56 are (from right to left) a large worm, a moth, a spider, a caterpillar, a butterfly, a frog and a snail: see lines 42–3, the 'living creatures starry and flaming' which include the worm and fly (in the eighteenth century a generic term for any flying insect).

99.1 *All . . . identifièd*] Cf. 71.15–19: 'All are men in eternity: rivers, mountains, cities, villages; / All are human, and when you enter into their bosoms you walk / In heavens and earths, as in your own bosom you bear your heaven / And earth; and all you behold, though it appears without, it is within, / In your imagination, of which this world of mortality is but a shadow.'   *even . . . stone*] Cf. 13.66–14.1: 'not . . . / One hair nor particle of dust, not one can pass away', and Blake's annotation of Thornton's 'Lord's Prayer': 'Everything has as much right to eternal life as God, who is the servant of man' (Bentley, *Writings*, 1516).

And then awaking into his bosom in the life of immortality.

And I heard the name of their emanations: they are namèd
Jerusalem.

The End of the Song of Jerusalem

[Plate 100: full-plate design]

99.5 *I heard*] Cf. 97.5 and note.

Plate 99 design. Below the text a naked young woman (seen by some commentators as hermaphroditic), her arms raised in an ecstatic posture, is embraced by a bearded, gowned and haloed patriarchal figure. The scene recalls the plate 96 design with the relation of the figures reversed, but the context here suggests that the figures should now be identified as the ultimate forms of female and male in the work, Jerusalem and the Divine Vision.

Plate 100 design. This shows the three aspects of Los: left, with his back to the viewer, the redeemed Spectre floats above the ground carrying the sun on his shoulder (cf. plate 97 design); right, Enitharmon draws from her distaff the fibres of blood from which human forms are created; centre, Los as blacksmith (his form throughout most of the poem) holds his hammer and tongs. Behind the three figures, beneath a night sky with stars and a crescent moon, a central stone circle of trilithons extends outwards to two smaller circles on either side: like other aspects of the fallen world the serpent temple of fallen religion is redeemed by Los's creative activities.

THE EVERLASTING GOSPEL

The Everlasting Gospel consists in its fullest form of nine fragments in Blake's Note-book and three on separate sheets bearing the watermark 1818 (reproduced in Erdman's edition of the Notebook, appendix III). Keynes and Bentley print all of these as belonging to the poem equally, identifying each by a letter and proposing an order (different letters and orders in the two editions). Bentley accepts an order first proposed by David Erdman as that of composition.[1] Erdman's more recent and different view of Blake's latest intentions about a selection from and ordering of the fragments is that three of the longer sections, considering in sequence Jesus as not humble, chaste, or gentle, should be preceded by two prefatory fragments and followed by an epilogue.[2] This view is accepted here.

Blake took his title from Revelation: 'And I saw another angel fly in the midst of heaven, having the everlasting gospel to preach unto them that dwell on the earth, and to every nation, and kindred, and tongue, and people' (14.6), a passage to which he had previously referred in the 1809 catalogue of his one exhibition: 'All [nations] had originally one language and one religion: this was the religion of Jesus, the everlasting gospel' (*A Descriptive Catalogue*, V; Bentley, *Writings*, 851). The everlasting gospel means to Blake the religion of Jesus purified of accretions which neutralize its challenges to Hebraic and classical moral and social codes. This gives a view of Jesus broadly consistent with that of *The Marriage of Heaven and Hell*. That he is not humble or gentle means that he does not regard conventional social and religious hierarchies, as exemplified by his plain dealing with the Pharisees – an antithesis to the obedience to established authority urged by more conventional Christianity drawing on Saint Paul (Romans, 13.1–7; Titus, 3.1; cf. 1 Peter, 2.13–16). His opposition to the Mosaic Law is epitomized in *The Everlasting Gospel* by the rejection of its ethic of sexual abstinence because that is seen not as a purifying but as a corrupting of love. Behind these specific oppositions there is a more general idea: Blake's Jesus does not conform to established moral norms, Jewish or pagan, because these encourage the central Blakean sin of self-righteousness. What is central to Blake's later view of Jesus is the gospel of unconditional forgiveness. This is established in a prose fragment in the Notebook which Erdman sees as possibly the seed of the poem:

---

[1] David Erdman, '"Terrible Blake in his Pride": An Essay on *The Everlasting Gospel*', *From Sensibility to Romanticism*, ed. Frederick W. Hilles and Harold Bloom (New York, 1965), 331–56. In his hypotheses about the order of composition Erdman admits to building at times an 'impression from rather megre evidence' (347). Erdman's proposed ordering is criticized by Randel Helms, 'The Genesis of *The Everlasting Gospel*,' *Blake Studies*, 9 (1980), 122–60.

[2] The poem was first printed in this form in the 1982 revision of *Complete Poetry and Prose*; see 1988 edn., 874–80.

There is not one moral virtue that Jesus inculcated but Plato and Cicero did inculcate before him. What then did Christ inculcate? Forgiveness of sins. This alone is the gospel, and this is the life and immortality brought to light by Jesus; even the covenant of Jehovah, which is this: If you forgive one another your trespasses, so shall Jehovah forgive you, that he himself may dwell among you; but if you avenge you murder the divine image, and he cannot dwell among you because you murder him. He arises again, and you deny that he is arisen, and are blind to spirit.[3]

Because this issue is so central, but is not developed in general terms by the poem as printed by Erdman, I have given as a supplement fragment [c] (Bentley's lettering) which Blake at some stage of composition himself saw as central, labelling it '1: this to come first.'

---

[3] Bentley, *Writings*, 1054 (Keynes and Bentley punctuate, '... he cannot dwell among you: because you murder him he arises again ...'). Cf. fragment [b] (Bentley, *Writings*, 1054–5), and *Jerusalem*, Chapter 3, preface (plate 52), 'To the Deists'.

The Everlasting Gospel

[Preface] [m]

I will tell you what Joseph of Arimathea
Said to my fairy. Was not it very queer?
Pliny and Trajan, what, are you here?
Come listen to Joseph of Arimathea.
5   Listen patient and, when Joseph has done,
'Twill make a fool laugh and a fairy fun.

[n]

What can be done with such desperate fools
Who follow after the heathen schools?
I was standing by when Jesus died:
What I called Humility they called Pride.

[k]

The Everlasting Gospel

Was Jesus humble, or did he
Give any proofs of humility?

---

[m]: Written on page 52 of the Notebook; not printed as part of 'The Everlasting Gospel' in the arrangements of either Keynes or Bentley.

m.1 *Joseph of Arimathea*] A disciple of Jesus who is reported in all four gospels as responsible for Jesus's burial (Matthew, 27.57–60; Mark, 15.42–6; Luke, 23.50–53; John, 19.38). Blake illustrated the legend that Joseph brought Christianity to Britain ('Joseph of Arimathea Preaching to the Inhabitants of Britian', c. 1793–96; Essick, *The Separate Plates of William Blake*, XI (Princeton, NJ, 1983).)

m.2 *fairy*] A spiritual being who inspires Blake and is even thought of as writing his poems; cf. 'My fairy sat upon the table and dictated *Europe*' (*Europe*, 3.24), and *The Book of Urizen*, 2.6 note.

m.3 *Pliny . . . Trajan*] Pliny the Elder (23–79), author of *Natural History*, and type of the natural scientist; Trajan (Marcus Ulpius Trajanus, c. 53–117), emperor of Rome from 98. Perhaps simply representative 'heathens' (n.2), one a scholar the other a ruler; but Blake may have chosen Trajan rather than any other notable emperor to contradict the sophistical developments by which, for moral reasons, he became accepted in legend as a Christian (see Dante, *Paradiso*, XX). For Blake's opposition to conceiving Christianity in terms of moral virtues, see the Notebook passage quoted in the headnote and supplementary fragment [c].

[n]: Written on page 52 of the Notebook; lines 21–4 of section [d] in Keynes's arrangement (lines 21–4 of the same fragment, called [k], in Bentley's arrangement).

n.2 *heathen schools*] Cf. m.3 note.

n.3 *I*] Joseph of Arimathea; but his voice is blended with Blake's own.

[k]: Written on pages 52–4 of the Notebook; fragment [d] in Keynes's arrangement.

k.1–2 *humble . . . humility*] In certain obvious senses in each of the gospel accounts Jesus does teach humility: see, for example, Matthew, 18.1–6; Mark, 9.33–7; Luke, 22.24–7; John,

Boast of high things with humble tone,
And give with charity a stone?
5   When but a child he ran away
And left his parents in dismay.
When they had wandered three days long
These were the words upon his tongue:
'No earthly parents I confess:
10   I am doing my Father's business.'
When the rich learnèd Pharisee
Came to consult him secretly,
Upon his heart with iron pen
He wrote, 'Ye must be born again.'
15   He was too proud to take a bribe;
He spoke with authority, not like a Scribe.
He says with most consummate art,

13.14–17. And fragment [n] (whether in Blake's voice or Joseph of Arimathea's scarcely makes any difference) admits that something that can be called 'humility' is a supreme virtue. What Blake contests here is the passivity which some traditional accounts of Jesus have derived from the teachings on humility in the gospels. He attempts to define a legitimate pride which he sees as basic to the prophetic spirit's ability to act on its sense of vocation: humility, insofar as it encourages self-doubt, is antithetical to this.

k.4 *give . . . stone*] (Jesus speaks) 'What man is there of you, whom if his son ask bread, will he give him a stone?' (Matthew, 7.9; substantially repeated in Luke, 11.11).

k.5–10 *When . . . business*] This incident from the childhood of Jesus is reported in Luke, 2.42–50; when Jesus is found he does not (as here) explicitly repudiate his parents, though his reply indicates a more primary allegiance to the divine and to his mission: 'wist ye not that I must be about my Father's business?' Matthew, 12.46–50, Mark, 3.31–5, and Luke, 8.19–21 report another incident in which Jesus affirms spiritual ties of greater importance than those to his natural mother. Cf. *Laocoön* [23] and note.

k.10 *business*] The trisyllabic pronunciation (bus-i-ness) for the modern sense which now requires a disyllabic pronunciation (bus'ness) was still current in the early nineteenth century.

k.11–14 *When . . . again*] The Pharisee Nicodemus came to Jesus by night: John, 3.1–21. The saying reported in line 14 comes from John, 3.7. Nicodemus acknowledged Jesus's authority as a teacher, but the Pharisees generally were opponents of Jesus noted for their strict interpretation of Mosaic Law. Jesus often arraigns them as hypocrites who combine an excessive concern for form with an inadequate awareness of the substance forms are intended to embody.

k.15 *bribe*] The gospels report no attempts in the ordinary sense to bribe Jesus. Blake presumably intended Jesus's rejection of Satan's offers made during the temptation in the wilderness, particularly his offer of worldly power to be given in exchange for being worshipped (Matthew, 4.1–11; Luke, 4.1–13).

k.16 *He spoke . . . Scribe*] Matthew, 7.29: 'For he taught them as one having authority, and not as the scribes.' Also Mark, 1.22.   *Scribe*] The Scribes were (like the Pharisees) teachers of the Mosaic Law and upholders of ceremonial tradition.

k.17 *consummate*] Accented on the second syllable.

'Follow me, I am meek and lowly of heart,'
As that is the only way to escape
20   The miser's net and the glutton's trap.
He who loves his enemies betrays his friends:
This surely is not what Jesus intends,
But the sneaking pride of heroic schools,
And the Scribes' and Pharisees' virtuous rules,
25   For he acts with honest triumphant pride,
And this is the cause that Jesus died.
He did not die with Christian ease,
Asking pardon of his enemies.
If he had, Cai'phas would forgive:
30   Sneaking submission can always live.
He had only to say that God was the devil,
And the devil was God, like a Christian civil,
Mild Christian regrets to the devil confess
For affronting him thrice in the wilderness,
35   He had soon been bloody Caesar's elf,

---

k.18 *Follow . . . heart*] Matthew, 11.29 ('I am meek and lowly in heart'). For Blake this saying, inconsistent with his sense of Jesus's 'honest triumphant pride' (25), cannot be taken at face value: it is a blind designed to evade corrupt attentions.

k.21 *He who . . . friends*] Jesus directly enjoins loving one's enemies (Matthew, 5.44; Luke, 6.27, 35): as in the previous lines Blake is driven to contradict an apparently clear saying, which he does (with 'surely' perhaps indicating a residual doubt) in the spirit of another saying of Jesus, 'He that is not with me is against me' (Matthew, 12.30; similarly Luke, 11.23). Cf. 'I am no Homer's hero you all know; / I profess not generosity to a foe. / My generosity is to my friends, / That for their friendship I may make amends. / The gen'rous to enemies promotes their ends, / And becomes the enemy and betrayer of his friends.' (Notebook, page 31; Bentley, *Writings*, 942).

k.22–5] Though the syntax of these lines is elliptical (with a verb such as 'to rebuke' understood before 'the sneaking pride'), the sense is clear: the kind of pride exemplified by Jesus's own actions shows his condemnation of the kind of pride held up for admiration by classical and Hebraic conventions.

k.23–4 *sneaking . . . heroic schools . . . rules*] Pride arising from conscious rectitude in adherence to a moral code; 'sneaking' when the code (classical or Hebraic) forbids self-admiration and so the feeling presents itself in other terms. Jesus gives an example of corrupt pride arising from the conscious exercise of virtue through the parable of the Pharisee and the publican, with its conclusion, 'every one that exalteth himself shall be abased' (Luke, 18.9–14).

k.29 *Cai'phas*] The High Priest at the trial which led to Jesus's crucifixion.

k.32 *like a Christian civil*] In *Milton* (9.10–14) Satan proclaims himself God and is worshipped in what Blake probably intended as a parody of ordinary church-going.

k.34 *affronting . . . wilderness*] Cf. line 15 note.

k.35 *bloody Caesar*] stained with the blood of his conquests; murderous and cruel.

k.35 *elf*] A recognized but vague deprecatory sense is implied (*OED sb*[1] 5): creature (here, 'agent'). Cf. line 62, where the word is used to refer to the devil.

And at last he would have been Caesar himself,
Like Dr Priestley, and Bacon, and Newton.
Poor spiritual knowledge is not worth a button,
For thus the Gospel Sir Isaac confutes:
40   'God can only be known by his attributes,
And as for the indwelling of the Holy Ghost,
Or of Christ and his Father, it's all a boast,
And pride, and vanity of imagination
That disdains to follow this world's fashion.'
45   To teach doubt and experiment
Certainly was not what Christ meant.
What was he doing all that time
From twelve years old to manly prime?
Was he then idle, or the less
50   About his Father's business?
Or was his wisdom held in scorn
Before his wrath began to burn
In miracles throughout the land
That quite unnerved Lord Caiaphas' hand?
55   If he had been Antichrist, creeping Jesus,
He'd have done anything to please us;
Gone sneaking into synagogues,
And not used the elders and priests like dogs,
But humble as a lamb or ass
60   Obeyed himself to Caiaphas.
God wants not man to humble himself:
This is the trick of the ancient elf.
This is the race that Jesus ran:
Humble to God, haughty to man,

---

k.37 *Dr Priestley . . . Newton*] Joseph Priestley (1733–1804), the Unitarian minister, advocate of civil and religious liberty, and scientist (one of the discoverers of oxygen), may have been personally known to Blake, who possibly satirized him through the figure of Inflammable Gass the Windfinder in *An Island in the Moon* (*c*. 1784). The essays of the Renaissance statesman and scientist Sir Francis Bacon (1561–1626) Blake annotated with unremitting hostility, objecting among many other things that 'Bacon put an end to faith' (Bentley, *Writings*, 1427). Priestley, Bacon and Newton are Caesar's creatures because Blake understands the fundamental tendency of their work as materialist and non-spiritual (line 38 summarizes the implications of their work according to Blake).

k.41 *indwelling . . . Ghost*] Cf. 1 John, 4.16: 'God is love; and he that dwelleth in love dwelleth in God, and God in him,' quoted by Blake in his annotations of Lavater (Bentley, *Writings*, 1384).

k.45 *teach . . . experiment*] Cf. 'Auguries of Innocence', lines 85–96.

k.48 *twelve . . . prime*] The gospels contain no records of Christ's life after the age of twelve (cf. lines 5–10 note) until the beginning of his ministry (traditionally understood as at the age of thirty).

65	Cursing the rulers before the people,
	Even to the Temple's highest steeple,
	And when he humbled himself to God
	Then descended the cruel rod.
	'If thou humblest thyself thou humblest me:
70	Thou also dwell'st in eternity.
	Thou art a man; God is no more:
	Thy own humanity learn to adore,
	For that is my spirit of life.
	Awake, arise to spiritual strife,
75	And thy revenge abroad display
	In terrors at the Last Judgement day.
	God's mercy and long-suffering
	Is but the sinner to judgement to bring.
	Thou on the cross for them shalt pray,
80	And take revenge at the Last Day.'
	Jesus replied, and thunders hurled:
	'I never will pray for the world.
	Once [I] did so when I prayed in the garden:
	I wished to take with me a bodily pardon.'
85	Can that which was of woman born,
	In the absence of the morn,
	When the soul fell into sleep,

---

k.70 *dwell'st in eternity*] 'Thus saith the high and lofty One that inhabiteth eternity . . . I dwell in the high and holy place' (Isaiah, 57.15).

k.71 *Thou . . . more*] The unity of man and God is a central theme of Blake's work: cf. *Marriage*, 22.18–23.2 note.

k.75–80 *thy revenge . . . Last Day*] The Blakean doctrine of the preceding lines gives places to conventional and unBlakean views on punishment for sin and (epitomizing the divine sanction for this) the myth of a Last Judgement at which Jesus will allot final and irrevocable punishments. Cf. the headnote quotation on unconditional forgiveness as, in Blake's view, central to the gospel propounded by Jesus.

k.79 *on . . . pray*] 'Father, forgive them; for they know not what they do' (Luke, 23.34).

k.83 *when . . . garden*] Based on John, 17.9: 'I pray not for the world, but for them which thou hast given me.' Blake takes words of Jesus at the Last Supper (just before he enters the garden of Gethsemane), prior to his arrest and trial, though he inverts their sense. He presumably means that when, in his moment of weakness before the crucifixion, Jesus asked the Father 'if it be possible, let this cup pass from me' (Matthew, 26.39; cf. Mark, 14.36; Luke, 22.42) he was in effect offering to renege on his mission of transforming the world.

k.85 *of woman born*] The phrase 'born of a woman' is used three times in Job, in contexts which assert human frailty (14.1, 15.14, 25.4: the first of these passages is particularly well known because of its use in the burial service of the Book of Common Prayer).

k.86 *In . . . morn*] In the absence of spiritual illumination (cf. lines 89–90): birth is regarded as a fall.

k.87 *the soul . . . sleep*] The soul 'sleeps' when it is born into this world.

And archangels round it weep,
Shooting out against the light
90   Fibres of a deadly night,
Reasoning upon its own dark fiction
In doubt which is self-contradiction . . . ?
Humility is only doubt,
And does the sun and moon blot out.
95   Rooting over with thorns and stems
The buried soul and all its gems,
This life's dim windows of the soul,
Distorts the heavens from pole to pole,
And leads you to believe a lie
100   When you see with not through the eye,
That was born in a night, to perish in a night,
When the soul slept in beams of light.

[f]

Was Jesus chaste, or did he
Give any lessons of chastity?
The morning blushed fiery red:
Mary was found in adulterous bed.
5   Earth groaned beneath, and Heaven above
Trembled at discovery of love.
Jesus was sitting in Moses' chair:

---

k.91 *fiction*] perhaps 'fashioning' (*OED* 1a; last recorded use 1711); though in the context Blake may also mean that the fallen being is ultimately unreal.

k.92 *self-contradiction*] The syntax collapses at this point.

k.93–4 *Humility . . . out*] Cf. 'Auguries of Innocence', lines 109–10.

k.95–6 *Rooting . . . buried soul*] Cf. 'The Garden of Love', *Songs of Experience*, line 12 note.

k.97 *This . . . soul*] Perhaps a reminiscence of the proverb 'The eye is the window of the heart (mind)' (Tilley, E231).

k.99–102 *leads . . . light*] Cf. 'Auguries of Innocence', lines 125–8 and note.

[f]: Written on pages 48–52 of the Notebook; fragment [e] in Keynes's arrangement.

f.3ff.] The incident Blake refers to is recorded in John, 8.2–11. Cf. *Marriage*, 23.13 note. The woman in this incident is not Mary Magdalene (line 4), and the identification of her with Mary is not usual, though Mary is commonly identified with another prostitute to whom Jesus offers forgiveness, the unnamed woman in the story of Simon the Pharisee (Luke, 7.36–50).

f.5–6 *Earth groaned . . . Heaven . . . / Trembled*] The diction as well as the thought recalls Adam's completion of the Fall in *Paradise Lost* (9.1000–3), a contrary moment of human transformation: 'Earth trembled . . . / . . . Nature gave a second groan; / Sky loured.'

f.7 *sitting . . . chair*] Figuratively: Jesus is asked to interpret the Mosaic Law. Blake's figure is based on Christ's own words about the position of the Scribes and Pharisees: they 'sit in Moses' seat' (Matthew, 23.2). On the relation of Jesus to the Mosaic Law cf. *Marriage*, 23.11 note.

They brought the trembling woman there.
'Moses commands she be stonéd to death.'
10   What was the sound of Jesus' breath?
He laid his hand on Moses' Law;
The ancient heavens in silent awe,
Writ with curses from pole to pole,
All away began to roll.
15   The earth trembling and naked lay
In secret bed of mortal clay,
On Sinai felt the hand divine
Putting back the bloody shrine,
And she heard the breath of God,
20   As she heard by Eden's flood:
'Good and Evil are no more:
Sinai's trumpets, cease to roar.
Cease, finger of God, to write.
The heavens are not clean in thy sight.
25   Thou art good, and thou alone,
Nor may the sinner cast one stone.
To be good only is to be
A devil or else a Pharisee.

---

f.12–14 *heavens . . . roll*] Cf. the apocalypse as described in Revelation: 'The heaven departed as a scroll when it is rolled together' (6.14).

f.17 *Sinai*] The mountain on which Moses received the tables of the Law: Exodus, chapters 19 and 20. Exodus 19.13 mentions the trumpets (line 22) which signal that worshippers should approach the mountain.

f.18 *Putting . . . shrine*] In Old Testament ritual the central altar of the tabernacle was smeared with the blood of sacrificial animals (Exodus 29). It is in keeping with aspects of New Testament theology – the symbolic rending of the altar veil after Christ's death (Matthew, 28.51; Mark, 15.38; Luke, 23.45); Christ understood as replacing the Levitical priesthood of Aaron – that this ritual should be superseded (put back).

f.19 *breath of God*] Blake knew some Hebrew and may have known that in the biblical account of Creation the Hebrew *rûah*, which the Authorized Version translates 'Spirit [of God]' (Genesis, 1.2), also means 'breath'. It is so translated in Psalm 33 (v. 6): 'By the word of the Lord were the heavens made; and all the host of them by the breath of his mouth.' Cf. lines 41–2.

f.20 *by Eden's flood*] That is, at the Creation ('flood' here means 'river'): the moral judgement in which Christ abrogates the Law of Moses is an event as momentous as the original creation of humankind.

f.21ff.] The speaker is Jesus.

f.23 *finger of God*] 'He gave unto Moses . . . two tables of testimony, tables of stone, written with the finger of God' (Exodus, 31.18).

f.24 *heavens . . . sight*] 'The heavens are not clean in his sight'; 'the stars are not pure in his sight' (Job, 15.15, 25.5). Cf. line 36.

f.25 *Thou . . . alone*] 'And Jesus said . . . Why callest thou me good? there is none good but one, that is, God' (Mark, 10.18).

Thou Angel of the Presence Divine
30 That didst create this body of mine,
Wherefore has[t] thou writ these laws,
And created Hell's dark jaws?
My presence I will take from thee:
A cold leper thou shalt be.
35 Though thou wast so pure and bright
That Heaven was impure in thy sight,
Though thy oath turned Heaven pale,
Though thy covenant built Hell's jail,
Though thou didst all to Chaos roll
40 With the serpent for its soul,
Still the breath divine does move,
And the breath divine is Love.
Mary, fear not, let me see
The seven devils that torment thee.
45 Hide not from my sight thy sin,
That forgiveness thou may'st win.

---

f.29 *Angel of the Presence*] See *Laocoön*, headnote (p. 357, note 5). The usual moral and eschatalogical scheme of Christianity, which includes obedience to the Mosaic Law and an eternal Hell in which sinners are punished, is not (Blake implies) divinely appointed: it is the creation of an inferior angel.

f.34 *leper . . . be*] Reversing the usual healing miracles of Jesus, some of which specifically cure leprosy (Matthew, 8.2–4; Mark, 1.40–5; Luke, 5.12–15, 17.11–19). But in the Old Testament leprosy is inflicted by God as a punishment: Moses' sister Miriam is smitten with the disease for speaking against Moses (Numbers, 12.10); Elisha's servant Gehazi for his attempt to extort money from the Assyrian general Naaman when Elisa cures his leprosy (2 Kings, 5.15–27); and King Uzziah as a punishment for sacrilege (2 Chronicles, 26.19–21). Cf. i.28, 30.

f.39 *Chaos*] In *Paradise Lost* (1.10) God is thought of as creating the world out of a primal Chaos: Blake argues that the Law reversed this process, introducing moral chaos, particularly because of the Law's negative attitude to sexual love.

f.40 *serpent*] Satan, who, disguised as a serpent, deceives Adam and Eve (Genesis, chapter 3) and so causes the Fall of humankind; what causes corruption in Blake's account is not the Fall but the Law.

f.43–4 *Mary . . . seven devils*] Cf. lines 3ff. note. Jesus is said to have cast out seven devils from Mary Magdalene (Mark, 16.9; cf. Luke, 8.2). The gospels do not explain these devils, but possession by devils in the gospels would normally be understood as implying madness rather than (on the conventional estimate) sexual impurity. In accordance with his account of Law as not a restraint of sin but its cause, Blake presents these devils not as impurity itself but as its source, the corruption of love by the mistaken doctrine of chastity (lines 71–2). Cf. *Laocoön* [28] and [30] and notes.

f.45–6 *Hide not . . . may'st win*] 'If we confess our sins, he is faithful and just to forgive us our sins' (1 John, 1.9), a verse particularly well known because of its use among the introductory sentences for the services of morning and evening prayer in the Book of Common Prayer. Blake implies a reversal of Genesis, chapter 3, where Adam and Eve hide from God because of their fear of punishment.

Has no man condemnèd thee?'
'No man, Lord.' 'Then what is he
Who shall accuse thee? Come ye forth,
50 Fallen fiends of heav'nly birth
That have forgot your ancient love,
And driven away my trembling dove.
You shall bow before her feet,
You shall lick the dust for meat,
55 And though you cannot love, but hate,
Shall be beggars at Love's gate.
What was thy love? Let me see it.
Was it love, or dark deceit?'
'Love too long from me has fled.
60 'Twas dark deceit to earn my bread.
'Twas covet, or 'twas custom, or
Some trifle not worth caring for,
That they may call a shame and sin
Love's temple that God dwelleth in,
65 And hide in secret hidden shrine
The naked human form divine,
And render that a lawless thing
On which the soul expands its wing.
But this, O Lord, this was my sin,
70 When first I let these devils in
In dark pretence to chastity,
Blaspheming Love, blaspheming thee.
Thence rose secret adulteries,
And thence did covet also rise.

---

f.47–9 *Has . . . thee*] Referring again to the episode in John of the woman taken in adultery: cf. lines 3ff. note.

f.49 *Come ye forth*] Jesus addresses Mary's 'seven devils'.

f.54 *lick the dust*] Cf. the punishment of the serpent in Genesis (3.14): 'dust shalt thou eat all the days of thy life'. In Micah (7.17) it is prophesied that the enemies of Israel 'shall lick the dust like a serpent.'

f.57 *thy*] Mary's.

f.61, 74 *covet*] Covetousness, avarice: one of the seven deadly sins of Christian tradition (deadly in that they cause spiritual death). In the traditional scheme Pride is the origin of all the rest. Here Blake sees other sins as arising from the Law's mistaken attitude to love.

f.64 *Love's . . . dwelleth in*] 'Your body is the temple of the Holy Ghost which is in you, which ye have of God' (1 Corinthians, 6.19); and cf. 1 Corinthians, 3.16, and 2 Corinthians, 6.16. The allusion is ironic: Paul's comment is made in the context of enforcing the sexual ethics Blake here opposes.

75   My sin thou hast forgiven me,
        Canst thou forgive my blasphemy?
        Canst thou return to this dark hell
        And in my burning bosom dwell,
        And canst thou die that I may live,
80   And canst thou pity and forgive?'
        Then rolled the shadowy man away
        From the limbs of Jesus to make them his prey,
        An ever-devouring appetite
        Glittering with festering venoms bright,
85   Crying 'Crucify this cause of distress
        Who don't keep the secrets of holiness.
        All mental powers by diseases we bind,
        But he heals the deaf and the dumb and the blind.
        Whom God has afflicted for secret ends
90   He comforts and heals, and calls them friends.'
        But when Jesus was crucified
        Then was perfected his glitt'ring pride.
        In three nights he devoured his prey,
        And still he devours the body of clay,
95   For dust and clay is the serpent's meat
        Which never was made for man to eat.

                        [i]

        Was Jesus gentle, or did he
        Give any marks of gentility?

---

f.81 *the shadowy man*] The false Jesus of Christian tradition, 'rolled . . . away' like the stone before Jesus's tomb because the living spirit is thus revealed.

f.82 *to make . . . prey*] Blake's expression is elliptical: the church's false picture of Jesus was intended to destroy his true significance.

f.85 *Crying 'Crucify*] As the crowd does when Pilate offers to release Jesus (Matthew, 27.22–3; Mark, 15.13–14; Luke, 23.21–3; John, 19.6).

f.87–90] For opposition to Jesus's miracles of healing see, for example, Matthew, 12.10–14; Luke, 13.14; John, 9.16ff.

f.92 *his*] Satan, the serpent's.

f.93 *three nights*] Jesus spent three days in his tomb, from Good Friday to Easter Sunday: during this time, before the resurrection, Satan apparently had power over him.

[i]: Written on pages 100–1 of the Notebook; fragment [b] in Keynes's arrangement.

i.1 *gentle*] Mild in disposition or behaviour (*OED a* 8); having the character appropriate to a person who is socially well-born (*OED a* 3a) – a meaning brought out by 'gentility'. Blake dissociates Jesus both from the conventional image of him as meek and mild and from the respectability of the church.

	When twelve years old he ran away
	And left his parents in dismay.
5	When after three days sorrow found,
	Loud as Sinai's trumpet sound:
	'No earthly parents I confess:
	My heavenly Father's business!
	Ye understand not what I say,
10	And angry, force me to obey.
	Obedience is a duty then,
	And favour gains with God and men.'
	John from the wilderness loud cried;
	Satan gloried in his pride.
15	'Come,' said Satan, 'Come away:
	I'll soon see if you'll obey.
	John for disobedience bled,
	But you can turn the stones to bread.
	God's high king and God's high priest
20	Shall plant their glories in your breast,
	If Caiaphas you will obey,
	If Herod you, with bloody prey,
	Feed with the sacrifice, and be
	Obedient: fall down, worship me.'
25	Thunders and lightnings broke around,
	And Jesus' voice in thunder's sound:
	'Thus I seize the spiritual prey:

---

i.3–8] Cf. k.5–10 and notes: the duplication indicates how far Erdman's putative 'final' version is from a finished work.

i.6 *Sinai*] Cf. f.17 note.

i.13 *John . . . wilderness*] John the Baptist, 'the voice of one crying in the wilderness' (Matthew, 3.3; cf. Mark, 1; Luke, 3; John, 1 and 3): John's ministry is presented in all four gospels as preparing for the ministry of Jesus. Blake implied a parallel between himself and John by subtitling his first illuminated work, *All Religions Are One*, 'the voice of one crying in the wilderness.'

i.17 *John . . . bled*] John was executed by Herod when he was imprisoned for denouncing Herod's marriage to his brother's wife, Herodias (Matthew, 14; Mark, 6). His 'disobedience' was a refusal to kowtow to and flatter authority.

i.18 *turn . . . bread*] One of the temptations to reveal his power, and so in effect to submit to Satan, to which Christ is subjected in the wilderness (Matthew, 4.3; Luke, 4.3).

i.22 *Herod . . . prey*] Referring to the Massacre of the Innocents – the children killed in Bethlehem by Herod in an attempt to ensure that the infant Jesus died (Matthew, 2.16): Blake takes this as epitomizing the tyrannous use of political power.

i.24 *fall down, worship me*] One of Satan's demands of Christ during the temptation in the desert (Matthew, 4.9; Luke, 4.7), in Matthew's account the final, climactic demand.

Ye smiters with disease, make way.
I come your king and god to seize.
30   Is God a smiter with disease?'
The god of this world ragèd in vain:
He bound old Satan in his chain,
And, bursting forth, his furious ire
Became a chariot of fire.
35   Throughout the land he took his course,
And tracèd diseases to their source.
He cursed the Scribe and Pharisee,
Trampling down hypocrisy.
Where'er his chariot took its way
40   There gates of death let in the day,
Broke down from every chain and bar,
And Satan in his spiritual war
Dragged at his chariot wheels. Loud howled
The God of this world, louder rolled
45   The chariot wheels, and louder still
His voice was heard from Zion's hill;
And in his hand the scourge shone bright:
He scourged the merchant Canaanite

---

i.28 *smiters with disease*] Cf. f.34 and note.

i.29 *king and god*] That is, Satan.

i.31 *god of this world*] The phrase is from Saint Paul: 2 Corinthians, 4.4. John's gospel three times uses 'prince of this world' (12.31, 14.30, 16.11): the Authorized Version marginal glosses make clear by cross-reference to Luke 10.18 that both are titles of Satan.

i.32 *He*] Jesus.   *bound old Satan*] 'He laid hold on the dragon, that old serpent, which is the Devil, and Satan, and bound him a thousand years' (Revelation, 20.2). Saint John the Divine means this as a prophecy of what will happen at the Last Judgement: Blake takes it as a consequence of the ministry of Jesus which has already come about.

i.34 *chariot of fire*] In conceiving of Christ's righteous wrath in terms of a fiery chariot Blake probably had in mind the 'chariot of paternal deity / Flashing thick flames' in which Christ defeats the devils in the war in heaven in *Paradise Lost* (6.750–1). The passage would be particularly notable to Blake because it is based on Ezekiel's vision of God which underlies Blake's own myth of four zoas (Ezekiel, chapters 1 and 10). Cf. *Milton*, 'And did those feet?', line 12 and note.

i.43 *Dragged . . . wheels*] Hazard Adams (*William Blake: A Reading of the Shorter Poems* (1963), 196) sees here an allusion to Achilles' treatment of the body of Hector (*Iliad*, XXII). If one accepts this it is more important to see differences than similarities between corporeal and spiritual war; but since, even in terms of the *Iliad*, Achilles is seen as behaving abominably, the supposed resemblance seems no more than a superficial similarity.

i.46 *His*] Jesus's.

i.48–9 *scourged . . . mind*] Referring to Christ's expulsion of the moneychangers and merchants from the temple in Jerusalem, but interpreting that symbolically (Matthew, 21.12–13; Mark, 11.15–17; Luke, 19.45–6; John, 2.13–17). In John, immediately following this incident, the temple is interpreted as symbolic of the body of Christ (2.21).

From out the temple of his mind,
50 And in his body tight does bind
Satan and all his hellish crew,
And thus with wrath he did subdue
The serpent bulk of Nature's dross,
Till he had nailed it to the cross.
55 He took on sin in the Virgin's womb,
And put it off on the cross and tomb,
To be worshipped by the Church of Rome.

[e]

The vision of Christ that thou dost see
Is my vision's greatest enemy.
Thine has a great hook nose like thine;
Mine has a snub nose like to mine.
5 Thine is the friend of all mankind;
Mine speaks in parables to the blind.
Thine loves the same world that mine hates;
Thy Heaven doors are my Hell gates.

---

i.48 *Canaanite*] The inhabitants of Canaan were heathens displaced or subjugated by the Jews. The Jews opposed to Jesus, Blake implies, were in effect heathens.

i.51 *hellish crew*] Milton constantly uses 'crew' for the devils in *Paradise Lost*.

i.53–4 *serpent . . . cross*] The serpent (the cause of the Fall in Genesis and so symbolic of sin) is often represented as nailed to the cross of Christ, showing that sin is overcome by the crucifixion. See, for example, *Paradise Lost*, 12.415–17: 'But to the cross he nails thy enemies, / The law that is against thee, and the sins / Of all mankind, with him there crucified'; cf. Blake's illustration of the lines: Butlin, *Paintings and Drawings*, 529.11. The interpretation of the serpent as representing Nature is Blake's: the crucifixion gives access to spiritual realities and so overcomes the illusions of the material world.

i.55 *took on sin*] In the Incarnation Jesus assumed the corrupt (material) nature of human beings.

i.57 *worshipped . . . Rome*] Blake argues as a Protestant: the Roman Catholic Church attends to religious symbols in the wrong way, becoming fixated upon the symbols themselves, not on the realities they embody. By the last line of this section Blake wrote a final couplet: 'I'm sure this Jesus will not do / Either for Englishman or Jew.'

[e]: Written on page 33 of the Notebook; fragment [a] in Keynes's arrangement.

e.4 *snub . . . mine*] 'I always thought Jesus Christ was a snubby or I should not have worshipped him if I had thought he had been one of those long spindle-nosed rascals' (Notebook, page 64; Bentley, *Writings*, 960).

e.6 *speaks . . . blind*] Blake has in mind those passages of the gospel in which Jesus describes his parables as deliberately inscrutable to those to whom it is not given 'to know the mysteries of the kingdom of heaven' (Matthew, 13.10–17; cf. Mark, 4.11–13, and Luke, 8.10).

Socrates taught what Melitus
10   Loathed as a nation's bitterest curse,
And Cai'phas was in his own mind
A benefactor of mankind.
Both read the Bible day and night,
But thou read'st black where I read white.

*

Supplement: Fragment [c]

If moral virtue was Christianity
Christ's pretensions were all vanity,
And Caiaphas and Pilate men
Praiseworthy, and the lions' den,
5   And not the sheepfold, allegories
Of God and Heaven and their glories.
The moral Christian is the cause
Of the unbeliever and his laws;
The Roman virtues' warlike fame
10   Take Jesus' and Jehovah's name;

---

e.9 *Melitus*] One of the three accusers of Socrates in the trial which led to his execution.

e.13 *Both*] That is, Blake and the conventional Christian of his day addressed in line 1.

e.14 *black . . . white*] Cf. *Marriage*, plate 5 on contrary readings of *Paradise Lost* and the Book of Job, and plate 24 on the Bible's 'infernal or diabolical sense'. Blake's re-working of John, 8.2–11 in fragment [f] above shows what a contrary reading of scripture means in practice: the 'sin' of the woman brought before Jesus is interpreted not as adultery but as acceptance of the sexual ethics on which the accusation of adultery is based.

[c]: Written on page 4 of the Notebook; supplementary fragment [1] in Keynes' arrangement. For the inclusion of this fragment, see the headnote.

c.2 *pretensions . . . vanity*] Cf. *Laocoön* [31].

c.3 *Caiaphas*] Cf. k.29 note. Blake wrote 'Caiphas' but the metre requires a trisyllable.   *Pilate*] The Roman governor of Judea at the time of Christ who, as the civil authority, was responsible for his crucifixion.

c.4 *lions' den*] The prophet Daniel was punished by being imprisoned in a den of lions as a result of praying to God and so violating a decree that only King Darius was to be petitioned. He is saved by God who sends an angel to shut the lions' mouths (Daniel, chapter 6). Blake presumably intends an analogy with Heaven conceived as an exclusive preserve of the righteous and as associated with punishment for the unrighteous.

c.5 *sheepfold*] Christ is the Good Shepherd (John, 10.14); his people are the sheep (John, 21.15–17); the sheepfold is an inclusive place for all those who follow him (John, 10.16).

c.9 *Roman virtues*] Cf. m.3 and k.21 notes.

> For what is Antichrist but those
> Who against sinners Heaven close
> With iron bars in virtuous state,
> And Radamanthus at the gate.

---

c.11 *Antichrist*] The great personal opponent of Christ and his kingdom expected by the early church (from 1 John, 2.18, 22, and 2 John, 7).

c.14 *Radamanthus*] One of the three judges who allots punishments in the classical underworld. Blake means that the same kind of figure is carried over into traditional Christian versions of Hell – for example, Minos, the assessor of punishments in the *Divina Commedia* (*Inferno*, canto 4), a figure taken over by Dante from Virgil (*Aeneid*, 6.432).

APHORISMS FROM
LAOCOÖN

Blake's *Laocoön* derives from one of the most famous of classical sculptures, which Blake knew from a life-size cast in the Royal Academy in London. Its subject is re-counted in the *Aeneid*, Book II. Laocoön, the priest of Neptune, warns the Trojans not to take into their city the wooden horse left by the Greeks apparently retreating from the siege of Troy. He and his two sons are crushed to death by two serpents sent by Minerva, and this is taken as a sign that Laocoön's true warning is false. Blake made two drawings of the cast – one now lost, the other one of his most beautiful and finished pencil drawings – in preparation not for his own engraving but for an engraved version to be used in illustration of the article on sculpture by John Flaxman in Abraham Rees's *The Cyclopaedia: or Universal Dictionary of Arts, Sciences, and Literature*. Blake's plate, which includes the Laocoön group alongside versions of two other well-known classical sculptures, the Venus de Medici and the Apollo Belvedere, is dated 1 October 1815 and was published in July 1816.[1] Blake returned to the subject *c.* 1824 when he produced a large pencil, pen and water-colour version, notably different in that the central figure is bearded and gowned (Butlin, *Paintings and Drawings*, 681), suggesting the beginnings of Blake's idiosyn-cratic interpretation of the myth.

Blake's attitudes to Greek and Roman culture developed and changed. In letters of 1799 and 1800 he is wholly enthusiastic: 'the purpose for which alone I live . . . [is] to renew the lost art of the Greeks'; he welcomes 'the immense flood of Grecian light and glory which is coming on Europe' (Bentley, *Writings*, 1524, 1534) – though in both cases Blake's view may have been influenced by what he knew of the tastes of his correspondents. He executed two watercolours on classical subjects, both re-lated (like Laocoön) to the Trojan War, *c.* 1811–12: 'The Judgement of Paris', and 'Philoctetes and Neoptolemus at Lemnos' (Butlin, *Paintings and Drawings*, 675–6). A drawing possibly of 'The Death of Hector' may also come from this time.[2] Other-wise Blake is characteristically antagonistic. In the preface to *Milton*, 'We do not want either Greek or Roman models'; and in works probably contemporary with the *Laocoön* he is yet more emphatic: 'Sacred truth has pronounced that Greece and Rome . . . were destroyers of all art' (*On Virgil*); and 'the Greek and Roman classics is the Antichrist' (marginalia to Thornton). Though many of the *Laocoön's* aphorisms indict classical culture as corrupt, as a whole the engraving (*Plate 9*) is more am-bivalent. 'The Greek fables originated in spiritual mystery . . . and real visions which

---

[1] The plate and associated materials are reproduced in Robert N. Essick, *William Blake's Com-mercial Book Engravings: A Catalogue and Study of the Plates Engraved by Blake after Other Artists* (Oxford, 1991).

[2] See Robert N. Essick, *Studies in Romanticism*, 27 (1988).

9. *Laocoön*

(Fitzwilliam Museum, Cambridge; original size: 16.4 × 19.6 cms)

are lost and clouded in fable and allegory' ('A Vision of the Last Judgement'; Bentley, *Writings*, 1008): the Greeks, that is, preserved symbolic myths of more ancient cultures genuinely in contact with the divine, though they adapted and trivialized, assigning significances appropriate to their own circumstances. Blake's aim in the *Laocoön* is, accordingly, to restore, not the lost art of the Greeks, but the lost meanings that lie behind Greek art. This means inventing (Blake would say recovering) what meaning the myth might have had in its supposedly original Hebrew context. The key to understanding this lies in Blake's inscriptions.[3]

Below the plinth on which the statue stands the whole group is described as 'Yahweh [indicated by the first two Hebrew characters only of the tetragrammaton, the Old Testament unutterable name of God: YH] and his two sons, Satan and Adam, as they were copied from the cherubim of Solomon's temple by three Rhodians, and applied to natural fact or history of Ilium [Troy]'.[4] Above the head of Yahweh is inscribed 'The Angel of the Divine Presence'[5] with below that what Blake presumably regarded as expressing this in Hebrew – all four of the Hebrew characters which form the sacred name, YHWH, followed by the four Hebrew characters meaning messenger, the term for what is usually translated 'angel'.[6] Above these inscriptions is 'He repented that he had made Adam (of the female, the adamah) and it grieved him at his heart'[7] – that is, that he had given form to the fallen, unimaginative consciousness (see aphorism [2]). Interpretation of the central figure has been

---

[3] Blake's attitudes to classical sculpture are set in their contemporary context by Morton Paley ('Wonderful Originals: Blake and Ancient Sculpture', Robert N. Essick and Donald Pearce, *Blake in his Time*, 1978). In context Blake's ideas about classical art deriving from Hebrew models seem less eccentric: they can be seen as embryonically present in the writings of his friend the sculptor John Flaxman and others, and as analogous to the widely held eighteenth-century view that Hebrew was the parent language from which all ancient and modern languages derived.

[4] 'The cherubim of Solomon's temple': cf. Blake's *Descriptive Catalogue* (1809; II): 'The artist having been taken in vision into the ancient . . . patriarchates of Asia, has seen those wonderful originals called in the sacred scriptures the Cherubim, which were sculptured and painted on the walls of temples, towers, cities, palaces . . . being originals from which the Greeks . . . copied . . . all the grand works of ancient art.' (Bentley, *Writings*, 830; cf. catalogue, p. 21, *Writings*, 839). Blake describes these 'wonderful originals' as 'all containing mythological and recondite meaning, where more is meant than meets the eye'. '. . . three Rhodians': Pliny, *Natural History*, describes the *Laocoön* as the work of 'Agesander, Polydorus, and Athenodorus, Rhodians' (trans. Philemon Holland, 1634, book 36, chapter 5).

[5] The title comes from a single reference in Isaiah, 63.9. The Authorized Version marginal gloss cross-references to Exodus 14.19, the angel who leads the Israelites through the wilderness as a pillar of cloud and a pillar of fire. Blake accepts this identification in 'A Vision of the Last Judgement' (Notebook, page 81; Bentley, *Writings*, 1017).

[6] These Hebrew characters with the same translation (Angel of the Divine Presence) also appear in plate 2 of Blake's Job engravings (1826). Cf. 'A Vision of the Last Judgement', where the Angel of the Divine Presence is identified as 'Jehovah Elohim', a combination of two of the names for God in Genesis (Bentley, *Writings*, 1017).

[7] This draws on Genesis, 6.6 ('it repented the Lord that he had made man') and 2.7 ('God formed man of the dust of the ground'); 'female' refers to the gender of the Hebrew noun 'adamah' (the ground), the material from which Adam was made.

disputed, but the Hebrew letters, the names, and the Genesis quotation suggest that Blake probably saw him as the Old Testament Creator caught in the toils of his creation, particularly – as the serpents, sons, and several of the inscriptions suggest – his ideas of Good and Evil. Immediately above the head of Yahweh is written in Greek the name of the central northern constellation Ophiucus, the serpent-bearer – whom, for obvious reasons, Blake might regard as a somewhat corresponding figure in classical mythology. Below the figure's left hand is written in Hebrew the name of Adam's first wife according to cabbalistic Judaism, Lilith. (No convincing explanation of this last detail has been suggested in terms of the plate itself: it is probably relevant that Blake's myth in *The Book of Urizen, The Four Zoas,* and elsewhere shows division into sexes as one of the first manifestations of the fallen condition.)

The serpent around the figure to the right is labelled 'Good'. Around the figure is written, 'Satan's wife, the Goddess Nature, is War and Misery, and Heroism a Miser' – military heroism, that is, is esteemed a virtue only in a system of values unredeemed by imagination: war, a cause of profit for the few, is a cause of poverty and suffering for the many.[8] The serpent around the figure to the left is labelled 'Evil'. Above the head and about the raised arm of this figure is written, 'Good and Evil are riches and poverty, a Tree of Misery propagating generation and death' – Blake returns, that is, to the attack begun in *The Marriage of Heaven and Hell* on the way good and evil are defined, here implying that values which masquerade nominally as moral qualities are in reality infected with materialism. But his attack on moral thinking is also more radical. Religion must not be identified, as it usually is, with moral ideas. That is the task of philosophy, and is likely to be a corrupt one because it will encourage self-righteousness. The aim of religion – in which it can be wholly identified with art – is a vision of the divine. 'The Last Judgement [will be] when all those are cast away who trouble religion with questions concerning good and evil . . . which hinder the vision of God'; 'moral virtues do not exist: they are allegories and dissimulations' ('A Vision of the Last Judgement'; Bentley, *Writings*, 1007, 1028). 'The moral virtues are continual accusers of sin and promote eternal wars and dominancy over others' (Marginalia to Berkeley's *Siris*; Bentley, *Writings*, 1504). This radical opposition between the gospel of Jesus and the ultimately Satanic moral virtues – conditions of being which can only be simulated because they are at odds with the energies that actually make life valuable – is analogous to the *Laocoön's* other oppositions: imaginative art is opposed to derivative art, empire and military power, and commercialism.

Both sets of inscriptions around the sons continue the criticism of the 'natural man' implied by the 'He repented . . .' inscription above Yahweh. Commentators do not agree on which figure represents which son. It would be paradoxical if the serpent labelled 'Evil' were not thought of as entwining Satan (left), and the name

---

[8] Cf. marginalium to Bacon: 'What do these knaves mean by virtue? Do they mean war and its horrors and its heroic villains?' (Bentley, *Writings*, 1429). 'The Goddess Nature' is the materialistic ethos that rules the fallen world: cf. 'Thus we see that the real God is the Goddess Nature, and that God creates nothing but what can be touched and weighed and taxed and measured: all else is heresy, and rebellion against Caesar, Virgil's only god' (annotations to Thornton; Bentley, *Writings*, 1518).

Lilith were not thought of as written next to Adam (right); but it is the issue of a twofold division – Good and Evil – not the particular identities, that is important. In *The Four Zoas*, *Milton* and *Jerusalem* Satan and Adam are paired: they represent complementary boundaries of the fallen condition which Blake in the poems calls the limits of 'opacity' and 'contraction' (*The Four Zoas*, 56.19–22; *Milton*, 11.20–1; *Jerusalem*, 35(31).1–2, 42.29–31). The aphorisms identify them in similar terms: they represent unenlightened intellect (epitomized by the accusation of sin: [26] and [30]) and purely corporeal existence (the 'natural man' without imagination: [2]).

The aphorisms expand the view of what the Loacoön myth embodies, implied by these identifications of the three figures. They proclaim the identity of art and religion; attack materialism and rationalism as destructive of art; oppose inspired Hebraic art to classical art vitiated by militarism and commercialism; expose the error of the accusation of sin as a cloak for violence which provokes violence; and set against this the necessity for unconditional forgiveness as the distinctive and central issue of the gospel of Jesus.

Like the Proverbs of Hell, the *Laocoön* aphorisms are cryptic or riddling statements which can often be understood in several ways; and (since the plate presents the aphorisms unsequenced and even in some cases without a clear division into units) even more than with the Proverbs of Hell connections between different individual items are for the reader to make. The aphorisms are printed here largely in the thematic arrangement in which they are given in the edition of David Erdman. They are numbered purely as a key to the annotations. Keynes (*Complete Writings* (1957/ 1966), 775–7) gives a different order and groups several sentences into units differently. Bentley (*Writings*, 664–6) gives another, again different, order and grouping.

Laocoön has been conventionally dated *c.* 1820, but the recent discovery that one of the only two extant copies is printed on paper watermarked 1826 makes it probable that it is Blake's last work in illuminated printing.

[*Laocoön*]

[1] What can be created can be destroyed.

[2] Adam is only the natural man and not the soul or imagination.

[3] The eternal body of man is the imagination, that is God himself, the divine body, Jesus: we are his members.

[4] It manifests itself in his works of art. (In eternity all is vision.)

[5] All that we see is vision from generated organs gone as soon as come, permanent in the imagination, considered as nothing by the natural man.

[6] Hebrew art is called sin by the Deist science.

[7] The whole business of man is the arts and all things common.

[8] Christianity is art and not money. Money is its curse.

[9] The Old and New Testaments are the great code of art.

---

[1] This is both threatening and consoling – threatening insofar as it applies to art (cf. [10]), consoling insofar as it applies to the limitations of the natural man's unimaginative consciousness, transcending which can restore a proper contact with the divine.

[3] *Jesus*] Given first in the form of the three Hebrew characters of the name 'Jeshua' or 'Joshua', meaning 'saviour', of which Jesus is the Greek form.

[6] *science*] 'Science' is always used negatively in the *Laocoön* (cf. aphorisms [10] and [11]). Eaves, Essick and Viscomi argue that Blake changed his views on science after completing *Jerusalem* (*William Blake: 'Milton, a Poem' and the Final Illuminated Works*, Tate/Princeton (1993), 242–3 and 276). But it may be that Blake intends here a special sense – 'Deist science', science which supposes that *all* phenomena have ultimately a material cause. Whereas for Blake, 'His opinion who does not see spiritual agency is not worth any man's reading' (*A Descriptive Catalogue*, V; Bentley, *Writings*, 852). Blake often uses 'science' positively in his late work (meaning both 'all kinds of knowledge' and in its modern sense): see, for example, *The Four Zoas*, 139.9–10: 'The war of swords departed now, / The dark religions are departed, and sweet science reigns'; or *Jerusalem*, plate 3: 'The primeval state of man was wisdom, art, and science'; or plate 77: 'expel from among you those who pretend to despise the labours of art and science, which alone are the labours of the gospel.' See also *Jerusalem*, 36(32).48, quoted in the note to aphorism [32] below. On the various meanings of 'science' in Blake's time, and how he exploits those, see Mark L. Greenberg, 'Blake's "Science"', *Studies in Eighteenth-Century Culture*, 12 (1983), 115–30.

[7] *all things common*] As in primitive Christianity: the phrase is used twice in Acts (2.44 and 4.32).

[9] *the . . . art*] Blake apparently adapts a phrase from Bishop Robert Lowth's translation of Isaiah (1779), in which Lowth refers to Aristotle's *Poetics* as 'the great code of criticism.'

[10] Jesus and his apostles and disciples were all artists. Their works were destroyed by the seven angels of the seven churches in Asia, Antichrist science.

[11] Science is the Tree of Death. Art the Tree of Life.

[12] God is Jesus.

[13] The gods of Priam are the cherubim of Moses and Solomon, the hosts of Heaven.

[14] The gods of Greece and Egypt were mathematical diagrams: see Plato's Works.

[15] There are states in which all visionary men are accounted mad. Such are Greece and Rome. Such is empire or tax: see Luke, ch. 2, v. 1.

[16] Art degraded, imagination denied, war governed the nations.

[17] Divine union deriding, and denying immediate communion with God, the spoilers say, 'Where are his works that he did in the wilderness? Lo,

---

[10] *seven angels . . . churches in Asia*] These angels and their churches are addressed in sequence (and most are in part reproved) in Revelation, chapters 2 and 3. In *Milton* (39.55) Blake presents them as types of the corrupt church in which Satan is worshipped as the God of this world. For the identification of religion and art cf. aphorisms [20], [22], and [23].

[13] *gods of Priam*] The gods of Homer and his age, Blake asserts, are degenerate realizations of Hebraic visions more closely in touch with the reality of the divine. Despite his culture's supposed Christianity, Blake saw it as in fact dominated by ethics derived from Greece. See, for example, *Milton*, plate 12, where Milton is presented as realizing that, despite *Paradise Lost's* apparent rejection of the ethos of classical epic (Book 9, proem), his supposedly Christian poem encourages its readers to 'follow after the detestable gods of Priam.'

[15] *Luke, ch. 2, v. 1*] 'And it came to pass in those days, that there went out a decree from Caesar Augustus, that all the world should be taxed.' Even before his birth Christ suffered the archetypal fate of the visionary at the hands of the commercial tyranny of empire.

[16] This sentence, inscribed centrally at the bottom of the plate, gives Blake's view of the fundamental situation from which the classical Laocoön sculpture derives, the context in which a proper understanding of its symbolism was corrupted.

[17] *the wilderness*] In which the Israelites wandered for forty years after the Exodus from Egypt. God's marvels include leading them by means of a pillar of cloud by day and a pillar of fire by night, the miraculous feeding with quails and manna, and the miraculous provision of water from a rock (Exodus, 13 and 16; Numbers, 20). Egypt and Babylon are Old Testament locations symbolizing tyranny and the captivity and enslavement of the Israelites, as recorded in the early chapters of Exodus, and in 2 Kings 25, 2 Chronicles 36, and Jeremiah 39 and 52. On Egypt as a symbolic location cf. the following aphorism. On the Goddess Nature see headnote, footnote 8. *Aeneid*, 6.848–53 (part of a speech by the shade of Aeneas's father,

what are these? Whence came they?' These are not the works of Egypt nor Babylon, whose gods are the powers of this world, Goddess Nature, who first spoil and then destroy imaginative art, for their glory is war and dominion. Empire against art. See Virgil's *Aeneid*, Lib. VI. v. 848.

[18] Spiritual war, Israel delivered from Egypt, is art delivered from nature and imitation.

[19] What we call antique gems are the gems of Aaron's breastplate.

[20] Prayer is the study of art. Praise is the practice of art. Fasting etc. all relate to art. The outward ceremony is Antichrist.

[21] Without unceasing practice nothing can be done. Practice is art. If you leave off you are lost.

[22] A poet, a painter, a musician, an architect: the man or woman who is not one of these is not a Christian.

Anchises), contrasts Rome and other nations, admitting that Rome may be inferior in various valuable activities, but predicting that Rome will make a distinct contribution in the moral sphere of good government. Blake also refers to this passage in *On Homer's Poetry* [and] *On Virgil* (c. 1822), and offers a decidedly free paraphrase, consistent with his reference to the passage in *Laocoön*: 'Let others study art: Rome has somewhat better to do, namely war and dominion.'   *Empire against art*] Cf. Blake's annotations of Bacon: 'Bacon calls intellectual arts unmanly. Poetry, painting, music are in his opinion useless, and so they are for kings and wars, and shall in the end annihilate them.' Also, 'it is not arts that follow and attend upon empire, but empire that attends upon and follows the arts' ('Public Address'; Bentley, *Writings*, 1440, 1043).

[18] On Egypt cf. [17]. This general comment on idealist art applies specifically to Blake's attempt to deliver the myth of Laocoön from reference to the legend of Troy (cf. the inscriptions on the central figure and aphorism [13]).

[19] The breastplate and gems of Aaron's ceremonial priestly garment are described in Exodus, 28.15–29. The breastplate's twelve jewels symbolize the tribes of Israel and are engraved with their names. As with *Laocoön* itself, Blake finds in the art of gem engraving Hebraic precedent for classical work. Cf. the marginalium to Reynolds: 'The Greek gems are in the same style as the Greek statues' (Bentley, *Writings*, 1477). Blake engraved a plate on classical gem engraving (dated 1819) for Abraham Rees's *Cyclopaedia* (for which he also executed an engraving of the classical Laocoön sculpture: see headnote). The accompanying article notes that gem engraving was carried on in ancient Israel and specifically cites Aaron's breastplate.

[20] Each of these sentences is engraved separately on the original plate. Despite their obvious relationship each might be printed as a separate aphorism. Two of these statements are almost exactly reduplicated in proofs of the first and last of Blake's Job illustrations (1826) now in the Beinecke Library, Yale University: 'Prayer to God is the study of imaginative art' (plate 1); 'Praise to God is the exercise of imaginative art' (plate 21).

[21] Cf. the marginalium to Reynolds: 'To learn the language of art copy for ever is my rule' (Bentley, *Writings*, 1431).

[23] You must leave fathers and mothers and houses and lands if they stand in the way of art.

[24] The unproductive man is not a Christian, much less the destroyer.

[25] The true Christian charity not dependent on money (the life's blood of poor families), that is on Caesar, or Empire, or Natural Religion.

[26] Money, which is the great Satan, or Reason, the root of good and evil in the accusation of sin.

[27] For every pleasure money <u>is useless</u>.

[28] Where any view of money exists art cannot be carried on, but war only (read Matthew, ch. X, 9 and 10 v.), by pretences to the two impossibilities, chastity and abstinence, gods of the heathen.

---

[23] Based on Luke, 14.26: 'If any man come to me, and hate not his father, and mother, and wife, and children, and brethren, and sisters, yea, and his own life also, he cannot be my disciple.'

[26] Satan is the archetypal accuser of sin, as in Revelation, 12.10. He is also, in Blake's view, 'the God of this world' (*The Gates of Paradise*, 'To the Accuser'). Cf. *Jerusalem*, 40.35, where 'moral virtue' is not a disinterested desire for justice but the cover for a corrupt desire for revenge, and fosters a society in which war is the occasional result of a perpetual state of conflict. Cf. *Jerusalem*, 47.13–15: 'the punisher / Mingles with his victim's spectre, enslavèd and tormented / To him whom he has murdered, bound in vengeance and enmity.' The accusation of sin is a central issue of the significance Blake sees in the whole Laocoön group. The complement to this analysis of religious corruption is the position in Blake's late work of forgiveness freely given as central to Christianity. Cf. aphorism [31]. Erdman prints this and the following aphorism in reverse order. However, aphorism [26] (as numbered here) is written immediately below [25] on the engraved plate, and may be syntactically continuous with it. Aphorism [27] is inscribed on the far right of the plate: it is grouped with [25] and [26] by Erdman for thematic reasons, but his placing of it between them interrupts what Blake may have intended as a single unit, as it is printed by Keynes (*Complete Writings* (1957/1966), 776) and by Bentley (*Writings*, 666).

[27] is useless] Underlined on the original plate.

[28] Matthew, 10.9–10 reads, 'Provide neither gold, nor silver, nor brass in your purses, Nor scrip for your journey, neither two coats, neither shoes, nor yet staves: for the workman is worthy of his meat.' Blake's application of this here assumes the identity of art and religion asserted in other aphorisms: see, for example, [10] and [23]. Blake means chastity literally, as in *Jerusalem*, 36.44–6, where the Eternals mock that 'a man dare hardly to embrace / His own wife for the terrors of chastity that they call / By the name of morality.' Sexual restraint is a tool of oppression. (The plate 36 speech of Eternals concludes with the lines quoted in illustration of aphorism [32].) Blake depicts repressed sexual desire as issuing in violence, and so as a cause of war, in *Jerusalem* (plates 63 to 69). The use of the word 'chastity' in *Jerusalem* (for example, at 94.23) also suggests a wider meaning similar to the biblical metaphor of 'uncircumcision': keeping from all forms of emotional openness and engagement. Blake twice uses 'chastity' in association with 'uncircumcised'/'uncircumcision' (*Jerusalem*, 49.64, 60.48). Since chastity is a virtue of both Catholic and Protestant Christianity 'the heathen' here means primarily non-Blakean Christians.

[29] Is not every vice possible to man described in the Bible openly?

[30] All is not sin that Satan calls so, all the loves and graces of eternity.

[31] If morality was Christianity Socrates was the Saviour.

[32] Art can never exist without naked beauty displayed.

[33] No secrecy in art.

---

[29] That is, the Bible is not a holy book in the sense in which holiness is usually thought of – not a book which presents only obviously elevating examples of moral 'purity'.

[30] Cf. [6], and the concluding comment on Lavater's *Aphorisms*: 'The origin of this mistake [the confusion of virtue and vice] in Lavater and his contemporaries is they suppose that woman's love is sin. In consequence all the loves and graces with them are sin.' Cf. also *Jerusalem*, plate 77: 'That which is sin in the sight of cruel man is not so in the sight of our kind God.'

[31] The present text largely follows the ordering of the aphorisms in Erdman's edition, but this sentence, inscribed below the plinth of the statue (though in a small, light script), could be thought of as central to the significance of the whole group. Blake repeated it in his annotations of Robert Thornton's 'Tory translation' of the Lord's prayer (1827) (Bentley, *Writings*, 1514), and in substance in 'The Everlasting Gospel': 'If moral virtue was Christianity / Christ's pretensions were all vanity' (Part c). Cf. the marginalium to Watson: 'The gospel is forgiveness of sin and has no moral precepts: these belong to Plato and Seneca and Nero' (Bentley, *Writings*, 1422). Blake was not antagonistic to Socrates. He suggests a parallel between Socrates and himself in text and design of *Jerusalem* plate 93: like Blake, whose one public exhibition was attacked by the journal run by the three Hunt brothers (*The Examiner*) who signed their work with a pointing hand, Socrates is there attacked by three false witnesses who point accusingly. Cf. Blake's 'Public Address' (Notebook, page 86; Bentley, *Writings*, 1045), where the same parallels are implied, and the late conversation about Socrates recorded by the diarist Henry Crabb Robinson: ' "I was Socrates". And then as if correcting himself: "a sort of brother".' (Bentley, *Blake Records* (1969), 310).

[32] Cf. *Jerusalem*, 36(32).48: 'Art and Science cannot exist but by naked beauty displayed.'

BIBLIOGRAPHY

TEXTS AND FACSIMILES

Collected and Selected Editions

Bentley, G. E., Jr. (ed.), *William Blake's Writings*, 2 vols. (Oxford, 1978).

Bindman, David (general editor), *The Illuminated Books of William Blake*, 6 vols. (London and Princeton, NJ, 1991–95) (vol. 1, *Jerusalem*, ed. Morton D. Paley, 1991; vol. 2, *Songs of Innocence and of Experience*, ed. Andrew Lincoln, 1991; vol. 3, *The Early Illuminated Books*, ed. Morris Eaves, Robert N. Essick and Joseph Viscomi, 1993; vol. 4, *The Continental Prophecies*, ed. D. W. Dörrbecker, 1995; vol. 5, *'Milton a Poem' and the Final Illuminated Works*, ed. Robert N. Essick and Joseph Viscomi, 1993; vol. 6, *The Urizen Books*, ed. David Worrall, 1995).

Bindman, David (ed.), *William Blake: The Complete Illuminated Books* (London, 2000).

Erdman, David V. (ed.), *The Complete Poetry and Prose of William Blake*, with a commentary by Harold Bloom (New York, 1965; rev. edn., 1988).

Erdman, David V. (ed.), *The Illuminated Blake* (London, 1975).

Grant, John, and Mary Lynn Johnson, *Blake's Poetry and Designs* (New York, 1979; rev. edn., 2008).

Keynes, Geoffrey (ed.), *The Complete Writings of William Blake* (London, 1957; rev. edn., 1966).

Mason, Michael (ed.), *William Blake*. The Oxford Authors (Oxford, 1988).

Ostriker, Alicia, *William Blake. The Complete Poems* (Harmondsworth, 1977).

Sloss, D. J., and J. P. R. Wallis (eds.), *The Prophetic Writings of William Blake*, 2 vols. (Oxford, 1926).

Stevenson, W. H. (ed.), *Blake. The Complete Poems*, text by D. V. Erdman (London, 1971; rev. edn., 1989; 3rd rev. edn., 2007).

Individual Works

Bentley, G. E., Jr. (ed.), *'Vala or The Four Zoas': A Facsimile of the Manuscript, a Transcript of the Poem, and a Study of its Growth and Significance* (Oxford, 1963).

Bogen, Nancy (ed.), *The Book of Thel: A Facsimile and a Critical Text* (Providence, RI, 1971).

Easson, K. P. and R. (eds.), *The Book of Urizen* (London, 1979).

Easson, K. P. and R. (eds.), *Milton* (London, 1979).

Emery, Clark, *The Book of Urizen* (Coral Gables, 1966).

Erdman, David (ed.), with the assistance of Donald K. Moore, *The Notebook of William Blake* (Oxford, 1973; rev. edn., 1977).

Erdman, David, and Magno, Cettina Tramontano (eds.), *'The Four Zoas' by William Blake: A Photographic Facsimile of the Manuscript with Commentary on the Illuminations* (Lewisburg, PA, 1987).

Keynes, Geoffrey (ed.), *The Letters of William Blake, with Related Documents* (London, 1956; 3rd edn., Oxford, 1980).

Keynes, Geoffrey (ed.), *Songs of Innocence and of Experience* (London, 1967).

Keynes, Geoffrey (ed.), *The Marriage of Heaven and Hell* (London, 1975).

Margoliouth, H. M. (ed.), *William Blake's 'Vala'* (Oxford, 1956).

Phillips, Michael (ed.), *The Marriage of Heaven and Hell* (Oxford, 2007).

Ryskamp, Charles (ed.), *The Pickering Manuscript* (New York, 1972).

Beginning with *Jerusalem* (1951), hand-coloured facsimiles of all Blake's works in illuminated printing (and his designs for the poems of Gray and for the Book of Job), made using stencils cut from originals, were published for the Blake Trust by the Trianon Press, Paris, almost all under the editorship of Sir Geoffrey Keynes.

The William Blake Archive, ed. Morris Eaves, Robert N. Essick and Joseph Viscomi, can be found at: http://www.blakearchive.org/blake
The Archive contains at least one copy of each of the illuminated books reproduced in colour, full bibliographical details and descriptions of each image, and tools for text- and image-searching. It also contains the Erdman edition (text and textual notes only) of *The Complete Poetry and Prose of William Blake*, and extensive other materials including drawings, paintings, engravings and bibliographical listings.

The Blake Digital Text Project, ed. Nelson Hilton, can be found at:
www.english.uga.edu/wblake/home1.html
This contains a graphical hypertext of *Songs of Innocence and of Experience*, the Erdman edition (text only) of *The Complete Poetry and Prose of William Blake*, and an on-line Blake concordance.

Graphic Works

Bindman, David, assisted by Deirdre Toomey, *The Complete Graphic Works of William Blake* (London, 1978).

Butlin, Martin, *The Paintings and Drawings of William Blake*, 2 vols. (New Haven, CT, 1981).

Essick, Robert N., *The Separate Plates of William Blake: A Catalogue* (Princeton, NJ, 1983).

Essick, Robert N., *William Blake's Commercial Book Illustrations: A Catalogue and Study of the Plates Engraved by Blake after Designs by Other Artists* (Oxford, 1991).

LITERARY SCHOLARSHIP AND CRITICISM

Biography and Bibliography

Ackroyd, Peter, *Blake* (London, 1995).

Bentley, G. E., Jr., *Blake Records* (Oxford, 1969; 2nd edn., New Haven, 2004).

Bentley, G. E., Jr., *Blake Books* (Oxford, 1977).

Bentley, G. E., Jr., *Blake Records Supplement* (Oxford, 1988).

Bentley, G. E., Jr., *Blake Books Supplement* (Oxford, 1995).

Bentley, G. E., Jr., *The Stranger from Paradise: A Biography of William Blake* (New Haven, 2001).

Erdman, David, et al., *A Concordance to the Writings of William Blake*, 2 vols. (Ithaca, NY, 1967).

Essick, Robert N., 'William Blake', *The Oxford Dictionary of National Biography* (Oxford, 2004).

Fuller, David, 'William Blake', *Literature of the Romantic Period: A Bibliographical Guide*, ed. Michael O'Neill (Oxford, 1998), 27–44.

Gilchrist, Alexander, *Life of William Blake, 'Pictor Ignotus'*, 2 vols. (London, 1863; rev. edn., 1880).

Johnson, Mary Lynn, 'William Blake', *The English Romantic Poets: A Review of Research and Criticism*, 4th edn., ed. Frank Jordan (New York, 1985), 113–253.

Keynes, Geoffrey, *Blake Studies: Essays on his Life and Work* (1949; 2nd edn., Oxford, 1971).

Wilson, Mona, *The Life of William Blake* (London, 1927; rev. edn., ed. Geoffrey Keynes, Oxford, 1971).

Literary Criticism

Adams, Hazard, *William Blake: A Reading of the Shorter Poems* (Seattle, WA, 1963).

Adlard, John, *The Sports of Cruelty: Fairies, Folk-Songs, Charms and Other Country Matters in the Work of William Blake* (London, 1972).

Ault, Donald, *Visionary Physics: Blake's Response to Newton* (Chicago, IL, 1974).

Beer, John, *Blake's Humanism* (Manchester, 1968).

Beer, John, *Blake's Visionary Universe* (Manchester, 1969).

Beer, John, *William Blake, 1757–1827*. Writers and Their Work (Windsor, 1982).

Beer, John, *William Blake: A Literary Life* (Basingstoke, 2005).

Behrendt, Stephen, *Reading William Blake* (Basingstoke, 1992).

Bellin, Harvey F., and Darrell Ruhl, *Blake and Swedenborg: Opposition is True Friendship* (New York, 1985).

Bentley, G. E., Jr. (ed.), *William Blake: The Critical Heritage* (London, 1975).

Bloom, Harold, *Blake's Apocalypse: A Study in Poetic Argument* (London, 1963).

Bronowski, Jacob, *A Man without a Mask (William Blake. 1757–1827)* (London, 1944; revised as *William Blake and the Age of Revolution*, New York, 1965).

Clark, Steve, and David Worrall (eds.), *Historicizing Blake* (Basingstoke, 1994).

Clark, Steve, and David Worrall (eds.), *Blake in the Nineties* (Basingstoke, 1999).

Cox, Stephen, *Love and Logic: The Evolution of Blake's Thought* (Ann Arbor, MI, 1992).

Curran, Stuart, and Joseph A. Wittreich, Jr. (eds.), *Blake's Sublime Allegory: Essays on 'The Four Zoas', 'Milton' and 'Jerusalem'* (Madison, WI, 1973).

Damon, S. Foster, *William Blake: His Philosophy and Symbols* (London, 1924).

Damon, S. Foster, *A Blake Dictionary: The Ideas and Symbols of William Blake* (1965; rev. edn., ed. Morris Eaves, Providence, RI, 1988).

Damrosch, Leopold, Jr., *Symbol and Truth in Blake's Myth* (Princeton, NJ, 1980).

De Luca, Vincent Arthur, *Words of Eternity: Blake and the Poetics of the Sublime* (Princeton, NJ, 1991).

Eaves Morris (ed.), *The Cambridge Companion to William Blake* (Cambridge, 2003).

Eliot, T. S., 'William Blake' (1920), *Selected Essays* (London, 1932; 3rd rev. edn., 1951).

Erdman, David V., 'Blake: The Historical Approach', in Alan S. Downer (ed.), *English Institute Essays: 1950* (New York, 1951).

Erdman, David V., *Blake: Prophet Against Empire: A Poet's Interpretation of the History of His Own Time* (Princeton, NJ, 1954; 3rd rev. edn., 1977).

Essick, Robert N. (ed.), *The Visionary Hand: Essays for the Study of William Blake's Art and Aesthetics* (Los Angeles, CA, 1973).

Essick, Robert N., *William Blake and the Language of Adam* (Oxford, 1989).

Essick, Robert N., and Donald Pearce, *Blake in his Time* (Bloomington, IN, 1978).

Ferber, Michael, *The Social Vision of William Blake* (Princeton, NJ, 1985).

Ferber, Michael, *The Poetry of William Blake* (Harmondsworth, 1991).

Frye, Northrop, *Fearful Symmetry: A Study of William Blake* (Princeton, NJ, 1947).

Frye, Northrop, 'Blake's Treatment of the Archetype', *English Institute Essays: 1950*, ed. Alan S. Downer (New York, 1951).

Frye, Northrop, 'Notes for a Commentary on *Milton*', in Vivian de Sola Pinto (ed.), *The Divine Vision: Studies in the Poetry and Art of William Blake* (London, 1957).

Frye, Northrop, *Blake: A Collection of Critical Essays* (Engelwood Cliffs, NJ, 1966).

Frye, Northrop, *Northrop Frye on Milton and Blake (The Collected Works of Northrop Frye*, vol. 16), ed. Angela Esterhammer (Toronto, 2005).

Fuller, David, '*Milton* and the Development of Blake's Thought', in J. R. Watson (ed.), *An Infinite Complexity* (Edinburgh, 1983).

Fuller, David, *Blake's Heroic Argument* (London, 1988).

Gardner, Stanley, *Blake's 'Innocence' and 'Experience' Retraced* (London, 1986).

Gardner, Stanley, *The Tyger, the Lamb, and the Terrible Desart: 'Songs of Innocence and of Experience' in its Times and Circumstance* (London, 1998).

Gleckner, Robert F., *The Piper and the Bard: A Study of William Blake* (Detroit, MI, 1959).

Gleckner, Robert F. and Mark L. Greenberg, *Approaches to Teaching Blake's 'Songs of Innocence and of Experience'* (New York, 1989).

Glen, Heather, *Vision and Disenchantment: Blake's 'Songs' and Wordsworth's 'Lyrical Ballads'* (Cambridge, 1983).

Gourlay, Alexander S., *Prophetic Character: Essays on William Blake in Honour of John E. Grant* (West Cornwall, Conn., 2002).

Greenberg, Mark L., *Speak Silence: Rhetoric and Culture in Blake's 'Poetical Sketches'* (Detroit, MI, 1996).

Hagstrum, Jean H., *William Blake, Poet and Painter: An Introduction to the Illuminated Verse* (Chicago, IL, 1964).

Harding, D. W., 'Experience and Symbol in Blake', *Experience into Words* (London, 1963).

Harper, George Mills, *The Neoplatonism of William Blake* (Chapel Hill, NC, 1961).

Hilton, Nelson, *Literal Imagination: Blake's Vision of Words* (Berkeley, CA, 1983).

Hilton, Nelson, (ed.), *Essential Articles for the Study of William Blake, 1970–84* (Hamden, CT, 1986).

Hilton, Nelson, and Thomas A. Vogler (eds.), *Unnam'd Forms: Blake and Textuality* (Berkeley, CA 1986).

Hirsch, E. D., Jr., *Innocence and Experience: An Introduction to Blake* (Chicago, IL, 1964; 2nd edn., 1975).

Hirst, Désirée, *Hidden Riches: Traditional Symbolism from the Renaissance to Blake* (London, 1964).

Hobson, Christopher Z., *Blake and Homosexuality* (London, 2000).

Holloway, John, *Blake: The Lyric Poetry* (London, 1968).

Larrissy, Edward, *William Blake*. Rereading Literature (Oxford, 1985).

Larrissy, Edward, *Blake and Modern Literature* (Houndmills, 2006).

Leader, Zachary, *Reading Blake's 'Songs'* (London, 1981).

Lincoln, Andrew, *Spiritual History: A Reading of William Blake's 'Vala' or 'The Four Zoas'* (Oxford, 1995).

Lucas, John, *William Blake*. Longman Critical Readers (London, 1998).

McGann, Jerome J., *Towards a Literature of Knowledge* (Oxford, 1989).

Makdisi, Saree, *William Blake and the Impossible History of the 1790s* (Chicago, 2003).

Mee, Jon, *Dangerous Enthusiasm: William Blake and the Culture of Radicalism in the 1790s* (Oxford, 1992).

Mellor, Anne Kostelanetz, *Blake's Human Form Divine* (Berkeley, CA, 1974).

Michael, Jennifer Davis, *Blake and the City* (Lewisburg, 2006).

Miller, Dan, Mark Bracher, and Donald Ault (eds.), *Critical Paths: Blake and the Argument of Method* (Durham, NC, 1987).

Mitchell, W. J. T., *Blake's Composite Art: A Study of the Illuminated Poetry* (Princeton, NJ, 1978).

Morton, A. L., *The Everlasting Gospel: A Study in the Sources of William Blake* (London, 1958).

Nemerov, Howard, 'Two Ways of the Imagination', *Carleton Miscellany*, 5 (1964), 18–41; reprinted in Nemerov's *Reflections on Poetry and Poetics* (New Brunswick, NJ, 1972).

Nurmi, Martin K., *William Blake* (London, 1975).

Ostriker, Alicia, *Vision and Verse in William Blake* (Madison, WI, 1965).

Paley, Morton D., *Energy and the Imagination: A Study of the Development of Blake's Thought* (Oxford, 1970).

Paley, Morton D., *The Continuing City: William Blake's 'Jerusalem'* (Oxford, 1983).

Paley, Morton D., *The Traveller in the Evening: The Last Works of William Blake* (Oxford, 2003).

Paley, Morton D., and Morris Eaves (eds.), *Blake: An Illustrated Quarterly* [formerly *Blake Newsletter*, 1967–77] (Rochester, NY).

Pierce, John B., *The Wond'rous Art: William Blake and Writing* (Madison, NJ, 2003).

Percival, Milton O., *Blake's Circle of Destiny* (New York, 1938).

Phillips, Michael (ed.), *Interpreting Blake* (Cambridge, 1978).

Phillips, Michael (ed.), *William Blake: The Creation of the 'Songs': from Manuscript to Illuminated Printing* (London, 2000).

Pinto, Vivian de Sola (ed.), *The Divine Vision: Studies in the Poetry and Art of William Blake* (London, 1957).

Punter, David, *William Blake*. New Casebooks (Basingstoke, 1996).

Raine, Kathleen, *Blake and Tradition*, 2 vols. (Princeton, NJ, 1968).

Raine, Kathleen, *Blake and the New Age* (London, 1979).

Raine, Kathleen, *Golgonooza, City of Imagination: Last Studies in William Blake* (Ipswich, 1991).

Rexroth, Kenneth, 'Classics Revisited LXIII: The Works of Blake' (1968), *The Elastic Retort: Essays in Literature and Ideas* (New York, 1973).

Roberts, Jonathan, *William Blake's Poetry: A Reader's Guide* (London, 2007).

Rosenfeld, Alvin, (ed.), *William Blake: Essays for S. Foster Damon* (Providence, RI, 1969).

Schorer, Mark, *William Blake: The Politics of Vision* (New York, 1946).

Spector, Sheila A., *'Glorious Incomprehensible': The Development of Blake's Kabbalistic Language* (Lewisburg, 2001).

Spector, Sheila A., *'Wonders Divine': The Development of Blake's Kabbalistic Myth* (Lewisburg, 2001).

Summerfield, Henry, *A Guide to the Books of William Blake: for Innocent and Experienced Readers* (Gerrards Cross, 1998).

Swinburne, A. C., *William Blake: A Critical Essay* (London, 1868).

Tannenbaum, Leslie, *Biblical Tradition in Blake's Early Prophecies: The Great Code of Art* (Princeton, NJ, 1982).

Thompson, E. P., *Witness Against the Beast: William Blake and the Moral Law* (Cambridge, 1993).

Vine, Steven, *Blake's Poetry: Spectral Visions* (Basingstoke, 1993).

Viscomi, Joseph, *Blake and the Idea of the Book* (Princeton, NJ, 1993).

Williams, Nicholas M., *Ideology and Utopia in the Poetry of William Blake*. Cambridge Studies in Romanticism (Cambridge, 1998).

Wright, Julia M., *Blake, Nationalism and the Politics of Alienation* (Athens, OH, 2003).

Yeats, W. B., 'William Blake and the Imagination', and 'William Blake and his Illustrations to the *Divine Comedy*' (1897), collected in *Ideas of Good and Evil* (London, 1903); reprinted in *Essays and Introductions* (London, 1961).

ART SCHOLARSHIP AND CRITICISM

Bindman, David, *Blake as an Artist* (Oxford, 1977).

Bindman, David (ed.), *William Blake: 'The Divine Comedy'* (Paris, 2000).

Blunt, Anthony, *The Art of William Blake* (London, 1959).

Butlin, Martin, *William Blake, 1757–1827* (Tate Gallery Collections: Volume Five; London, 1990).

Chayes, Irene H., 'Blake's Way with Art Sources: Michelangelo's "The Last Judgement"', *Colby Library Quarterly*, 20 (1984), 60–89.

Chayes, Irene H., 'Blake's Way with Art Sources II: Some Versions of the Antique', *Colby Library Quarterly*, 26 (1990), 28–58.

Eaves, Morris, *William Blake's Theory of Art* (Princeton, NJ, 1982).

Essick, Robert N., *William Blake: Printmaker* (Princeton, NJ, 1980).

Fuller, David, 'Blake and Dante', *Art History*, 11 (1988), 349–73.

Heppner, Christopher, *Reading Blake's Designs* (Cambridge, 1995).

Paley, Morton D., *William Blake* (Oxford, 1978).

Raine, Kathleen, *William Blake* (London, 1970).

Vaughan, William, *William Blake*, British Artists Series (London, 1999).

Warner, Janet, *Blake and the Language of Art* (Kingston, Ont., 1984).

Critical opinions which are discussed in the introductions, and information which appears in the annotation, have also been derived from the following sources.

Auden, W. H., 'A Mental Prince', *The Observer*, 17 November, 1957.

Baine, Rodney M., 'Thel's Northern Gate', *Philological Quarterly*, 51 (1972), 957–61.

Baine, Rodney M., 'Bromion's "Jealous Dolphins"', *BIQ*, 14 (1980–81), 206–7.

Baine, Rodney M., and Mary R. Baine, '"Then Mars thou wast our center"', *English Language Notes*, 13 (1975–76), 14–18.

Bateson, F. W., *Selected Poems of William Blake* (London, 1957; 2nd edn., 1961).

Butlin, Martin, 'A New Color Print from the Small Book of Designs', *BIQ*, 26 (1992–93), 19–21.

Cooper, Andrew M., 'Irony as Self-Concealment in *The Marriage of Heaven and Hell*', *A/B: Auto/Biography Studies*, 2 (1986–87), 33–44.

Cooper, Andrew M., 'Blake and Madness: The World Turned Inside Out', *ELH*, 57 (1990), 585–642.

Curran, Stuart, 'Blake and the Gnostic Hyle: A Double Negative', *Blake Studies*, 4 (1972), 117–33 (reprinted in Hilton, 1986).

De Luca, Vincent Arthur, 'Proper Names in the Structural Design of Blake's Myth-Making', *Blake Studies*, 8 (1978), 5–22 (reprinted in Hilton, 1986).

Dorfman, Deborah, '"King of Beauty" and "Golden World" in Blake's *America*', *ELH*, 46 (1979), 122–5.

Doxey, William S., 'William Blake. James Basire, and the *Philosophical Transactions*', *Bulletin of the New York Public Library*, 72 (1968), 252–60.

Eaves, Morris, 'On Blakes We Want and Blakes We Don't', *Huntington Library Quarterly*, 58 (1996), 413–39.

Ellis, Helen B., 'Added and Omitted Plates in *The Book of Urizen*', *Colby Library Quarterly*, 23 (1987), 99–107.

Enscoe, Gerald E., 'The Content of Vision: Blake's "Mental Traveller"', *Papers in Language and Literature*, 4 (1968), 400–13.

Erdman, David V., 'The Binding (et cetera) of *Vala*', *The Library*, 5th series, 19 (1964), 112–29.

Erdman, David V., '"Terrible Blake in his Pride": An Essay on *The Everlasting Gospel*', in *From Sensibility to Romanticism: Essays Presented to Frederick A. Pottle*, ed. Frederick W. Hilles and Harold Bloom (New York, 1965).

Essick, Robert N., '*The Four Zoas*: Intention and Production', *BIQ*, 18 (1984–85), 213–20.

Essick, Robert N., 'Variation, Accident and Intention in Blake's *Book of Urizen*', *Studies in Bibliography*, 39 (1986), 230–5.

Essick, Robert N., 'Blake's "The Death of Hector"', *Studies in Romanticism*, 27 (1988), 97–108.

Essick, Robert N., 'William Blake, Thomas Paine, and Biblical Revolution', *Studies in Romanticism*, 30 (1991), 189–212.

Ferber, Michael, '"London" and its Politics', *ELH*, 48 (1981), 310–38.

Ferber, Michael, 'Blake's *Thel* and the Bride of Christ', *Blake Studies*, 9 (1981), 45–56.

Ferber, Michael, 'Mars and the Planets Three in *America*', *BIQ*, 15 (1981–82), 136–7.

Fisher, Peter, 'Blake's Attacks on the Classical Tradition', *Philological Quarterly*, 40 (1961), 1–18.

Fox, Susan, 'The Female as Metaphor in William Blake's Poetry', *Critical Inquiry*, 3 (1977), 507–19 (reprinted in Hilton, 1986).

Gallagher, Philip J., 'The World Made Flesh: Blake's "A Poison Tree" and the Book of Genesis', *Studies in Romanticism*, 16 (1977).

Gleckner, Robert F., 'Blake's Swans', *BIQ*, 15 (1981–82), 164–9.

Greenberg, Mark L., 'Blake's "Science"'; *Studies in Eighteenth-Century Culture*, 12 (1983), 115–30.

Heffernan, James A. W., 'Blake's Oothoon: The Dilemmas of Marginality', *Studies in Romanticism*, 30 (1991), 3–18.

Helms, Randel, 'Proverbs of Heaven and Proverbs of Hell', *Paunch*, 38 (1974), 51–7.

Helms, Randel, 'The Genesis of *The Everlasting Gospel*,' *Blake Studies*, 9 (1981), 122–60.

Hilton, Nelson, 'Blake and the Perception of Science', *Annals of Scholarship*, 4 (1988), 54–68.

Hollander, John, 'Blake and the Metrical Contract', in *From Sensibility to Romanticism: Essays Presented to Frederick A. Pottle*, ed. Frederick W. Hilles and Harold Bloom (New York, 1965).

Johnson, Mary Lynn, 'Beulah, "Mne Seraphim", and Blake's *Thel*', *Journal of English and Germanic Philology*, 69 (1970), 258–77.

Kreiter, Carmen S., 'Evolution and William Blake', *Studies in Romanticism*, 4 (1965), 110–18.

Kumbier, William, 'Blake's Epic Meter', *Studies in Romanticism*, 17 (1978), 163–92.

Levinson, Marjorie, '*The Book of Thel* by William Blake: A Critical Reading', *ELH*, 47 (1980), 287–303.

Linkin, Harriet Kramer, 'Revisioning Blake's Oothoon', *BIQ*, 23 (1989–90), 184–94.

Mann, Paul, 'The Final State of *The Four Zoas*', *BIQ*, 18 (1984–85), 204–12.

Mellor, Anne K., 'Blake's Portrayal of Women', *BIQ*, 16 (1982–83), 148–55.

Mellor, Anne K., 'Sex, Violence and Slavery: Blake and Wollstonecraft', *Huntington Library Quarterly*, 58 (1996), 345–71.

Metcalf, Francis Wood, 'Reason and "Urizen": The Pronunciation of Blakean Names', *Blake Newsletter*, 6 (1972–73), 17–18.

Middleton, Peter, 'The Revolutionary Poetics of William Blake: Part I: The Critical Tradition', in *1789: Reading Writing Revolution*, ed. Francis Barker et al. (Colchester, 1982).

Middleton, Peter, 'The Revolutionary Poetics of William Blake: Part II: Silence, Syntax, and Spectres', *Oxford Literary Review*, 6 (1983), 35–51.

Mitchell, W. J. T., 'Visible Language: Blake's Wond'rous Art of Writing', in *Romanticism and Contemporary Criticism*, ed. Morris Eaves and Michael Fischer (Ithaca, NY, 1986), 46–86 (reprinted in Punter, 1996).

Murray, E. B., review of *William Blake's Writings*, ed. G. E. Bentley, Jr., *BIQ*, 14 (1980–81), 148–61.

Murray, E. B., 'Thel, *Thelyphthora*, and the Daughters of Albion', *Studies in Romanticism*, 20 (1981), 275–97.

Ostriker, Alicia, 'Desire Gratified and Ungratified: William Blake and Sexuality', *BIQ*, 16 (1982–83), 156–65 (reprinted in Hilton, 1986).

Otter, A. G. den, 'The Question of *The Book of Thel*', *Studies in Romanticism*, 30 (1991), 633–55.

Paley, Morton D., '"A New Heaven is Begun": William Blake and Swedenborgianism', *BIQ*, 13 (1979–80), 64–90 (reprinted in Bellin and Ruhl, 1985).

Pearce, Donald R., 'Natural Religion and the Plight of Thel', *Blake Studies*, 8 (1978), 23–35.

Peterfreund, Stuart, 'Blake, Priestley, and the "Gnostic Moment"', *Literature and Science: Theory and Practice* (Boston, MA, 1990).

Reiman, Donald H., and Christina Suttleworth Kraus, 'The Derivation and Meaning of "Ololon"', *BIQ*, 16 (1982), 82–5.

Reisner, Thomas A., and Mary Ellen Reisner, 'Blake's "Auguries of Innocence"', *The Explicator*, 35.3 (1977), 32–3.

Santa Cruz Blake Study Group, review of Erdman and Bloom, *The Complete Poetry and Prose of William Blake* (1982 edn.), *BIQ*, 18 (1984–85), 4–31 (partially reprinted in Hilton, 1986).

Spector, Sheila A., 'The Reasons for "Urizen"', *BIQ*, 21 (1987–88), 147–9.

Spector, Sheila A., 'Hebraic Etymologies of Proper Names in Blake's Myth', *Philological Quarterly*, 67 (1988), 345–63.

Tayler, Irene, 'The Woman Scaly', *Bulletin of the Midwest Modern Language Association*, 6 (1973), 74–87 (reprinted in Grant and Johnson, 1979).

Tayler, Irene, 'Blake's *Laocoön*', *Blake Newsletter*, 10 (1976–77), 72–81.

Tolley, Michael J., 'Blake's Use of the Bible in a Section of *The Everlasting Gospel*', *Notes and Queries*, n.s. 9 (1962), 171–6.

Villalobos, John C., 'A Possible Source for William Blake's "The Great Code of Art"', *English Language Notes*, 26 (1988), 36–40.

Villalobos, John C., 'William Blake's "Proverbs of Hell" and the Tradition of Wisdom Literature', *Studies in Philology*, 87 (1990), 246–59.

Viscomi, Joseph, 'The Evolution of *The Marriage of Heaven and Hell*', *Huntington Library Quarterly*, 58 (1996), 281–344.

Viscomi, Joseph, 'The Lessons of Swedenborg: or, The Origin of William Blake's *The Marriage of Heaven and Hell*', in Thomas Pfau and Robert F. Gleckner (eds.), *Lessons of Romanticism: A Critical Companion* (Durham, NC, 1998).

Warner, Janet, 'Blake's "Auguries of Innocence"', *Colby Library Quarterly*, 12 (1976), 126–38.

Weinroth, Michelle, 'Blake's *Book of Thel*', *McGill Literary Journal*, 1 (1979), 40–64.

Worrall, David, 'William Blake and Erasmus Darwin's *Botanic Garden*', *Bulletin of the New York Public Library*, 78 (1974–75), 397–417.

Worrall, David, 'Blake and the Night Sky I: The "Immortal Tent"', *Bulletin of Research in the Humanities*, 84 (1981), 273–95.

INDEX OF TITLES AND
FIRST LINES